COMMON GROUNDWORK

A Practical Guide to Protecting Rural and Urban Land

Third Edition

COMMON GROUNDWORK

A Practical Guide to Protecting Rural and Urban Land

A Handbook for Making Land–Use Decisions

Third Edition

A Joint Project of

Western Reserve Resource Conservation and Development Council
Ohio Office of Farmland Preservation
Seventh Generation
Chadbourne & Chadbourne, Inc.

Joseph H. and Mary M. Chadbourne

CHADBOURNE & CHADBOURNE
INCORPORATED

Chagrin Falls, Ohio

Nondiscrimination Clause

All Western Reserve Resource Conservation and Development Council, Ohio Office of Farmland Preservation, Seventh Generation, and Chadbourne & Chadbourne, Inc., programs and services are available without regard to race, color, national origin, religion, sex, age, marital status, or handicap.

Notice

The third edition was financed in part by a grant from the Lake Erie Protection Fund, with contributions from the Western Reserve Resource Conservation and Development Council, the Ohio Office of Farmland Preservation, Seventh Generation, and Chadbourne & Chadbourne, Inc.

Disclaimer

The information presented in this manual does not necessarily reflect the policies and procedures of the Western Reserve Resource Conservation and Development Council or the Ohio Office of Farmland Preservation. The opinions and conclusions are the authors' alone and should not be relied upon as creating any right in litigation in Ohio.

Credits

This publication includes images from Corel Photo House Version 3.1, which are protected by the copyright laws of the U. S., Canada, and elsewhere. Used under license.

First edition 1993 by the Institute for Environmental Education
Second edition 1995 by Chadbourne & Chadbourne, Inc.
Third edition 2000 by Chadbourne & Chadbourne, Inc.

CHADBOURNE & CHADBOURNE
INCORPORATED

18554 Haskins Road
Chagrin Falls, OH 44023-1823
Tel: 800-484-7949 + 1993 or 440-543-7303; Fax: 440-543-7160
Web Site: <<http://www.chadbourneinc.com>>

Contact Chadbourne & Chadbourne, Inc., for ordering information.

ISBN (paper): 1–930156–00–1

Library of Congress Catalog Card Number: 99-96206

Annotated Table of Contents

Quick Alphabetical Locator for Land Management Tools
in Section IV   xi

Acknowledgments   xiii

A Brief Introduction   xvii

Section I: The Problem   1

Section II: The Role of Planning in Land Preservation   9

Section III: Implementation — Zoning and Subdivision
        Regulations for Open Space and Farmland Preservation   23

Section IV: Land Management Tools   33

    IV–A–1: Private Initiatives — Individual and Group   33

        Agricultural Conservation Easement — Conservation
        easements that specifically restrict farmland from
        development and give farmers income, property, and
        estate tax reductions   35

        Bargain Sale — The sale of land to a conservation
        organization at less than market value   39

        Conservation Easement — A legal agreement between
        a landowner and a qualified conservation agency that
        transfers development rights from the owner to the agency
        to protect natural and cultural features in perpetuity   41

        Estate Management Strategies — To help preserve family
        lands, including farmland, a number of estate management
        strategies may be enacted during a landowner's lifetime
        or upon death   40

        Land Trust — A private, nonprofit organization that
        protects natural and cultural resources through
        conservation easements, land acquisition, and education   49

        Limited Development — The development of one portion
        of a property to finance the protection of another portion   52

        Outright Donation — The donation of land to a qualified
        charitable land conservation management organization   55

IV–A–2: Private Initiatives — Federal & State Programs 59

Access Management — U.S. Department of Transportation's standards support community planning efforts to reduce traffic congestion and improve pedestrian and vehicular safety 61

Agricultural District — A legal designation that allows qualifying farmers to defer utility assessments if farming is continued on the land 68

Agricultural Economic Development — The creation and stimulation of new marketing strategies to improve the sales and profitability of agricultural products help promote the goal of farmland preservation 73

Brownfields — Ohio's Voluntary Action Program — The restoration of contaminated urban sites reduces sprawl, retains jobs for inner cities, and slows industrial development of farmland and sensitive natural areas 80

Conservation Reserve Program — A program that pays farmers to convert erodible cropland to resource–preserving vegetative cover 87

Current Agricultural Use Value — A program that calculates farmland value based on soil type and product markets, rather than on development values, thereby reducing taxes on agricultural land 94

Farmland Protection Program — A federal program matching state funds to purchase conservation easements on prime farmlands 98

Forest Tax — A program that reduces property taxes if the owner maintains approved forest management practices on the land 103

National Conservation Buffer Initiative — Farmland buffers that reduce runoff and soil erosion and increase wildlife habitat qualify for financial assistance from state and federal programs 106

Storm Water Management — NPDES Phase II — Small municipalities and small construction sites previously exempted under Phase I will now be required to develop and implement storm water management programs 110

Wetlands Mitigation and Banking — When wetlands, which prevent pollution, flooding, and provide habitat, are irrevocably lost to dredging or fill, constructed or restored replacement wetlands may be purchased to maintain their net value to the country 115

Wetlands Reserve Program — Federal program with state partnering to restore the functions and values of wetlands and to preserve riparian areas through payments to landowners for conservation easements and wetland reconstruction practices 121

Wildlife Habitat Incentives Program — Private landowners may improve habitat for wildlife and fisheries with federal cost–sharing funds awarded after installation 125

IV–B–1: Public Initiatives — Acquisition 129

Land and Water Conservation Fund — A 50% / 50% matching fund program to expand and improve public outdoor recreation areas 131

Land Banking — The obtaining, holding, and subsequent release of lands by a local government for controlled development or for conservation purposes 134

Outright Purchase — The acquisition of lakeshores, river corridors, or other lands by individuals, land trusts, government organizations, and others for the benefit of the public 137

Purchase of Development Rights — A public / private government initiative that acquires the development rights of property to limit development 141

Transportation Enhancements — The federal highway transportation program contributes funds to enhance cultural, aesthetic, and environmental aspects of local transportation and transit systems 145

IV–B–2: Public Initiatives — Zoning 153

Agricultural Zoning — A method for protecting agricultural land use by stipulating minimum lot sizes or limitations on nonfarm uses 155

Cluster Development Zoning — A plan which concentrates development on one part of a property in

order to protect the remainder of the parcel as open space
without changing the overall density of the development   160

Conservation Development Zoning — A type of cluster
development which emphasizes a planned unit
development for preserving open space, wetlands,
natural landscaping, floodplains, and other priority
resources, as well as for preventing storm water runoff   163

Large–Lot Zoning — A requirement that each new house
be constructed on a minimum number of acres, generally
at least 5 or more   166

Overlay Zoning — An overlay of additional land–use
restrictions on top of existing ones to protect specific
resources such as reservoirs and historic districts   169

Performance Zoning — A requirement that any new
development be reviewed based on its projected impact
on specific features of the community, such as farming,
traffic flow, and storm water management   171

Planned Unit Development Zoning — A mechanism for
cluster development zoning and conservation development
zoning in the Ohio Revised Code that may allow more
creative designs and mixed use plans   174

Quarter / Quarter Zoning — A specification that limits
nonfarm development to one house per 40 acres, that is,
¼ of ¼ of the original 640–acre tract   179

Sliding Scale Zoning — The enactment of a ratio of
dwelling units to land acreage that concentrates
development on smaller lots by increasing the minimum
lot size for houses built on larger parcels   182

**IV–B–3: Public Initiatives — Special Protection
& Conservation Regulations**   185

Capital Improvement Programming — The scheduling
of budgetary expenditures for infrastructure, thereby
guiding and pacing development   187

Cooperative Agreement — An agreement between
two or more organizations to share in financing,
maintaining, or managing a property   192

Environmental Impact Ordinance — An assessment
of the potential harmful effects of a pending development

upon the environment so that steps to prevent damage
can be taken before the project begins   196

Growth Management — Pacing the rate of development
or controlling the location of development so that laws can
be passed on a very selective basis to manage a
community's growth   199

Impact Fees and Exactions — Fees or infrastructure
improvements required from a developer to offset the
costs to a community of new development   204

Moratoria — Legal actions that temporarily freeze
development so that adequate planning and follow–up
ordinances can be put into place   208

Special Designation — The protection of scenic river
corridors and other valuable resources through state or
federal recognition and technical assistance   211

Transfer of Development Rights — A technique for
guiding growth away from sensitive resources and toward
controlled development centers through the transfer of
development rights from one area to another   218

**SECTION V: How Your Local Government Works with
    Respect to Land Use**   223

SECTION VI: Action Center Resources   237

   **VI–A: Funding Sources for Protecting Rural
            and Urban Land**   239

   **VI–B: Agencies, Organizations, Publications, and Internet
            Start–Up & Use**   251

       Community Supported Agriculture Programs   251
       **Computer–Based Resources: The Internet &
               World Wide Web**   254
       Conservancy Districts   259
       Farm Bureaus   261
       Farmers' Markets in Ohio   262
       Historic Preservation Resources   274
       Land Trusts   275
       Metropolitan Planning Organizations   279
       Ohio's Forests   282
       Ohio's Nature Preserves   284
       Ohio's Scenic Rivers   289

Ohio State University Extension Offices   290
Organizations & Publications with Land–Use Interests   300
Park Districts   322
Parks   328
Planning Commissions & Councils—County & Regional   335
Resource Conservation & Development Councils   346
Soil and Water Conservation Districts and Natural
   Resources Conservation Service Offices   347
Watershed Protection Organizations   354

VI–C: Glossary of Land–Use Terms   357

VI–D: Map of Ohio Counties   373

Index   375

Quick Alphabetical Locator for Land Management Tools in Section IV

Access Management	61
Agricultural Conservation Easement	35
Agricultural District	68
Agricultural Economic Development	73
Agricultural Zoning	155
Bargain Sale	39
Brownfields — Ohio's Voluntary Action Program	80
Capital Improvement Programming	187
Cluster Development Zoning	160
Conservation Development Zoning	163
Conservation Easement	41
Conservation Reserve Program	87
Cooperative Agreement	192
Current Agricultural Use Value	94
Environmental Impact Ordinance	196
Estate Management Strategies	46
Farmland Protection Program	98
Forest Tax	103
Growth Management	199
Impact Fees and Exactions	204
Land and Water Conservation Fund	131
Land Banking	134
Land Trust	49
Large–Lot Zoning	166
Limited Development	52
Moratoria	208
National Conservation Buffer Initiative	106
Outright Donation	55
Outright Purchase	137
Overlay Zoning	169
Performance Zoning	171
Planned Unit Development Zoning	174
Purchase of Development Rights	141
Quarter / Quarter Zoning	179
Sliding Scale Zoning	182
Special Designation	211
Storm Water Management — NPDES Phase II	110
Transfer of Development Rights	218
Transportation Enhancements	145
Wetlands Mitigation and Banking	115
Wetlands Reserve Program	121
Wildlife Habitat Incentives Program	125

ACKNOWLEDGMENTS

Background

In 1993, *Common Groundwork: A Practical Guide to Protecting Rural and Urban Land* was conceived as a joint project by the Institute for Environmental Education, the Lake and Geauga Soil & Water Conservation Districts, and the Western Reserve Resource Conservation & Development Council. That publication was financed in part through a grant from the Ohio Environmental Protection Agency under provisions of Section 319 of the Clean Water Act as amended in 1987.

At the time, we—Joseph and Mary Chadbourne—were the principals of the Institute, and we wrote the book, along with Institute subcontractor Benjamin Hitchings. When the Institute was scheduled to close its operations in December 1993 after 22 years, we formed a Subchapter S Corporation, Chadbourne & Chadbourne, Inc. (C&C), in August 1993. C&C is an environmental consulting firm that continues much of the Institute's work.

The Institute printed the first edition of *Common Groundwork* in 1993. Chadbourne & Chadbourne, Inc., made minor revisions to that first edition in October 1995, issuing a second edition in 1996.

In 1999, a revision, update, and expansion of *Common Groundwork* by C&C was proposed by the Officers of the Western Reserve Resource Conservation & Development Council, Seventh Generation, and the recently created Office of Farmland Preservation within the Ohio Department of Agriculture. These organizations wanted the book to address the growing problem of sprawl and its impact on the loss of farmland, open space, and vital urban centers, as well as the actions citizens could take to redress these problems and prevent future losses. In light of the changes in land–use practices and resources available over the past 6 years to help protect sensitive rural and urban areas, we found *Common Groundwork* required a major rewriting rather than a revision.

The work was financed by a grant from the Lake Erie Protection Fund as well as contributions from each of the three sponsors and Chadbourne and Chadbourne, Inc. This version of *Common Groundwork* includes much that is new: a discussion of planning, zoning, and subdivision regulations in preserving farmland and open space; a number of new programs and legal techniques available to help protect sensitive areas; many updated case histories; a section on how to use the land–use focused computer

resources on the Internet; e–mail and Web site addresses for new
and old contacts; a completely revised "Action Center Resources";
and a section on how individuals, groups, and jurisdictions can fund
land–protection projects. Experts in the field, cited below,
recommended new content as well as corrections and
enhancements in reviewing various drafts of the manuscript.

References

We telephoned, faxed, and e–mailed many people who held
special knowledge of new land–use tools, modifications of earlier
planning and management techniques, or had initiated those
practices themselves. Their names are associated in the guide with
the actual information they provided, either directly in the text or as
footnotes. They have given us permission to identify them and their
contact information, and have extended an invitation to readers to
call them about subjects that require a deeper discussion than
could be presented here. This opportunity helps to perpetuate the
guide as a living document to help keep readers current.

The Internet has given us nearly instant access to current,
previously unavailable information about land–use practices
throughout the country. So, with our information sources we are
also providing e–mail and Web site addresses where possible,
along with conventional contact information. And, to further
readers' use of this document and to help them take advantage of
these electronic resources, we have included a brief "how–to–do–it"
instructional guide for computer or Internet novices in the "Action
Center Resources" section titled "Computer–Based Resources:
The Internet & World Wide Web."

Reviewers

We mailed various drafts of the guide to those who volunteered or
who were selected to critique all or part of the work. Since we
cannot cite the many individual suggestions they made, we list their
names here, with our gratitude.

Chuck Ashcroft, Executive Director, Grand River Partners, Painesville,
  OH
Mary Bielen, Ohio State University Sea Grant Extension Office, Toledo,
  OH
Tom Blaine, District Specialist, Community Development, Ohio State
  University Extension, Wooster, OH
John Brandt, Editor-in-Chief, *Industry Week*, Cleveland, OH
Lana Brandt, resident, Shaker Hts., OH
Edith Chase, President, Ohio Coastal Resources Management Project,
  Kent, OH
Kirby Date, Director, Countryside Program, Beachwood, OH

Thomas Denbow, Executive Director, Chagrin River Watershed Partners, Inc., Willoughby Hills, OH
Kyle Dreyfuss-Wells, Assistant Director, Chagrin River Watershed Partners, Willoughby Hills, OH
George Espy, Executive Director, Seventh Generation, Elyria, OH
Joseph Hadley Jr., Executive Director, Northeast Ohio Four County Regional Planning & Development Organization, Akron, OH
Bryn Jones, Geographic Information Specialist, Chardon, OH
Lawrence Libby, Professor and C. William Swank Professor in Rural–Urban Policy, Department of Agricultural Economics, The Ohio State University, Columbus, OH
Larry Long, Executive Director, County Commissioners Association of Ohio, Columbus, OH
Steve Madewell, Assistant Director of Natural Resource Management and Planning, Lake Metroparks, Concord Township, OH
Elaine Marsh, Director, Friends of the Crooked River, Akron, OH
John Niedzialek, Vice President, Western Reserve Resource Conservation & Development Council, and Soil Conservationist, Natural Resources Conservation Service, U.S. Department of Agriculture, Painesville, OH
Sara Pavlovicz, former Medina County Commissioner, Seville, OH
Tom Quintrell, Attorney, Arter & Hadden, Cleveland, OH
Tom Rapini, Board Supervisor, Lake County Soil & Water Conservation District, Painesville, OH
Caitlin M. Roberts, resident, Cleveland Hts., OH
Richard Roddie, conservation easement donor, Bainbridge Township, OH
Sharon Schnall, resident, Bainbridge Township, OH
Jim Skeeles, Extension Agent, Agriculture & Natural Resources, Community Development, OSU Extension Office, Elyria, OH
Howard Wise, Executive Director, Ohio Office of Farmland Preservation, Ohio Department of Agriculture, Reynoldsburg, OH

One Final Acknowledgment

Since the first edition of this book, we have heard many heartening first– and second–hand stories from people who have learned they can make a difference in shaping what their communities are, what they will become. Usually, we think of stakeholders as people with political or economic interests, but the most powerful stakeholders of all are those ordinary citizens who care deeply about quality–of–life issues right where they live *and* in the greater world—and act on them. They are people working hard for small and sustainable uses of the land.

We want to acknowledge their efforts to make protection of sensitive rural and urban lands a priority in their daily lives. Their success to date and tomorrow benefits all of us. We hope this third edition of *Common Groundwork* helps them in their work.

—*Joseph H. Chadbourne & Mary M. Chadbourne*
January 2000

A BRIEF INTRODUCTION

Who Should Read This Guide?

We wrote this guide for anyone who is now or will become involved in land use and development decisions—both privately and publicly. Those who can act privately on their own behalf include individual citizens, land owners, environmentalists, farmers, developers, lawyers, consulting planners and engineers, land trust managers, realtors, and citizen groups, to name a few. And, those who can act on the public's behalf encompass elected and appointed officials, such as planning commission, zoning commission, and zoning board of appeals members; protection, preservation, and enforcement agency specialists; other participants in local, state, and federal government; as well as nonprofit and charitable organizations concerned with land–use issues.

While the guide was funded, written, reviewed, printed, and published in Ohio for its citizens especially, the many land–use issues and the means for addressing them apply nationwide.

How is the Guide Organized?

Sections I through III provide the rationale for this guide today: the problem of sprawl and the accompanying loss of farmland, open space, and vital urban centers; the importance of comprehensive plans and the methods for creating them; and the legal structure for achieving and enforcing fair, practical, and scientifically supportable land–use management tomorrow.

Section IV contains privately and publicly initiated ordinances, programs, and individual options or choices, i.e., the land management tools that citizens and officials can use to achieve the goals of the comprehensive plans in their communities.

Section V briefly reviews how local governments work with respect to land–use issues at the county, municipal, and township levels.

Section VI provides information for taking action. Funding sources, computer–based resources, support agencies and organizations, a technical glossary, and a map of Ohio counties extend the background provided in Section IV. From these resources, readers interested in land–use issues will have places to go for practical help in achieving their goals.

Note: For the reader's convenience, the names of land management tools are annotated in Section IV of the Table of Contents. Following the Table of Contents is a Quick Alphabetical Locator with page numbers for each of the tools. In the running text, tool names appear in parentheses. In the Glossary they are marked by an asterisk. Finally, boldfaced page numbers in the Index refer to the location of the full description of a given tool.

I. The Problem

I. THE PROBLEM

This guide addresses the problem of sprawl and the resulting loss of natural resources, farmland, open space, and vital urban centers. It provides citizens and officials with the rationale for adopting comprehensive plans in their local communities and explains over 40 land management tools for protecting a community's natural and manmade assets.

Sprawl is population migration from densely settled urban centers to rural areas. It creates problems for both the urban and the rural communities involved. First, it depletes the cities of their skilled workers, which erodes the tax base and in turn reduces infrastructure support, leading to racial polarization, diminished cultural diversity, and loss of economic vitality. Second, the development of rural land degrades natural resources, reduces farmland and open space, adds to infrastructure costs—waterlines, sewers, highways—and upsets the environmental balance upon which both urban and rural citizens depend.[1]

As one example of outmigration in Ohio, between 1960 and 1990 the City of Cleveland lost 70,000 households. And, its real estate value lost $1,500,000,000, or 25% of its total worth. These households have moved to the five–county region surrounding the city (Cuyahoga, Geauga, Lake, Lorain, and Medina). The Ohio Housing Research Network indicates that from 1980 to 2010 these five counties will see a 30% increase in residential land.[2] Such shifts in population are occurring in all seven major urbanized areas in Ohio.

To illustrate the concurrent loss of natural resources, from 1960 to 1990 that five–county region around Cleveland lost 40% of its farmland. The seven counties in the Columbus metropolitan area (Franklin, Delaware, Fairfield, Licking, Madison, Pickaway, and Union) account for the state's largest amount of farmland loss—425,101 acres, just over 1,000 acres a month, a 23% change. And, all of Ohio lost 4,358,827 acres in farms, a rate of 10,755 acres per month, according to the U.S. Census of Agriculture. Of course, not all farmland loss is due to sprawl alone. But, in a more recent sampling period, 1982 to 1992, about 60% of 472,000 acres—28,000 acres per year, or 77 acres per day—were developed on farmlands with prime or unique soils, which are those soils that meet the U.S. Department of Agriculture's highest productivity standards.[3]

This is significant because Ohio is one of only four states that has more than 50% of its land classified as "prime farmland." In fact, agriculture, and all of the support services—food packaging and delivery, farm equipment manufacture, storage—is the state's largest industry, contributing some $67,700,000,000 annually, and one in every six jobs, according to a recent Ohio State University study.

The long–term implications are troubling, not only to Ohio but also to the nation. In 50 years, the population could increase 50% to more than 390,000,000, while at the same time farmers and ranchers would have 13% fewer acres of high quality farmland for food production. Pessimistically, within this time, the United States could become a net food *importer*, instead of a net food *exporter*. And, this makes us dependent upon the resources of other countries that are already unsustainable—to say nothing about the trade balance.[4]

The record on sprawl in Ohio and across the country is clear. Outmigration from cities and suburbs has led to devastation of *unique rural community resources*: the erosion of agricultural soils, the filling of wetlands, flooding, contamination of surface and underground water supplies, the destruction of natural habitats, and, with this last, the loss of diversity in both plant and animal species.

"Unique rural community resources" is a generic expression, since no two communities are identical. However, those resources are easily recognized:

● **Prime farmland:** Farmland classified by the Natural Resources Conservation Service as best for row, forage, and fiber crop production. Factors include level of topography, drainage, moisture supply, soil texture and depth, and susceptibility to erosion and runoff. Because of these characteristics, prime farmland affords the least cost to the farmer and least cost to natural resources.

● **Open space:** Undeveloped stretches of natural land that because of their capacity to store water and restore aquifers, provide habitat, preserve scenic views and forestlands; or because of their limit on safe development due to steep slopes, erodible soils, or floodplains, should be preserved in the public interest and, therefore, protected from development.

- **Groundwater:** Subsurface waters in rock, sand, or gravel which are the present or future sources of public or private water supplies. The holding area, or aquifer (i.e., water–bearing area), is recharged from precipitating rain and snow. Recharge land may become contaminated, which could pollute the aquifer; or, it might be covered over when buildings, roads, and parking areas are constructed, thereby reducing the amount which could be taken in and later withdrawn.

- **River corridors:** Natural rivers, streams, or creeks and adjacent land that possess important water conservation, flood prevention, storm water erosion control, and scenic, biologic, historic, or outdoor recreation value.

- **Wetlands:** Marshes, swamps, bogs, fens, and other wetlands with characteristic wet soil and vegetation that aid in flood protection and pollution abatement and that provide critical nursery areas and primary habitat for a variety of plants and animals.

- **Coastal zones:** Limited and irreplaceable stretches along freshwater and saltwater bodies that are rich in natural, commercial, recreational, industrial, and aesthetic resources and opportunities.

- **Geologic areas:** Land forms subject to hazardous downward movement of soil and / or rock masses, slope failure, or landslides because of erodible soils, steep slopes, or unique geologic, hydrologic, or topographic conditions.

- **Flood zones:** Areas of past or planned development where life and property are threatened by documented flood damage, as in 100–year flood zones.

- **Historic, cultural, and scenic sites:** Usually local, state, or federally designated buildings or places of importance because of their association with history, architecture, special culture, or extraordinary visual character.

What is the answer to preserving these "unique rural community resources"?

Everywhere, the popular answer is "smart growth." It expresses the need for policies and practices to channel sprawl into more sustainable forms, including fiscal responsibility, land stewardship, environmental quality, social justice and equity, and fairness to the majority of property owners. In 1998, the publication *EcoCity Cleveland* commissioned The American Planning Association to prepare a study, now published, *Working Paper: A Smart Growth Agenda for Ohio*. The authors listed these "ingredients for success":[5]

•   Agreement on direction–setting visions or goals for the state that are concrete and capable of being implemented.

•   A long–term commitment by the governor and state legislature to make the Smart Growth program work.

•   The governor clearly communicating to state agencies the commitment to the program and holding them accountable for changes in agency policies and practices.

•   Extensive public involvement and education.

•   An adequate package of incentives to local governments to ensure constructive participation in the program.

Both cities and rural areas, but especially farmlands, will need financial assistance on a substantial scale to accomplish the goals of smart growth.

For cities, some progressive initiatives have been undertaken by federal, state, and local governments and agencies. These include the Jobs Bill III, a $90,000,000 fund to help cities acquire and clean up brownfields (contaminated sites) for private sector reinvestment; the Urban Schools Initiative Agenda to resolve educational challenges to city schools; the Ohio Housing Trust Fund to address low and moderate income housing; and others reported in Section IV. These and other initiatives will help to retain urban populations and enhance the quality of life in these critical cultural and economic centers.

For farmland preservation, Senate Bill 223 was signed on January 4, 1999, authorizing the Ohio Department of Agriculture, local governments, and charitable organizations to hold, acquire, and accept agricultural easements to ensure continued farmland use in perpetuity. That law authorizes local governments to levy or raise sales taxes, increase property taxes, and/or issue bonds to pay for farmland protection. In addition, the law requires the Department of Agriculture to establish procedures and eligibility criteria for making matching grants to local governments and charitable organizations to purchase agricultural easements.

The Department's Office of Farmland Preservation is currently drafting rules to the matching grant program and is expected to submit them to the Ohio General Assembly's Joint Committee for Agency Rule Review (JCARR) for approval in late 1999. Assuming that JCARR approves the rules, the Director of Agriculture will then need to request funding from the governor and the legislature in order to implement the matching grant program.[6] If successful, these actions will preserve farmland and manage development in a sustainable way.

Smart growth can work for Ohio, the American Planning Association maintains. It points to another state to support its claim, Maryland's "Smart Growth and Neighborhood Conservation Initiative," a comprehensive investment and land–use strategy to slow sprawl. The heart of the plan is a law that directs state agencies to invest public funds for economic development in existing cities and towns and to deny most allocations that encourage suburban sprawl. In short, the Maryland program is not a regulatory plan that prohibits development; rather, it is an incentive system that uses the power of the state's investment potential to promote development in desirable locations. It both helps to rebuild urban neighborhoods and to preserve rural farmland.

This example of smart growth and the case histories in the land management tools section of this guide emphasize the practical approaches that can be taken to achieve these goals—to address the issues of sprawl and the loss of natural resources, farmland, open space, and vital urban centers.

It all begins with planning

NOTES

[1] Ohio State University Extension (A. Prindle & T. Blaine), *Costs of Community Services*, CDFS-1260-98 (July 1998), 1-2. Available from the "Land Use Series" of Fact Sheets, Ohio State University Extension, Community Development, 700 Ackerman Road, Columbus, OH 43202-1578; Web Site: <<http://ohioline.ag.ohio-state.edu>>.

[2] "Saving Farms by Saving Cities," *EcoCity Cleveland Journal*, No. 4 (Spring 1997), 5.

[3] "Cleveland in Greater Cleveland: Defining a Regional Role for Our Central City," *EcoCity Cleveland Journal*, No. 4 (Spring 1997), 14. For subscriptions to

this publication with a bioregional focus, contact David Beach, Editor, 2841 Scarborough Rd., Cleveland Hts., OH 44118, Tel: 216-932-3007; Fax: 216-932-6069; E-mail: <<ecocleveland@igc.org>>; Web Site: <<http://www.ecocleveland.org>>.

[4] American Farmland Trust (A. Sorenson, et al.), *Farming on the Edge* (DeKalb, IL: Northern Illinois University, Center for Agriculture in the Environment, March 1997), 2. Contact the American Farmland Trust at 1920 N St. NW, Ste. 400, Washington, DC 20036; Tel: 202-659-5170; Fax: 202-659-8339; Web Site: <<http://www.farmland.org>>.

[5] Ibid., 15.

[6] Howard Wise, Executive Director, Ohio Office of Farmland Preservation, Department of Agriculture, 8995 E. Main St., Reynoldsburg, OH 43068; Tel: 614-728-6238; Fax: 614-466-6124.

[7] Stuart Meck, AICP, with Jason Wittenberg, "Working Paper: A Smart Growth Agenda for Ohio," *Citizens' Bioregional Plan for Northeast Ohio*, a special issue of the *EcoCity Cleveland Journal*, No. 6 (Spring 1999), 5. Web Site: <<http://www.ecocleveland.org>>.

II. THE ROLE OF PLANNING IN LAND PRESERVATION

II. THE ROLE OF PLANNING IN LAND PRESERVATION

What We Are Talking about When We Talk about "Land"

Many of us think of land as just the soil and grass we walk on and can lay title to by purchasing and marking ownership with posts after surveys have been done. But, in this guide, the word "land" means everything that makes up what really is in a parcel, no matter its size: soils, the underlying geology, groundwater, plant and animal species, valleys, hills, rivers, lakes, streams, wetlands, floodplains, views, even the air quality associated with a particular area. You might argue that these are features of a parcel of several hundred acres, but what about only one acre? A half acre? A quarter of an acre? Even these smallest parcels of land have plant and animal life, soils, views, air quality, water running across and under them, some measurable slope, an underlying geology.

Together, all these parts make land what it is. And when we harm or destroy or cover over one part, it is only a matter of time until other parts decline. Stripped of all vegetation—trees, other plant life—and many above– and below–ground animals will leave the land; soils will erode in rain, wind, and snow. Air quality will be compromised and views obscured by the ensuing dust.

It follows logically that planning the use of land requires that we know what *all* of these parts are, how they function in a given area, and the services they provide, so that any one part can be modified with the *least* harm to the other parts. Therefore, any plan for land use, including preservation of open space for habitats or scenic views or farming, must also include the technical, professional inventories of these parts, including but not limited to these: soil sampling and analysis, water flow (hydrology) measurement, water quality tests, inventories of plant and animal life, soil percolation tests, evaluations of the quality and quantity of groundwater stores, contour mapping of terrain, patterns in business and residential inflow and outflow, the tax–rate competitiveness of the area compared to other nearby jurisdictions, etc.

These data provide the scientific justification for recommendations in the comprehensive plan. Later, if the plan is contested in court, the data provide the basis for defense, and they are currently given greater weight than arbitrary or judgmental arguments. As an example, note the Clinton County case cited below and the reference to "highly fertile soil and abundant ground water."

Without this information, we proceed blindly, in ignorance, in a direction or with an idea or a hope, but certainly not with a plan. So, when appointed and elected public officials and citizens and planning consultants draw up land–use plans *without* a thorough knowledge of these parts and an understanding about how they interact, they may be acting on the public's behalf, but they are not acting for the public's benefit.

Introduction: Comprehensive Planning versus Other Approaches

Several names for planning appear in land–use vocabulary today. The most widely used is *comprehensive* planning and, in Ohio, it is this type of planning that is generally supported by the courts as a legal instrument to regulate development.

Watershed planning uses a critical natural feature of an area—its existing hydrology, or watercourses and reserves—to define its site and the political entities in or tangential to that defined site to determine the players in the planning process. On the other hand, *regional* planning most commonly uses multiple political areas to define its area of activity, such as a three–county or five–county planning agency for coordinating transportation projects. *Bioregional* planning, as its name suggests, pertains to planning for large–scale land areas defined by specific natural resource features, functions, and boundaries.

In contrast to these other types of planning, *comprehensive planning* specifically exists under state law in terms defined in the Ohio Revised Code (ORC, see Chapter 713). It applies to a process undertaken by existing political jurisdictions—counties, municipalities, and townships—a hallmark of which is citizen participation. None of the other types of planning yet hold this status.

A. Comprehensive Planning

A comprehensive plan, also known as a master plan or general plan, outlines a local government's policies, objectives, and decision guidelines. It serves as a blueprint for development. Plans usually identify areas targeted for various land uses, including agriculture, forestry, open space, and historic preservation, as well as residential, commercial, industrial, and recreational uses. Comprehensive plans provide the rationale for zoning and subdivision regulations and promote the orderly development of public services. In the ORC, Section 303.02 for townships and counties, the statutory purpose of zoning is to promote "public health, safety, and morals." In municipalities, ORC Section 73.06, the purpose of zoning is for "the interest of public health, safety, convenience, comfort, prosperity, or general welfare." As an all–inclusive approach to addressing future community growth, the final document should be:

❒ Comprehensive in the scope of information it considers

❒ Long–range in its time frame

❒ General

❒ Focused on physical development

❒ Related to community goals and social and economic policies established in frequent citizen participation sessions

❒ Regarded as a guide, not as a regulation[1]

The elements, such as land–use patterns, housing conditions, population, roadways, and other infrastructure, however, can vary from one community to another. Therefore, each plan follows the results of studies of existing local conditions, projection of future trends, as well as the goals and objectives for each governmental jurisdiction. Ultimately, the comprehensive plan should conclude with a set of recommendations, in the form of goals and objectives, with specific strategies to address each goal. It is these characteristics—a plan that is complete, appropriately involves the public at all stages, and is thorough and scientific in its methods—that have allowed comprehensive plans to carry great weight in the courts.

Cost of Community Services

One relatively new set of information available to the planning process is "cost of community services" calculations. Its inclusion in the planning process can contribute to the technical objectivity of the final comprehensive plan.

Numerous studies on the cost of community services conclude that residential development in any area invariably leads to increased per capita demand for publicly provided services. This places increased burdens on local infrastructure and public agencies and therefore on the tax payers, since local tax rates tend to follow growth. With small growth rates, around 1 to 2% per year, costs do not escalate rapidly; but with higher growth rates, above 3% per year, per capita spending begins to increase dramatically.[2]

The community costs vary with use, but studies have documented that residential land costs the local government *more* than it receives in taxes from the new development. Public services cost between $1.15 to $1.50 in services for every $1 in taxes collected. Therefore, the new residential tax base does not cover the cost of the community services needed to support it. Instead, new residential development puts the entire community at a net revenue loss as expenses exceed tax income. In contrast, for commercial and industrial use, the local government pays about $.35 to $.65 in services for each $1 received. And for agricultural and open space use, the services cost from $.30 to $.50 per $1 paid in taxes.

A major expense item in the cost of community services associated with residential development is education. The public school system accounts for about 60% to 70% of total governmental spending. Commercial and industrial development and land left as open space do not place a direct burden on the school system— and farmland places only a slight burden. Thus, the cost of public services is lower for them than for residential land use.

Cost of community services studies should be considered by all communities as they determine the goals of their comprehensive plans. In so doing, community members should understand that these studies do not judge the public good or long–term merits of land use or the taxing structure. Rather, they help citizens and officials to know, realistically, what the *actual* costs will be as they work to strike a balance among affordable housing, jobs, land conservation, and the use of resources.[3]

A Word about Legal Challenges

To illustrate the legal force of a comprehensive plan, a recent common pleas court decision recognized comprehensive planning, even in the absence of zoning. On October 20, 1998, the Common Pleas Court of Clinton County, Ohio, Civil Division, decided on the "merits on consolidated administrative appeals," which involved an application by Martin Marietta to create and operate a new limestone quarry on 262 farmland acres which it owns in Wilson Township, Clinton County, Ohio.[4] The land was not zoned, but it was already subject to a county comprehensive plan adopted in May 1995, under Ohio Revised Code (ORC) Chapter 713. The land was designated for agricultural protection by the plan, based on its highly fertile soil and abundant ground water. The Court concluded that the Reclamation Commission of Ohio ". . . acted in a legally proper fashion under the applicable statutes in determining that the Chief (of the Division of Mines and Reclamation) should have denied a mining permit to Martin until such time as the permit applicant could adequately demonstrate that the mining plan was no longer in conflict with a pre–existing comprehensive land–use plan."

The decision of the Reclamation Commission was "AFFIRMED," the Clerk of Courts file reads.

However, it should also be noted that the ruling record on comprehensive plans in Ohio has not been consistent. Although comprehensive planning and zoning are two of the most important tools available to help local governments influence growth and development, not every Ohio government entity has adopted these planning tools. The Ohio State University's September 1999 study, *The Ohio Zoning and Land Use Survey*, revealed that 24 (28%) of Ohio's 88 *counties* have never had comprehensive plans. Additionally, many of the counties with *no zoning* also have no comprehensive plans. And, only 162 (25%) of the 654 *townships* responding to the survey—out of a state total of 1,373 townships—have a township plan.[5] Furthermore, many of these comprehensive plans have not been updated within five years, the recommended period for plan revisions. This alone suggests considerable laxity by these governments in protecting rural and urban land, and makes their communities vulnerable to development without the guidance of an appropriate comprehensive plan.

B. Watershed Planning

As mentioned earlier, *watershed planning* uses a critical natural feature of an area—its existing hydrology, or watercourses and reserves—to define its site, and the political entities in or tangential to that defined site to determine the players in its planning process. Watershed–based planning is not new to Ohio. In the 1890s, the U.S. Inland Waterways Commission reported to Congress "that rivers must be treated as integrated systems."[6] This approach refers to an extensive effort to address multiple causes of water quality and habitat degradation in a watershed.

For example, locally in Northeast Ohio, the Chagrin River Watershed Partners (CRWP) works with numerous county, municipality, and township jurisdictions as well as park districts to promote activities that protect the Chagrin River Watershed and to protect and preserve the local natural resource base.[7] The CRWP has a number of model ordinances, fact sheets, and other materials to help individuals and political jurisdictions to solve or prevent water–quality and quantity problems, such as establishing buffers along rivers.

Everyone lives within a watershed—an area of land from which surface water drains into a common river, lake, or wetland. The Ohio Environmental Protection Agency (OEPA) has identified approximately 5,000 water body segments in the state and has grouped them into 326 watersheds. Of these watersheds, 276 contain water body segments that have been classified as "impaired."

"Impaired water body segments" do not meet Clean Water Act standards for use (aquatic life habitats, water supply, recreation), water quality criteria (toxicity and aquatic life support), and antidegradation policy (ensuring protection of high quality water). Impairment at any one point in a watershed originates from natural and human activities above that physical point. Therefore, a watershed plan identifies sources of nonpoint pollution problems, such as runoff from impervious, or nonabsorbing, surfaces— sidewalks, parking lots, etc.—so that citizens and public officials can, together, undertake effective responses.[8]

The Ohio EPA's Division of Surface Water, in cooperation with the U.S. Department of Agriculture's Natural Resources Conservation Service (USDA's NRCS), the Ohio Department of Natural Resources (ODNR), the Ohio State University Extension, the Maumee Valley Resource Conservation and Development, Inc., and the Miami Valley Regional Planning Commission, prepared the watershed–based planning document, *A Guide to Developing Local Watershed Action Plans in Ohio.* It details the steps and the content areas for developing an action–based watershed plan.[9]

Nationally, the Center for Watershed Protection has compiled a list of resources on the following watershed protection tools: land–use planning, land conservation, aquatic buffers, improved site design, erosion and sediment control, storm water management, nonstorm water discharges, and stewardship programs. The Center also posts model ordinances that cover a variety of watershed protection issues. At their Web site they also have a *Consensus Agreement on Model Development Principles to Protect Our Streams, Lakes and Wetlands,* a compendium of 22 principles for watershed protection to use when developing residential streets and parking lots (habitat for cars), lot development (habitat for people), and conservation of natural areas (habitat for nature).[10]

C. Regional Planning

The Northeast Ohio Areawide Coordinating Agency (NOACA) and the Northeast Ohio Four County Regional Planning & Development Organization (NEFCO) are just two of some 100 planning agencies in Ohio. Some are county agencies, while others are multi–county or regional. NOACA was organized by commissioners from Cuyahoga, Geauga, Lake, Lorain, and Medina Counties in 1968 to coordinate planning for the five–county region. It later merged with the Cleveland Seven–County Transportation Land Use Study, expanding its mission to the continuous, inclusive, coordinated transportation planning necessary to qualify the region for federal funding for transportation. It is now the region's federally designated Metropolitan Planning Organization (see Section IV–B–1, "Transportation Enhancements [ISTEA & TEA–21])". Today, it has transportation, water quality, and air quality planning functions.[11]

Critical to land–use planning, one of NOACA's principal transportation functions is to "Produce a long–range (20 to 25 years), multi–modal (highways, transit, air, water, rail) transportation plan with due consideration to: comprehensive long–range land–use plans; development objectives; overall social, economic and environmental goals; system performance and energy conservation objectives; alternative transportation system management (short range, low cost efficiency improvements); and investment strategies to make more efficient use of existing transportation facilities."

For water quality management, among other assignments, NOACA assists Designated Management Agencies with plans and programs that address public wastewater treatment, home sewage, package plants, storm water permits, nonpoint source pollution management (such as storm water management and sediment control programs in urban areas and erosion control practices in rural ones), groundwater protection, wetlands, and other water quality strategies.[12]

Its responsibility for air quality relates primarily to air pollution generated by transportation–related sources. Here, the goal is to attain compliance with Ohio and federal air quality standards.

Additionally, NOACA created the Land Use Analysis project to promote land use policies that encourage efficient, compact land development that helps bring about mobility, saves environmentally sensitive and agricultural lands, and enhances the economic viability of existing communities. That Land Use Analysis provided some of the data about land zoned for development in Medina County, as described in *Citizens' Bioregional Plan for Northeast Ohio* discussed below.

NOACA's powers reside in allocating state and federal transportation money and in vetoing highway and transit projects that its board opposes. It does *not* have jurisdiction over the control of road siting, sewers, and development.

D. Bioregional Planning

As stated earlier, *bioregional planning* pertains to large–scale land areas defined by specific natural resource features, functions, and boundaries. *EcoCity Cleveland Journal*'s special Spring 1999 issue, *Citizens' Bioregional Plan for Northeast Ohio*, which covers a seven-county area, offers this perspective: "A bioregion, or life–place, is a geographic area of interconnected natural systems and their characteristic watersheds, land forms, species and human cultures. It's a place that 'hangs together' in ecological and human terms."[13] A bioregional plan, the issue states, helps citizens think about such questions as:

- What lands in our region are likely to be developed in the next decade?

- Where might a regional greenbelt be created?

- Where should new development be concentrated to promote livable communities and mixed land uses?

- How could the building industry's legitimate need for buildable land be satisfied in the most sustainable manner possible?

- Where should transportation improvements be focused to link town centers and reduce dependence on the automobile?

- How might sensitive natural areas and open spaces be preserved for future generations and to protect the region's biological diversity?

- How can farming have a viable future in . . . Ohio?[14]

The *Bioregional Plan* assembles maps to illustrate some of the sprawl sequences described earlier in this guide's Section I. These maps show the river drainage basins and land cover in the seven–county area, outmigration, shifting wealth, transportation projects, lands at risk from development, urban cores, and current zoning patterns. In the last instance, for example, in Medina County, all of the so–called "vacant land" in townships—165,000 acres now used mostly for agriculture—is zoned for development. If the current pace of building continues, all of this land will be completely developed by 2045, bringing in 47,000 new homes and eliminating agriculture entirely.[15] The report concludes that a bioregional plan should be the product of a public planning agency and its citizens working closely together on the plan elements and goals.

Finally, one other mechanism of planning and land protection has come to the forefront in Ohio. Park districts are forming voluntary partnerships with local agencies and communities to protect unique community resources. These partnerships are responsible for about 80% of the current land preservation action in the state. The park districts already have a tax base and a preservation mission. Therefore, they have greater flexibility to form and implement preservation plans than do other jurisdictions. A large–scale example appears in the case history about the Ohio & Erie Canal National Heritage Corridor in Section IV, "Special Designation."

Summary

All of these levels of planning bear upon "The Problem" described in Section I of this guide. But, to date, *watershed–based, regional,* and *bioregional planning* do *not* yet have the authority to control the critical factors involved in sprawl and farmland loss. So, is one type of planning better than others? If better means what is legally defensible in Ohio courts, then, historically, comprehensive planning is currently the best planning tool of the four. But from an environmental perspective, from the wisest ecological perspective, even the local comprehensive planning done at the township level should extend its scientific analysis to those concerns of watershed, regional, and bioregional planning. Those comprehensive plans would inventory the land's many features, consider the watershed, the multi–jurisdictional areas of land use, the natural biological features, and the carrying capacities of the greater, biologically defined region. Extended logically, Ohio township trustees would give priority in their comprehensive planning activities to the local air quality, water quality and quantity, and the impact of the township's land use on its downstream watershed: for some areas in northeast Ohio that is the Mississippi River, for others, it is where 20% of the earth's available fresh water resides—the Great Lakes.

NOTES

[1]See the "Land Use Series" of fact sheets available from the Ohio State University Extension, Community Development, 700 Ackerman Road,

Columbus, OH 43202-1578; Web Site: <<http://ohioline.ag.ohio-state. edu>>. The *Comprehensive Planning* issue, by John B. Conglose, CDFS-1269-99, was issued in April 1999.

[2] Ohio State University Extension, *Cost of Community Services*, Fact Sheet CDFS–1260–-98, 1-2.

[3] Farmland Information Center, American Farmland Trust, *Cost of Community Services*, Fact Sheet, 1-7. Downloaded May 4, 1999 from Web Site: <<http://www.farm.fic.niu.edu/fic–ta/tafs–cocs.html>>.

[4]The legal argument cited here is based on the "Decision on the Merits on Consolidated Administrative Appeals," Case No. 97CVF–12–11096 (Martin Marietta Materials, Inc., appellant, vs. Reclamation Commission of Ohio, et al., appellees) and Case No. 98CVF–01–238 (Division of Mines and Reclamation, appellant, vs. Board of County Commissioners of Clinton County, Ohio, appellees, rendered October 20, 1998, Judge Beverly Y. Pfeiffer, presiding).

[5]John Stamm, OSU Extension, Franklin County, reported these data in *The Ohio Planning and Zoning Survey: Determining the State of Basic Land Use Tools*, 1999. 1945 Frebis Ave., Columbus, OH 43206-3793; Tel: 614-462-6700; Fax: 614-462-6745; Web Site: <<http://www.ag.ohio-state.edu/~fran/index.html>>.

[6]*A Guide to Developing Local Watershed Action Plans in Ohio* (Columbus, OH: Ohio Environmental Protection Agency, Division of Surface Water, June 1997), 1. Copies are available upon request from OEPA, Tel: 614-644-2001 and at the OEPA Web Site: <<http://www.epa.state.oh.us>>. In addition, the Division of Surface Water also maintains a listing of Ohio–based watershed protection organizations. Copies are available from Laurel Hodory, Tel: 614-644-3020; E-mail: <<laurel.hodory@epa.state.oh.us>>. A selection of local, state, regional, national, and international groups appears in Section VI–B, "Action Center Resources," under " Watershed Protection Organizations."

[7] Chagrin River Watershed Partners, 2705 River Rd., Willoughby Hills, OH 44094-9445; Tel: 440-975-3870; Fax: 440-975-3871; Web Site: <<http://www.crwp.org>>.

[8]This discussion of impaired water bodies comes from the Ohio Farm Bureau's publication, *Speak Out* 54 (May 1999), prepared by John Wargowsky and Julie Grimes. Download from Web Site: <<http://www.ofbf.org>>.

[9] *A Guide to Developing Local Watershed Action Plans in Ohio*, 1-2.

[10]Center for Watershed Protection, 8392 Main Street, Ellicott City, MD 21043; Tel: 410-461-8323; Fax: 410-461-8324; E-mail: <<mrrunoff@pipeline.com>>; Web Site: <<http://www.pipeline.com/mrrunoff>>.

[11] Information about NOACA in this regional planning section comes from its online publications, "About NOACA," "Mission Statement," and "Statement of Planning Functions" at Web Site: <<http://www.noaca.org>>.

[12] Ibid.

[13]From *Citizens' Bioregional Plan for Northeast Ohio,* a special issue of the *EcoCity Cleveland Journal,* No. 6 (Spring 1999), 5. Web Site: <<http://www.ecocleveland.org>>.

[14] Ibid., 4.

[15] Ibid., 13.

III. FROM PLANNING TO PROTECTION: ZONING AND SUBDIVISION REGULATIONS

III. FROM PLANNING TO PROTECTION: ZONING AND SUBDIVISION REGULATIONS

(*Authors' Note:* For further background on zoning and subdivision regulations, please see Section V, "How Your Local Government Works with Respect to Land Use")

This section shows the basis for the assumption that a thorough comprehensive plan with recommended zoning and detailed subdivision regulations can produce an effective legal instrument to control sprawl and preserve natural resources, farmland, open space, and vital urban areas.

Expanding upon the general concept of comprehensive planning in preceding Section II, the six steps of a local comprehensive plan are these:

STEP 1. Identify the Problems and Opportunities; Set Goals

Problems might include an inadequate tax base to fund schools; rampant development that is rapidly changing the character of the community; lack of parks and recreational areas; road and utility costs that have exceeded the community's tax base; conflict between septic system versus sewer / water line advocates; etc. Opportunities might include a large land gift to the community for parks and recreation, or an economic windfall, such as the recent payment of over $15,000,000 to Bainbridge Township, Ohio, from the estate taxes of Paul Frohring. Goals might include the designation of an open space sub–plan. It would identify land for open space preservation using a variety of tools, such as a *planned unit development* designation. Other areas of open space could be designated for preservation using other tools, such as *outright purchase, conservation easement, agricultural zoning*, and other means described in Section IV. And, the sub–plan could prescribe areas for concentrating development, thus minimizing sprawl, through the use of such tools as *transfer of development rights.*

STEP 2. Collect Community Information

The community information collected provides the scientifically supportable data and documentation that may be needed for legal challenges to the plan or, later, to its zoning resolution or ordinance. Community information includes (1) inventories of the natural resources—soils, water, animals and plants, drainage areas, riparian areas [stream banks], groundwater recharge spaces, wetlands, floodplains, etc.; (2) human resources—demographics, including education of residents, income, family composition, etc.; (3) economic resources—taxes, property and other levies; (4) cost of community services—overall budgets and infrastructure costs, highways, utilities, etc.[1]; (5) community land–use composition—residential, industrial, including agricultural percentage, other business types, open space—parks, etc.; (6) maps of the entire area showing existing land use practices, as well as significant soil types and other natural features. Lists of pending projects or commitments that can not be cancelled or placed on hold must also be collected. Ideally, all of the community information should be of three kinds: historic, contemporary, and projected. Where available, similar information for jurisdictions in outlying communities should also be gathered for comparative purposes.

STEP 3. Compare Scenarios

Creating various maps, determining revenue flow from taxes, assessing "build outs" (maximum development) versus maintaining the existing balance of development and open space—all these scenarios allow participants to weigh the effects of the various plans and their effects. From such comparisons they can isolate the characteristics of a community they most want to attain and most want to avoid.

STEP 4. Select a Plan

The comprehensive plan will actually be a set of sub–plans for each of the goals the community wishes to achieve. One sub–plan might address housing; another, transportation; still another, open space for parks, for habitat, and water quality protection, etc. Still another sub–plan might include encouraging certain kinds of industry in the community, such as farming, by creating incentives for farmers to keep their land in agriculture or animal husbandry, rather than selling it for development. As such, this particular sub–plan—as well as any others—would directly address the goal versus the economic factors necessary to achieve it.

STEP 5. Implement the Plan

Once the comprehensive plan and its sub–plan parts are complete, planning participants then turn to the existing tools to apply to realize the plan goals. The variety of tools described in this guide in Section IV will give most communities the framework necessary to help them achieve their plans.

STEP 6. Monitor Progress

A series of benchmark events tied to dates for achieving them should be reviewed by a body of citizens and public officials at regular intervals so that problems, if any, can be solved and progress measured against the goals of the plan.

With a comprehensive plan in hand, the next step is to write (or rewrite) zoning regulations to carry out the specific goals and objectives of the plan.

The Comprehensive Plan and Zoning

Ideally, the comprehensive plan with its specific goals and objectives is expressed by the public through zoning regulations. The state delegates three broad types of power to local governments—taxation, eminent domain, and police power. Zoning is a police power. As noted in Section II, zoning is not a community requirement, and many jurisdictions do not have any zoning regulations. Ohio's enabling legislation allows municipal zoning, that for villages and cities, which are incorporated governments, and rural zoning for townships, which are unincorporated governments. Since the focus of this guide is on outmigration to suburban areas creating sprawl and, in most instances, the resulting loss of farmland and open space, this Section primarily addresses rural zoning regulations. Under the ORC, that is the purview of counties and townships.[2]

Counties and townships were originally viewed by the state as essentially farmland and thus were governed as an extension of the state, whereas municipalities were seen as virtually autonomous. Now, many counties and townships are faced with urban development situations, but they do not have the full authority to respond in ways that are appropriate to the health and welfare of their citizens. Whatever the development challenges, counties and townships must follow the zoning process established by the Ohio Revised Code. They are not free to adopt their own process for establishing or enforcing zoning codes. Therefore, redress of this problem at the *state level* is critical. Some help is forthcoming in certain recent and proposed changes in land–use regulation, and those are discussed later in this Section. They provide new opportunities for local governments to control the effects of urban population movements and the loss of farmland to development.[3]

County zoning may include all or any number of townships in the county, but the zoning text is the same for all townships. Township zoning is the responsibility of township trustees, while county zoning falls under the jurisdiction of the county commissioners. A township administers its own zoning regulations unless it has voted to let the county administer it.

The enactment of county and township zoning, and the relationships among their respective zoning commission, the board of zoning appeals, and the zoning inspector are detailed in publications noted at the end of this Section and in Section IV. But, put simply, this is how it works. Township trustees (1) adopt a resolution (called an ordinance in municipalities) to proceed with zoning, (2) appoint an advisory zoning commission which prepares zoning text and maps, (3) hold a public hearing, (4) seek a county or regional planning commission comment, (5) hold a second public meeting and a review of the text and maps, then (6) submit the resolution to local referendum where it becomes law with a majority vote. With this process, townships can customize zoning in their communities so that it reflects the natural and cultural resources of the area and their residents' special needs and interests.[4]

The Four Major Zoning Districts

There are several different types of zoning districts, but the four major categories are: (1) agricultural, (2) residential, (3) business, and (4) industrial.[5] As mentioned above, in Ohio the state allows some new flexibility in zoning regulations in the form of *planned unit development*, which includes *cluster development zoning* and *conservation development zoning.*

Flexible Zoning

Flexible zoning, or development, emerges in a variety of projects, originating primarily from the philosophy, values, or needs of a landowner and from those same determining factors expressed by a community through its comprehensive plan—or lack of it—and its zoning—or the lack of it (see Section II, The Role of Planning in Land Preservation).

The major forms have similar characteristics, and their names are often used interchangeably. Therefore, they are distinguished briefly in a group here but detailed in Section IV where they are referenced alphabetically in five separate categories. The order below progresses from the type of project that *least* manages open space, the protection of natural resources, and sustainable development to those which prioritize those characteristics the *most*. The range and degree to which these priorities are addressed in each zoning type can vary greatly by community.

Traditional Zoning: Typically 0 to 5% open space, maximum number of housing units allowed, permitted by township, or in its absence, county zoning.

Planned Unit Development Zoning: Usually 10 to 40% open space; uniform lot sizes and frontages; encourages creative design; can allow mixed use units — residential, retail, office, commercial; enabled by the state's *planned unit development* legislation.[6, 7]

Cluster Development Zoning: Variably 20 to 95% open space; like *conservation development zoning,* concentrates dwelling units, open space generally shared by homeowners association; natural areas given some protection; can be enabled under *planned unit development zoning.*

Conservation Development Zoning: At least 25 to 40% open space; a type of *cluster development zoning* that emphasizes scientific studies to achieve preservation of natural features and protection of soils, vegetation, waterways, etc.; can be enabled by *planned unit development zoning.*

Limited Development: Generally 50 to 90% open space; intended to balance the landowner's dual goals of maximizing conservation while generating some cash flow to cover costs of conservation and/or to meet other financial needs.

Townships and Subdivision Regulations

In Ohio townships there is yet another challenge for managing natural resources and farmland preservation planning. With or without its own zoning, townships must adhere to the subdivision regulations issued and enforced by the county or the regional planning commission. In short, Ohio townships may not control the subdivision of their land: counties control it.

Subdivision regulation directs the actual physical layout and design of property at the time it is initially developed or for any new single–family residential development that, under *Ohio Planning and Zoning Law*, involves the creation of more than five new lots, at least one of which is less than five acres, or which involves the opening, widening, or extension of a public street. Complementary site–plan review is normally required for new and expanded or altered multi–family, retail, office, institutional, and industrial developments.

Both subdivision and site–plan regulations require that the local government review the layout and design of new, expanded, or altered developments to insure that they meet appropriate standards. These standards apply to such details as location, design, construction of streets, sidewalks, parking lots, landscaping, sewers, water lines, parks, and open spaces.[8]

While comprehensive planning, zoning, and subdivision regulations provide the framework for the community vision, the means for making that vision a reality lie in the application of appropriate land management tools. Those tools come in many forms: as legal instruments, federal and state–funded programs, voluntary incentives, or other special practices.

Over forty tools are detailed in Section IV. With them communities realize the goals identified in their comprehensive plan. Most of the tools apply in Ohio; those that do not have been applied successfully in other states. Each is accompanied by case histories to provide readers with a direct connection to individuals who have used or are using the tools in their own communities. Finally, each tool includes additional information sources at agencies, in publications, and at Web sites. By consulting these resources, citizens, public officials, and other interested parties can determine which tools are best for achieving the desired goals of their communities.

NOTES

[1]The Conservation Fund, *Pilot Conservation Development Evaluation System*, Revised Draft, Version June, 2, 1999 (Chicago, IL: 1999), 3-10. See also *Community Choices: Thinking through Land Conservation, Development, and Property Taxes in Massachusetts*, the Trust for Public Land's New England Region report, 1998. Downloaded July 19, 1999 from Web Site: <<http://www.tpl.org/tpl/nero/comchoices>>. See as well the American Farmland Trust's *Fiscal Costs and Public Safety Risks of Low-Density Residential Development on Farmland: Findings from Three Diverse Locations on the Fringe of the Chicago Metropolitan Area*, March 1998. Downloaded May 4, 1999 from Web Site: <<http://farm.fic.niu.edu/cae/wp/98-1/wp98-1.html>>.

[2] Office of Local Government Services, Ohio Department of Development, *Ohio Rural Zoning Handbook*, Fourth Edition (Columbus, Ohio: Ohio Department of Development, 1991); Ohio Department of Development, 24th - 29th Floors, 77 S. High St., Columbus, OH 43215-6108; Tel: 614-466-3379; Fax: 614-644-0754.

[3] Richard C. Brahm, "Zoning and Property Rights," a presentation at OSU Extension's "Better Ways to Develop Ohio" conference on June 25, 1999, at the Columbus Athenaeum, Columbus, OH.

[4] *Ohio Revised Code*, Section 519.12. Downloaded June 2, 1999 from Web Site: <<http://orc.avv.com/title-5/sec-519/whole.htm>>.

[5] Ohio State University Extension, *Zoning Types*, No. CDFS--302 (April 1999), 2.

[6] *Ohio Revised Code*, Section 519.12.

[7] *Ohio Revised Code*, Section 303.022. Downloaded July 20, 1999 from Web Site: <<http://orc.avv.com/title-3/sec-303.022..htm>>.

[8] Western Reserve Resource Conservation and Development Council (Kirby Dale, et al.), *The Countryside Program: Conservation Development Resource Manual* (Painesville, OH: 1998), 1C-4, 2C-1. Tel: 216-295-0511; Fax: 216-295-0527; E-mail: <<ninmile@en.com>>.

IV. LAND MANAGEMENT TOOLS

IV–A–1: Private Initiatives — Individual and Group

Agricultural Conservation Easement

Bargain Sale

Conservation Easement

Land Trust

Limited Development

Outright Donation

Estate Management Strategies

AGRICULTURAL CONSERVATION EASEMENT (ACE)

OBJECTIVE: *Agricultural conservation easements (ACEs)* compensate landowners for keeping their land in agricultural production.

WHO ENACTS IT: The individual landowner in conjunction with a public agency, such as a local government, or a private conservation organization, often a *land trust.*

HOW IT WORKS: *ACEs* are actually *conservation easements* specifically directed at protecting productive agriculture. Some states differentiate between *agricultural conservation easements* and *conservation easements,* while others do not. Ohio does, and we have therefore included a separate entry for both of these easements. *ACEs* generally limit subdivisions, nonfarm development, and other uses that are inconsistent with commercial agriculture. Some *ACEs* permit commercial development related to the farm operation and the construction of farm buildings. Most do not restrict farming practices, although some easement holders ask landowners to implement soil and water conservation plans. Landowners who receive federal funds for *ACEs* must implement conservation plans developed with the USDA's Natural Resources Conservation Service.[1]

Most *ACEs* are permanent, though some have extended minimum term limits, such as 30 years. There are some exceptions in which the easement is rescinded, such as neighborhood changes which make farming untenable or if the land is taken by eminent domain. However, certain legal procedures obtain, and the relevant parties must agree to rescind. After the easement is granted, landowners retain all other property rights—privacy, farming, leasing or selling the land (on which the easement is carried, regardless of a new owner). The land is reassessed by the county auditor, usually to a lower value, but it is still subject to local taxation.

The easement holders' responsibilities are the same as those listed for *conservation easements.*

The tax benefits can be several. Donated *ACEs* that meet Internal Revenue Code 170(h) criteria are treated as charitable gifts. Thus, donors can deduct an amount equal to 30% of their adjusted gross income in the year of the gift.[2] Other requirements and benefits are described in the *conservation easement* tool section. The American Farm and Ranch Protection Act of 1997 added Section 2031(c) to the code. This permits the executor of an estate or an owner of land subject to a *conservation easement* meeting the requirements of Section 170(h) to elect to exclude for federal estate tax purposes up to 40% of the value of the land. There is a cap of $300,000 in 2001, $400,000 in 2002, and $500,000 in 2003 and thereafter. The full benefit offered by this law is available for easements that reduce the fair market value of a property by at least 30%; smaller deductions are available for easements that reduce property value by less than 30%.[3]

Fund sources to purchase *ACEs* are many. General obligation bonds (see the case history in the *farmland protection program* tool unit) are the most popular source; property taxes usually require a public referendum for a dedicated levy; real estate transfer taxes are generally paid by the buyer at the time of the transaction; sales taxes by local governments are authorized in about half of the states; annual appropriations are used in some instances; federal funds normally require matches up to 50%, but they are not assured from year to year. Other attempts to raise money to buy *ACEs* are listed by the American Farmland Trust's Farmland Information Center. They include a cellular phone tax; a voluntary local tax check–off box; state–sponsored credit cards; lottery proceeds; development taxes in special districts; mitigation ordinances, either granting an *ACE* or paying the equivalent for future *ACEs*; and other possibilities which have their own pros and cons.[4]

ADVANTAGES: *Agricultural conservation easements* permanently protect important farmland while keeping the land in private ownership and on local tax rolls. They can be custom–designed to meet the needs of individual farmers, ranchers, and unique properties. They provide farmers with income, property, and estate tax reductions, with the last making the transfer to heirs more affordable.

DISADVANTAGES: *ACEs* cannot guarantee that farming will continue: neighborhood changes and agricultural economics may force cessation. Therefore, the terms of the agreement must be flexible to allow farmers to adjust to these circumstances. Also, the farmland can be taken by eminent domain. Donating the development rights may be financially difficult for a farmer, and for this same monetary reason, a prospective buyer may not wish to be limited by the *ACE*. And, as in all *conservation easement* management, the holder of an *ACE* has continuing oversight responsibilities and expenses.

CASE HISTORY: *American Farmland*, the Spring 1999 issue, contained an example of farmland protection using an *agricultural conservation easement* in an article by JoJo Gehl, "The Farm Legacy Program, How AFT Helps Private Landowners Protect Their Farms and Ranches." Virginia Dalnodar and her sister each inherited 50% of her great grandfather's farm in Ohio. In 1997, after her sister passed away, Dalnodar who lives on the east coast, wanted to keep the land in farming and provide income for her children and her co–owning sister's children. She donated her 50% interest in the farm to AFT and also gave AFT appreciated securities, which the Trust sold to purchase the remaining 50% from her niece and nephews. With full title to the farm, AFT took over the lease with the long–term tenant farmer.

Gehl writes, "For the next several years, Dalnodar will receive a monthly payment from AFT out of rent from the farm. In 2001, or possibly sooner, AFT will sell the land, subject to a *conservation easement* to be held by AFT, to the current tenant or another farmer. AFT will take proceeds from this sale and buy an annuity that will provide Dalnodar and her successors with income for 20 years. With money left after the annuity purchase, AFT will establish a fund to protect other farms in Ohio."[5] (*Case History Source:* For additional details, contact AFT's Director of Land Protection at 800-370-4879.)

ACTION STEPS: Obtain a copy of *Fact Sheet: Status of State Pace Programs*, available from the Farmland Information Center, American Farmland Trust (AFT), 1200 18th St., NW, Suite 800, Washington, DC 20036; Tel: 202-331-7300; Fax: 202-659-8339; Web Site: <<http://www.farmland.org>>. In addition, see the AFT's Fall 1999 *American Farmland* issue. A quarterly publication, this issue summarizes the national status of farmland protection efforts. Information on membership in AFT is available at the above address and Web site, and it includes an annual subscription to the magazine.

NOTES

[1] Farmland Information Center, American Farmland Trust, *Fact Sheet: Agricultural Conservation Easements*, 2. Downloaded from Web Site: <<http://farm.flc.niu.edu/flc-ta/tafs-ace.html>>.

[2] Ibid., 2.

[3] Ibid., 2.

[4] Farmland Information Center, American Farmland Trust, *Fact Sheet: Purchase of Agricultural Conservation Easements: Sources of Funding*

(January 1999), 4. Downloaded from Web Site <<http://farm.fic.niu.edu/fic-ta/tafs-acefund.html>>.

[5] American Farmland Trust (J. Gehl), "The Farm Legacy Program," *American Farmland*, Vol. 20, No. 1 (Spring 1999), 21.

BARGAIN SALE

OBJECTIVE: To provide permanent protection for land by selling it to a conservation organization at a price lower than the market value.

WHO ENACTS IT: The individual landowner, in conjunction with a government agency or a private conservation organization such as a land trust.

HOW IT WORKS: A *bargain sale* strikes a compromise between selling a property at fair market value and donating the property outright. The former option makes the transaction more expensive for the conservation organization, while the latter makes the arrangement more expensive for the landowner. Instead, the landowner sells the land to a conservation organization at a reduced price while still making some income on the property. In addition, the landowner can claim the difference between the full market value and the selling price as a charitable gift that is tax–deductible.

In some cases, the landowner and the recipient organization may negotiate an installment sale in which the property is transferred over an extended period of time.

ADVANTAGES: A *bargain sale* allows a landowner to place the property under the protection of a conservation organization while receiving some monetary compensation. In addition, the landowner is generally eligible for income and capital gains tax benefits on the percentage of the land's value that was donated. These features make it attractive to landowners who cannot afford *outright donation*. Finally, the conservation organization, in turn, does not have to pay the full market value for the property.

DISADVANTAGES: The landowner does not receive as much compensation as the property would bring if sold at its fair market value. However, the conservation organization still has to come up with a substantial amount of money to acquire the land.

CASE HISTORY: In the 1960s, the American Electric Power Company (AEP) purchased 3,000 acres of land along Sandusky Bay. The site's proximity to Lake Erie and the vast supply of cooling water that it affords made the location an attractive one for a new power plant. Over the next two decades, as heavy industry began to leave northern Ohio and the demand for electricity declined, AEP could no longer justify constructing the plant. By the early 1980s, it was ready to sell the property.

Two centuries before, the land had formed part of a vast network of marshes that stretched all the way to Toledo. Subsequent draining and development activity had transformed much of the area to farm fields, industrial sites, and marinas. The AEP property, however, remained largely undeveloped and continued to provide critical habitat for a number of wetland species, including a wide variety of birds. In particular, it contained nesting habitat for bald eagles.

These biological assets attracted The Nature Conservancy (TNC), a nonprofit conservation organization. In 1986, AEP and TNC agreed to a *bargain sale* for the entire property. While the land had a fair market value of $4.2 million, AEP sold the parcel for $2.8 million. TNC did not have to pay the full price, and AEP got a tax deduction on the $1.4 million worth of property value that it donated.

In 1987, TNC sold the land to the State of Ohio for management as the Pickerel Creek Wildlife Area. (**Case History Source:** Adapted from a write–up by Jeff Knoop, former Director of Science and Stewardship, The Nature Conservancy, Ohio Chapter; see TNC Ohio Chapter contact details below.)

ACTION STEPS: The Nature Conservancy, Ohio Chapter, Jan Burkey; Scott Davis, Assoc. Dir., Jeff Newberg, Dir. of Acquisitions, 6375 Riverside Drive, Ste. 50, Dublin, OH; 43017; Tel: 614-717-2770; Fax: 614-717-2777. Web Site: <<http://www.tnc.org/Infield/State/Ohio>>. Obtain the booklet, *A Landowner's Guide to Preserving Natural Areas*, from the Ohio Department of Natural Resources, Division of Natural Areas & Preserves, 1889 Fountain Square Ct., Columbus, OH 43224; Tel: 614-265-6453; Fax: 614-265-3096; Web Site: <<http://www.dnr.state.oh.us/odnr/dnap/dnap.html>>. Contact your local land trust (see listings in the **Action Center Resources**) about the potential of a given property for a *bargain sale.* For a case history about some of the issues in the valuation of land in a *bargain sale*, see Todd D. Mayo's "Tax Court Determines Value of Natural Lands in a Bargain Sale" at this Web Site: <<http://mayo.mayolawfirm.com/ Philanthropy/Glick.html>>. Wisconsin's Gathering Waters has information about conservation options for landowners—visit its Web Site: <<http://www.gatheringwaters.org/resource_options. html>>.

CONSERVATION EASEMENT

OBJECTIVE: A *conservation easement* is a restriction placed on a piece of property to protect the resources—natural or manmade—associated with the parcel.

WHO ENACTS IT: The individual landowner, in conjunction with a government agency or a private conservation organization, such as a *land trust*, voluntarily either sells or donates a *conservation easement* on the parcel and signs a legally binding agreement that prohibits certain types or amounts of development (residential and / or commercial) from taking place, while retaining title to the parcel.

HOW IT WORKS: This land protection technique is based upon the legal definition of land ownership, which bestows a "bundle of rights" on the property owner. By placing a *conservation easement* on the land, the owner agrees to give us some of those rights, since such an easement restricts development. Examples of easements include utility easements, access easements, and mining easements. A qualified recipient organization holds the easement and is required to monitor and enforce the adherence of current and future property owners to the terms of the easement.

Conservation easements may be placed on some parts of a property and not others and may allow the owner to retain certain rights with respect to the property, such as the continuation of farming, cutting of firewood, and even building an additional house. The owner retains all other property rights, such as the right to lease or sell the property, and the right to privacy—though some government–initiated easements, such as *farmland protection programs*, may allow the party holding the *conservation easement* to enter the property to monitor its management obligations.

In most cases, donating a *conservation easement* makes the landowner eligible for certain tax benefits. These include a potential reduction in federal income tax (IRS 170(h)) and estate tax.[1] Ohio law (ORC 5713.01) requires the county auditors to take into account the diminution in value as a result of the imposition of the *conservation easement* (ORC 5713.04), often resulting in a lower property tax assessment.

In general, an owner who contributes less than the entire interest in a property is *not* allowed a deduction under ORC Section 170(f)(3)A. However, an exception to this rule is provided in Section 170(f)(3)(B)(iii) for a "qualified conservation contribution." It must meet these criteria:

❏   The transfer is a qualified real property interest

❏   It goes to a qualified organization

❏   The future designated use is exclusively for conservation purposes

❏   The duration of the contribution is in perpetuity

❏   And, if it is valued over $5,000, the claim for a deduction must be confirmed with a qualified appraisal certified on Form 8283[2]

These requirements are defined in Section 170(h) as follows:

❏   "Qualified real property interest" includes any of the following interests in real estate: (1) entire interest of the donor (other than a qualified mineral interest); (2) a remainder interest (made at the time of death); (3) a qualified restriction granted in perpetuity on the use of the property, namely, a *"conservation easement."*

❏   "Qualified organizations" include publicly supported charitable organizations which meet 501 (c) (3) rules and the public support test of Section 509(a). A private foundation does *not* qualify. Land trusts, governmental units, and regional and national organizations such as The Nature Conservancy and The Audubon Society also qualify. The organization must make a commitment to protect the conservation purposes of the donation and have the resources to enforce those restrictions.

❏   "Conservation purpose" means: (1) the preservation of land for outdoor recreation by, or the education of, the general public; (2) the protection of a relatively natural habitat of fish, wildlife, or plants, or similar ecosystems; (3) the preservation of open space (including farmland or forestland) where such preservation is (a) for the scenic enjoyment of the general public, or (b) pursuant to a clearly defined federal, state, or local governmental conservation policy and will yield a significant public benefit; (4) the preservation of a wild or scenic river or to protect the scenic, ecological, or historical character of the property that may be contiguous to existing conservation sites; or (5) the preservation of an historically important land area or a certified historic structure.

❏   "In perpetuity" requires the essential conservation purpose must be preserved forever.

❏   A "qualified appraisal" is required, and the appraiser must verify the amount of the deduction on Form 8283 for deductions over $5,000.

Additionally, where the donor reserves certain rights that might impair the conservation interest of the property, the donor must:

• Document the condition of the property at time of the gift
• Grant the donee the right to inspect and enforce legal remedies
• Subordinate a mortgage on the property[3]

Other land protection programs employ *conservation easements* to restrict activities in perpetuity, such as the *farmland protection program*, *purchase of development rights*, *conservation reserve program*, the *wetlands reserve program*, and others.

ADVANTAGES: An easement allows a landowner to protect valuable resources on the property while retaining ownership of the land. Although relinquishing some or all of the development rights, the owner generally reserves all other rights to the land.

DISADVANTAGES: To receive tax benefits, the law requires that landowners donate the easement in perpetuity. This means that landowners have no legal grounds for recovering the rights granted by the *conservation easement* if they later change their minds. (Certain programs, such as the *farmland protection program*, allows reversion of farmland to the owner if, because of some nearby conflict such as development, farming becomes impossible.) Donors release the opportunity to develop the land and reap any economic benefit from that action. For the easement holder, there are supervisory expenses to fulfill holder responsibilities.

CASE HISTORY: In 1980, Lake County, Ohio, resident James P. Storer deeded a *conservation easement* on 58 acres of wooded land on the south side of the Grand River to the Ohio Chapter of The Nature Conservancy. His easement limits land use on the property to minimal trail maintenance, cutting of firewood, and removal of dead trees. The terms forbid use of the land for construction, hunting, fishing, or camping.

Mr. Storer said he wished to protect the hardwood stand from lumbering or development. About 40 of the 58 acres are covered with mature stands of second–growth red oak, white oak, and beech that are 75 to 100 years old; white maple, hickory, tulip, and sassafras are among other tree species on the parcel.

This plot may be one of the oldest and healthiest woodlots left in the Lake County area. It is a cornerstone in a larger Grand River Preservation Project with the Ohio Department of Natural Resources, the Lake County Soil and Water Conservation District, Lake Metroparks, the Natural Resources Conservation Service, and the Ohio Chapter of The Nature Conservancy.

When the easement was complete, Mr. Storer took a significant deduction for the donation on his tax return for the year. He added that he hoped that his experience will encourage others to grant *conservation easements* on their lands. (*Case History Source:* For further information, contact Scott Davis, Assoc. Dir., The Nature Conservancy, Ohio Chapter, 6375 Riverside Drive, Ste. 50, Columbus, Ohio 43017; Tel: 614-717-2770; Fax: 614-717-2777. Or, contact James P. Storer, 5330 Blair Road, Perry, Ohio 44081; Tel: 440-254-4952.)

ACTION STEPS: For *conservation easement* contract forms, contact The Nature Conservancy, International Headquarters, 1815 North Lynn Street, Arlington, VA 22209. Tel: 703-247-3724. Forms are also available from the Ohio Department of Natural Resources, Division of Natural Areas & Preserves, Tel: 614-265-6453, along with information about conservation along Ohio's designated scenic rivers. Additional details are available in *Model Conservation Easement and Historic Preservation Easement, 1996* by Thomas S. Barrett and Stefan Nagel, published by the Land Trust Alliance. Readers who want to know about managing easement programs may obtain *The Conservation Easement Handbook, Managing Land Conservation and Historic Preservation Easement Programs* by Janet Diehl and Thomas S. Barrett from the Land Trust Alliance. For tax benefits, consult *Preserving Family Lands: Book I—Essential Tax Strategies for the Landowner* (October 1998) and *Book II* (March 1997), by Stephen J. Small, published by Landowners Planning Center.

NOTES

[1] Thomas Quintrell, "Conservation Easements, Land Trusts, Tax Incentives, & Estate Planning," a presentation at OSU Extension's "Better Ways to Develop Ohio" conference on June 25, 1999, at the Columbus Athenaeum, Columbus, OH. E-mail: <<Tquintrell@arterhadden.com>>; and subsequent telephone and written communications from T. Quintrell to J. Chadbourne, June through October 1999.

[2] Ibid.

[3] Ibid.

ESTATE MANAGEMENT STRATEGIES

OBJECTIVE: To address tax implications that may significantly affect a landowner's ability to conserve land and / or pass it on to heirs.

WHO ENACTS IT: In consultation with a legal adviser, the individual landowner initiates an appropriate estate plan.

HOW IT WORKS: Stephen J. Small, an attorney, has written two books introducing and detailing a number of techniques for preserving family lands, including several amplified in this guide, such as *conservation easements* and *outright donation*. In Chapter 3 of *Preserving Family Lands: Book II—More Planning Strategies for the Future*, he introduces "the basic rules" for estate planning.[1] These provide the essential background information with which a landowner, in consultation with a legal adviser, can proceed to preserve family lands. Therefore, we have abstracted the essentials of Small's basic tax rules here and referred his publications below to encourage taking the next steps.

Small begins by stating that the federal tax law starts with the proposition that "every gift, every transfer of wealth or value, is potentially subject to gift tax or estate tax." There are four exceptions to this concept that provide the basis for preserving family lands:

❏ **Annual Exclusion:** Each year, you can give away $10,000 to as many different people as you like without you or the recipient being subject to taxation. If you are married, your spouse may also give another $10,000 so, together, you may give any one person up to $20,000 per year without a tax consequence. This exclusion does not prevent you from paying additionally for someone's medical bills or tuition costs, provided they are paid directly to the medical service provider or to the qualifying educational institution (Section 2503[e]). The actual gift may be in some form other than cash, such as interests in a ranch, or farm, or corporate stock—it is the dollar value that counts.

❏ **Marital Deduction:** Spouses can give each other unlimited gifts, unlimited transfers of value, either during lifetime or at death, with no gift or estate tax charged.

❏ **Charitable Gift:** If you give a *conservation easement*, or an *outright donation*, or cash, to a qualified organization, you can take an income tax deduction of up to 30% of your adjusted gross income and the remaining amount over the following five years, and that asset is no longer counted in the value of your estate.

☐ **Unified Credit:** In addition to gifts under annual exclusion, marital deduction, and charitable transfers under the 1997 Taxpayer's Relief Act, every individual can give to other people—during the individual's lifetime or at death—a total of $650,000 (for 1999; see chart below, as this threshold rises), all without any federal gift tax or estate tax. This credit increases over the next several years as follows:

1999	$650,000	**2004**	$850,000
2000–2001	$675,000	**2005**	$950,000
2002–2003	$700,000	**2006**	$1,000,000

Small gives the following example to illustrate the application of these exceptions. "Bill, a widower, has $1,000,000 in the bank. Bill gives the $1,000,000 to his daughter tomorrow. There is no gift tax on the first $10,000 of the gift because of the annual exclusion. There is no gift tax on the next $650,000 because of the annual exclusion. There is a gift tax on the remaining $340,000." But, in another situation, Bill has $1,000,000 in the bank. He dies. He leaves the $1,000,000 to his daughter. There is no federal estate tax on the first $650,000 because of the unified credit. The $10,000 annual exclusion does not apply since Bill died. Therefore, there is a federal estate tax on the remaining $350,000. Gift and estate tax rates are the same: 30% for gifts and estates of $100,000 to $150,000, and up to 55% on gifts and estates over $3,000,000.[2]

Significantly, Small points out what he calls "the most common tax planning mistake." It occurs when, say, a husband and wife own a property jointly with right of survivorship, or JWROS, with simple wills. One of them dies, leaving everything to the other. There is no estate tax at that time, because now the survivor owns all of the property. But, when that second person dies, the whole estate is treated as one, and the estate is entitled to only a $650,000 tax credit. But, if the two owners had divided their ownership so they each owned half, for example, by changing their ownership to "tenants in common," then with new wills they each may use a unified credit of $650,000. If the property were worth $1,300,000, the estate tax would be charged on the difference between $1,300,000 and the one unified credit of $650,000, or on the remaining $650,000. In the second case there would be no tax, since the $1,300,000 estate would be entitled to two unified credits, reducing the taxable estate value to zero.

The book then offers further ideas that may be considered and practical examples to illustrate the advantages of those approaches to preserving family lands.

In all cases, consult your tax law attorney before making any transactions.

CASE HISTORIES: These are included with each of the land management tools in this guide, such as *conservation easement, outright donation*, as well as with the tax incentive tools described, such as *purchase of development rights, current agriculture use value*, etc.

ACTION STEPS: Obtain a copy of both of Stephen Small's books: *Preserving Family Lands: Book 1—Essential Tax Strategies for the Landowner* (Boston, MA: 1998) and *Preserving Family Lands: Book II—More Planning Strategies for The Future* (Boston, MA: 1997); both are published by and available from the Landowners Planning Center, P.O. Box 4508, Boston, MA02101-4508; Tel: 617-357-1644.

NOTES

[1] Stephen J, Small, *Preserving Family Lands: Book II—More Planning Strategies for The Future* (Boston, MA:, 1997), 17 - 21.

[2] Ibid., 19.

LAND TRUST

OBJECTIVE: To protect important natural and cultural resources in the community.

WHO ENACTS IT: Local citizens, in most cases.

HOW IT WORKS: *Land trusts* are conservation organizations that work to protect some or all of the following community assets: productive agricultural and forestland, scenic and recreational resources, such as lakes and rivers, wildlife habitat, historic sites, community open space; and ecologically sensitive areas, such as groundwater recharge areas, wetlands, river banks, and coastal zones.

Also known as "conservancies," *land trusts* are community–based, private, and nonprofit. They protect land by acquiring outright ownership, by receiving a *conservation easement*, or by facilitating the transfer of ownership or easements to other conservation organizations that will ensure protection.

Specific techniques used by *land trusts* to protect land include *bargain sale, conservation easement, limited development, cooperative agreement,* and *outright donation.* Other commonly used tools are land exchange, preacquisition, revolving fund, rights–of–first refusal, and purchase / leaseback agreements (see Section VI–C, Glossary of Land–Use Terms). This diversity of techniques allows conservancies to develop creative protection plans that meet the needs of the individual landowner, the *land trust,* and the community at–large.

ADVANTAGES: Since most *land trusts* are run by local citizens, they are often more responsive to the needs of the community than are national organizations or government agencies. Because they are private, they possess a flexibility that governments often lack. And, as nonprofits, they do not pay taxes. In addition, donations made to a trust are tax–deductible.

DISADVANTAGES: *Land trusts* are often underfunded and rely heavily on volunteer labor. For those without paid staff, administrative continuity can be a problem. Many *land trusts* also encounter ignorance about their value on the part of the general public. As a result, conservancies must dedicate some of their funds to community education about how *land trusts* can benefit the local region.

CASE HISTORY: About 15 years ago, residents of Russell Township in Geauga County, Ohio, became concerned about the changing character of the area. As the township developed into a bedroom community, prime parcels of open space were disappearing. To confront this problem, a group of citizens formed the Russell Land Conservancy in 1985 to identify and protect important natural resources in the township.

Establishing the Conservancy took about six months. During this time, volunteers identified trustees, achieved nonprofit status, and produced a brochure and press releases. Considerable help was provided by the Trust for Public Land (TPL), a national conservation organization based in San Francisco. Using grants from local foundations, TPL provided technical assistance and covered some of the legal costs of incorporating the Conservancy.

Once this process was complete, the Conservancy set two goals for its preservation efforts: (1) to protect the Chagrin River corridor and (2) to preserve large tracts of open space in the local area. With a staff consisting entirely of volunteers and a budget of between $2,000 and $3,000 annually, the Conservancy had to be creative in putting together its initiatives. It had to rely heavily on a "directed marketing" approach to fund its projects. This involves requesting assistance from individuals who might have a special interest in protecting a tract of land due to their personal relationship or physical proximity to the property.

Former president of the Conservancy, Thomas Stanley, stated that the greatest asset of the Conservancy had been the commitment of its trustees over the long term. However, ongoing needs included more money for acquisitions and more volunteers with legal, financial, and real estate expertise.

In 1995, the Russell Land Conservancy merged with the Chagrin River Land Conservancy, a very successful *land trust* with a paid staff and an annual budget (over $1,000,000 in 1998), and now operates collaboratively under the latter name. As of the fall of 1999, the combined holdings are projected to total approximately 2,000 acres along the Chagrin River. (**Case History Source:** Thomas Stanley, President, Russell Land Conservancy; current contact: Rich Cochran, Exec. Dir., Chagrin River Land Conservancy, P.O. Box 148, Chagrin Falls, OH 44022; Tel: 440-247-0880; Fax: 440-247-0881. E-mail: <<crlc148@aol.com>>.)

ACTION STEPS: For online lists of *land trusts* in the U.S. and Canada, see The Land Trust Alliance's list at Web Site: <<http:////www.lta.org/listing.html>> or write or call the Alliance at 1319 F

St., NW, St. 501, Washington, DC 20004; Tel: 202-638-4725; Fax: 202-638-4730. Also see Todd D. Mayo's list of *land trusts* at his firm's Web Site: <<http://www.mayolawfirm.com/Conservation/ LandTrustsAlpha. html>>, or write or call him at Mayo Law Firm P.C., 92 Boston Post Rd., P.O. Box 23, Amherst, New Hampshire 03031-0023; Tel: 603- 673-6607; Fax: 603-672-9394; E-mail: <<tmayo@mayolawfirm. com>>. Other *land trust* information is available from the Trust for Public Land, National Office, 116 New Montgomery St., 4th Floor, San Francisco, CA 94105; Tel: 415-495-4014; Fax: 415-4954103; E-mail: <<mailbox@tpl.org>>; Web Site: <<http://www.tpl.org>> and through TPL's Cleveland Field Office, 1836 Euclid Ave., Ste. 800, Cleveland, OH 44115; Tel: 216-694-4416; Fax: 216-696-2326; E-mail: <<info@tpl.org>>. Contact Tom Quintrell for a copy of his paper, *Conservation Easements: Land Trusts, Tax Incentives and Estate Planning*, from a presentation at the OSU Extension's "Better Ways to Develop Ohio" conference on June 25, 1999, at the Columbus Athenaeum, Columbus, OH—T. A. Quintrell, Arter & Hadden LLP, 1100 Huntington Bldg., 925 Euclid Ave., Cleveland, OH 44115-1475; Tel: 216-696-1100; Fax: 216-696-2645; E-mail: <<Tquintrell@arterhadden.com>>. Write for or download the Ohio State University Extension Fact Sheet, *Land Trusts*, CDFS-1262-98; Community Development, 700 Ackerman Rd., Columbus, OH 43202-1578, downloadable at Web Site: <<http://ohioline.ag.ohio-state.edu/cd-fact/1262. html>>. Contact your local Soil and Water Conservation District for a copy of its introductory booklet, *Land Trusts: A Primer*. For an in–depth, "how–to" handbook with case histories and sample documents, see *Starting a Land Trust*, published by the Land Trust Alliance. And, for an overview of the tax and other consequences of gifting land, see Stephen Small's *Preserving Family Lands: Book 1—Essential Tax Strategies for the Landowner* (Boston, MA: 1998) and *Preserving Family Lands: Book II—More Planning Strategies for The Future* (Boston, MA: 1997), both available from the Landowners Planning Center, P.O. Box 4508, Boston, MA02101-4508; Tel: 617-357-1644. For a brief look at the *land trust* movement and the role trusts can play in preserving community character, see William Poole's "In Land We Trust," *Sierra*, March / April 1992, 52-58. John Emmeus Davis' "Reallocating Equity: A Land Trust Model of Land Reform," *Land Reform, American Style* (Totowa, NJ: Rowman & Allanheld, 1984), 209-232, reflects on the social and economic ramifications of *land trusts* in the community. Contact the *land trusts* in your area (see **Action Center Resources**). Obtain a copy of *Everybody Wins!: A Citizen's Guide to Development* by Richard D. Klein, 1990, APA Planners Bookstore.

LIMITED DEVELOPMENT

OBJECTIVE: To finance the protection of land by developing a small portion of it.

WHO ENACTS IT: The landowner, in conjunction with a *land trust* or other qualified conservation organization.

HOW IT WORKS: In many cases, landowners would like to protect their property but can not afford the costs. Farmers in particular are often land–rich and cash–poor.

It is a type of *conservation development zoning* typically involving residential densities lower than would be allowed by local codes. *Limited development* provides a means of balancing land preservation with the financial needs of the landowner. The owner sells or develops the part of the property with the least natural or cultural significance, while protecting the area with the greatest importance. Protection can be achieved by means of a *conservation easement* or an outright transfer of land to a conservation organization (see *outright donation*). Conservation organizations generally only use this technique as a last resort.

ADVANTAGES: *Limited development* can make land preservation affordable. It also has less environmental impact than density–neutral *cluster development zoning*. In addition, if the landowner places a *conservation easement* on the land or donates the property to a conservation organization, that owner should be entitled to a charitable income tax deduction equal to the value of the *conservation easement* or property given.

DISADVANTAGES: From a conservation standpoint, some of the property is lost to development.

CASE HISTORY #1: When a developer outbid the Gates Mills Land Conservancy for 102 acres of land overlooking the Chagrin River, many people thought that another stretch of valuable open space was gone for good. The Conservancy, however, was not ready to give up. Instead, it hired a landscape architect from William Behnke & Associates to draft an alternative development plan. Then Conservancy members met with the developer, Louis J. Marino of Chagrin Falls, and showed him the alternative. Marino agreed to work with the Conservancy and the Village of Gates Mills to modify the original plan and minimize any detrimental impacts on the landscape. The result was a more environmentally sensitive development that also brought distinct benefits for the developer.

On the 43.3 acres of the parcel that lay in Gates Mills, Marino scaled back the number of house lots from 14 to 10. He then granted a *conservation easement* on 20.2 of these acres to the Gates Mills Land Conservancy, thus permanently protecting the steep hillside overlooking the Chagrin River. In addition, through redesign, the project planners managed to reduce the number of times the access road crossed a creek from two to one, thereby reducing the development's impact on this tributary of the Chagrin River.

In return for lowering the number of house lots in his project, Marino received greater cooperation from the Village of Gates Mills, which approved his plan more rapidly than normal. By granting an easement on part of the parcel, Marino made himself eligible for a tax deduction, while at the same time protecting the scenic value of the hillside for the new landowners.

Marino also saved money on construction costs by reducing the number of bridges that had to be built. Lastly, he helped to build his reputation as a developer who is willing to work *with* communities to craft a better development. In this way, the Conservancy, the Village, and the developer managed to protect an environmentally sensitive area in a manner that was acceptable to all three parties (**Case History Sources:** Louis J. Marino, Heartland Development, Inc., 29425 Chagrin Blvd., Pepper Pike, OH 44122; Tel: 216-292-6020; and Thomas Quintrell (former President, Gates Mills Land Conservancy), Attorney, Arter & Hadden, Cleveland, OH; now contact Rob Galloway, Pres., Gates Mills Land Conservancy, P.O. Box 13, Gates Mills, OH 44040; Tel: 440-423-0421 or 216-861-7423; E-mail: <<rgalloway@bakerlaw.com>>.)

CASE HISTORY #2: Standing in contrast to the preceding case history is the purchase of land by the Sustainable Conservation (SC) group in partnership with the Watershed Institute and the Conservation Fund. The 37–acre parcel at 466 Elkhorn Road, Monterey, CA, had been overgrazed and, due to the fragility of the soil base, had eroded and caused substantial water quality degradation to the nearby Elkhorn Slough. After the purchase, the organizations began restoration of the habitats that had suffered during its use as rangeland—wetlands and oak woodlands—in an effort to improve the Elkhorn Slough water quality. They also subdivided some of the property into three residential parcels, and placed the remaining land under *conservation easements*. As the first sustainable development in the area, the Elkhorn experiment disappointed its investors for two reasons: a drastic slide in real estate values in the area in the early 90s and the weak "buying power" of the local residents who are of low and moderate income levels.

Although the group has finally located a "moderate income housing developer," initial private investors in this *limited development* experiment have had to take personal losses on the venture. SC points out that the habitat restoration was clearly a success. And it maintains that an *outright purchase* by a group such as The Nature Conservancy or Trust for Public Land would have been very costly compared to SC's net on the project, even with its loss in equity.[1] As a result, groups looking at *limited development* ventures should be sensitive to the overall real estate market as well as the demographic profiles of likely potential buyers in the area of the project. (**Case History Source:** Sustainable Conservation's *Sustainable Conservation: Conservation Based Land Development*, 109 Stevenson St., Fourth Floor, San Francisco, CA 94105; Tel: 415-977-0380; Fax: 415-977-0381; E-mail: <<suscon@igc.org>>; Web Site: <<http://www.suscon.org>>.)

ACTION STEPS: Download *Sustainable Conservation: Conservation Based Land Development* from the Sustainable Conservation Web Site: <<http://www.suscon.org/projects/cbld._ cbld.html>>. Contact a local conservation organization (see **Action Center Resources**) that can help you to identify the areas of your property that are most worthy of protection. Obtain a copy of Stephen Small's *Preserving Family Lands: Book 1—Essential Tax Strategies for the Landowner* (Boston, MA: 1998), and the Urban Land Institute's 1985 book, *Working with the Community: A Developer's Guide*, as well as *Everybody Wins!: A Citizen's Guide to Development* by Richard D. Klein, 1990, APA Planners Bookstore. In addition, contact your local *land trust* (see **Action Center Resources**) to discuss options for your property that it may be able to help implement.

NOTES

[1] Sustainable Conservation, *Sustainable Conservation: Conservation Based Land Development* (San Francisco, CA: 1999), 2-3. Downloaded August 31, 1999 from Web Site: <<http://www.suscon.org/projects_cbld.html>>.

OUTRIGHT DONATION

OBJECTIVE: *Outright donation*, or gift, "is a very desirable method of property conveyance because it is simple and it gives the entrusted party relative freedom to vary the uses of the property to meet changing needs or conditions."[1] And, donation avoids further real estate or estate taxes, while maximum tax savings can be realized from the donation.

WHO ENACTS IT: An individual landowner (the donor), and a receiving federal, state, government, or conservation organization (the donee).

HOW IT WORKS: While an *outright donation* is desirable and simple and may lead to the greatest tax deduction for the donor, Thomas A. Quintrell, Attorney, strongly advises potential donors to be aware of two concerns:

> The donee must be a "qualified" organization under the Internal Revenue Code.

> The donee should be a well established and reliable organization.[2]

His argument is summarized in his quote from Stephen A. Small (*estate management strategies*), who says, "never trust an unrestricted piece of land." Quintrell explains that time and circumstances change, so that a donee who receives unrestricted land can sell it for any purpose, including development, or just to raise funds for the organization. The donor's purpose in donating the property may thereby be thwarted.[3]

To prevent that sale, the donor might give the property subject to restrictions as to its use and development. But, in that case, the donor would only be entitled to the reduced value of the property subject to the restrictions imposed in the deed.

Quintrell recommends how it *should* work. First, grant a *conservation easement* on the property to a qualified charitable organization. Second, deed the property to a different qualified organization. "In this way, the owner–donor first gets the deduction for the reduced value of the property by reason of the *conservation easement*, and then he gets the balance when he deeds the fee to another qualified charitable organization."[4] This two–step procedure results in the deduction of the full value of the property and protects the donor against unauthorized uses in the future.

To learn about qualifications for granting a *conservation easement*, refer to that title in this guide.

If the property is an outright gift—not a sale—the owner–donor gets a charitable deduction in the donor's income tax return equal to the fair market value of the property at the time of the gift up to 30% of the taxpayer's adjusted gross income. If there is an excess, it carries forward for an additional five years.

ADVANTAGES: *Outright donation* gives landowners a maximum deduction for the value of their property and, if done correctly, can also afford them protection from development. They continue to enjoy the property, e.g., the scenic view, or biking, and it may serve as a buffer for the property retained. The donor no longer has responsibility or liability for the property given, and it is not includable in the donor's estate.

DISADVANTAGES: The landowner does not receive immediate monetary compensation for the donation; rather, it is postponed through tax reductions. There may be some risks associated with the recipient organization's use of the property and long–term stability, so some care is in order to select one with a solid record.

CASE HISTORY #1: Joan Greig owns 24 acres of land in Aurora, Ohio, that she and her husband purchased in 1971. Now a widow, Mrs. Greig decided that her property's assets should remain pristine—a pine forest they had once used for Christmas tree sales, a wetland created by a beaver dam. And she also counts as an added value her land's proximity to a neighboring parcel on Town Line Rd., the Novak Sanctuary, which is owned by the Audubon Society of Greater Cleveland. When given the choice between selling over two–thirds of the property to a developer so he could run a sewer line through it for a proposed development, Mrs. Greig opted instead to make on *outright donation* to the Audubon Society in the form of a *conservation easement* on the property. It "will guarantee that the 15.5 acres will never be developed."[5]

Darhl Foreman of the Audubon Society of Greater Cleveland says that although Mrs. Greig will enjoy a tax benefit from the easement, she would have made more by selling to a developer. However, the easement gives the Novak Sanctuary "an enormous amount of protection."[6] Had the property been sold, the developer would have had to drain the wetland to run the sewer line to the proposed development site.

Mrs. Greig says that she believes her husband would have made the same decision had he been alive, since "he just loved having the land."[6] (**Case History Source:** Barry Kawa, *The Plain Dealer*, reported March 4, 1999. See Note 5, below.)

CASE HISTORY #2: William and Emily Benua faced an interesting dilemma. Lifelong conservationists, they wanted to make sure that their 520–acre property in Fairfield County, Ohio, received permanent protection as a nature preserve. At the same time, they wanted to ensure their own well being for the remainder of their lives. To work out a solution, they turned to the Ohio Chapter of The Nature Conservancy (TNC), a nonprofit conservation organization.

From the outset, TNC was interested in protecting the land. Adjacent to the Clear Creek Valley Preserve, the parcel contained an array of hardwood forest communities, sandstone formations cut by Clear Creek and the Hocking River, and nesting habitats for several rare bird species. Together, these scenic and biological attributes made the land an outstanding candidate for preservation.

After careful planning, the Benuas and the staff from TNC agreed upon an *outright donation* with reserved life estate. Here's how it worked. When Mrs. Benua died, her interest in the property went to TNC. Mr. Benua's share was also transferred to TNC subject to the conditions of a reserved life estate. This arrangement allowed him to continue to live in the house and enjoy the property as long as the land's scenic and biological resources were not damaged. When Mr. Benua died, his remainder interest in the property went to TNC, making it the sole owner of the parcel.

Through this arrangement, the Benuas achieved their wish of protecting the property. They also reaped immediate tax savings and minimized the financial burden on their heirs. In return for their donation, the Benuas received a deduction from their state and federal income tax equal to the value of the charitable gift subject to the reserved life estate. The gift also reduced the value of their estate, saving their heirs considerable inheritance tax.

In 1992, The Nature Conservancy transferred the William Ellsbury Benua and Emily Platt Benua Nature Preserve to The Columbus and Franklin County Metropolitan Park District for ongoing protection and management. (**Case History Source:** Adapted from a write–up by Jeff Knoop, former Director of Science and Stewardship, the Ohio Chapter of The Nature Conservancy.)

ACTION STEPS: Contact Scott Davis, Assoc. Dir., or Jeff Newberg, Division of Acquisitions, Ohio Chapter of The Nature Conservancy, 6375 Riverside Dr., Ste. 50, Dublin, OH 43017; Tel: 614-7176-2770; Fax: 614-717-2777. Contact the ODNR, Division of Natural Areas & Preserves, for a copy of *A Landowner's Guide to Preserving Natural Areas,* Tel: 614-265-6453. Obtain a copy of the American Farmland Trust's Farmland Information Center's *Farm Transfer and Estate Planning,* available from AFT Technical Assistance, Herrick Mill, One Short St., Northampton, MA 01060; Tel: 413-586-4593; Fax: 413-586-9332; Web Site: <<http://www. farmlandinfo.org>>. There are also useful descriptions about the advantages of *outright donation* in three states' Web sites— California, South Carolina, and Texas: (1) *Methods of Land Conservation,* Web Site: <<http://www.iceucdavis.edu/guide_to_ california_programs_for_biodiversity_conserv . . ./Methods.htm>>; (2) South Carolina's Congaree Land Trust document, *Conservation Easements: How They Can Work for You* at Web Site: <<http:// //www.congareelt.org/easements.html>>; (3) and for wetlands areas, Texas Parks and Wildlife's *Wetlands Assistance Guide—General Landowner Options* at Web Site: <<http://www. tpwd.state.tx.us/conserve/wetlands/downopt.htm>>.

NOTES

[1] Information Center for the Environment, College of Agriculture and Environmental Sciences, University of California at Davis, *Methods of Land Conservation—California Programs for Biodiversity Conservation,* 4. Available from the University of California at Davis; downloaded August 18, 1999 from Web Site: <<http://www.ice.ucdavis/edu/guide_to_california_programs_for_ biodiversity_conserv.../methods.htm>>.

[2] Thomas A. Quintrell, letter of June 15, 1999, to J. Chadbourne and telephone conversation between Quintrell and Chadbourne on August 8, 1999, and subsequent fax, Quintrell to Chadbourne, dated August 18, 1999. T. A. Quintrell, Arter & Hadden LLP, 1100 Huntington Bldg., 925 Euclid Ave., Cleveland, OH 44115-1475; Tel: 216-696-1100; Fax: 216-696-2645; E-mail: <<TQuintrell@arterhadden.com>>.

[3] Quintrell, communications on June 15, 1999, August 8, 1999, and August 18, 1999.

[4] Thomas A. Quintrell, letter of June 15, 1999, to J. Chadbourne.

[5] Barry Kawa, "Aurora Woman Gives Rare Easement for Conservation to Audubon Group," *The Plain Dealer* (March 4, 1999), 1-B.

[6] Ibid.

IV. LAND MANAGEMENT TOOLS

IV–A–2: Private Initiatives—Federal & State Programs

Access Management

Agricultural District

Agricultural Economic Development

Brownfields

Conservation Reserve

Current Agricultural Use Value

Farmland Protection Program

Forest Tax

National Conservation Buffer Initiative

Storm Water Management

Wetlands Mitigation and Banking

Wetlands Reserve Program

Wildlife Habitat Incentives Program

ACCESS MANAGEMENT

OBJECTIVE: *Access management* combines roadway engineering with land–use planning to give local governments a means for minimizing the effects of urban sprawl, maintaining intended service levels for different classes of roadways, reducing traffic congestion and travel delay, enhancing vehicular and pedestrian safety, and coordinating land–use and transportation decisions.

WHO ENACTS IT: County and municipal planning commissions, township trustees, zoning commissions, and other public and private development officials who have a role in coordinating land use management and the public highway system.

HOW IT WORKS: To balance the conflicting goals of rapid traffic movement with safe site accessibility, the Ohio Department of Transportation (ODOT) has developed standards that manage the number and spacing of driveways, traffic signals, medians, and intersections. The standards are specified in a *State Highway Access Management Manual On–Line,*[1] adopted by ODOT September 1, 1998 as "best management practices" and are recommended— before development—for inclusion in zoning regulations, subdivision and site–plan reviews, and minor subdivision and lot split regulations that are typically exempt from subdivision regulations.

When vehicular traffic is highly regulated—e.g., four–lane highways, shoulder exits, synchronized stop lights, median strips— it moves rapidly and safely. But, when those same vehicles need to enter and exit a driveway to a single residence, shopping mall, or gas station—and there are no regulations of the location, spacing, and frequency of access points—traffic moves very slowly and unpredictably, creating delays to other vehicles and increasing the likelihood of accidents. John Heilman from the Ohio Kentucky Regional Council of Governments notes these issues:[2]

❑ *Access management* is a safety issue—50 to 60% of accidents are access related, i.e., involving vehicles turning in and out of driveways and across streets.

❑ Of all network–wide fuel consumption, 40% is attributable to vehicles stopped and idling at traffic signals.

❑ Frequent and poorly spaced traffic signals can reduce roadway capacity by over 50%.

Access management, derived from powers conferred to the Director of the Department of Transportation by Section 5501.31 and 5515.01 of the ORC, is a more efficient way of dealing with traffic management. The *State Highway Access Management Manual On–Line*, Section 1.5.1, states basically that all vehicular access and connections to the state highway system should be regulated in accordance with the provisions of the *Manual* or those adopted by local municipalities that meet or exceed the Department's standards.[3] ODOT may review those policies, standards, and requirements to determine whether or not they are consistent with the purpose and standards of the *Manual*. And, it may work with the local authority in implementing standards for permitting access to state highways within the municipality. These "best management practices" can be implemented through conventional applications of zoning, subdivision, and traffic regulations. ODOT also provides some examples illustrating how *access management* standards can be integrated into local land–use regulations.

Zoning: Requirements affecting minimum lot size, frontage, and building setback can be used to achieve desired levels of access and safety within each zoning district, i.e., to quote from ODOT's 9–page overview, *Land Use Regulations Supporting Access Management:*[4]

❑ Lot frontage (facing the main highway) requirements and the minimum size of corner lots should be increased to allow for greater corner clearance.

❑ Desired lot depth, width, and size should be established to ensure there will be adequate space for on–site circulation, parking, driveway throat length, and service drives.

Overlay zoning can provide alternatives to the one–house–one–driveway typical of an existing zoning regulation and can be tailored to the specific circumstances along a particular route. Again from the reference just cited:

❑ Overlay requirements may address any issues, e.g., joint access (shared driveways), parking lot cross access, reverse frontage (also called backage roads, i.e., the principal entry road is behind buildings), minimum lot frontage, driveway spacing, and limitations on the number of new driveways or subdivisions.

❒ An overlay concept along emerging commercial or residential corridors can manage curb cuts by minimizing the number of permitted driveways to one per parcel or by other means, such as with interior road access.

❒ Existing parcels with larger frontages should be permitted more than one driveway and additional driveways should be permitted by special use permit.

❒ Existing parcels with minimal frontage may be permitted a driveway or shared driveway or may require alternative means of access.

❒ Joint access may be required at the time of site–plan approval or subdivision for abutting lots with inadequate frontage.

❒ Land uses should coordinate pedestrian and vehicular access with adjacent properties and design access drives so they do not hinder traffic flow.

Subdivision and Site–plan Review: Subdivision regulations guide the division and subdivision of land into lots, blocks, and public ways. *Access management* review allows planning and engineering staff to advise developers on access standards and issues before they have invested in plat preparation and before problems occur. Access related issues that should be addressed in the subdivision or site–plan review process include the following from ODOT's *Land Use Regulations Supporting Access Management.*[6]

Subdivision Regulations

❒ The roadway system as a whole should meet the projected traffic demand and the individual roads should be designed according to their desired function. The distances between driveways and intersections should be adequate to maintain the needed level of access and safety.

❒ Housing units should front on residential access streets rather than on major roadways.

❒ The site plan should allow enough space for on–site vehicular circulation without causing overflow onto surrounding major roadways.

❐ The pedestrian and bicycle path system should link desired destinations such as residential lots, parking areas, surrounding developments, open space, and recreational and other community facilities.

Site–Plan Reviews

The following illustrates a typical list of access related information that may be required of applicant residential and commercial developers for the site–plan review:

❐ Location of driveways and intersections on both sides of the road.

❐ Distances between driveways, intersections, median openings, traffic signals, and other transportation features on both sides of the property.

❐ Number and direction of lanes to be constructed on the driveway.

❐ Striping and signing plans for both the road and the driveway.

❐ All proposed transportation features (such as auxiliary lanes, signals, median treatments).

❐ Appropriate traffic studies, including trip generation data.

❐ Parking and internal circulation plans.

❐ Plat map showing property lines, rights–of–way, easements, and abutting owners.

❐ A detailed description of any requested variance, the reason, proof of necessity.

❐ A cross–section of the main road.

Minor Subdivision & Lot Splits: Current practice applies minor subdivision or lot splits to land divisions of up to five lots, any one of which is under five acres in area. Since any parcel under five acres in area is subject to minor subdivision regulations, they can be an effective tool in managing development. Since lots greater than five acres are not subject to the subdivision regulations, large "bowling alley" and "flag" lots may be created that cause a variety of problems for owners and local governments. These regulations provide a mechanism to prevent the creation of nonconforming lots that compromise safe and efficient access.

The ODOT *Manual* presents some design options, such as reverse frontage (or backage) roads, parallel frontage roads, medians, driveway spacing and location, joint and cross access, retrofitting nonconforming access, and transit / bicycle / pedestrian access. ODOT emphasizes the term "options," stating that "The complexity of today's transportation system calls for unique solutions to common problems. The right combination of elements can help local officials achieve a safe and efficient highway system."[7]

ADVANTAGES: Fewer delays and accidents cut transportation costs for businesses, and business locations remain more accessible and attractive to customers when there is less congestion. Taxpayers benefit because access managed highways can carry more traffic, reducing the need for more highways. Studies over several decades have shown that *access management* can reduce accidents as much as 50% while safely increasing travel speeds by as much as 40%.[8]

DISADVANTAGES: *Access management* regulations apply to state highways, not to municipal or county highways. ODOT can only encourage and support local governments to adopt their policies and principles. And, if they do not, once development plans have been approved, it is too late to take advantage of the potential for greater safety and traffic efficiency. Close attention should be given to policies and practices that increase impervious surfaces without compensating open space.

CASE HISTORY #1: The Licking County, Ohio, Planning Commission has included *access management* provisions in its subdivision regulations, using national standards similar to those in the ODOT *Manual*. These provisions apply to any development or increase in access points as of July 1, 1996. They are specified in a 20–page document that details, for example, the classification of roads and then the driveway spacing for each type of road—such as 550 feet between driveways on a "major arterial" roadway. This adoption of *access management* was the first in Ohio. It now applies extensively throughout the county. (***Case History Source:*** Jerry Brems, Planning Dir., Licking County Planning Commission, County Planning Department, 205 Second Street, Newark, Ohio 43055. Tel: 740-349-6555. Fax: 614-349-6552.)

CASE HISTORY #2: Findlay, Ohio, by contrast, used overlay zoning in 1997 to control access on U.S. 224. Findlay's Zoning

Regulation Chapter 1170, "TA–O Tiffin Avenue Overlay District," applies to lands lying on the south side of Tiffin Avenue (U.S. 224), between Bright Road and County Road 236, in Hancock County, Ohio. After heavy development on the north side of Tiffin Avenue, it became apparent that the south side "will be redeveloped into more intense land–use forms than the existing single–family residential pattern."[9]

Findlay prepared overlay zoning to manage a number of features the city wished to protect: (1) uses—restricted to retail businesses and services, e.g., restaurants, offices, banks, clubs, theaters; and (2) development standards—setbacks on Tiffin Avenue as well as side and rear yards, structure heights, screening requirements, exterior lighting. Access to the individual properties is by a service drive system and is prohibited directly from Tiffin Avenue. The service entries and exits are opposite those signalized access roads on the north side—essentially precluding new turning points on Tiffin Avenue. Findlay's "Tiffin Avenue Development Plan" map, revised June 4, 1999, displays the result of the overlay.[10] (*Case History Source:* Bruce D. Cochran, Assistant City Engineer, City of Findlay, City Engineering Department, Municipal Building, Room 304, Findlay, Ohio 45840–3346; Tel: 419-424-7121; Fax: 419-424-7120.)

CASE HISTORY #3: Tom King, Planning Director for Hudson, Ohio, does not include *access management* practices either in zoning or subdivision regulations. Rather, in reviewing initial development proposals, he promotes the policies of the ODOT *Manual.* He requires developers to complete a traffic impact study with their proposals so that Hudson can evaluate this additional information in making choices for the community. For example, Hudson has chosen to accept more traffic congestion, in preference to constructing the ODOT *Manual's* recommended number of extra turn lanes. This general approach has worked out well. The policy has good criteria, and it is being well accepted by developers, King summarized. (*Case History Source:* Tom King, Planning Dir., Hudson Community Development, 46 Ravenna Street, Ste. D3, Hudson, Ohio 44236. Tel: 330-342-1790.)

ACTION STEPS: To acquire the Ohio Department of Transportation's *State Highway Access Management Manual On–Line*, download it from its Web Site: <<http://www.dot.state.oh.us/traffic/accessmgmt/Manual_Default.htm>>. For questions, contact Gary Coburn, Access Management Coordinator, Office of Traffic Engineering, Ohio Department of Transportation, Columbus, OH; Tel: 614-644-8153.

NOTES

[1] Ohio Department of Transportation, *State Highway Access Management Manual On–Line*, Section 1.2. Downloaded June 8, 1999 from Web Site: <<http://www.dot.state.oh.us/traffic/accessmgmt/Manual_Default.htm>>.

[2] John L. Heilman, Ohio Kentucky Regional Council of Governments, Technical Service, Cincinnati, OH, reported in his presentation, *Access Management: A Solution to Urban Traffic Congestion,* at OSU Extension's "Better Ways to Develop Ohio" conference on June 24–25, 1999, at the Columbus Athenaeum, Columbus, OH.

[3] ODOT, *State Highway Access Management Manual On–Line*, Section 2.12.5.

[4] Ohio Department of Transportation, *Land Use Regulations Supporting Access Management: Problems, Solutions, Combining Roadway Engineering with Land Use & Development Regulations* (No date), 3.

[5] Ibid., 4.

[6] Ibid., 9.

[7] Ohio Department of Transportation, *The Road to Access Management* (September 1, 1998), 2. Downloaded from Web Site: <<http://www.dot.state. oh.us/traffic/accessmgmt/Road_to.htm>>.

[8] City of Findlay, *Chapter 1170 TA-O Tiffin Avenue Overlay District* (1999 Replacement), Sections 1170.01 through 1170.06, 79-01.

[9] City of Findlay, *Tiffin Avenue Development Plan* (map dated June 4, 1999), unpaginated.

AGRICULTURAL DISTRICT

OBJECTIVE: To form special areas where commercial agriculture is encouraged and protected by offering farmers a deferral of new utility assessments to help achieve the same goals as regulating strategies.

WHO ENACTS IT: Sixteen states have authorized farmers to apply for an *agricultural district* designation on a voluntary basis through their county auditor's office, or if the land is within a municipality, through the city or village administration. The authorizing states are CA, DE, IL, IO, KY, MD, MA, MN, NJ, NY, NC, OH, PA, TN, UT, and VA.[1]

HOW IT WORKS: *Agricultural district* eligibility is the same as *current agricultural use value*, which allows farmland to be assessed at its *current agricultural use value* for real estate purposes rather than at the higher development value. Eligible are: (1) lands of at least 10 acres (but 11 acres with a dwelling on it, since 1 acre is subtracted for a residence on the property), (2) land smaller than 10 acres but having generated at least $2,500 in gross income for three years prior to application, or (3) land for which the owner can present evidence of an anticipated gross income of $2,500 for the year of application but subject to individual county auditor's evaluation. The land has to be devoted exclusively to commercial animal or poultry husbandry, aquaculture (raising of fish), apiculture (raising of bees), field crops, tobacco, fruits, vegetables, nursery stock, ornamental trees, sod, or timber. The land does not have to be contiguous, but it does have to be farmed as one economic unit (i.e., with the same equipment and personnel).[2]

If the farm meets the eligibility criteria, the auditor must certify the application (ORC 929.02[A]). Once approved, the *agricultural district* is in effect for five years; at the end of this time, the owner may elect to extend the term of the *district* for the entire parcel or for a portion of the land. Renewal is made between the first Monday in January and the first Monday in March, as in the case of *CAUV.*[3] If the property is sold before the five–year term expires, the next owner may assume continued enrollment until the conclusion of that term. If the new owner wishes to terminate participation, the back penalty will be asessed.

As an *agricultural district*, the law states that no public entity can collect an assessment for sewer, water, or electrical service on that property, unless it is a residential dwelling of the owner or other nonagricultural structure which may be located in the *district.*[4] The tax is deferred until withdrawal from the program. Since utility assessments are usually based on a frontage and / or total acreage, the costs to a farm may be seriously draining.

Removal of the land from the *district* can have two consequences. First, the deferred assessments become due when the land is withdrawn from an *agricultural district*, and this applies even to a *partial* withdrawal or change in use. And, an additional penalty will be assessed which is one–fourth of the penalty assessed under the *CAUV* program, but the penalty is computed only for the land converted to other uses—not for all the land in the *agricultural district*. If the land is entered into both an *agricultural district* and *CAUV*, a withdrawal could impose double penalties.

The money lost by the county due to the deferred assessment can be made up by the Water and Sewer Commission (ORC 1525) with loans that are paid back when the farmer withdraws from the *district* and pays the deferred amount plus interest. Unfortunately, the General Assembly has not provided new funds to this program in over a decade.

In addition to deferred utility assessments, the *agricultural district* protects enrollees from any civil action regarding nuisances (odors, noises) involving agricultural activities. To many landowners this protection is becoming increasingly important, particularly with livestock operations, as developments crowd farmlands.

Another help to the *agricultural district* enrollee is a provision of an additional review of land value and extra consideration of its necessity and alternatives if the land is to be taken by eminent domain. This assures a fair judgement of compensation to the landowner.

A 1996 survey revealed that in Ohio 3,300,000 acres out of 15,200,000 eligible acres (21%) were enrolled in *agricultural districts*. This is a 50% increase since a prior survey in 1991.

ADVANTAGES: Like *CAUV*, the *agricultural district* incentives help to restore fairness to farmers in the real estate tax system. Ironically, since Ohio farmers own the largest amount of land in a taxing district, they are assessed the greatest tax, yet they use fewer community services than residential land. The suspension of utility assessment helps buy time for farmers and delays conversion of farmlands to nonagricultural uses.

DISADVANTAGES: As a voluntary program, farmers may withdraw from the program, pay the deferred taxes and penalty, and then sell the land for development. To prevent that, additional regulatory tools must be used, such as *agricultural zoning, purchase of development rights*, or *agricultural conservation easement*.[3]

CASE HISTORY #1: Mark and Deborah Mackovjak of Madison Township, Ohio, once owned the Northcoast Perennials Nursery. They were notified they would be assessed for construction of a "water main and necessary appurtenances thereto in County Line Road . . . ," even though it did not benefit their agricultural business. The tentative assessment totaled $29,724.06 for 907 running feet of property, assessed at a rate of $32.77 per foot. But, since they had already enrolled in the *agricultural district* program, their assessment was deferred as long as they continued to farm the land and maintain their enrollment. That bill will become due if the Mackovjaks, or their heirs, sell their land for nonagricultural uses or leave the program. Without the deferment, they might have been forced to sell some of that land to raise the $29,724.06. Mark added that a neighbor was enrolled in the *CAUV* program only, but not the *agricultural district* program. She discovered, too late, that this same waterline assessment was levied against her property at a cost of $72,000. (***Case History Source***: Mark Mackovjak, 7533 South Ridge Rd., Madison, Ohio 44057; Tel / Fax: 440-428-2033.)

CASE HISTORY #2: Mike McGrath, Chief of Planning, Delaware Agricultural Lands Foundation, uses a two–step program to protect farmland in that state. First, he enrolls farmland into the *agricultural district* program, with the usual 10–year minimum enrollment period subject to 5–year renewal. In Delaware's program, the utility assessments are deferred forever; the right–to–farm protection and review of land taken by eminent domain (for a higher compensation) are both included. There is no recoupment upon leaving the *agricultural district* before the contract conclusion except if developed within 5 years after termination. The farmer receives no payments from the Foundation. Next, with enrollment in the *agricultural district* completed, farmers may offer to sell their development rights to the Foundation. This assures preservation in perpetuity. The rationale for selecting properties for *purchase of development rights* (*PDR*) enrollment is based upon soil, zoning, adjacent housing, strategic mapping, and individual farm characteristics. The final judgement rests upon deciding if the selection is objective, understandable, and defensible.

The price paid for *PDR* acreage is the difference between the standard appraised market value of the land only (not housing, barns, or other improvements)—say $2,500 per acre—and the calculated agricultural value, say $800 per acre, which equals $1,700 per acre. The Foundation then invites farmers to offer, or "bid," by stating a discount, such as 50% off the *PDR* acreage value. That would be an offer that would receive a payment of $850 per acre. Since any one farm would differ in value from another, the Foundation chooses to award funds based upon the discount.

The Foundation now enrolls 115,000 acres out of a possible 500,000 acres in Delaware in the *agricultural district* program. And, it has *purchased development rights* of 36,800 acres from the *agricultural district's* 115,000 acres, and projects 44,000 acres by the end of Fiscal Year 2000.

Funding for the effort has been from several sources: the federal *farmland protection program*, a total of $2,330,000; a direct appropriation from the State of Delaware General Assembly following a court settlement with the State of New York, $40,000,000; and, pending, current revenue surplus through the bond bill, $25,000,000 over two years.

Mike concludes that his two–step program works because it is user–friendly, has minimum qualifications, results in straightforward written agreements, focuses on preserving the land, and it is fairly priced. A final benefit to Delaware is the calculation that for every $1 spent on farmland preservation, the state saves $10 on infrastructure costs. (*Case History Source*: Mike McGrath, Chief of Planning, Delaware Agricultural Lands Foundation, Delaware Department of Agriculture, 2320 South DuPont Ave., Dover, Delaware 19901; Tel: 302-739-4811; Fax: 302-697-4465.)

ACTION STEPS: For a copy of the text for a model zoning ordinance, *Model Agricultural Zoning Ordinance, Lancaster County, Pennsylvania,* contact the Center for Excellence in Sustainable Development, U.S. Department of Energy, Office of Energy Efficiency and Renewable Energy, Denver Regional Support Office, 1617 Cole Boulevard, Golden, CO 80401; Tel: 800-363-3732; Fax: 303-275-4830; Web Site: <<http://www.sustainable.doe. gov>>. Also, see Findlay, PA's *agricultural zoning*, including authorized uses, exceptions, conditional uses, and dimensional standards for residential uses, at its Web Site: <<http://www.town.findlay.pa.us/ FINWEB/117403_a.htm>>. The Farmland Information Center of the American Farmland Trust also has a Fact Sheet (September 1998), *Agricultural District Programs*, which reviews the history of the program, its functions, benefits and drawbacks, and provides a summary status of provisions, by state, for U.S. *agricultural districts* at its Web Site: <<http://www.farmlandinfo.org>>.

NOTES

[1] Farmland Information Center, American Farmland Trust, *Fact Sheet: Agricultural District Programs* (September 1998), 1-4. Web Site: <<http://www.farmlandinfo.org>>.

[2] See the "Land Use Series" of Fact Sheets available from the Ohio State University Extension, Community Development, 700 Ackerman Road, Columbus, OH 43202-1578; Web Site: <<http://ohioline.ag.ohio-state.edu>>. The *Agricultural Districts in Ohio* by John D. Rohrer, CDFS-1268-99, was issued in February 1999, 1.

[3] Ibid., 2.

[4] Ibid., 2-3.

AGRICULTURAL ECONOMIC DEVELOPMENT

OBJECTIVE: To improve farmland sustainability by enhancing its economic viability, both before and after other voluntary and regulatory tools are employed to protect it from nonagricultural use.

WHO ENACTS IT: Various levels of government and institutions make loans and grants to support direct wholesale and retail marketing and new value–added farm products to increase agricultural economic productivity.[1]

HOW IT WORKS: The following are economic development strategies for farmers, ranchers, and agricultural communities that provide technical assistance and facilitate access to capital for agricultural business development and expansion. The following twelve strategies are verbatim from the American Farmland Trust's Farmland Information Center pamphlet, *Agricultural Economic Development.*[2]

❐ *Planning for Agricultural Viability:* Some local governments are incorporating agricultural business strategies into their traditional economic development plans. Four local governments in Maryland employ economic development specialists who advise farmers on new products, services, marketing strategies, and management techniques to increase profitability. New York's county Agricultural and Farmland Protection Boards have the authority to receive state matching funds to develop and implement county agricultural and farmland protection plans. Many of these plans include the promotion of economic development initiatives for agriculture.

❐ *Business Planning and Capital Investment:* Preparing a business plan can allow farmers and ranchers to examine a range of strategies to increase profits. A new Massachusetts program gives farmers access to a team of agricultural, economic, and environmental consultants. Team members assess farm operations and make recommendations to improve performance. Farmers may receive state grants for capital improvements based on their business plans. In return, farmers agree to sign five– or ten–year covenants restricting development of their land. The plans and grants are designed to make farms more profitable; the covenants give the strategies time to work.

Canada has a national program that provides incentives for farmers to develop business plans through cost–sharing and grants.

❐ *Loan Programs and Economic Development Incentives:* Twenty–four states offer public agricultural financing programs. Many of these are targeted to beginning farmers. Few, if any, have the capital to meet the demand for credit among farmers. One promising approach is a private initiative in Maryland that is experimenting with getting commercial banks to participate in an agricultural loan program through the commitment of Community Reinvestment Act funds.

❐ *Direct Marketing:* Growers who market agricultural products directly to customers usually receive higher prices than farmers and ranchers who sell wholesale. Counties and towns can encourage the development of agricultural retail businesses by specifically permitting roadside stands, pick–your–own operations, nurseries, and other agricultural uses in their zoning bylaws. Many communities also have developed and distributed maps showing the location of farmstands, pick–your–own operations, and farmers' markets. Some have posted signs directing drivers to farm businesses.

❐ *Farmers' Markets:* Farmers' markets give growers access to a large base of customers. Most markets are open–air public spaces where farmers gather to sell home–grown products. Farmers may travel hundreds of miles to downtown markets in big cities. The markets are good for the city as well as the farmers, as they attract customers who patronize other downtown businesses. (For markets in Ohio, see *Ohio Farmers' Markets*[2] and *Ohio Farmers' Markets Directory.*[3])

❐ *Marketing to Restaurants and Food Retailers:* Much of the retail price of food pays for marketing and distribution. By selling directly to food retailers, farmers and ranchers can capture more profit. A growing number of natural and specialty food stores are expressing interest in selling local farm products. Several nonprofit organizations are working to establish links between growers and chefs. Encouraging restaurants to use local produce and meats and to promote them on their menus may help build a retail customer base for both local farms and dining establishments. Contact with restaurants and food retailers also helps keep farmers informed about trends in the food industry.

❑ *Community Supported Agriculture:* Community supported agriculture (CSA) is a relatively new form of direct marketing. CSA farm customers pay for a share of the harvest at the beginning of the year and receive a weekly bundle of vegetables and fruits throughout the growing season. This system takes some of the risk out of farming and shifts the time that growers must spend on marketing to the beginning of the year. Some organizations are working to build CSA networks that would allow individual growers to offer a larger selection of farm products to their customers and discounts on food prices in exchange for volunteer labor. The two case histories, below, discuss two different kinds of CSAs in Ohio.

❑ *Diversification:* Agricultural operations that specialize in commodities such as corn or milk are vulnerable to economic shocks caused by low prices or bad weather. State Departments of Agriculture, Extension Program agents, and economic development agencies promote diversification to reduce risk and increase profits. Diversification can mean planting new crops or shifting to a different mix of crops and livestock, developing new products or services or targeting new markets.

❑ *New Products and Marketing Strategies:* State and local governments and agricultural organizations are helping growers create and market specialty products such as cheese, wine, preserves and sauces, potato chips and cereals. These products can be sold year–round—a big advantage in cold climates—and some can be marketed through the mail. Several states are investigating the feasibility of public commercial kitchens that could serve as incubators for farm–based food businesses. An organization in Virginia is developing a brand of local farm and seafood products, and an organization in Maine is experimenting with selling farm products on the Internet.

❑ *Agritourism:* Several state and local governments offer workshops for farmers who are interested in developing recreational businesses. Agricultural tourism is increasingly popular in farming communities near urban areas. Entrepreneurial growers are offering educational and recreational services such as school tours, hay and sleigh rides, crop mazes, petting zoos, restaurants, ranch vacations, and bed–and–breakfast facilities. These services bring in new customers and promote farm products.

❒ *Grower Cooperatives:* Growers who sell wholesale can increase their access to lucrative markets by forming cooperatives. High–volume retailers such as supermarkets that find it too difficult to buy from individual producers may welcome the opportunity to purchase locally grown food from a well organized cooperative. Cooperatives can also offer a diverse selection of products to retailers at a competitive price.

❒ *Reducing the Costs of Production:* Most agricultural economic development strategies are designed to help producers increase revenues, but a few help them cut costs. A project in Vermont is training dairy farmers to implement pasture–based management. By switching from growing and storing feed crops to grazing, dairy farmers can cut costs and improve their quality of life. Other organizations promote the use of integrated pest management and organic farming, which reduce the cost of inputs and may increase the prices that growers can demand for their products. Purchasing cooperatives for seeds and other agricultural supplies also can reduce production costs.

ADVANTAGES: The American Farmland Trust reports that in the past two years, the number of state–registered farmers' markets has grown 20% to more than 2,400, and by projecting and adding nonregulated markets, the actual number is probably twice that high. Direct marketing now serves more than a million customers every week, producing an estimated $1,100,000,000 in gross income for farmers.[5]

DISADVANTAGES: Coordinating agencies, such as the farmland preservation task forces some Ohio counties are forming with the support of local soil and water conservation districts, require funds to staff and equip services before they can become fully functional. Also, they confront possible resistance from other groups that see these centers as an anti–development force.[6]

CASE HISTORY #1: Molly and Ted Bartlett established Silver Creek Farm, in Hiram, Ohio, 16 years ago, and since 1992 have run it as a community supported agriculture (CSA) project, the oldest and largest CSA in the state. On a 75-acre working farm, with 18 acres in organic fruits and vegetables, they host member families, school groups, and others who "join the farm" to work and to learn about its many commodity and social benefits. The gardens, greenhouse, sheep, chickens, turkeys, ponds, forests, and wetlands together demand much labor to sustain, but also they provide uncommonly rich opportunities to educate others about the benefits of keeping land as productive farmland.

The success of Silver Creek stems from its working membership. There are three categories: (1) a "Working Core," who pay $325 per year and must work eight half–days to pick, wash, sort, and pack the many different vegetables grown; (2) "Grazers," who pay $375 per year, and who may pick their own produce whenever they wish but must have been associated with the farm for a minimum of one year; and (3) "Regular" members, who are not able to spend working hours on the farm, and pay $425 per year for weekly shares of vegetables—one share serving two people for one week. The Bartletts have limited the number of regular members to 100 per year to concentrate on the quality of the farms' products and services rather than its quantity of food.

Their summer crops include blueberries, squash, kale, chard, peas, heirloom tomatoes, sweet corn, peppers, herbs, eggplant, beets, broccoli, and garlic, while fall offerings are turkeys, winter squash, root crops, pumpkins, and potatoes.

In 1999, Silver Creek offered CSA optional shares to its members at various prices for quantities of blueberries, eggs, chicken, lamb, sweaters knit from Silver Creek sheep's wool, and certified organic Ohio beef, goat cheese, and flowers from other nearby CSAs and farms.

In addition to supplying its members, Silver Creeks sells vegetables to buyers' clubs, food co–ops, and restaurants. Other products available at Silver Creek Farm include certified Ohio organic beef, farm–raised chicken and lamb, as well as local maple syrup, certified organic heirloom seedlings, herb plants, organic gardening aids, pottery, sheepskins, and yarn. They have been serving wholesale markets at various area stores since 1984. Their farm market is open Wednesday through Saturday, 10:00 a.m. to 5:00 p.m., May through October, and then Saturday only 10:00 a.m. to 5:00 p.m., November through April.

The farm is also available to schools, garden clubs, and other interested groups for educational activities that include wildflower and bird walks and classes in organic gardening. If desired, Silver Creek's services can extend to providing box lunches as well as catered dinners for these groups. (*Case History Source:* Molly and Ted Bartlett, 7097 Allyn Road, P.O. Box 126, Hiram, Ohio 44234-0126. Tel: 330-569-3487; Fax: 330-569-7076; E-mail: <<silvrcf@aol.com>>.)

CASE HISTORY #2: Brad Masi at the Oberlin Sustainable Agriculture Project (OSAP) in Oberlin, Ohio, coordinates a nonprofit venture to promote economic development of farmlands. OSAP is another CSA project which grows 3 acres of vegetables, row crops, and flowers and then distributes these through a local farmers' market, several restaurants (including the Black River Café in Oberlin), as well as through Oberlin College. OSAP also conducts on–site education for farmers to emphasize the importance of economics to sustain agriculture. In 1998 the project received a grant from the Nord Foundation and the USDA's Sustainable Agriculture Research and Education (SARE) Program.

OSAP sells "shares" of produce to "shareholders." A "full" share, intended for large families, is $450; a "large" share, for a family of 4 to 5, is $350; a "small" share totals $175; and a "mini" share—the most popular—is $90. Payment is due April 1st. The purchaser of a mini share, for example, shops at the Oberlin Farmers' Market on Tuesdays and Saturdays. Upon selection, the produce is bundled in units valued at $1.00 each, and unit values are checked off the shareholder's membership card. A CSA dollar buys more than a Farmers' Market dollar.

OSAP plans to double its share sales next year to help sustain the project, but Brad may also turn over the Farmers' Market component to the local community because it takes considerable time and effort to run it.[8] (*Case History Source:* Brad Masi, Oberlin Sustainable Agriculture Project, MPO Box 357, Oberlin, Ohio 44074. Tel: 440-775-8409; Fax: 440-775-8124).

ACTION STEPS: Review the Ohio State University Extension's list, "Community Development Publications" for business development opportunities and procedures. It is available from the Ohio State University Extension, Community Development, 700 Ackerman Rd., Ste. 235, Columbus, OH 43202-1578, Tel: 614-292-1868, or download documents from its Web Site: <<http://ohioline.ag.ohio-state.edu.>>.[7]

NOTES

[1] Farmland Information Center, American Farmland Trust, *Fact Sheet: Agricultural Economic Development*, 1-4. Downloaded August 2, 1998 from Web Site: <<http://farm.fic.niu.edu/fic-ta/tafs-aed.html>>.

[2] Ibid., 1-4.

[3] *Ohio Farmers' Markets*, an Internet listing downloaded May 4, 1999 from Web Site: <<http://www.ams.usda.gov/farmersmarkets/states/ohio.htm>>.

[4] Ohio Department of Agriculture, *Ohio Farmers' Markets Directory* (Columbus, OH: June 1998). E-mail: <<wwwagri@ohio.gov>>; Web Site: <<http://www.state.oh.us/agri/>>.

[5] American Farmland Trust, *American Farmland*, Vol. 18, No. 2 (Fall 1997), 18-19.

[6] Alan Achkar, "Architect to Try to Save Farmland," *The Plain Dealer* (June 1, 1999), 5-B.

[7] Ohio State University Extension (T. Pritchard), *Community Development* (April 28, 1997), 1-6. Downloaded from Web Site: <<http://www-comdev.ag.ohio-state.edu/cdpubs.html>>.

[8] Kenneth Sloane, "Oberlin Sustainable Agriculture Project," faxed on August 11, 1999 to J. Chadbourne by by Oberlin College Stenographic Services.

BROWNFIELDS—OHIO'S VOLUNTARY ACTION PROGRAM

OBJECTIVE: Ohio EPA's *Voluntary Action Program* (VAP) targets brownfields (lands contaminated by spills or leaks of either hazardous materials or petroleum) "to restore abandoned urban factory sites, rebuild the economy of our cities, and keep industrial development from eating up Ohio's farmland and green spaces."[1]

WHO ENACTS IT: Begun in 1994 and administered by the Ohio EPA, the VAP—or S.B. 221, the Ohio Real Estate Cleanup and Reuse Program—depends on property owners to assess voluntarily the contamination levels at their site and then to hire Ohio EPA–certified environmental professionals to inspect and test the site, then perform cleanup (if that is required) to meet the applicant's intended use—as an industrial or residential area, for example. [2]

HOW IT WORKS: The goal of the *VAP* is to help brownfield owners clean up their property to appropriate levels of safety consistent with the likely future commercial, industrial, or residential use of the land. The design of *VAP* minimizes red tape, allowing land owners to concentrate their efforts on effective clean–up and redevelopment.

Parties responsible for site cleanup apply to the *VAP* for a permit according to future–use standards. Ohio EPA has developed protective standards appropriate to the intended use of the restored property. For example, cleanup standards are more strict for a site intended for residential development than for housing a machine shop. The responsible party then hires consultants and testing facilities that certify whether or not the site meets those standards for future use. Testing may show that the site will meet the intended use standard without actual cleanup occurring. In such cases, a deed restriction is required to limit the owner to that use only.[3]

During site examination, owners of the property are subject to criminal penalties if they violate permit agreements or falsify or withhold any information about the voluntary cleanup. Once a site has been cleaned up, an EPA–certified examiner files a "No Further Action" letter requesting a "Covenant Not to Sue." The covenant releases the property owner from civil liability to the State of Ohio for additional cleanup of the site. It does not offer the same protection from either the federal government or other parties, however. As a result, a number of state *VAP* applicants enter

"Memorandums of Agreement" with the U.S. EPA to "dissuade" federal action against a property owner. *VAP* covenants are filed with county recorders and remain permanently attached to the title of the property, affording future owners the same liability protection. The program gives Ohio EPA access to all cleanup documents and properties as well as the authority to audit project records to confirm that standards have been met. The cleanup standard imposed by EPA may require deed restrictions on the property specifying use only for the purposes allowed under the cleanup agreement.[4] As of June 2, 1999, Ohio EPA has issued 32 covenants. Some 34 recent applications are now pending.[5]

In Ohio, participation in the *VAP* is necessary if a land owner is to be eligible for the following fund–assistance programs: (1) projects that benefit water quality—ground and surface waters—may qualify for low–interest loans from Ohio EPA's Water Pollution Control Loan Fund and the Ohio Water Quality Authority; (2) businesses can earn state income tax or corporate franchise tax credits for brownfield projects that clean up sites and reuse property for economic development (under the Brownfield Site Cleanup Tax Credit Program); and (3) once cleanup is complete, brownfield sites are eligible for state property tax abatements.[6]

Many communities have creative financial incentives to help investors with the costs of brownfields redevelopment. They include (1) setting aside local monies for redevelopment projects; (2) establishing revolving loans; (3) using tax increment financing to raise public monies; (4) issuing bonds to underwrite redevelopment, and then applying new revenues from the completed project to pay off the bond debt; (5) offering tax abatements to investors; and (6) giving preferential utility rates to the project in acknowledgment of the savings to the community from the use of existing power lines and other utility infrastructure.[7]

Economic tools available on the federal level to encourage use of brownfield sites for economic development include: the Department of Housing and Urban Development's Community Development Block Grants and Section 108 loans, and the Economic Development Administration's Title I Public Works Grants and Title IX Economic Adjustment Assistance. Future options will include "tax credits, federally supported revolving loan funds to state voluntary cleanup programs, and low interest loans and grants."[8]

Under a special circumstance, a certified professional may submit a request to the director of the Ohio EPA for an "Urban Setting Designation" for a property meeting these minimum criteria:

❑ Lying within a township or city limits and having at least 20,000 residents

❑ Having community water connections to a minimum of 90% of the parcels

❑ Lying outside any Ohio–EPA wellhead protection area

❑ Having no drinking water wells within ½ mile of the site[9]

In May 1999, the Ohio EPA granted a request from Cleveland, Ohio, for an "Urban Setting Designation" allowed under 1995 and 1996 state rules to encourage voluntary cleanups of brownfield sites. OEPA agreed not to enforce rules requiring developers to clean up contaminated water underneath six tracts of land in the city totaling 18 square miles, effectively most of Cleveland's industrially zoned land that contains some 14,000 individual brownfields. The main argument for the waiver is that Cleveland draws all of its drinking water from Lake Erie. Groundwater under Cleveland is scarce, and what is there moves slowly through the underlying clay and rock that trap it. Therefore, the odds are low that the contaminants will reach drinking water elsewhere. The designation makes cleanup in Cleveland's brownfields considerably less costly and time consuming than before.[10, 11]

The Voluntary Action Program procedure is not required for brownfield development. An owner may proceed privately, foregoing the state's fund–assistance, described above, and the "Covenant Not to Sue," but using the *VAP's* cleanup standards and professional certification. Use of these standards has been accepted by bank loan officers to warrant their investments in such privately initiated brownfield projects.

ADVANTAGES: In addition to the environmental and economic benefits cited above, brownfield redevelopment could encourage further central city revitalization efforts. For example, downtown or waterfront brownfield sites are often economical and resource-efficient development sites because they use existing infrastructure—bridges, roads, utility rights–of–way—and don't siphon off public monies for duplicate structures elsewhere. Thus, urban brownfield redevelopment discourages sprawl to outlying areas.[12]

DISADVANTAGES: Remediation and other redevelopment costs may exceed the value of the property. In addition to the environmental problems, existing buildings on the site may have structural weaknesses or there may be a lack of access to major transportation routes. And, businesses are likely to forego remediation of a brownfield in areas where taxes are higher than in outlying locales, or if quality–of–life factors are low—such as poor quality schools, high levels of crime and racial tension, a weak local business environment, or other elements that make life difficult for employers and employees. Furthermore, remediating a site does not guarantee success for the redeveloped property or that it will meet other goals, such as bringing jobs back to the central city.[13]

Uncertainty about liability is still the most frequent deterrent to brownfield redevelopment. Others are the complexity and expense of cleanup itself and the standard of cleanup required for the intended use. Lack of uniformity between federal and state laws and their enforcement policies add to the confusion and uncertainty. As a result, banks and other potential financing sources may be reluctant to lend money for projects.[14]

CASE HISTORY #1: In September 1997, Ohio EPA issued a "covenant not to sue" to Nakki Partners, Inc. With that covenant, it released the company "from state civil liability associated with the cleanup of property at 5055 Nike Drive, Columbus."[15] From 1988 until 1994, Chemserve Environmental occupied the site. Chemserve, an industrial cleaning and hazardous / special waste transportation services company, was also registered under Ohio law as a large quantity hazardous waste generator. An Ohio EPA–certified environmental service, Epsys Corporation, investigated the site and performed a risk assessment that examined, among other factors, "the use of ignitable hazardous wastes produced on the property during on–site decontamination of tanker trucks."[16] Epsys required the company to close down its hazardous waste drum storage area. This move allowed Epsys to certify that the site then met standards for industrial use. As part of the VAP, the property now holds a deed restriction limiting its use to "industrial, light industrial, and nonretail commercial and heavy industrial uses."[17]

CASE HISTORY #2: In a case dated April 1998, the Ohio EPA issued a "covenant not to sue" to Columbiana County Port Authority after the Authority cleaned up a former brickyard near 2400 Clark Ave., Wellsville, OH. The covenant released the Port Authority from any state civil liabilities associated with the cleanup. The 23.4 acre site had been a brick manufacturing facility for nearly a century. Several interconnected buildings and other structures remained after owners discontinued brick manufacturing in the late 1970s. Structures included kilns, ovens, office and maintenance areas, and above–ground storage tanks. The Buckeye Coal Company also had used the site for coal storage. The Port Authority currently uses the site for temporary storage of its Australian bar steel and refractory brick inventories. Civil & Engineering Consultants, a state–certified examiner, investigated the site. All hazardous materials found during its assessment were subsequently removed, and C&EC was able to certify that no contamination had been released to the environment. The property is now ready for industrial use.[18]

CASE HISTORY #3: Similarly, Ohio EPA issued a "covenant not to sue" to HBE Corporation after it disposed of asbestos and hazardous and nonhazardous chemicals that included paints and swimming pool chemicals at the former downtown Sheraton Hotel, 50 North Third Street, Columbus. The disposal occurred after Lawhon & Associates hired a state–certified environmental professional to determine if there were significant environmental problems associated with the site. The asbestos and chemicals were cited. After refurbishing the property, HBE reopened it as the Adam's Mark Hotel in the spring of 1999.[19]

CASE HISTORY #4: Ohio EPA also issued the Southern Ohio Port Authority a "covenant not to sue" for 16.8 acres of the former Empire Detroit Steel Company in New Boston, OH. Previously run as a steel mill for nearly a century, the Port Authority removed approximately 26,000 cubic yards of soil and waste materials contaminated with PCBs, asbestos, and petroleum. The certified environmental professional hired by the Port Authority sampled the soil and ground water. They confirmed that cleanup standards had been met and that there were no significant environmental problems associated with the site. The Authority subsequently sold the property to OSCO Industries. OSCO will construct a new facility that will bring in over 100 new jobs to the area.[20]

ACTION STEPS: For the *VAP* Web page, which is updated monthly, see Web Site: <<http.//www.epa.state.oh.us/derr/volunt. html>>, or contact Frank Robertson, Tel: 614-644-2924; E-mail: <<frank.robertson@epa.state.oh.us>>. For additional information regarding Ohio EPA's Water Pollution Control Loan Fund, contact Dave Reiff with the Ohio Division of Environmental and Financial Assistance at 614-644-2798; for financing from the Ohio Department of Development, contact Brad Biggs at 614-644-8201; and for financing available from the Ohio Water Development Authority, call Steve Grossman at 614-466-5822. Additional finance information is available in *Fact Sheet #5, Ohio EPA Financial Assistance for Voluntary Action Program Remediations* and also in *Financial Assistance for Voluntary Action Program Remediations— Ohio Brownfield Partnership.*

NOTES

[1] Christopher Jones, Dir., Ohio EPA in Ohio EPA's *Re-Use News, Vol. 5. Issue 2, Summer 1999.*

[2] Ohio EPA *Voluntary Action Program,* No. 1 (December 1997), 1. Downloaded June 8, 1999 from its Voluntary Action Program Web Site: <<http://www.epa.epa.state.oh.us/derr/vap/factsheets/fact1.html>>

[3] Ibid., 1.

[4] Ibid., 1-3.

[5] Ohio EPA, *Summary of NFAs Received and Covenants Issued* (June 2, 1999), 1-6. Downloaded from June 8, 1999 from its *Voluntary Action Program* Web Site <<http://www.epa.state.oh.us/derr/vap/factsheets/fact1.html>>.

[6] Ohio State University Extension (M. Bielen), *Brownfields and Their Redevelopment,* CDFS-1527-96, 5. Available from Ohio State University Extension, Community Development, 700 Ackerman Road, Columbus, OH 43202-1578; Web Site: <<http://ohioline.ag.ohio-state.edu>>.

[7] Ibid., 5.

[8] Ibid., 5.

[9] Ohio EPA, *Urban Setting Designation Fact Sheet,* No. 8 (February 1998), 1-2. Downloaded June 8, 1999 from Web Site: <<http://www.epa.state.oh.us/derr/vap/factsheets/fact8.html>>.

[10] Jim Nichols, "EPA Oks Brownfield Development," *The Plain Dealer* (May 11, 1999), B-1.

[11] Ohio EPA, *Urban Setting Designation Fact Sheet,* 1-3.

[12] Ohio State University Extension (M. Bielen), *Brownfields and Their Redevelopment,* 3.

[13] Ibid., 3-4.

[14] Ibid., 4.

[15] Ohio EPA, *Nakki Partners of Columbus to Benefit from State Brownfields Laws* (September 4, 1997) 1. Downloaded June 8, 1999 from Web Site <<http://www.epa.ohio.state.gov/derr/vap/news-releases/nakki.html>>.

[16] Ibid., 1.

[17] Ibid., 1.

[18] Ohio EPA, *Columbiana County Port Authority to Benefit from Voluntary Action Program* (Updated May 5, 1999), 1. Downloaded from Web Site <<http://www.epa.ohio.state.gov/derr/vap/news-releases/columbiana.html>>.

[19] Ohio EPA, *HBE Corporation, Columbus, Ohio* (Updated May 25, 1999), 1. Downloaded June 8, 1999 from Web Site <<http://www.epa.state.oh.us/derr/derr/vap/leg_report/adamsmark.html>>.

[20] Ohio EPA, *Southern Ohio Port Authority, New Boston, Ohio* (Updated May 25, 1999), 1. Downloaded June 8, 1999 from Web Site <<http://www.epa.ohio.gov/derr/vap/leg_report/sopa.html>>.

CONSERVATION RESERVE PROGRAM

OBJECTIVE: The *Conservation Reserve Program* (*CRP*) converts active cropland to passive by covering it with grasses, shrubs, or trees. These plantings prevent soil erosion, increase wildlife habitat, improve air quality, and protect water bodies. The program pays compensatory rent to the farm owner and cost–shares conversion expenses. The "Regular Sign–up" component enrolls volunteers during a designated period of the year.

WHO ENACTS IT: *CRP* was authorized by the Food Security Act of 1985, amended in 1990, 1994, and last in 1996 as the Federal Agriculture Improvement and Reform Act. The "New CRP," with the final rule published in the Federal Register February 19, 1997, refocused on only the most environmentally sensitive land. *CRP* is administered by the U.S. Department of Agriculture's (USDA) Farm Service Agency through the Commodity Credit Corporation and in cooperation with the Natural Resources Conservation Service, Cooperative State Research, Education, and Extension Service, state forestry agencies, and local Soil and Water Conservation Districts.[1]

HOW IT WORKS:

A. REGULAR SIGN–UP

CRP is the largest and most comprehensive conservation program ever undertaken by the federal government. Erosion control remains a top priority, but water quality and wildlife habitat improvement are now emphasized as well. Through 2002, to cap enrollment, Congress set a maximum of 36,400,000 acres for the entire fifty states, but through October 1, 1999 the enrollment was 32,500,000, leaving only 3 4,000,000 acres available for the next Regular Sign–up period, the 20th year, during the fall of 1999.

Therefore, with only a small amount of the eligible cropland to enroll for 2000 (the exact acreage will not be known until final re–enrollment and termination contracts are returned), a new Environmental Benefits Index (EBI) was developed to identify lands offering the greatest environmental value. The EBI consists of these factors:

❏ Wildlife habitat benefits
❏ Water quality benefits from reduced erosion, runoff, and leaching
❏ On–farm benefits of reduced erosion
❏ Long–term retention benefits

❏ Air–quality benefits from reduced wind erosion
❏ The land's location in a Conservation Priority Area, if applicable
❏ Cost of enrollment per acre[2]

The Natural Resources Conservation Service calculates the EBI based upon these factors.

Conservation Priority Areas are regions targeted for enrollment, such as the Long Island Sound, the Chesapeake Bay, an area adjacent to the Great Lakes, and the Prairie Pothole region. In addition, in a given state the Farm Service Agency Committee may designate up to 10% of its remaining cropland as a Conservation Priority Area.

The cost of enrollment is determined by a "bid" from the applicant. If it is above the bid cap, the enrollment is denied; if it is less, the likelihood of acceptance is increased. The bid cap is approximately $100 per acre per year. However, certain lands qualify for certain bonuses. Under the *buffer initiative*, for example, because of the water quality benefit realized from filter strips and riparian buffers (see B–1, below) established next to water bodies, the USDA will add 20% to the annual rental.

The "New CRP" increases emphasis on the enrollment and restoration of cropped and noncropped wetlands and highly erodible soils. For example, all cropland within the Great Lakes watershed is eligible, though land with orchards, vineyards, and ornamental plantings are not. As the terms of prior enrollment conclude—usually after 10 to 15 years—less vulnerable farmland will return to production, thereby maximizing both conservation benefits to sensitive lands and economic benefits to productive land.

Upon receiving a *CRP* contract, the farmer must develop a conservation workplan and have it approved by the local soil and water conservation district. The USDA will contribute up to 50% of the costs incurred in planting vegetative cover on the enrolled land. However, farmers may not receive economic benefit from these plantings while the land is under the *CRP* contract. But, they may withdraw certain land at any time with a 60–day notice to USDA and replace it with land that meets more rigorous standards for erosion control, water quality, tree–planting, or wildlife benefits. Again, this flexibility helps preserve the most sensitive lands and return the least sensitive properties enrolled in *CRP* back to productivity.

B. CONTINUOUS SIGN–UP

1. High Priority Conservation

On September 4, 1996, an additional part to *CRP* was added for certain high priority conservation practices that yield highly desirable environmental benefits. Under this new option, farmers may sign up at any time, rather than wait for an announced sign–up period. Continuous sign–up allows flexibility in starting these practices. Unlike the Regular Sign–up selection process, acreage is automatically accepted at fixed rental amounts based on soil characteristics and the prevailing rental rates. These special practices are quoted here from USDA's *The Conservation Reserve Program*:[3]

❒ **Filter Strips:** Area of grass, legumes, and other vegetation that filter runoff and waste water by trapping sediment, pesticides, organic matter, and other pollutants. Filter strips are planted on cropland at the lower edge of a field or adjacent to bodies of water.

❒ **Riparian Buffers:** Areas of trees and / or shrubs next to ponds, lakes, and streams that filter out pollutants from runoff as well as provide shade for fish and other wildlife. The vegetations' natural litter also provides food and shelter for valuable wildlife.

❒ **Shelter Belts, Field Windbreaks, and Living Snow Fences:** Belts of trees or shrubs planted in single or multiple rows. Such tree rows and hedges reduce wind erosion, improve air quality, protect growing plants, and provide food, shelter, and breeding territory for wildlife.

❒ **Grass Waterways:** Channels, either natural or constructed, that are planted with suitable vegetation to protect soil from erosion. Grass waterways can help heal gullies and washouts while greatly reducing the loss of topsoil and the sedimentation of streams, ponds, and lakes.

❒ **Shallow Water Areas for Wildlife:** Small areas whose purpose is to provide cover and a water source for wildlife. Water is impounded using embankments, berms, or other methods, and then surrounded by a small area planted with permanent cover.

❒ **Salt–Tolerant Vegetation:** Vegetation planted to reclaim areas in which saline (salt) water is seeping to the surface. Planted areas upstream reduce the amount of water recharging the seep, and salt–tolerant plants reclaim contaminated seepage areas.

❒ Certain EPA–Designated Wellhead Protection Areas:
Wellhead Protection Areas help assure the safety of municipal
water supplies drawn from wells. Vegetation planted in an area
surrounding the wellhead helps to protect the water supply from
contamination.

2. Conservation Reserve Enhancement Program (*CREP*)

On May 26, 1998, the USDA invited state governors to submit
proposals for the *CREP*, a continuous enrollment plan to focus on
"significant" environmental problem areas within the state
recognized by agencies collaborating on agricultural impacts.[4] As of
July 31, 1999, only these states have signed an agreement with the
USDA to offer the program: Delaware, Illinois, Maryland,
Minnesota, New York, North Carolina, Oregon, and Washington.
Landowners will receive payment on an "enhanced" basis, that is
based on 155% of the *CRP* rental rate per acre (locally determined)
for planting grass filter strips, and 175% per acre for wetlands,
riparian forest buffers, and field windbreaks. The major reason for
enhancing the rental rates is to retain former *CRP*–enrolled land
that is terminating its contract and therefore will be "released" from
conservation to production.

Ohio's *CREP* proposal to protect the Western Lake Erie
watershed, June 8, 1999, reports that, "At the Ohio–Indiana–
Michigan intersection, just four counties have more than 125,000
acres enrolled in *CRP*. Release of this land will require
conservation treatment to prevent increased erosion and
sedimentation within the Western Lake Erie watershed. This loss
will need to be mitigated by new *CRP* enrollments or accelerated
conservation planning and application efforts for wildlife practices.
Release of the *CRP* land will also result in increased nutrient and
pesticide loading to the stream system and Lake Erie."[5]

Ohio proposes *CREP* agreements with farmland owners in all or
part of the following 27 counties: Allen, Ashland, Auglaize,
Crawford, Defiance, Erie, Fulton, Hancock, Hardin, Henry, Huron,
Lucas, Lorain, Marion, Medina, Mercer, Ottawa, Paulding, Putnam,
Richland, Sandusky, Seneca, Shelby, Van Wert, Williams, Wood,
and Wyandot. The collective agreements totaling 67,000 acres will
"improve water quality by reducing sediment pollution, nutrient
loading, and field runoff by installing riparian buffers, filter strips,
windbreaks, wetlands, and other best management practices." The
improved water quality will enhance terrestrial and aquatic wildlife
habitat, especially for federally listed candidates for the endangered
species list.[6]

The agreements proposed are these:

1. 30 years for riparian buffers / wildlife habitat / tree plantings / windbreaks and 15 to 20 years for wetland restorations and shallow water sediment control basins. (USDA will pay owners 175% of the *CRP* rental rate for the first 15 years, and an increased rate for the next 15 years. And ODNR will add a one–time sign–up incentive of $500 per acre enrolled.)

2. 20 years for all other filter strips (see list under B–1, above). USDA will pay 155% of the rental rate for the first 15 years, and more for the last 5 years. ODNR will contribute $200 per acre enrolled and $40 per acre to cost–share the installing of warm–season grasses.[7]

Additional conditions and compensations provide incentives for long–term riparian area maintenance with ODNR joining for enrollment of shallow water areas for wildlife.[8]

Overall, the Ohio *CREP* proposes to complete 12,000 agreements with farmers in the 27–county region. Ultimately, the plan projects reduction of 130,000 cubic yards of soil erosion per year within the watershed, saving $800,000 per year in dredging costs—all primarily by installing best management practices on 67,000 acres "to enhance farm conservation planning through soil erosion control, water management, pesticide and fertilizer management, livestock waste nutrient management, wildlife management, and forest management."[9]

ADVANTAGES: USDA estimates economic benefit ranges for the life of the initial 36,400,000 acre enrollment—which includes both regular and continuous sign–up components—as follows:

❐ Increases in net farm income: $2.1 to 6.3 billion
❐ Value of future timber resources: $3.3 billion
❐ Preservation of soil productivity: $ 0.6 to 1.7 billion
❐ Improved surface water quality: $1.3 to 4.2 billion
❐ Reductions in damage from wind–blown dust: $0.3 to 0.9 billion
❐ Enhanced small game hunting: $1.9 to 3.1 billion[10]

The Natural Resources Conservation Service (NRCS) estimates annual reductions in topsoil loss nationwide for acres under contract to be some 700 million tons, or an average of 19 tons per acre. This is a 21% decrease in erosion on cropland compared to the pre–*CRP* erosion rate.[11]

DISADVANTAGES: There is little remaining acreage available under the program at this time. The 1996 Act continued the *CRP* maximum enrollment to 36,400,000 acres through 2002, and with nearly all of that already enrolled, 32,500,000 acres, except for acres to be released annually from earlier 10 to 15 year contracts, very few acres of new land can be converted to passive growth. Thus, one of the most effective conservation programs promoted by the federal government is legislatively capped.

CASE HISTORY #1: John Duncan bought farmland in Wapakoneta, Ohio, Auglaize County, in 1992. He wanted to build a home there, improve the habitat for wildlife—especially pheasants—but continue to have it farmed. Because the terrain was rolling land, just south of the glacier's terminus, he installed windbreaks to limit erosion as well as to improve habitat diversity. After three years of farming, the land qualified for enrollment in the Regular Sign–up *CRP* as well as the *buffer initiative* for an additional financial compensation. He plans to extend the *CRP* contract after the 1–year term. John added that east of his property, in flat country, he noticed that farmers had cut down fence rows and planted in the recovered space. He heartily disapproved of that attempt to gain a few acres of growth. (*Case History Source:* John Duncan, 22582 State Route 87, Wapakoneta, Ohio 45895; Tel: 419-568-7472.)

Case Histories—Others: See the *national conservation buffer initiative* case histories.

ACTION STEPS: Obtain a copy of the Farm Service Agency's 40–page booklet, *The Conservation Reserve Program*, by contacting the Farm Service Agency, United States Department of Agriculture, Conservation Environment Program Division, STOP 0506, 1400 Independence Ave., SW, Washington, DC 20250-0506; Tel: 202-720-9563; Fax: 202-690-0691; Web Site: <<http://www.fsa.usda.gov>>. In Ohio, contact Chris Kauffman, Grants Coordinator for programs supported by the Ohio Department of Natural Resources, Division of Soil and Water Conservation; Tel: 614-265-6914; E-mail: <<chris.kauffman@dnr.state.oh.us>>.

NOTES

[1] Farm Service Agency, U. S. Department of Agriculture, *The Conservation Reserve Program*, Document PA–1603 (May 1997), 15-19.

[2] Ibid., 21.

[3] Ibid., 22-23.

[4] Farm Service Agency, USDA, "USDA Announces Details of a Nationwide Environmental Conservation Effort," News Release No. 0222.98 (May 1998), 1-2. Downloaded July 29, 1999 from Web Site: <<http://www.fsa.usda.gov/pas/news/releases/1998/05/0222.txt>>.

[5] Draft memorandum dated June 8, 1999 from Chris Kauffman, CREP Coordinator, Division of Soil and Water Conservation to USDA-FSA, S. Maurere et al.; USDA-NRCS, P. Wolf, et al.; ODNR, L. Vance, et al., Regarding the "Western Lake Erie Watershed Project / Conservation Reserve Enhancement Program (CREP) Proposal," 8.

[6] Ibid., 1.

[7] Ibid., 14.

[8] Ibid., 15.

[9] Ibid., 13.

[10] Ibid., 13.

[11] Ibid., 18.

CURRENT AGRICULTURAL USE VALUE

OBJECTIVE: A voluntary program offering farmland owners the opportunity to have their parcels taxed according to a lower agricultural tax value, rather than at a higher market, or "development," value.

WHO ENACTS IT: Enabling legislation passed April 1974 authorizes the Ohio Department of Tax Equalization to administer the *CAUV* program through the auditors in all of Ohio's 88 counties, according to ORC 5713.30–38.

HOW IT WORKS: All states except Michigan use this program, where it is variously called "current use assessment," "current use valuation," "farm use valuation," "use assessment," "use value assessment," or a "deferred taxation form of differential assessment." It is the same as "preferential assessment," except that *CAUV* has a tax recovery penalty if enrolled farmland reverts to nonagricultural use.

Farmlands qualify for *CAUV* if they are larger than 10 acres (it must be at least 11 acres if the property includes a house, since 1 acre is deducted for a residence) and are devoted exclusively to commercial animal or poultry husbandry, aquaculture (fish), apiculture (bees), field crops, tobacco, fruits, vegetables, nursery stock, ornamental trees, sod, or timber. Noncommercial timberlands may qualify if they are part of a parcel of land, or adjacent to a parcel of land, owned by that same person who otherwise independently qualifies for the *CAUV* program. Tracts of timber of 10 acres or more and not adjacent to or part of a parcel qualifying for the program must demonstrate commercial use to qualify.[1]

A parcel of less than 10 acres can qualify if it generated an average of at least $2,500 per year for three years before application. In addition, the land has to be devoted exclusively to agriculture. The land does not have to be contiguous, but it does have to be farmed as one economic unit (i.e., with the same equipment and personnel). Woodlots can be included in the program.

A recent provision concerns idle or fallow land which provides some leeway to the farmer for showing good cause for discontinuing production and/or remaining in the *CAUV* program. And, as in the determination of eligibility for *agricultural districts*, the auditor's office may employ some flexibility in the "acreage" and "usage" qualification criteria.

Agricultural values of participating farmland are based upon soil data, production costs, and commodity prices. In each county, these values are updated every three years to reflect changes in those factors.

ADVANTAGES: *CAUV* corrects inherent "unfairness" to farmland owners in the real estate tax system. Though Ohio farmers generally own the largest amount of land in a taxing district and since public services are funded largely through local real estate taxes, farmland owners provide most of the funding for public services. Yet cost of community services studies show that farmers use fewer community services than nonfarm residences. *CAUV* tends to help redress that imbalance. Lower taxes help farmers economically, and in turn stronger economics help sustain the industry.[2] *CAUV* assists young landowners by making farming more affordable since the land is taxed at a lower rate.

Over 6,000,000 acres of farmland in Ohio have been enrolled in *CAUV* throughout the 1990s.

DISADVANTAGES: To enroll, farmers must fill out and file an application with the county auditor and pay a one–time fee of $25. To remain in the program, they must renew annually between the first Monday in January and the first Monday in March, but no subsequent fee is required. If an enrolled farmer changes the land use to something other than agriculture, the county auditor will collect a penalty equal to the tax savings received over the prior three years plus interest, unless there are extenuating circumstances—which could extend the *CAUV* status for up to three years.

CASE HISTORY: The Lake County Nursery in Perry, Ohio, paid the enrollment fee for *CAUV*. The owners farmed 77 acres and met qualification criteria. The auditor's office calculated the new tax for the land, based under the *CAUV* program. The comparison between a full year's taxes without and with *CAUV* is shown in the table below.

The assessed value of the land *without* the *CAUV* allowance was $55,300. *With* the *CAUV* program, the auditor assessed the Lake County Nursery's land the total of $2,440. These calculations and comparisons illustrate the benefits of the program to the nursery owner.

CAUV Allowance Calculation for Lake County Nursery

	Full Year Without CAUV	Full Year With CAUV
Assessed value	$55,300.00	$ 2,440.00
Tax rate	x .09926	x .09926
Gross tax	$ 5,489.08	$ 242.19
Gross tax	$ 5,489.08	$ 242.19
Reduction factor	x .397948	x .397948
Tax credit	$ 2,184.37	$ 96.37
Gross tax	$ 5,489.08	$ 242.19
Tax credit	- 2,184.37	- 96.37
Adjusted tax	$ 3,304.71	$ 145.82
Adjusted tax	$ 3,304.71	$ 145.82
10% rollback tax credit	- 330.47	- 14.58
Net taxes	**$ 2,974.24**	**$ 131.24**

A neighbor volunteered, "We can count the non–nursery farmers on our hands." Lake County is the smallest county in Ohio in actual area, but it leads the state in cash receipts for nursery and greenhouse stock, fresh market crops, and other agricultural products.[2] That is because of the nursery business. Yet without the *CAUV* program benefits to these owners, their businesses might not be sustainable. (*Case History Source:* Maria Zampini, Lake County Nursery, P.O. Box 122, Perry, OH 44081; Tel: 440-259-5571; Fax: 440-259-3114.)

ACTION STEPS: For a comparison in Ohio counties of the tax value of agricultural real property qualifying for *CAUV* and that same property's value under "highest and best use value method," see the Ohio Department of Taxation's "Taxable Current Agricultural Use Value of Real Property, Taxable Value of Real Property before CAUV, and Number of CAUV Acres and Parcels, by County, Calendar Year 1997," in Table PD-32 (Lotus format, downloadable) at Web Site: <<http://www.state.oh.us/tax/stats/pd32cy97.htm>>. More on *CAUV* is available in the Ohio Revised Code, Sections 5713.30-5713. 36, available on line at Web Site: <<http://orc.avv.com>>. Also, see Larry DeBoer & John Sindt's "Use Value Assessment of Agricultural Land," a publication of the Indiana State Board of Tax Commissioners, October 31, 1996;

E-mail: <<rolaleye@tcb.state.in.us>>; Web Site: <<http://www. state.in.us/taxcomm/html/publistb.html>>. And, see American Farmland Trust's *Saving American Farmland: What Works* (Northhampton, MA: 1997), 145-166, Web Site: <<http://www. farmland.org>>.

NOTES

[1] *Crossection*, Vol. XIII, First Quarter 1999, Lake County Soil and Water Conservation District for the Friends of Conservation in Lake County, 125 E. Erie St., Painesville, Ohio 44077; Tel: 440-350-2730.

[2] Ohio State University Extension (G. Jeffers & L. Libby) *Current Agricultural Use Value Assessment in Ohio*, CDFS-1267-99 (February 1999), 1-2. Available from the "Land Use Series" of Fact Sheets, Ohio State University Extension, Community Development, 700 Ackerman Road, Columbus, OH 43202-1578; Tel. 800-589-8292 (Ohio only) & 614-292-1868. Web Site: <<http://ohioline.ag.ohio-state.edu.>>.

FARMLAND PROTECTION PROGRAM

OBJECTIVE: *FPP* is a voluntary program that helps farmers keep their land in agriculture. *FPP* funds 50 / 50 state, local, or tribal entities with existing *farmland protection programs* to purchase *conservation easements.*

WHO ENACTS IT: The 1996 Farm Bill established a *Farmland Protection Program* to protect farmland from conversion to nonagricultural uses. The Federal Agriculture Improvement and Reform Act authorized up to $35,000,000 in matching funds from 1996 to 2002. Funding is from the Commodity Credit Corporation, and the USDA's Natural Resources Conservation Service (NRCS) implements the program.[1] S. 333 and H.R. 1950 reauthorize the *FPP* at $55,000,000 and add conservation nonprofit organizations to the current entities which can purchase easements with *FPP* and 50% matching funds.

HOW IT WORKS: NRCS starts the process by publishing a request for proposals in the *Federal Register.* When a state, tribal, or local application for matching funds is approved, NRCS executes a *cooperative agreement* on behalf of the Commodity Credit Corporation. The agreement describes the transaction, the parcel, the easement, project cost, and the federal share.[2]

Enrollment in the *FPP* limits the land to agricultural use for a minimum of 30 years. Preference is given to projects that protect farmland in perpetuity through *conservation easements.* The applicant's farmland must be prime or locally unique farmland, which meets certain USDA soil, slope, and climatic criteria for optimal agricultural production. The owner must: (1) establish that it is part of a pending offer from a state, tribe, or local farmland protection program, such as the *conservation reserve program* or *wetlands reserve program*; (2) prove that it is privately owned; (3) submit a conservation plan; (4) assure that it is large enough to sustain agricultural production; (5) have access to markets for its products; (6) confirm existence of adequate infrastructure and agricultural support services; (7) prove surrounding lands can support long–term agricultural production; (8) confirm development pressure; (9) demonstrate a commitment to farmland protection through the use of incentive–based or regulatory farmland protection techniques; (10) and, finally, the applicants must prove the capacity to monitor and enforce *conservation easements.*[3]

The *cooperative agreement* spells out the role of the NRCS in developing and implementing the conservation plan. That plan must be implemented on all of the acreage enrolled. Failure to do so is considered a violation of the agreement. A reversionary clause in the agreement requires the state or local government to reimburse the federal government if the terms of the agreement are not enforced or if the easement is terminated.

ADVANTAGES: The *FPP* provides financial support to state and local *farmland protection programs*. It protects farmland from residential and commercial development by acquiring *agricultural conservation easements* on productive farmland. By transferring federal dollars to local farmers, producers can use the capital for reinvestment in their operations, invest for retirement, or reduce debt. By removing the speculative value of the land, compensatory programs help keep farmland affordable for beginning farmers. Finally, the *FPP* encourages good land stewardship by requiring and monitoring conservation plans.

DISADVANTAGES: No money. Ohio did not pass a law authorizing its 50% match in time to qualify for the federal share of the *FPP*. And, the U.S. Congress has not authorized any new funds for FY 2000. In 1996, 37 entities in 17 states signed cooperative agreements and received just under $14,500,000 in federal matching funds. And, some of the provisions listed above, especially the conservation plan, place an added burden on the landowner, which may discourage participation.[4] For states, a drawback requires their purchase of the easements before *FPP* pays them.

Case History #1: In New Jersey, under the Agriculture Retention and Development Act, the State Agriculture Development Committee—which is in, but not of, the Department of Agriculture, did qualify for and receive *farmland preservation program* funds: $1,000,000 in 1996, $200,000 in 1997, and $1,400,000 in 1998. If 1999 funds—$55,000,000 was authorized—become available, the Committee will apply once more. But, with state bond issues in 1981, 1989, 1992, and 1995, they have received $200,000,000 with which to purchase *agricultural conservation easements* for enrollment in their "Easement Purchase Program." And, in 1999, the Garden State Preservation Trust Act, passed June 1999, has approved $98,000,000 each year for 10 years for four programs—Open Space "Green Acres," Historic Sites, the Committee's state office, and Farmland Preservation. The bond issues and the Trust Act monies are a portion of the state's sales tax (6%). The Trust Act 10–year amount will be "leveraged", i.e., by purchasing bonds, to perhaps $140,000,000 and divided among the four programs. The net effect for the Committee is that they will have about $50,000,000 each year for 10 years starting in 2000 to purchase *agricultural conservation easements*—doubling or tripling their past rate of acquisition.

There are three ways the Committee has acquired agricultural farmland easements: (1) The local county owns the easement and cost–shares. The Committee provides 65% and the county 35% of the total cost (342 easements on 49,671 acres); sixteen counties with over 99% of New Jersey's available agricultural lands have established county Agricultural Development Boards to develop agricultural programs; (2) The Committee buys the land on a fee–simple basis (private ownership of real estate in which the owner has the right to control, use, and transfer the property at will) then auctions it off for the farmland value (14 easements on 3,330 acres); (3) Landowners donate either to the county or to the Committee (6 easements on 1,174 acres).

The costs per acre have ranged from $1,667 in the southern part of New Jersey, which is mostly farmland, to $10,500 in the northern part, which is heavily developed. Since the program is voluntary, a county wishing to cost–share with the Committee must generate its own monies. Most counties have a county tax of about ½ cent per $100 of valuation dedicated to this match; therefore, the selection of lands to purchase is not biased in favor of spending where the land is least costly since the counties balance the land value difference. (*Case History Source:* Gregory Romano, Exec. Dir., State Agriculture Development Committee, Health / Agriculture, Warren and Market Streets, PO Box 330, Trenton, New Jersey 08625-0330; Tel: 609-984-2504; Fax: 609-633-2004; E-mail: <<agsroma@ag.state.nj.us>>.)

Case History #2: The Vermont Housing and Conservation Board received $1,000,000 in 1996 plus $1,800,000 in state and private foundation funds and local fund raising, so that with a combination of *bargain sales, conservation easements,* donations, and *outright purchases,* they acquired *agricultural conservation easements* on 14 farms. The farms are in Addison, Franklin, Orleans, and Windsor counties and total 4,235 acres.

Since then, they have acquired 81,784 acres on 240 farms, with a total of $42,508,830 in a combination of funds: (1) Vermont Housing and Conservation Board funds, $30,100,000; (2) Farms for Future, $10,100,000; (3) *Farmland Protection Program,* $2,300,000. And, for FY 2000, the farmland conservation target with Conservation Board and Farms for Future monies totals $3,087,000. (*Case History Source:* Jim Libby, General Counselor, Vermont Housing and Conservation Board, 149 State Street,

Montpelier, Vermont 05602; Tel: 802-828-3250; Fax: 802-828-3203.)

Case History #3: The Maryland Agricultural Land Preservation Foundation in Baltimore County found that participation in the *FPP* helped resolve two problems with their farmland acquisition plans. First, the *FPP* staff greatly simplified and shortened (from 2 ½ years to 1 year) the time to contract for *agricultural conservation easements.* Second, the federal staff shifted the Baltimore County from a legally binding requirement that they purchase easements based on the discount offered by the landowner, rather than upon the agricultural value of the land. The County found that wealthier owners could afford to offer a greater discount than a working farmer. Now, with the revised contract developed with the federal staff, the County has been able to purchase "real," family–owned, working farms. There is still a problem, however. If an enrolled farmer wishes to give property to his children, then he must pay back to the *FPP* that share of the total property transferred to the children. This results in complicated paperwork, extra time, and a loss of money. A preferable alternative is to use money from a property transfer tax rather than the federal money. Also, the County found that money from the *Intermodal Surface Transportation Efficiency Act* could be used to purchase farmland along highways. Altogether, with *FPP* funds, bond issues, and private donations, Baltimore County has the largest contiguous area under *agricultural conservation easements* on the East Coast, about 10,000 acres. (*Case History Source:* Wally Lippincott, Land Preservation Program Administrator, Baltimore County Department of Environmental Protection and Resource Management, 401 Bosley Ave., Room 416, Towson, MD 21204; Tel: 410-887-4488, ext. 241.)

ACTION STEPS: Contact the local Soil and Water Conservation District office (see **Action Center Resources**) about questions regarding the *farmland protection program,* as well as the Ohio Office of Farmland Preservation, Howard Wise, Exec. Dir., 8995 E. Main St., Reynoldsburg, OH 43068; Tel: 614-466-2732; Fax: 614-466-6124; E-mail: <<farmland@odant.agri.state.oh.us>>. Also, the American Farmland Trust has numerous publications and reports in hard copy and online. Web site resources include AFT's Technical Assistance Center, LandWorks, Farmland Protection Tools, Federal Policy, AFT's list of regional offices, its Center for Agriculture and the Environment, the Farmland Information Library, and a list of AFT publications. Contact them at American Farmland Trust, 1200 18th St., NW, Ste. 800, Washington, DC 20036; Tel: 202-331-7300; Fax: 202-659-8339; E-mail: <<Info@farmland. org>>; Web Site: <<http://www.farmland.org>>. For additional electronic sources of information, begin those listed in "Notes," below.

NOTES

[1] Natural Resources Conservation Service, U.S. Department of Agriculture, *1996 Farm Bill: Conservation Provisions Summary*, 1-5. Downloaded June 8, 1999 from Web Site <<http://www.nhq.nrcs.usda.gov/OPA/FB96OPA/Sum96FB.html>>.

[2] Natural Resources Conservation Service, U.S. Department of Agriculture, *1996 Farm Bill: Conservation Provisions—Farmland Protection Program Request for Proposals*, 6. Downloaded June 3, 1999 from Web Site: <<http:////www.nhq.nrcs.usda.gov/OPA/FB96OPA/FPP_rfp.html>>.

[3] Farmland Information Center, American Farmland Trust, *Farmland Protection Program Fact Sheet*, 1. Downloaded May 4, 1999 from Web Site: <<http://farm.fic.niu.edu/fic-ta/tats-fpp.html>>.

[4] *1996 Farm Bill: Conservation Provisions—Farmland Protection Program Request for Proposals*, 8.

FOREST TAX

OBJECTIVE: To provide tax relief to landowners with forested land.

WHO ENACTS IT: Landowners, through the Ohio Department of Natural Resources, Division of Forestry.

HOW IT WORKS: Under the Ohio Forest Tax Law, landowners are eligible who own woodland tracts of 10 acres or more in size, or 11 acres, if the parcel contains a dwelling, since 1 acre is subtracted for a residence. For forestland to be certified, there must be 10 acres of contiguous forest not less than 120 feet wide, and it must be inspected by the state forester to qualify for a tax credit.

Under 1993 requirements, the land must have been managed as a woodlot, which may include commercial cutting, and cannot be used for grazing. It must be protected from fire, and cannot currently be enrolled in the *current agricultural use value program*.

Eligible landowners can apply to the Ohio Department of Natural Resources, Division of Forestry. Landowners who gain approval for their application receive a 50% reduction in the amount of taxes due on the certified land. There is a one–time $50 filing fee, but no annual reapplication is required. In addition, there is no penalty if the land is removed from the program.

Before the forestland can be certified, the owner must demonstrate the intent to engage in forest management by completing a prescribed forest practice, such as replanting or pruning in the area, which will be reviewed every five years thereafter.[1]

ADVANTAGES: The program is easy to initiate and provides landowners with a financial incentive to keep their land forested.

DISADVANTAGES: The program only applies to forestland. Farmers with woodlots often receive greater tax relief by enrolling their land in the *CAUV* program. Any changes in land use or in the deed to the property require recertification to participate.

The program is not particularly effective as a growth management tool, since no penalty is assessed if land is withdrawn from the program. As a result, the payoff from developing a given parcel of land will generally far outweigh the financial inducement to keep the land forested.

CASE HISTORY: The Geauga County Auditor's Office prepared the table below to illustrate the estimated tax credit for property with forestlands certification. The example is for 21.28 acres, of which 18 acres is currently in woodlot, qualifying it for certification for tax credit in 1999. (*Case History Source:* Tracy A. Jemison, Geauga County Auditor, Chardon, OH 44024-1293; See contact information in Note 2, below.)

**Estimated Forestland Certification Tax Credit for 1999[2]
(Figures rounded to Nearest Whole Dollar Values)**

Assessed Value at 35% (State Law) of Market Worth	Without Forest Land Certification	With Forest Land Certification
Land	$24,680	$16,070
House	$21,700	$21,700
TOTAL	**$46,380**	**$37,770**

Tax Computation
Full rate 113.25
Effective rate .057166862

Effective rate x assessed worth	$ 2,651	$ 2,159

Credits

Income tax rollback (10%)	$(265)	$(216)
2.5% tax credit	$(15)	$(15)

Tax Due for Year

Tax computed less tax credits	$ 2,371	$ 1,928

**1999 Estimated Savings with Forestlands Certification:
$2,371 - $1,928 = $443**

ACTION STEPS: For the number of your regional forester, contact the Ohio Department of Natural Resources, Chief of the Division of Forestry, Fountain Square, Columbus, OH 43224; Tel: 614-265-6694.

NOTES

[1] Document from Land Owner Assistance, Division of Forestry, Ohio Department of Natural Resources, *Ohio Forest Tax Law*, downloaded May 10, 1999 from Web Site: <<http://www.hcs.ohio-states.edu/ODNR/Landownerasst/tax.htm>>

[2] Estimate for a Geauga County property of 21.28 acres, of which 18 acres is in woodlot, qualifying it for Forestland Certification Tax Credit for 1999; calculations by the Geauga County Auditor's office, October 4, 1999. Contact Tracy A. Jemison, Geauga County Auditor, 231 Main St., Courthouse Annex, Chardon, OH 44024-1293; Tel: 440-285-2222; Fax: 440-286-4359; E-mail: <<geaugaauditor@mwweb.com>>; Web Site: <<http://www.geaugalink.com/auditor>>.

NATIONAL CONSERVATION BUFFER INITIATIVE

OBJECTIVE: Nationally, the *national conservation buffer initiative* (*NCBI*) establishes 2,000,000 miles of conservation buffers— plantings, manmade structures, and farming practices defined in the *conservation reserve program* to reduce farmland runoff and soil erosion and increase wildlife habitat and plant and animal diversity. The Ohio NCBI, called the Lake Erie Buffer Program, forecasts an enrollment of 100,000 acres by the year 2002.[1]

WHO ENACTS IT: Farmers, ranchers, and other landowners may use conservation buffers to improve soil, water, and air quality while enhancing fishing and wildlife habitat. Some buffer practices qualify for financial assistance from federal and state programs, e.g., the *conservation reserve program* and the *wetland reserve program*.

HOW IT WORKS: The *national conservation buffer initiative* promotes the concept of buffer practices, which include riparian buffers (stream, pond, and lake shorelines), filter strips (plantings to reduce runoff and soil erosion), grassed waterways, shelter– belts / field windbreaks, living snow fences, contour grass strips, cross–wind trap strips, shallow water areas for wildlife, wellhead protection areas, field borders, alley–cropping herbaceous wind barriers, vegetative barriers, streambank plantings, among others. To promote the concept, *NCBI* employs basically three activities: (1) information and marketing through publications and training, (2) research and monitoring through erosion studies and water monitoring, and (3) financial assistance by working through *conservation reserve program, wetlands reserve program*, as noted above, as well as the environmental quality incentives program, and the stewardship incentives program.[2]

In Ohio, a Lake Erie Buffer Team, a 22 member organization representing 20 public and private conservation partners, has formulated 10 strategic elements that comprise the "Lake Erie Buffer Team Strategic Plan" (also called the Lake Erie Buffer Program). These elements are:

1. Implement a basin–wide marketing and information program that promotes the benefits of conservation buffer practices throughout the Lake Erie watershed and that supports implementation of the Ohio *conservation reserve enhanced program*, a special extension of the *conservation reserve program* to focus on "significant" environmental problems in prime farmland or unique soils areas.

2. Provide additional field–level technical assistance to help landowners within the watershed plan to apply conservation buffer practices.

3. Demonstrate innovative conservation buffer practices and use institutional partnerships to create programs that accelerate the adoption of these practices.

4. Monitor progress in conservation buffer installations and collect watershed data to assess the benefits of the installations.

5. Originate a basin–wide recognition program to publicize buffer accomplishments and create awareness about the importance of conservation buffers.

6. Use the agribusiness community to broaden support for and promotion of the Lake Erie Buffer Initiative.

7. Identify long–term strategies that increase the potential of conservation buffers to generate income and become self sustaining.

8. Encourage watershed or county–based local *buffer initiatives.*

9. Develop an urban conservation buffer program.

10. Provide for administrative coordination and fiscal assistance to the buffer team.[3]

As mentioned above, there are several federal / state programs that offer financial assistance for buffer practices. One of them is through the *CRP*'s continuous sign–up component. Farmers can enroll at any time, without having to submit a competitive offer. First, the Natural Resources Conservation Service or conservation district office will help identify buffer practices that are appropriate for the farmland and that qualify for assistance. Next, the landowner submits an offer to the agency; if eligibility requirements have been met, it will be accepted automatically. If the farmland is already enrolled in the regular *CRP* and the contract is expiring, selected portions of that land can be enrolled in the continuous sign–up *CRP*.[4]

The USDA publication, *Buffers: Common–Sense Conservation,* describes the payment rates for continuous sign–up enrollment as follows: "The annual rental payments are based on the relative productivity of the soil type being offered and the average dryland cash rental rate for comparable land in the county."[5] The program adds 20% to that payment for field windbreaks, grassed waterways, filter strips, and riparian buffers; and 10% is added for land within designated wellhead protection areas. Cost–share is also provided for these measures, including site preparation, temporary cover until permanent cover is established; grading or shaping; planting seeds, trees, or shrubs; and installing plastic mulch, and supplemental irrigation and fencing.

ADVANTAGES: The benefits of buffers have been known for years, but their installation has been resisted because landowners would have to take farmland out of production, thereby losing income. Now, the financial compensation makes it attractive to construct buffers to help preserve and restore increasingly unproductive land while consolidating farming operations to fewer acres but more productive land.

DISADVANTAGES: The *buffer initiative* depends upon funds from existing federal / state programs, e.g., the *CRP*, the *WRP,* etc. Some, like *CRP*, have acreage limits, 34,600,000 nationwide for *CRP*, with 32,500,000 acres already taken. There are 100,000 acres in each state for the *CREP*, and of this total, in Ohio 67,000 acres have already been reserved for the Western Lake Erie Watershed. In other words, there are very few acreage units available to furnish the money to pay for newly buffered lands.

CASE HISTORY #1: Lyle and Phil Shaffer, father and son, of Wood County, Ohio, have installed buffer strips on their farmland for over 30 years. With mostly swamplands that drain into Lake Erie, the farm has many ditches that, unprotected, carry soil and fertilizer from the fields. Therefore, the Shaffers have planted grasses along 4½ miles of ditches and 5 miles of windbreaks. Because the Shaffers were already practicing "high priority conservation" measures, they qualified for the continuous sign–up *CRP* and now have 18 acres enrolled. So far, they say, it has been "All pluses." (*Case History Source:* Lyle and Phil Shaffer, 7580 Huffman Road, Cygnett, Ohio 43413; Tel: 419-655-3849.)

CASE HISTORY #2: Bill Frankart owns farmland in Sandusky and Seneca Counties. Unlike the Shaffers, he had not constructed buffers because he could not afford them. He had to get some return from the land. Now, with the commencement of the *buffer initiative* program, in the last two years Frankart has constructed ditch bank grass filters using clover, fescue, timothy, rye, and other grasses. Seventy acres qualified for enrollment in the continuous sign–up *CRP*, and he is receiving payments annually, as well as half the buffer construction costs. Frankart recognized that he was not being a good land steward when he felt it was economically necessary to plant crops right up to the drainage ditch banks, but, now, with the financial compensation, he can afford to protect his farmland and the adjacent waterways. (*Case History Source:* Bill Frankart, 7731 N. Township Road 32, Clyde, Ohio 43410; Tel: 419-639-2492; Fax: 419-639-0059.)

ACTION STEPS: Request a copy of *Riparian Buffers: Technical Information for Decision Makers*, 1999, from Chagrin River Watershed Partners, 2705 River Rd., Willoughby Hills, OH 44094-9445; Tel: 440-945-3870; Fax: 440-975-3865. Order the USDA's *Buffers, Common–Sense Initiatives*, No. 576-666 (Washington, DC: U.S. Government Printing Office, 1997), no pagination, available from the U.S. Department of Agriculture, 14th & Independence Ave. SW, Washington, DC 20250; Tel: 202-720-2791. See other materials available at Web Site: <<http://rigis2. nhq.nrcs.usda.gov:80/CCS/Buffers.html>>. Obtain the *National Conservation Buffer Initiative: Questions and Answers*, USDA Natural Resources Conservation Service from the USDA at the Washington, DC, address above or download Web Site: <<http:// rigis2.nhq.nrcs.usda.gov.80/BCS/aqua/buffer.pdf>>. Order "Conservation Practice Job Sheets" on filter strips, grassed waterways / vegetated filter systems, riparian, buffers, etc. Write the Natural Resources Conservation Service, USDA, Conservation Communications Staff, P.O. Box 2890, Washington, DC 20013; download from Web Site: <<http://www.nrcs.usda.gov>>.

NOTES

[1] "New Lake Erie Buffer Team Strives Toward Improving Water Quality in Ohio's Farmlands," *Northcoast Newsletter: News and Information from the Ohio Lake Erie Commission* in *Twine Line*, Vol. 20, No. 6 (November / December 1998), NCN-1 through NCN-3.

[2] Steve Davis, Resource Conservationist & Team Leader—Lake Erie Buffer Team, Natural Resources Conservation Service, USDA, 3900 Campus Dr., Ste. A, Lima, OH 45840; Tel: 419-222-0614; Fax: 419-224-3415. Fax memorandum on the National Conservation Buffer Initiative to J. Chadbourne, August 8, 1999.

[3] Steve Davis, Resource Conservationist, and Team Leader—Lake Erie Buffer Team, 3900 Campus Drive, Lima, Ohio 45801. Proposal for National Conservation Buffer Initiative to the Lake Erie Protection Fund (July 1999), 3-4.

[4] U. S. Department of Agriculture, *Buffers: Common–Sense Conservation*, No. 576-666 (Washington, DC: U.S. Government Printing Office, 1997), 8-fold brochure, no pagination, at Web Site: <<http://rigis2.nhq.nrcs.usda.gov.80/ CCS/Buffers.html>>.

[5] Ibid., no pagination.

STORM WATER MANAGEMENT— NPDES PHASE II

(*Author's Note:* This material may facilitate the development of comprehensive plans in those communities that do not already have them–please see Section II, The Role of Planning in Land Preservation).

OBJECTIVE: To regulate storm water discharges in small municipalities and from small construction sites not now regulated by the National Pollution Discharge Elimination System (*NPDES*) Phase I regulations.

WHO ENACTS IT: Small municipalities (about 280 in Ohio) in urban areas with separate storm sewer systems and small construction site owners and operators "disturbing" between 1 to 5 acres for new facilities.[1]

HOW IT WORKS: As of August 1999, it is proposed—with a final ruling due October 29, 1999 and publication of the rules in November 1999—that nationwide, starting in early 2003, the U.S. EPA will regulate storm water discharge sources that were not included in Phase I of the *NPDES* Program, including some that do not now release pollutants listed under Phase I.

Small Municipalities: The Ohio EPA, under the currently proposed regulation 40CFR122.26, will issue a general permit to small municipalities in urban areas that operate municipal sewer systems. Combined sewer systems are not subject to these regulations.[2] As proposed, those recipients must submit within 90 days a Notice of Intent (NOI) for Coverage Under Ohio Environmental Protection Agency Storm Water General Permit[3] and a storm water management plan to comply with the stipulations of the general permit.

The NOI is a simple, one–page form requesting basic information. The storm water management plan proposes six minimum control measures and the use of best management practices (BMPs) for storm water management implemented during land development.[4] The six "Minimum Control Measures" are cited here from the Ohio EPA's Information Sheet, as presently proposed:[5]

❐ **Public Education and Outreach Program** on the impacts of storm water on surface water and possible steps to reduce storm water pollution. The program must be targeted at both the general community and commercial, industrial, and institutional dischargers.

❏ **Public Involvement and Participation** in developing and implementing the Storm Water Management Plan.

❏ **Elimination of Illicit Discharges** to the MS4 (i.e., separate <u>s</u>torm <u>s</u>ewer <u>s</u>ystems).

❏ **Construction Site Storm Water Runoff Ordinance** that requires the use of appropriate BMPs, preconstruction review of <u>s</u>torm <u>w</u>ater <u>p</u>ollution <u>p</u>revention <u>p</u>lans (SWP3s), site inspections during construction for compliance with the SWP3, and penalties for noncompliance.

❏ **Post–Construction Storm Water Management Ordinance** that requires the implementation of structural and nonstructural BMPs within new development and redevelopment areas, including assurances of the long–term operation of these BMPs.

❏ **Pollution Prevention and Good Housekeeping** for municipal operations such as efforts to reduce storm water pollution from . . . open space, and parks, as well as the maintenance of vehicle fleets.

In this proposed rule, the U.S. EPA supports a storm water management plan that takes into account the watershed in which the applicant is located, and especially commends policies and ordinances that accomplish the following goals:

- Protecting sensitive areas such as wetlands and riparian areas
- Minimizing imperviousness
- Maintaining open space, and/or
- Minimizing the disturbance of soils and vegetation.[6]

There *are* waiver possibilities proposed for small municipalities, but they require meeting all of these conditions: (1) the population is less than 1,000, (2) the separate sewer system contributes no pollution to a physically interconnected system which does carry pollution, and (3) the municipality certifies that storm water controls are not needed for reasons that address pollutants of concern.[7]

Small Construction Sites: While Phase I of the *NPDES* regulates construction on 5 or more acres, Phase II will regulate construction on sites of 1 to 5 acres.

Municipally–Owned Industrial Facilities: Certain of these facilities were excluded from Phase I of the *NPDES* Program, such as wastewater treatment plants discharging a minimum of 1,000,000 gallons of water per day and some construction sites larger than 5 acres which were exempt from regulation by another federal program. One, the *Intermodal Surface Transportation Efficiency Act of 1991*, excluded municipalities of 100,000 or less in population. These facilities must now apply for permit coverage by August 7, 2001.

Under *Phase II*, there are opportunities for some industrial processes that do not pollute with chemicals or products on the Phase I list, that is, that have "no exposure," to become exempt from Phase I permit requirements. The number of qualifying facilities may be as high as 70,000 nationwide.[8]

ADVANTAGES: For communities that do not have a comprehensive plan and / or effective zoning, *Phase II* provides an opportunity to develop a community–wide plan that protects natural resources with cost–effective best management practices. An important measure is the requirement of a public education and outreach program, which enhances the potential effectiveness of *Phase II* practices serving as a community's equivalent of a comprehensive plan.

DISADVANTAGES: Some communities are alarmed by the probable cost of best management practice constructions within their jurisdiction. These will no doubt require the generation of new income to offset those expenses.

CASE HISTORY #1: Chagrin River Watershed Partners, Inc. (CRWP), has produced *Consensus Agreement on Model Development Principles to Protect Our Streams, Lakes, and Wetlands.* The document's objective is "to provide planners, developers, and local officials with benchmarks to investigate where existing ordinances may be modified to reduce impervious cover, conserve natural areas, and prevent storm water pollution." The principles address streets and parking lots, lot development, and conservation of natural areas. The publication may help communities work toward a storm water management plan. It is available from CRWP. (*Case History Source:* Tom Denbow, Exec. Dir., Chagrin River Watershed Partners, Inc., 2705 River Rd., Willoughby Hills, OH 44094; Tel: 440-975-3870; Fax: 440-975-3865.)

CASE HISTORY #2: The consequences of failing to use best management practices to control runoff during a construction project are reflected in a recent settlement between the Ohio EPA and Hermitage Builders, Inc., over erosion in Concord Township, Ohio. A 260–acre golf course under construction is nearly complete, and utility hook–ups for the 80 one–acre residential lots are scheduled for completion in the fall of 1999.

Earlier in the project, EPA inspectors had ordered the "elimination of erosion gullies and the movement of sediment traps to enhance the control of runoff."[9] But, as work proceeded on the golf course and the subdivision, Hermitage Builders' construction activities led to serious silting of Ellison Creek, normally green in color but turned milky brown from runoff.

In the settlement between Ohio EPA and Hermitage, the company must pay a $35,000 fine and "take several erosion abatement measures, such as placing seed, matting and straw, reinforcing and replacing sediment fencing and installing a settling pond to collect runoff."

The erosion control problems were so serious at the Hermitage site and one other development project in Lake County that county commissioners drafted erosion control regulations that they hope to have approved by the end of 1999. They used existing regulations from nearby Geauga County as well as assistance from the soil and water conservation districts and Chagrin River Watershed Partners to develop the proposed Lake County regulations.[10]

With local erosion control regulations based on best management practices on the books, communities enhance their ability to protect their water quality, habitat, and other natural features during the site disturbances that accompany development. (**Case History Source:** James Lawless, "Developer, EPA Settle Erosion Battle," *The Plain Dealer* (August 12, 1999) See contact information below.)

ACTION STEPS. Contact Bob Pholpe, Mgr., Storm Water Section, Division of Surface Waters, Ohio EPA, P.O. 1049, 122 South Front Street, Columbus, Ohio 43216-1049. Tel: 614-644-2001; Fax: 614-644-2745. Web Site: <<http://www.chagrin.epa.state.oh.us>>; federal Web Site: <<http://www.access.gpo.gov/su-docs/aces/aces140.html>>; Phase I, <<http://www.epa.gov/owm/new.htm>> or <<http://www.epa.gov/owmitnet/pipes/2-.htm>>; Phase II Web Site: <<http://www.epa/owm/sw/phase2/htm>>. Obtain copies of the following documents: *Better Site Design: A Handbook for Changing Development Rules in Your Community* as well as *Nutrient Loading from Conventional and Innovative Site Development*, Center for Watershed Protection, 8392 Main St.,

Ellicott, MD 21043; Tel: 410-461-8323; "Reviewing Site Plans for Stormwater Management," Nonpoint Education for Municipal Officials (NEMO) Project, c/o Chester Arnold, University of Connecticut CES, 1066 Saybrook Rd., Haddam, CT 06438-0070; Tel: 860-345-4511; Fax: 860-345-3357; E-mail: <<carnold@canr1. cag.uconn.edu>>; and "Muddy Water In—Muddy Water Out," *Watershed Protection Techniques*, Vol. 2, No. 3 (February 1997), 393-403. (This article is available from Chagrin River Watershed Partners; contact information is in the first case history, above.)

NOTES

[1] Ohio EPA, "Expansion of the NPDES Storm Water Permit Program—Phase II," Information Sheet (no date), 1-2.

[2] Ibid., 1.

[3] Ohio EPA, "Notice of Intent (NOI) for Coverage under Ohio Environmental Protection Agency Storm Water General Permit," Application Form, EPA Form No. 4494 (June 25, 1993).

[4] Dan Mecklenberg, Storm Water Engineer (ODNR, Division of Soil and Water Conservation), *Rainwater and Land Development: Ohio's Standards for Storm Water Management, Land Development, and Urban Stream Protection*, Second Edition (Columbus, OH, 1996), 190 pp.

[5] Ohio EPA, "Expansion of the NPDES Storm Water Permit Program—Phase II," 1.

[6] Ibid., 2.

[7] Ibid., 2.

[8] Ohio EPA, "Expansion of the NPDES Storm Water Permit Program—Phase II," 2.

[9] James Lawless, "Developer, EPA Settle Erosion Battle," *The Plain Dealer* (August 12, 1999), 3–B.; Tel: 1-800-275-5253; E-mail: <<jlawless@plaind. com>>.)

[10] Telephone conversation October 13, 1999, between Tom Denbow, Chagrin River Watershed Partners, and J. Chadbourne.

WETLANDS MITIGATION AND BANKING

OBJECTIVE: To protect land by preserving the many valuable functions of wetlands—i.e., pollution prevention, flood protection, and habitat preservation—from loss to dredge or fill material by requiring permits which include appropriate compensatory mitigation, the minimization of adverse impacts, either on the project site or at an off–site location.

WHO ENACTS IT: The principal federal program regulating wetlands is the Federal Water Pollution Control Act Amendments of 1972, Section 404. It is administered jointly by the U.S. Army Corps of Engineers and the U.S. Environmental Protection Agency under the advisement of the U.S. Fish and Wildlife Service and the National Marine Fisheries Service.[1] Most states also conduct wetland protection programs for areas not under federal regulatory jurisdiction.

HOW IT WORKS: Under Section 404(b)(1) guidelines, the Corps reviews and decides upon standard, project–specific permit applications submitted by a developer. If the Corps decides that the project cannot reasonably be expected to avoid a wetland area, the Section 404(b)(1) Guidelines sequence three steps for a permit grant: (1) no discharge can be permitted if there is a practicable alternative to the proposed development that would have less adverse impact on the aquatic environment; (2) the applicant must take all "appropriate and practicable" steps to minimize unavoidable wetland impacts; and lastly (3) replacement of the wetlands to be impacted, called compensatory mitigation, may be provided by either restoring former wetlands, and / or enhancing existing wetlands. If restoration or enhancement cannot be accomplished on–site and in–kind, this mitigation may include the creation of new wetlands at another site where the functions of the impacted site can be successfully recreated and sustained.[2]

The compensatory mitigation requirements are established by assuring that the "wetland functions lost at the impacted site are replaced by the functions made available at the mitigation site."[3] As the Section 404 Program has grown from the 1990 emphasis of on–site mitigation to compensate for unavoidable wetland impacts, it has recognized off–site mitigation as an acceptable alternative, in some instances, to ensure mitigation success. There are several categories of off–site mitigation. One of these alternatives is called "Wetlands Mitigation Banking."

In December 1995, the Corps and the U.S. EPA finalized the Federal Guidance defining mitigation banking as "the restoration, creation, enhancement, and, in exceptional circumstances, preservation of wetlands or other aquatic habitats expressly for the purpose of providing compensatory mitigation in advance of discharges into wetlands permitted under the Section 404 regulatory program."[4] The guidelines stress that regulators should establish bank sites in advance of project impacts, so that mitigation credits—a credit is equivalent to one acre of restored wetland—can be traded for units of permitted wetland loss preferentially within the watershed of the impacted site. As wetland losses are permitted by the regulatory agency, debits are made to the bank, reducing its credit balance. The trading ratio is set by the regulators to achieve a no–net–loss in wetland function and acreage. In Ohio, a typical ratio might specify that one acre of impacted wetlands requires the construction of two acres of new, off–site wetlands to offset the loss.

Applications to construct *wetlands mitigation* banks are examined by a Mitigation Bank Review Team. The Team consists of the U.S. Army Corps of Engineers, the U.S. Environmental Protection Agency, the U.S. Fish & Wildlife Service, the U.S. Department of Agriculture's Natural Resources Conservation Service, and the National Marine Fisheries Service, as appropriate. Also, the Team will include pertinent state tribal, local regulator, and resource agencies. In Ohio, the state agencies include the Ohio Environmental Protection Agency and the Ohio Department of Natural Resources.

There are several forms of mitigation banks.

❏   **Single–User Mitigation Banks:** These are usually large, private developers or state or local agencies planning for their own future needs who can afford the up–front investment.

❏   **Public Commercial Banks:** Generally, these banks are managed by government agencies and established nonprofit conservancies or land trusts or museums. They subsidize the construction and operation of public banks. They sell credits, and may or may not apply the proceeds to offset their initial and continuing management costs.

❏   **Private Commercial Banks:** Privately owned corporations may design and, with approval by the Mitigation Banking Review Team, construct mitigation wetlands and then sell credits competitively at market value. These are intended to broaden the use of large–scale wetlands by attracting entrepreneurs who are more likely to be able to afford up–front construction expenses than are public agencies and nonprofit institutions.[5]

Different from "banking," another approach to off–site mitigation is the "in–lieu–fee system," which primarily addresses small–scale projects, perhaps ½ to 3 acres in size. In this case, in lieu of providing compensation directly, the impacted site owner pays a fee to a conservation organization that has agreed with the Corps of Engineers to establish a trust fund for restoration, enhancement, and / or preservation of aquatic resources. The agreement might establish a clear time table for the replacement wetland project. The hypothesis is that the conservation organization will be able to pool monies from several small mitigants in order to create or complete a large project.[6]

ADVANTAGES: Mitigation banking provides high quality, large wetland ecosystems that afford more functions and values than those of the impacted wetland. Mitigation banks usually end up being owned by a public agency and can be used by the public for recreational and educational opportunities. With mitigation banking, the development community has a cost effective, high quality wetlands mitigation option, and the regulatory agencies have one large site to monitor as opposed to numerous, small isolated sites, thereby reducing operating expenses.

DISADVANTAGES: Mitigation banks are not available in all watersheds, and small watersheds may never be able to support a mitigation bank economically. And, in some cases, the availability and economics of off–site mitigation may overlook on–site remedies. In either situation, the loss of wetlands in these small watersheds permanently removes their benefits to the area—flood reduction, water quality protection, toxics filtration, and erosion control.

Some investigations have found mitigation to be nearly a complete failure. In 1997, the Ohio EPA's Division of Surface Waters published a study documenting problems. In *A Functional Assessment of Mitigation Wetlands in Ohio: Comparisons with Natural Systems*, Drs. Siobhan Fennessey and Joanne Roehrs of that Division found that manmade wetlands have many different characteristics than natural systems, and that manmade constructions are not replacing the functions of those natural wetlands.[7]

CASE HISTORY: The Ohio Wetlands Foundation, a private nonprofit 501(c)3 corporation established in 1992 by the Ohio Home Builders Association, initially agreed in 1993 with the Ohio Department of Natural Resources, Division of Wildlife, to select, design, restore, and construct wetlands on state–owned land that would be managed and maintained by the Division of Wildlife.

Since then, working with other agencies, the Foundation has developed four mitigation banks. A fifth is under review by the Mitigation Bank Review Team and is expected to be approved by the end of 1999. The Corps retains all permit authority and determines whether the use of a bank is acceptable on a case–by–case basis. The following is a short description of each bank, the last still under approval review.

❐ **Hebron:** The Foundation paid a fee to the Ohio Department of Natural Resources to develop a 33–acre mitigation bank at ODNR's Hebron Fish Hatchery. The Foundation paid for all design and construction costs, sold the 33 mitigation rights to various private and public clients who needed compensatory mitigation (at a range of $7,000 to $10,000 / acre), and monitored the site for 5 years. In June 1999, after the required 5–year performance period, the Corps relieved the Foundation of any further responsibility for the Hebron bank's performance.

❐ **Big Island:** Again, with a fee–paid agreement with ODNR, the Foundation restored and enhanced 350 acres at ODNR's Big Island Wildlife Area, west of Marion, Ohio. Credited with 288 acres, the Foundation sold credits to 90 clients for $16,000 per acre.

❐ **Sandy Ridge:** With a similar agreement, the Foundation designed and constructed a 115–acre mitigation bank on property owned by the Lorain County Metro Park District in North Ridgeville, Ohio. The bank received 87 credits, which were sold within 2 years.

❐ **Slate Run:** The Foundation then constructed a 156–acre bank on land owned by the Columbus and Franklin County Metro Park District in central Ohio. Construction was completed in June 1999.

❐ **Three Eagles:** The Foundation has submitted a mitigation plan to the Mitigation Bank Review Team for approval of a 158–acre wetlands restoration project. Upon completion of construction and the required 5–year monitoring period, the site will be placed in a *conservation easement* for wetlands preservation in perpetuity and donated to a public entity as manager. The credit price is expected to range between $13,000 and $16,000 per credit. Three Eagles will serve Wood, Lucas, Sandusky, and Ottawa counties.

Other information, including additional case histories, are available from the Ohio Wetlands Foundation. (*Case History Sources:* Jim Sutliff, Pres., Ohio Wetlands Foundation, 3675 Africa Road, Galena, Ohio 43021; Tel. 740-548-0484; Fax: 740-548-4393; Web Site: <<http://www.Ohiowetlands.org>>.)

ACTION STEPS: Obtain a copy of *Guidelines for the Development of Wetland Replacement Areas*, NCHRP Report 379, National Cooperative Highway Research Program, Transportation Research Board, National Research Council (Washington, DC: National Academy Press, 1996); copies are available from the Transportation Research Board, National Research Council, 2101 Constitution Ave., Washington, DC 20418, ISBN 0-309-05708–6. For wetlands mitigation information, contact Alan Anacheka–Nasemann, U S Army Corps of Engineers, Buffalo District, 1776 Niagara St., Buffalo, NY, 14207-3199, Tel. 716-879-4319; and, Steve Metivier, Biologist, Regulatory Branch (same address), Tel. 716-879-4314. For national information, contact Bob Brumbaugh, U.S. Army Corps of Engineers, Alexandria, VA, Tel. 703-428-7069.

NOTES

[1] National Wetland Mitigation Banking Study, *Expanding Opportunities for Successful Mitigation: The Private Credit Market Alternative*, IWR Report 94-WMB-3 (Alexandria, VA: Institute for Water Resources, U.S. Army Corps of Engineers, January 1994), 9.

[2] Ibid., 9-10.

[3] Ibid., 11.

[4] Ibid., 12.

[5] Ibid., 13-14.

[6] *Alternative Mechanisms for Compensatory Mitigation: Case Studies and Lessons about Fee-Based Compensatory Wetlands Mitigation* (Alexandria, VA: Institute for Water Resources, U.S. Army Corps of Engineer, March 1993), 2.

[7] National Audubon Society, Great Lakes Region Office, "Ohio EPA Finds Mitigation Wetlands Are Not Measuring Up," *Ohio Wetlands Update*, Vol. 4, No. 6 (July 1997), 1.

[8] J. Chadbourne telephone conversation on June 28, 1999 with Jim Sutliff, Ohio Wetlands Foundation, and subsequent fax from Sutliff to Chadbourne. Contact: See case history source, above.

WETLANDS RESERVE PROGRAM

OBJECTIVE: The *wetlands reserve program* is a voluntary program to protect, restore, and enhance wetlands in all states, with the goal of improving migratory and other wildlife habitat, upgrading water quality, filtering sediment from runoff water, aiding in flood water retention and ground water recharge, increasing open space, enhancing aesthetics, and expanding opportunities for environmental education. Farmers who restore and protect existing farmed wetlands and landowners along stream corridors are compensated for value lost and / or restoration expenses.[1]

WHO ENACTS IT: Authorized by the Food Security Act of 1985 with amendments in 1990 and 1996, the U.S. Department of Agriculture's National Resources Conservation Service (NRCS) administers the *WRP*, consulting on program matters with the Farm Service Agency,[2] and—in Ohio—with assistance from the Ohio Department of Natural Resources (ODNR). The individual landowner, working with the NRCS, prepares a plan in which the wetland and any adjacent lands must be restored and maintained [3]

HOW IT WORKS: Currently, landowners submit a signed enrollment application at any time of the year to the local NRCS office. The NRCS, in consultation with the U.S. Fish & Wildlife Service (FWS), evaluates the land's eligibility. Next, the landowner prepares a preliminary plan for restoring the wetland—with help from NRCS, FWS, ODNR, and the local conservation district. The plan contains practices, structures, and estimated costs to be used in a competitive selection of projects to be funded. In 1999, Ohio underwrote $2,000,000 in *WRP* costs and projects; $2,000,000 may become appropriated for 2000

If the application is tentatively selected, NRCS determines the *current agricultural use value* of the land (approximately $750 to $1,000 / acre, with up to an additional $500 / acre from bonus funds available) and then can offer three options to the landowner:

❏ **Permanent Easement:** This is a *conservation easement* in perpetuity. Payment to the landowner will be the least of the *current agricultural use value* of the land, or an established payment cap, or an amount offered by the landowner. USDA also pays 100% of any wetland restoration costs.

❏ **30–year Easement:** This *conservation easement* lasts 30 years. Payments are 75% of what would be paid for a permanent easement. In this case, USDA pays 75% of the restoration costs.

❑ **Restoration Cost–Share Agreement:** An agreement for a minimum of 10 years re–establishes degraded or lost wetland habitat. The USDA pays 75% of the cost of restoration only, while the landowner does not place an easement on the property, and is not reimbursed for the land value of the restoration site.[4]

Additionally, the ODNR's Division of Wildlife's Streambanking Program, through NatureWorks funding, will offer cost–share dollars for wetland restorations up to 25% of the costs, not to exceed $250 / restoration acre, for W*RP's* second and third options, above. This makes it possible to reimburse 100% of the restoration expenses. The ODNR contract is for a minimum of 15 years, not 10 as in *WRP*.[5, 6]

Also, ODNR's Division of Soil and Water Conservation, through The NatureWorks Program, will offer the following to encourage "riparian area enhancements," as funding permits:[7]

❑ **Perpetual Easements:** The NatureWorks Program will pay 50% of the amount paid by the *WRP* in its first option, above, as a bonus, not to exceed $500 maximum / riparian acre.

❑ **30–year WRP Conservation Easements:** The NatureWorks Program will pay 25% of the amount paid by *WRP*, its second option above, as a bonus, not to exceed a $250 maximum / riparian acre.

The *WRP* applications may be used for the ODNR applications.[7]

Eligibility for the *WRP* requires the landowner to offer an easement, to have owned the land a minimum of 12 months prior to enrollment—unless the land was inherited, or to prove the land was not obtained for the purpose of enrolling it in the *WRP*. Further, the land itself must be restorable and suitable for wildlife benefits. These include:

- Wetlands farmed under natural conditions
- Farmed wetlands
- Prior converted cropland
- Farmed wetland pasture
- Farmland that has become a wetland as a result of flooding
- Rangeland, pasture, or production forestland where the hydrology has been significantly degraded and can be restored
- Riparian areas that link protected wetlands

- Lands adjacent to protected wetlands that contribute significantly to wetland functions and values, and
- Previously restored wetlands (see *conservation reserve program*); property is eligible if it meets *WRP* requirements.[8]

Landowners enrolling riparian areas that connect wetlands may be required to establish an additional *conservation easement* with another entity that includes those wetlands.

Ineligible land includes wetlands converted after December 23, 1985; lands with timber stands established under a *CRP* contract; federal lands; and lands where conditions make restoration impossible.[9]

ADVANTAGES: The *WRP* compensates a landowner while providing the benefits of wetland conservation. The landowner controls access to the property, but allows NRCS to enter for inspection and management. The *WRP* easement does not open the area to public hunting, fishing, or other forms of recreation unless desired by the owner. Harvesting timber is allowed if included in the *WRP* plan. Land restricted by a *WRP* easement may be leased or sold by the owner, but the easement still applies to the property.

DISADVANTAGES: *WRP* funding has been irregular, unpredictable, and inadequate to meet the demand. By July 1999, Ohio expended most of its 1999 allocation for *WRP*. Although authorized through 2002, the availability of 2000 funds will not be known until the beginning of the year.[10]

CASE HISTORY: Neil Babb in London, Madison County, Ohio, enrolled 85 acres of land into the *WRP* in 1996. It qualified for a perpetual *conservation easement*. The acreage had been farmed and was a "little wet" with a one–acre lake, probably left by someone removing gravel some time ago. Later that year, he constructed a 5–acre wetland, and in 1997, a 3–acre wetland within the easement area. The wetlands fit well with 35 additional, adjacent wooded acres and a nearby 5–acre lake. The 85 acres are now restored wetlands with a dramatic increase in the duck and geese populations and upland pheasants and quail. There are a number of red–tailed hawks that now nest in the wooded section of the property. For some reason the deer population, however, has decreased, and Neil has no explanation for this.

Occasionally, "four–wheelers" have entered his property and damaged the area; once he caught a poacher on the land. Hunters have not caused any problems. Overall, Neil is very pleased with his decision to enroll in the *WRP*. (*Case History Source:* Neil Babb, Landowner, P.O. Box 374, London, Ohio 43140; Tel: 740-852-9404 [w] and 740-852-2158 [h].)

ACTION STEPS: For *WRP* information and updates, contact John Armentano, *WRP* Coordinator, 200 North High Street, Room 522, Columbus, OH 43215-2478; Tel: 614-255-2469; Fax: 614-255-2548. For Ohio Department of Natural Resources' NatureWorks and other ODNR–sponsored grant application procedures, contact Chris Kauffman, Grants Coordinator for programs supported by ODNR's Division of Soil and Water Conservation; Tel. 614-265-6914, E-mail: <<chris.kaufmann@dnr.state.oh.us>> or Mike Cook, Tel: 614-265-6395.

NOTES

[1] National Resources Conservation Service et al., *The Wetlands Reserve Program*, WRP-1 (October 1997), 8-fold brochure, no pagination. The NRCS Web Site is <<http://www.nhq.nrcs.usda.gov>>.

[2] National Resources Conservation Service, U.S. Department of Agriculture, *Fact Sheet: Wetland Reserve Program* (no date), 1. Downloaded June 8, 1999 from Web Site: <<http://www.nhq.nrcs.usda./gov/OPA/FB96OPA/WRPfact.html>>

[3] Ibid., 2.

[4] Ibid., 2.

[5] National Resources Conservation Service, U.S. Department of Agriculture, *Fact Sheet: Wetland Reserve Program* (October 1998), 3.

[6] J. Chadbourne telephone communication with C. Kaufmann. See Ohio Department of Natural Resources, *NatureWorks, Nonpoint Source Pollution Control— Streambanking: Reserving Riparian Areas to Enhance Water Quality*, (no date), 3-5. Available from ODNR; contact Chris Kaufmann, E-mail: <<chris.kaufmann@dnr.state.oh.us>> or Jill Deibel, E-mail: <<jill.deibel@dnr.state.oh.us>>.

[7] National Resources Conservation Service, U.S. Department of Agriculture, *Fact Sheet: Wetland Reserve Program* (October 1998), 3.

[8] National Resources Conservation Service, U.S. Department of Agriculture, *Fact Sheet: Wetland Reserve Program* (No date), 2-3. Downloaded June 8, 1999 from Web Site: <<http://www.nhq.nrcs.usda.gov/OPA/FB96OPA/WRPfact.html>>

[9] Ibid., 3.

[10] National Resources Conservation Service, U.S. Department of Agriculture, *Fact Sheet: Wetland Reserve Program* (no date), 3.

WILDLIFE HABITAT INCENTIVE PROGRAM

OBJECTIVE: To develop and improve habitat for upland wildlife, wetland wildlife, endangered species, fisheries, and other wildlife.

WHO ENACTS IT: *WHIP* is budgeted for $50,000,000 through 2002 by the 1996 U.S. Department of Agriculture (USDA) Farm Bill of 1996. Private landowners or land managers voluntarily apply to their USDA service center or local soil and water conservation district (SWCD) office for installation and maintenance cost–sharing funds.[1]

HOW IT WORKS: The applicant prepares an installation and maintenance plan with technical assistance from the Natural Resources Conservation Service (NRCS) and the SWCD. Every plan answers these basic questions:[2]

- Does the plan provide specific assistance for the species of fish or wildlife the landowner is trying to help?
- Are the recommended practices technically feasible?
- Does the participant understand the plan, including obligations, practice standards and specifications, installation schedule, and maintenance requirements?
- How will adjacent land use activities impact the project site?
- Does the plan encourage the use and development of native plants and habitats?
- Does the plan encourage plant diversity?

Upon approval of the plan, the landowner agrees to a 5– to 10 year contract to construct the proposed habitat improvements. Upon their completion, the USDA pays up to 75% of the installation and anticipated maintenance costs to the landowner. The owner retains all property rights but does allow monitoring by the NRCS or its designated agent.

Award of the agreement is based upon individual state–specified goals and objectives for habitat improvement. All lands are eligible for consideration except:

- Federal land.
- Land currently enrolled in the water bank program, *conservation reserve program*, *wetlands reserve program*, or other similar programs.

- Land subject to an Emergency Watershed Protection Program floodplain easement.
- Land where USDA determines that impacts from on–site or off–site conditions make the success of habitat improvement unlikely.[2]

Participation in *WHIP* may qualify the owner for enrollment in the *current agricultural use value program*—depending on the county auditor's decision. *CAUV* allows land to be taxed at a lower agricultural value, rather than at a higher market, or development, value.

ADVANTAGES: *WHIP* encourages habitat improvement not only through cost–sharing but also by allowing the opportunity to enroll or maintain eligibility in the *CAUV program*. That means that the *CAUV* eligibility for less than 10 acres—i.e., proof of $2,500 gross income per year for three prior years—may be met through USDA payment from the *wildlife habitat incentives program*. As a result, more private landowners are likely to be brought into the state's plan for encouraging habitat improvement.

DISADVANTAGES: Cost–sharing does not cover all aspects of improvement expenses. And, the USDA payment arrives after the owner has incurred and paid those costs.

CASE HISTORY: Jeffrey and Maurine Orndorff, an attorney and a Soil Conservationist, respectively, rented 30 acres of their land to a neighbor, John Nelson, for growing crops. When John's father died and his children were not interested in continuing the farm, he took an outside job and was unable to operate the farm himself. Thus, he no longer needed the Orndorff's pastureland. This gave Jeffrey and Maurine the opportunity to enroll in *WHIP*, preserving their land with cold– and warm–season grasses, a long held hope. They did not realize then that in Geauga County they automatically qualified for *CAUV*, in which they had already participated.

Jeffrey's brother, Perry Orndorff, a Soil Conservationist in Circleville, Ohio, has enrolled 6 to 8 landowners in *WHIP*. (*Case History Source:* Jeffrey and Maurine Orndorff, 17366 Wing Rd., Chagrin Falls, Ohio 44023; Tel: 440-543-5780; Fax: 440-285-3363.)

ACTION STEPS: Obtain further information on *WHIP, CAUV*, and other USDA programs from the National Resources Conservation Service, USDA, at Web Site: <<http://www.nhq.nrcs.usda.gov>>.

NOTES

[1] USDA 1996 Farm Bill Conservation Provisions, "Wildlife Habitat Incentives Program (WHIP)—Questions and Answers," 1. Downloaded June 8, 1999 from Web Site: <<http://www.nhq.nrcs.usda.gov/OPA/FB96oPA/WhipQ%A.html>>.

[2] Ibid., 2.

IV. LAND–USE MANAGEMENT TOOLS

IV–B–1: Public Initiatives — Acquisition

Land and Water Conservation Fund

Land Banking

Outright Purchase

Purchase of Development Rights

Transportation Enhancements (ISTEA & TEA–21)

LAND AND WATER CONSERVATION FUND

OBJECTIVE: To expand and improve public outdoor recreational facilities nationwide by providing matching funds to state and local governments for land acquisition and park improvements.

WHO ENACTS IT: State and local park agencies, in conjunction with the federal government.

HOW IT WORKS: The federal government provides up to 50% in matching reimbursement funds for the acquisition or improvement of recreational facilities. Each state is allocated money on an annual basis, which it can keep for state parks or share with local governments. The Ohio branch of the program is administered by the Ohio Department of Natural Resources (ODNR) through the Midwest Regional Office of the National Park Service.

One interesting aspect of the program is that state and local agencies can substitute donations for their share of the project cost. For example, if someone intends to contribute a parcel of land worth $50,000 to ODNR for use as a nature preserve, ODNR can then apply to the *land and water conservation fund* for $50,000 to protect or improve the same, or another, property. All requests for funding must meet the guidelines outlined in Ohio's Statewide Comprehensive Outdoor Recreation Plan drafted by ODNR.

ADVANTAGES: The program reduces the cost to state and local park agencies of funding new acquisitions and improvements.

DISADVANTAGES: The program provides no money up front. Local governments must first obtain approval and acquire the land or make improvements before submitting receipts for partial reimbursement. The program monies allocated to Ohio and all other states have dropped considerably in the last decade. In 1979, Ohio received nearly $14.5 million. By 1988, that amount had fallen to about $500,000. In 1991, Ohio received just over $1 million through the program, and from 1992 to 1995 approximately $850,000 per year.[1] A markup of H.R. 701 and H.R. 798, proposed for action November 9–10, 1999, dedicates $900,000,000 annually for the *land and water conservation fund*.

The Clinton administration had initially proposed a $1 billion in FY 2000 for the Fund to acquire and protect open space. As a federal trust for land acquisition, the *land and water conservation fund* was set up to be financed by proceeds from leases for offshore oil and gas wells on federal land. However, for years it has been underfunded, leading the Clinton administration in 1999 to propose full and permanent funding for the program.[2]

CASE HISTORY: The Ashtabula County Metropolitan Park District added park land and improved recreational opportunities in the county with a budget of $11,000 a year using the *land and water conservation fund.* In 1989, the Ohio Water Service Company (OWS) offered to donate 10 acres of land to the Park District. The offer was attractive because it was a donation and the property was adjacent to the Harpersfield Covered Bridge Metropolitan Park that runs along the Grand River.

The property that OWS wanted to transfer to the Park District included a four–acre reservoir behind the Harpersfield Dam. OWS could write off the donation as a charitable gift and stop paying property tax on land that it was no longer using. The Ashtabula Park District, in turn, could then expand its existing park at no cost. However, there were no funds to make improvements on the donated property. So Charles Kohli, the Park District's chairman of the Board of Commissioners, began to look around for help. What he found was the *land and water conservation fund.*

Kohli learned that through the *land and water conservation fund* he could use donated property as a "gift credit." In other words, the OWS gift could serve as the Park District's 50% contribution, allowing it to obtain a 50% funds match from the Ohio Department of Natural Resources (ODNR). First he had to get permission from ODNR. Then Kohli got approval for a park improvement project using *land and water conservation fund* money. In June 1992 the property was finally transferred from OWS to the Park District.

A private appraiser valued the donated property at $60,000. Thus, the Park District was able to access a matching $60,000 through the *land and water conservation fund* program. This money is being used to build restrooms and a new picnic pavilion on the donated land. With one success under its belt, the Park District is now pursuing other sources of funding to make additional improvements. In the process, it has demonstrated that even with limited funds organizations can find ways to finance their conservation projects. (**Case History Source:** Charles Kohli, Chmn. of the Board of Park Commissioners, Ashtabula County Metropolitan Park District, 5491 Route 307 West, Geneva, OH 44041.)

ACTION STEPS: Contact Mike Cook, Administrator of Land Management Section, Division of Real Estate & Land

Management, Ohio Department of Natural Resources, Building C, 1952 Belcher Drive, Columbus, OH 43224-1386; Tel: 614-265-6395; Web Site: <<http://www.dnr.state.oh.us/odnr/relm/relm.html>>.

NOTES

[1] Telephone conversation June 9, 1999 between J. Chadbourne and Mike Cook, Administrator of Land Management Section, Ohio Department of Natural Resources; Tel: 614-265-6395.

[2] See the National Resources Defense Council's "Briefings" section of *The Amicus Journal* , 21 (Spring 1999), 15.

LAND BANKING

OBJECTIVE: To manage growth, protect open space, and control land pricing in rural and urban areas by acquiring and temporarily holding land or by financing or actively participating in, for example, the redevelopment of blighted urban areas. Thus, *land banking* can be a tool for economic development and infrastructure preservation.

WHO ENACTS IT: Local government.

HOW IT WORKS: Local government initiates the program by acquiring a number of undeveloped properties in the community. Like a person's savings, each property is "deposited" in the *land bank* where it is held until the local government decides to put it on the market. By carefully timing the sale of the bank's different holdings, government officials can influence the rate and location of growth. The *land bank* can also be used to help discourage speculation and keep down the price of land by preventing a group of private investors from acquiring a monopoly on developable land.

Local officials can also protect land by placing development restrictions on it before putting it up for resale. Some communities have also used land banking to freeze development temporarily on certain parcels of land until a comprehensive plan for land use has been completed.

ADVANTAGES: The technique provides government with a potent tool for managing growth and minimizing speculation. In addition, any increase in the value of banked lands goes back to the community–at–large when that land is sold, instead of going to a private individual.

DISADVANTAGES: A large amount of capital is needed to start the program.

CASE HISTORY # 1: The Nantucket Land Bank Act of Massachusetts became effective on February 1, 1984. Directed by five legal residents, it may purchase and dispose of land in the interest of conservation.[1] More stringent than eminent domain, which might be invoked when dealing with unreasonably resistant land owners, the Act requires the Land Commission to retain its property predominantly in its scenic or natural condition.[2]

Nantucket's Land Commission may incur debt by issuing bonds, but most of the *land bank* funding comes from a 2% fee imposed on real estate transfers. These fees are the liability of the buyer. *Land bank* purchases are projected at some 15% of the entire island, with its activities becoming increasingly popular as development pressures rise. Protection of land values works advantageously for developers and residents. Preservation increases land values, and the 2% fee does not stem demand. (**Case History Source:** Jean O. Melious, *Land Banking Revisited: Massachusetts Breaks the Mold*, Lincoln Institute of Land Policy, Land Policy Roundtable, Basic Concept Series, Number 107; see ordering information below.)

CASE HISTORY #2: In the face of unmanaged land use practices that were changing the character of the island of Martha's Vineyard, in 1986 island voters created the Martha's Vineyard Land Bank Commission. Its function was to "reverse the losses" that permanent island residents experienced when an untrammeled building boom led to fencing and gating of community trails, beaches, hunting areas, and other formerly open spaces.[5] The Commission's revenue is a 2% surtax on most real estate transfers in the Vineyard's six towns. With that revenue, from 1986 to 1996, the Commission conserved some 1,100 acres to support the activities of farmers, hunters, birders, beach users, and others.[6] The Martha's Vineyard Land Bank property is "neither a sanctuary program nor a park system, it is a middle ground where the highest virtues of conservation can be realized: public enjoyment of nature, where limits and restraint secure the natural world's future."[7] *Land bank* property is available for public use during daylight hours, with hunting permits distributed by a lottery system. As of 1998, there were 32 individual properties in the *land bank*, with nine available for hunting. Holdings range in size from 0.6 to 104.9 acres. Depending on the property, permitted activities include sunbathing, swimming, birding, hunting, horseback riding, hiking, picnicking, fishing, canoeing, farming, and access to scenic vistas. (*Case History Source:* Martha's Vineyard Land Bank Commission, P.O. Box 2057, 167 Main St., Edgartown, MA 02539; Tel: 508-627-7141.)

ACTION STEPS: To order the Nantucket Land Commission case history, contact the Lincoln Institute of Land Policy, 113 Brattle St., Cambridge, MA 02138-3400; Tel: 617-661-3016 or 800-526-3873; Fax: 617-661-7235 or 800-526-3944; Web Site: <<www.lincolninst.edu>>. The Institute has three recent publications of interest: *Using Assisted Negotiation to Settle Land Use Disputes: A Guidebook for Public Officials*; *Lincoln Institute's Second Annual Review—The Value of Land*; and Harvey M. Jacobs' *State Property Rights Laws:*

The Impacts of Those Laws on My Land. For further details about the Martha's Vineyard Land Bank Commission, write, call, or visit the Commission at: P.O. Box 2057, 167 Main St., Edgartown, Massachusetts 02539; Tel: 508-627-7141 (Meetings, open to the public, are held at 5 p.m. every Monday. While there, visitors may view the open space plans, past and current newsletters, and the *land bank* gallery of paintings and photos of its properties.) Other downloadable materials on *land banking* include these: *Transfer Tax? Don't Bank on It* at Web Site: <<http://www.walpole.ma.us/nwalpoletimeslandbank80797.htm>>; *Neighborhood Development Zone Initiative* at Web Site: <<http://www.floridacdc.org/coa-zone.htm>>; "HUD Secretary's Best in American Living Award Winners in 1998," *Alamodome Affordable Parade of Homes* at Web Site: <<http://www.huduser.org/research/ 2998awards4.html>>; and "Blue Ribbon Practices in Community Development, *City Sponsored Land Banking—City of Rock Hill, South Carolina* at Web Site: <<http://www.hud.gov/ptw/docs/sc13.html>>.

NOTES

[1] Jean O. Melious, *Land Banking Revisited: Massachusetts Breaks the Mold*, Land Policy Roundtable Basic Concepts Series Number 107 (Cambridge, MA: Lincoln Institute of Land Policy), 24.

[2] Ibid., 24.

[3] Ibid., 30.

[4] Ibid., 39.

[5] Martha's Vineyard Land Bank Commission, *Conservation Lands Map—1998*, 14-panel map/brochure (Edgartown, MA: 1998), no pagination. (Individual copies are available gratis; bulk orders are available for a fee. See contact information in the second case history source.)

[6] Ibid.

[7] Ibid.

OUTRIGHT PURCHASE

OBJECTIVE: To protect important resources in the community by bringing them under public ownership.

WHO ENACTS IT: Any government entity, from the local to the state to the federal level.

HOW IT WORKS: Also known as "fee simple acquisition," this technique has traditionally been used by local governments to acquire land for public facilities such as parks, schools, or water treatment plants. However, the procedure can also be used to provide protection for sensitive lands. It can be done through the powers of eminent domain or on a voluntary basis.

In general, a government entity can acquire land only if it is designated for public use or if it serves a public purpose. *Outright purchase* provides local governments with a mechanism for protecting valuable community resources such as lakefront beaches and river corridors. The technique can also be used to control the rate of growth through creative funding mechanisms. Nantucket, Massachusetts, and Block Island, Rhode Island, for example, have placed a 2% tax on real estate transfers, with all proceeds being used to purchase open space. Every time a property changes hands, more revenue is generated to protect important features of the local landscape.

To illustrate the growing public acceptance of *outright purchase*, The Nature Conservancy's September / October 1999 newsletter, *Nature Conservancy*, states:

> In their November 1998 trip to the polls, voters in 26 states were presented with 148 ballot measures aimed at generating public funding for land acquisition and other conservation initiatives. In an overwhelming show of support, they approved 124 measures—or 04 percent—even though many involved explicit tax increases. These measures collectively created more than $5 billion for conservation.[1]

Other communities, such as Palo Alto, California, have determined through land–use studies that it is actually less expensive to purchase land in the surrounding foothills than to pay the infrastructure and public service costs that would result from the development of these areas.

ADVANTAGES: Of all the tools available to local governments, *outright purchase* provides them the surest means of restricting potentially harmful uses of the land. Since land is acquired permanently, the technique is not subject to the political changes that sometimes compromise zoning regulations.

DISADVANTAGES: The technique is expensive since the government agency acquires all rights to a property, not just the development rights. In addition, the government assumes responsibility for the maintenance and management of the property. The technique has the added disadvantage of removing the land entirely from the public tax rolls.

CASE HISTORY #1: In the fall of 1999, Twinsburg, Ohio, residents faced a choice between increasing parklands or increasing their local population due to development. Earlier in the year on August 10, 1999, the Summit County Council voted to place a $10.5 million 20–year bond issue on the ballot November 2nd to make an *outright purchase* of 908 acres for conservation and public park areas in Reminderville and Twinsburg Townships. Unless purchased, the current owners of 638 of the 908 acres had asked the Council to approve the annexation of their land to Reminderville for residential development at a density of three homes per acre.

If the land were to be developed, a recent Reminderville ordinance would require a 15% set aside of land for open space, but an even higher percentage if environmentally sensitive features were present. Already documented are tracts of rare plants, one of the longest sandstone ledges in the state, and large tracts of bird–filled forests.

However, Council representatives reported publicly that even if those sensitive areas were also set aside for conservation, a residential development would lead to a major increase in Twinsburg's population. As a result, the bond issue on the November 2nd ballot asked voters which they would prefer: to pay $50 to $100 more [per homeowner] each year for 20 years for a park or to see their roads, schools, and businesses become more crowded if the land were developed.

With Council members going on record saying that the community would have to build more schools and roads if development occurred, Twinsburg's Mayor Karabec reported that "residents he had spoken with supported the issue once they learned they would have to pay more for schools and services if the land were developed" than they would if the acreage were purchased for parkland and left as open space.[2] Studies nationwide by the

American Farmland Trust and others have documented the substantial penalties to taxpayers of infrastructure development costs versus leaving land open and undeveloped.

This particular case history is one of many across the country that reflected carry–over of voter interest in "smart growth," which was so widely supported in the fall 1998 elections. In Twinsburg, Ohio, on November 2, 1999, citizens approved the bond issue to purchae parklands by a vote of 2,664 to 1,214.[3] (*Case History Source:* Karen Farkas, "Twinsburg Vote Pits Tax Now vs. Higher Taxes Later," *The Plain Dealer* (August 12, 1999), 1–B and 6–B; Tel: 800-628-6689; E-mail: <<kfarkas@plaind.com>>.)

CASE HISTORY #2: The City of Akron's Water Supply Division in Summit County ensures a continuous quantity of high quality drinking water for an estimated 350,000 consumers in the Greater Akron area. The source water for this supply is the Upper Cuyahoga watershed in Geauga and Portage Counties. All of the raw drinking water is withdrawn for treatment from Akron's Lake Rockwell, located in Portage County. Thus, what happens in this source water area is of vital concern to the Division. As land use in the watershed becomes increasingly intense through development, both point and nonpoint sources of pollution from roads, sewage plants, septic tanks, combined sewer overflows, industry activities, forestry, recreation, livestock, and agricultural operations threaten to contaminate the source waters. Akron's Water Supply Division, therefore, spends considerable energy monitoring and protecting these source waters. One means is to acquire environmentally sensitive lands and protect them.

Akron has purchased significant areas of land, and currently owns about 12% of its 207 square–mile source water area. In 1991, the Division acquired the White Oaks property in Portage County. It consists of 393 acres in Hiram and Mantua Townships. Shaped like an hourglass, the property stretches for nearly two miles along the Upper Cuyahoga River, which outlets into Lake Rockwell 12 miles downstream. In 1994, a 250–acre parcel of uplands and wetlands located near Akron's Wendell R. LaDue Reservoir was acquired by trade. Environmentally sensitive, this parcel adds a large vegetative buffer to the reservoir. More recently, in 1999, the Division purchased 27 acres along the river within the floodplain that has one–quarter mile of river frontage. All of these areas are managed to promote a mature forest canopy that provides storm water runoff filtration and retention. Controlled public hunting is permitted on much of Akron's land that is not environmentally sensitive.

Managed to be in its natural state of mature forest, Akron's land also enhances the recreational value of the Upper Cuyahoga River. This is particularly significant, since a 25–mile reach of the river upstream of Lake Rockwell is a state–designated Scenic River.

By acquiring land within its source water area, the Division can ensure that the land will continue to serve its natural purifying function while retaining its scenic attributes. (**Case History Source:** Kim C. Coy, Watershed Supt., Akron Water Supply, 1570 Ravenna Rd., Kent, OH 44240-6111; Tel: 330-678-0077; E-mail: <<coyki@akron.oh. us>>.)

ACTION STEPS: Contact local and state park districts to learn about how *outright purchases* contribute to parkland holdings. See Russell L. Brenneman and Sarah M. Bates, eds., *Land-Saving Action*, Island Press, 1984, for case histories on *outright purchase* and other acquisition options. Contact the Midpeninsula Open Space District to obtain a copy of its booklet, *Land Acquisition Policies and Procedures*, Old Mill Office Center, Ste. C-135, 201 San Antonio Circle, Mountain View, CA 94040; Tel: 415-949-5500.

NOTES

[1] Audrey Pritchard, "Greenbacks, Green Space: Public Spending Mirrors Growing Public Concern," *Nature Conservancy*, Vol. 41, No. 5 (September / October 1999), 6.

[2] Karen Farkas, "Twinsburg Vote Pits Tax Now vs. Higher Taxes Later," *The Plain Dealer* (August 12, 1999), 1–B and 6–B; Tel: 800-628-6689; E-mail: <<kfarkas@plaind.com>>.

[3] "Election '99," *The Plain Dealer* (November 3, 1999), B–7.

PURCHASE OF DEVELOPMENT RIGHTS

OBJECTIVE: A voluntary program to preserve important resources, such as river corridors, aquifer recharge areas, open space, but notably farmland, by paying for and retiring the *development rights* of the land and restricting the deed to agreed activities, such as farming.

WHO ENACTS IT: The individual landowner originates an offer to sell the property's *development rights*. Eighteen states authorize *purchase of development rights* (*PDRs*). Ohio's enabling legislation S.B. 223, specifically allowing *agricultural conservation easements* (*ACE*), passed in the fall of 1998 and by the House in January 1999, authorized the Director of Agriculture, municipalities, counties, and nonprofits to *purchase development rights* through an *ACE. Conservation easements*, which also allow for the *purchase of development rights*, had been a part of state law for a number of years. *Conservation easements* can be held by certain special districts, including soil and water conservation districts, conservancy districts, and park districts, in addition to the Department of Natural Resources, local governments, and nonprofits.[1]

HOW IT WORKS: Local governments, or their representatives comprised of elected officials, members of agriculture, industry, etc., review applications from landowners wishing to sell their *development rights*. Just as "mineral rights" can be bought from the landowner's "bundle of rights," prohibiting digging for minerals, so "development rights" can be sold, thereby prohibiting the landowner from developing the property or selling it for that purpose. The entity purchasing the *development rights* retires them and places a deed restriction on the property so that it can never be developed, although the land could be taken by eminent domain. Local governments can lease *development rights* for a specified period of years, but only for agricultural land.

Responding to the community's priorities (in the case of farmland, proximity to other agrarian lands, overall fertility of the land, development pressure, etc.), the *PDR* representative seeks appraisals, negotiates agreements, purchases the rights, and then enforces deed restrictions. In the case of agricultural land, a purchase price is basically the difference between the land's market value, i.e., development value, say $5,000 / acre, and its assessed *current agricultural use value*, say $2,000 / acre. That is, the purchase price is $3,000 / acre. Now, the landowner has the development value, the $3,000 / acre in cash, and with retained ownership can sell the land as agricultural property, receiving the $2,000 / acre. In short the farm has generated a total return of $5,000 / acre for the owner, but the land now cannot be developed.

The owner has the remaining rights without loss of the property. Therefore, the farmer has the right to privacy, to sell or lease it, and in the case of farmland preservation programs, the right to continue farming; and, he has new money for equipment or services, or income to reserve for retirement. If the farmer sells the property, the deed restriction goes to the buyer, thus preventing any future development. Most of the successfully executed *PDRs* create large, contiguous open spaces or farmlands. These are especially helpful to farmers because they concentrate suppliers of farm equipment, services, and transportation, yielding economies of scale.[2]

ADVANTAGES: *PDR* is completely voluntary, and the landowner is not deprived of any value of the property—the owner receives cash for *development rights* and retains all of the other rights and the property. With the sale or lease of *development rights*, the land is now valued at *current agricultural use value*, lowering its property tax and substantially reducing its inheritance tax liability. When taxed at full development value, farmlands often have to be sold by the heirs to pay the inheritance taxes—and, too frequently, they are sold for development.

PDRs have proven to be more effective in perpetuating open space and continued farming than other programs, such as *current agricultural use value*, which give small tax breaks, or zoning, which often changes. And, *PDRs* are less expensive than *outright purchase*.

DISADVANTAGES: But, in all cases, *PDRs* cost money. Where does the money come from? In all of the 18 states with *PDRs*, some sort of tax, ranging from sin taxes at the state level to local property, income, and sales taxes have been levied to make the purchases possible. Although Ohio has a *PDR* program for agricultural land, it has not yet generated a source of funding for any purchases. The levying of new taxes as the source of monies for *purchasing development rights* can be difficult and contentious to promote, both to the lawmakers who must pass them and to the citizens who must support them with tax dollars.

Additionally, taxes alone probably won't generate enough revenues to make the *PDR* programs as effective as they need to be. In some cases, the very name of the program has proven to be confusing to citizens, leading them to oppose a program they actually want in concept. In the case history below, Massachusetts found that citizens sometimes believe the state is actually buying up rights so that it can *conduct* development, i.e., interpreting the program name as meaning "the purchase of rights in order to develop the property." In actuality, the *development rights* are being retired and not used for development. The State of Massachusetts' legal counsel is presently working on a new name for the program, one that clearly conveys what the program does, i.e., it limits development.

CASE HISTORY: From 1967 to 1977, the Commonwealth of Massachusetts lost an estimated 300,000 acres, or 45%, of its prime farmland to development. In response, the state legislature established a special Agricultural Preservation Restriction Program in 1977, designed to *purchase development rights* from landowners with prime farmland. Through July 21, 1999, the program has purchased rights on 43,825 acres held by 487 farms. (*Case History Source:* Richard Hubbard, Chief of the Bureau of Land Use, Massachusetts Department of Food and Agriculture, Lancaster Field Office, 142 Old Common Road, Lancaster, MA 01523; Tel: 508-792-7711.)

ACTION STEPS: For a case history in the Ann Arbor / Ypsilanti, MI, area, see "Buying the Right to Build: The Benefits of PDR," in *Creating Livable Communities: Alternatives to Urban Sprawl*, a special issue of *Ecology Reports*, Vol. XXIX, No. 1 (1997), 6-7, at Web Site: <<http://www.hvcn.org/info/ecaa/landuse.html>>. In Kentucky, "a new section of KRS Chapter 67A is created to allow a public referendum in urban government counties for the *purchase of development rights* program in an effort to prevent development of rural properties. Purchases made under the program may be funded through an occupational license tax, an urban county property tax, or a transient room tax. The property tax, if approved by the voters, could be up to an additional 5 cents per $100 of value." Text for the bill is available at Web Site: <<http://www.state.ky.us/agencies/revenue/bills/hb644.htm>>. See also T. Daniels & D. Bowers, *Holding Our Ground: Protecting American Farms and Farmlands*, Island Press, 1997, as well as T. Daniels, "The Purchase of Development Rights: Preserving Agricultural Land and Open Space," *Journal of the American Planning Association*, 57 (Autumn), 421-431.

NOTES

[1] J. Chadbourne, telephone conversation with contact at American Farmland Trust, July 1999. AFT, P.O. Box 96982, Washington, DC 20077-7048; Tel: 800-431-1499; Web Site: <<http://www.farmland.org>>.

[2] Ohio State University Extension (J. Daubenmire and T. Blaine), *Purchase of Development Rights*, CDFS-1263-98 (July 1998): 1-3. Available from the "Land Use Series" of Fact Sheets, Ohio State University Extension, Community Development, 700 Ackerman Road, Columbus, OH 43202-1578; Web Site: <<http://ohioline.ag.ohio-state.edu>>.

TRANSPORTATION ENHANCEMENTS (ISTEA & TEA–21)

OBJECTIVE: Transportation and transit enhancements programs of the Federal Highway Administration are designed to strengthen the cultural, aesthetic, and environmental aspects of the nation's intermodal transportation system.

WHO ENACTS IT: State departments of transportation, local governments, and private conservation organizations.

HOW IT WORKS: In 1991, the *Intermodal Surface Transportation Efficiency Act (ISTEA)* reauthorized the federal transportation program; and, in 1998, the *Transportation Equity Act for the 21st Century (TEA–21)* reauthorized transportation legislation for six more years, FY 1998–FY 2003. The latter authorized $217,781,000,000 (an increase of 43% over the prior six years) from the Highway Trust Fund's Highway Account, its Mass Transit Account, and the General Fund to be administered by five agencies: the Federal Highway Administration, the National Highway Traffic Safety Administration, the Federal Transit Administration, the Research and Special Programs Administration, and the Federal Railroad Administration. Over 70 separate programs are authorized by *TEA–21*, under 6 titles:[1]

- ☐ Title I—Federal–Aid Highways ($171,000,000,000)
- ☐ Title II—Highway Safety ($1,711,000,000)
- ☐ Title III—Federal Transit Administration Programs ($41,000,000,000)
- ☐ Title IV—Motor Carrier Safety ($644,000,000)
- ☐ Title V—Transportation Research ($2,881,000,000)
- ☐ Title VI—Miscellaneous ($545,000,000)

Significantly, *TEA–21* changes the Federal Budget Act to link Highway Trust Fund expenditures to actual gasoline tax receipts. This guarantees a spending floor that is independent of the congressional budget. It also eliminates some administrative levels of management and oversight and increases states' flexibility in project selection.

The "enhancements" provisions of *TEA–21* continue and strengthen ISTEA's emphasis on the environment, particularly in these areas:[2]

☐   It increases funding by 35% over FY 1997 to $1,350,000,000 for the Congestion Mitigation and Air Quality Improvement Program.

☐   It creates a new transit enhancements program for projects such as pedestrian facilities and art in and around transit stations.

☐   It provides encouragement to use alternative modes of transportation, such as bicycles.

☐   The Act allows states to permit low emission vehicles to use high occupancy vehicle lanes.

☐   Improvements and increased funding, a total of $270,000,000, is provided for the Recreational Trails program.

The enhancement programs that pertain to protecting rural and urban land are summarized here.

Transportation Enhancements: Ten percent of the Surface Transportation Program (a six–year total of $33,332,000,000) must be allocated by each state for transportation enhancements now— unlike *ISTEA*, which required 20% match with nonfederal funds—other federal programs may be used to match the 80% provided by *TEA–21*. In Ohio, the state's 1999 TEA-21 allocation was given to 16 Metropolitan Planning Organizations (see **Action Center Resources**, "Planning Commissions and Councils—County & Regional"). They represent "urbanized" centers defined by the latest population census, while nonurbanized areas are overseen by the Ohio Department of Transportation (ODOT). Most MPOs are hosted by Regional Planning Organizations, such as the Northeast Ohio Areawide Coordinating Agency (NOACA). Others are separately housed but coordinate planning with their local Planning Organization. Each MPO received the additional 10% for "enhancements," and they can apply for a share of the $5,000,000 "taken off the top of the federal award," which is open to competitive bidding from all MPOs and nonurbanized areas. Eligible activities include:

☐   Safety and educational activities for pedestrians and bicyclists

☐   Acquisition of scenic easements and scenic or historic sites, including provision of tourist and welcome center facilities

❐　　Environmental mitigation to address water pollution due to highway runoff or reduce vehicle–caused wildlife mortality while maintaining habitat connectivity
❐　　Transportation museums
❐　　Historic preservation
❐　　Preservation of abandoned railway corridors, including conversion to hike / bike trails
❐　　Control and removal of outdoor advertising
❐　　Archaeological planning and research, landscaping, and other scenic beautification.[3]

Transit Enhancements: A one percent set aside provides new funds of $20,840,000 in FY 1998 up to $32,610,000 in FY 2003 for transit enhancements. The nine eligible categories are:

❐　　Historic preservation, rehabilitation, and operation of mass transportation buildings, structures, and facilities, including historic bus and railroad facilities
❐　　Bus shelters
❐　　Landscaping and other scenic beautification, including, tables, benches, trash receptacles, and street lights
❐　　Public art
❐　　Pedestrian access and walkways
❐　　Bicycle access, including bicycle storage facilities and installation equipment for transporting bicycles on mass transportation vehicles
❐　　Transit connections to parks within the recipients' transit service areas
❐　　Signage
❐　　Enhanced access for persons with disabilities to mass transportation.[4]

In addition to the 10% Surface Transportation Program and the 1% Transit Enhancement funds, bicycle and pedestrian projects are broadly eligible for funding from almost all the major federally aided highway, transit, and safety programs included in the "over 70 separate programs" list authorized by TEA–21.[5]

Additionally, *TEA–21* reauthorized the Recreational Trails Program. With $30,000,000 for 1998, $40,000,000 for 1999, and $50,000,000 thereafter through 2003, states may use these funds from maintenance and restoration of existing trails, construction of new trails, acquisition of easements for trails, and other trail–use amenities.[6]

TEA–21 introduced a new program, the Transportation and Community System Preservation Pilot Program (TCSP), with

$20,000,000 for 1999 and $25,000,000 for the following four years. In general, and unlike other programs, TCSP is a "comprehensive initiative including planning grants, implementation grants, and research to investigate and address the relationships between transportation and community and system preservation and to identify private sector–based initiatives."[7] These funds are directed to high growth areas where "traffic calming" measures and corridor preservation activities are necessary, including establishing urban growth boundaries, green corridors that provide access to major highway corridors for efficient and compact development, reducing traffic impact on the environment, reducing the cost of future infrastructure, and encouraging private sector investment.[8]

Application for all funding requires an official government sponsor. Neighborhood groups or developers are not eligible and should partner with a town, city, public transit agency, air resource board, school board, or park district. And, the project must have a direct relationships to the nation's transportation system. Priorities generally obtain for applicants whose projects:

❐   Meet the requirements of Title 23 and Chapter 53 of Title 49 USC.

❐   Are coordinated with state and local adopted preservation or development plans

❐   Promote cost–effective and strategic investment in transportation infrastructure that minimize adverse impacts on the environment

❐   Promote innovative private sector strategies.

ADVANTAGES: *TEA–21* funds can be used to purchase *agricultural easements* because they provide floodwater storage and scenic vistas along transportation routes. A considerable amount of predictable money—now locked into a fixed gas–tax floor—over a six–year period of time allows opportunities for long–range planning not common to many other federally funded programs.

DISADVANTAGES: Fund application requires prior public participation, coordination with many other agencies, and multiple reviews—and all of these incur expenses with no guarantee of a grant award or cost compensation.

CASE HISTORY #1: The City of Dayton, Ohio, received a TCSP planning grant of $300,000 for FY 1999 to establish a precision metalworking park on under–used industrial property in downtown Dayton. This concept was created during the development of the comprehensive plan for the City of Dayton. The proposal abstract states that in the next 20 years, the park, "Tool Town," will house over 80 tooling and machining businesses, representing 5,500 jobs and still having the capacity for additional growth. The property is well served with existing transportation and utility infrastructure that is currently not being used to capacity.

With the TCSP, Dayton will be able to complete the evaluation of the existing buildings, transportation infrastructure, utilities, and develop a schematic campus master plan with capital costs, an implementation schedule, and funding strategies. Implementation activities already underway include the award of a U.S. EPA brownfields pilot grant, the construction of a business incubator in Tool Town, funds allocated to acquire property in Tool Town, efforts to gain public control of additional property, and the private–sector formation of the Tool Town Foundation to implement recommendations that focus on the tooling and machining industry. (*Case History Source:* Contact Eileen Enabnit, Planner, Department of Planning, Tool Town, City of Dayton, Dcpr. of Planning, 101 West Third Street, P.O. Box 22, Dayton, Ohio 45401; Tel: 937-443-3671; Fax: 937-443-4281. E-mail: <<enabnit_ eileen@planning.ci.dayton.oh.us>>.)

CASE HISTORY #2: Woodmere Village, Ohio, a suburb of Cleveland, has received a $195,000 TCSP grant to improve traffic flow and make "Chagrin Boulevard a 'Place' Instead of a Dividing Road." Presently Chagrin Boulevard is a two–lanc roadway pressed by heavy traffic into the equivalent of a four–lane highway. It is difficult for pedestrians to cross, its sidewalks are blocked by cars triggering traffic signals, and business access is choked and unsignalled. To relieve these problems, the Ohio Department of Transportation proposed to tear up the existing roadway and replace it with a five–lane highway that uses the center lane for left turns only. However, Woodmere citizens objected to the loss of parking spaces under the plan, and the village then issued a request for proposal in 1997 to address the problem. After competitive reviews, the partnership of Clint & Greene and People for Public Spaces was awarded a grant to plan a boulevard. They will first construct a test section of frontage road for business access with shared entries for parking. ODOT is willing to wait for this demonstration work, with the expectation of funding its completion.

The planning to integrate the interests of home, place, and business will set the stage to adopt new zoning and land use policies to encourage denser, more sustainable development in the future.[9, 10] (*Case History Source:* Contact Ed Hren, Village Engineer, Chagrin Valley Engineering, Ltd, 24850 Aurora Road, Unit A, Bedford Heights, Ohio 44146; Tel: 440-439-1999; Fax: 440-439-1969; or contact Barbara Clint, Clint & Greene, 17825 Windward Rd., Cleveland, OH 44119; Tel: 216-481-1539.)

ACTION STEPS: For an Ohio Federal Highway Administration contact, call or write Joe Werning, U.S. Department of Transportation, Federal Highway Administration, 200 North High St., Room 328, Columbus, OH 43215; Tel: 614-280-6839; Fax: 614-280-6876. Mail or phone inquiries to FHWA's Transportation and Community and System Preservation Pilot Program (TCSP) may be made to the following: Susan B. Petty, Office of Environment and Planning, HEP–20, Tel: 202-366-6577; or to Reid Alsop, Office of the Chief Counsel, HCC–31; Tel: 202-366-1371; at the Federal Highway Administration, 400 Seventh St. SW, Washington, DC 20590. The voice mail telephone number for the TCSP is 800-488-6034. Online, visit the Federal Highway Administration's Web site for more information, including the complete text of the legislation, fact sheets, and e-mail contacts for questions about TEA–21; Web Site: <<http://www.fhwa.dot.gov/Tea–21>>. Of particular value is the *Federal Register* notice for TEA–21, *FHWA Docket No. FHWA–98–4370: Transportation and Community and System Preservation Pilot Program: Implementation of the Transportation Equity Act for the 21ˢᵗ Century*, a 13–page summary of the funding guidelines, priorities, and state contacts for applicants; downloadable from Web Site: <<http://www.fhwa.dot.gov/tea21/fedreg3.htm>>.

NOTES

[1] *TEA–21 Fact Sheet, Transportation Equity Act for the 21ˢᵗ Century —Authorization Table*, which breaks out dollar allocations by the seven Titles of funding, 1-14. Downloaded August 31, 1999 from the FHWA Web Site: <<http://www.fhwa.dot.gov/tea21/factsheets$.htm>>.

[2] *A Summary of the Transportation Equity Act for the 21ˢᵗ Century (TEA–21)*, 1-6. Downloaded August 31, 1999 from the House of Representatives Web Site: <<http://www.house.gov/transportation/bestea/tea21sum.htm>>.

[3] *TEA–21 Fact Sheet, Transportation Equity Act for the 21ˢᵗ Century— Transportation Enhancements*, 1-3. Downloaded August 31, 1999 from the FHWA Web Site: <<http://www.fhwa.dot.gov/tea21/factsheets/te.htm>>.

[4] *TEA–21 Fact Sheet, Transportation Equity Act for the 21ˢᵗ Century—Transit Enhancements*, 1-2. Downloaded August 31, 1999 from the FHWA Web Site: <<http://www.fhwa.dot.gov/tea21/factsheets/transenh.htm>>.

[5] *Planning & Environment—Intermodal and Statewide Programs*: Bike/Ped *Technical Summary*, August 25, 1998, 1-9. Downloaded form the FHWA Web Site: <<http://www.fhwa.dot.gov/hep10/biped/bpbro.html>>.

[6] *Planning & Environment—Intermodal and Statewide Programs*: Recreational *Trails Brochure*. Downloaded form the FHWA Web Site: <<http://www.fhwa.dot.gov/hep10/rec/rtbro.htm>>.

[7] *TEA–21 Fact Sheet, Transportation Equity Act for the 21ˢᵗ Century— Transportation and Community and System Preservation Pilot Program*, 1-3. Downloaded June 8, 1999 from the FHWA Web Site: <<http://www.fhwa.dot.gov/tea21/factsheets/t-csp.htm>>.

[8] Ibid., 1-3.

[9] "Notices—Woodmere Village, Cleveland: Making Chagrin Boulevard a 'Place' Instead of a Dividing Road: A Greater Cleveland Demonstration Project in Woodmere Village, Ohio, $195,000," *Federal Register*, Vol. 64, No.89, Monday, May 10, 1999, 25111.

[10] "Boulevard Is Focus of Woodmere Plans," *Chagrin Valley Times*, July 22, 1999, 5.

IV. LAND MANAGEMENT TOOLS

IV–B–2: Public Initiatives — Zoning

Agricultural Zoning

Cluster Development Zoning

Conservation Development Zoning

Large–Lot Zoning

Overlay Zoning

Performance Zoning

Planned Unit Development Zoning

Quarter / Quarter Zoning

Sliding Scale Zoning

AGRICULTURAL ZONING

OBJECTIVE: *Agricultural zoning* is a special application of zoning to one of four districts, or zones—residential, industrial, commercial, and agricultural. It designates areas where farming is the primary land use and discourages nonagricultural uses in those areas.

WHO ENACTS IT: The Ohio Revised Code (ORC), Chapters 303.519 and 713, authorize protection of farmland under the state zoning enabling statutes. Local governments may write *agricultural zoning* ordinances to "prevent farmland from being converted to nonagricultural uses, prevent the fragmentation of farms, prevent land–use conflicts, and protect agricultural producers from nonfarm intrusion into agricultural areas as well and as vigorously as residential zoning can protect housing areas from commercial or industrial intrusions."[1]

HOW IT WORKS: In *agricultural zoning* ordinances or resolutions, control over the number of residential dwellings in a district is established by specifying a minimum lot size that corresponds to the amount of land needed to support a farm. Densities will vary with the type of farming within that district, or zone. If, for example, 160 acres are required for a viable livestock or row crop operation, the landowner may build only one dwelling on those 160 acres. Another type of farming, such as horticulture, might require only 25 acres for self–supporting operation; therefore, the residential density would be set at one dwelling per 25 acres. Other factors may enter into the determination of the final formula, but "the permitted uses within an agricultural zone should be consistent with the viable farming alternatives."[2]

Agricultural zoning complements *agricultural districts* and *current agricultural use value (CAUV)* by clearly defining areas of agricultural production. *Agricultural districts* (ORC Chapter 929) protect farmers from water, sewer, and electric assessment charges when these utilities intersect the protected farmland enroute to other developments. The zoning also offers some shielding from eminent domain and lawsuits and from nuisance complaints. The districts are initiated by individual landowners. Similarly, *CAUV*, which lowers taxable land use to its *current agricultural use value*, begins with the individual owner. In contrast, *agricultural zoning* requires action by township trustees or county commissioners and includes, optimally, a substantial number of farmland owners operating over a large area of land.

The National Agricultural Lands Study reported 270 counties with *agricultural zoning* in 1981. By 1996, there were 700 jurisdictions in 24 states with some form of this management practice. And, as another example of its use, in Lancaster County, Pennsylvania, all but two of its 41 townships have adopted some form of *agricultural zoning* provisions covering 320,000 acres of farmland. Many townships followed the nonbinding 1978 Lancaster County model ordinance, but not all—resulting in varying degrees of actual compliance.[3]

ADVANTAGES: *Agricultural zoning* is more effective than individually initiated programs. As a community–developed plan, its members know that the zone is protected and, therefore, proposed development must conform to the zoning. And, by definition, the zone is a consolidated agricultural region, rather than a scattering of individual farmers, as is the case for *agricultural districts* and *CAUV*. Another argument in its favor is that it is also less expensive for the community than other programs, such as *purchase of development rights*, which requires up–front cash to purchase the rights.

DISADVANTAGES: Zoning, in general, is politically unstable because of changes in leadership, circumstances, and landowners. Therefore, *agricultural zoning* should be reenforced with other land–use protection tools, such as some of those described in this guide.

CASE HISTORY #1: From 1963 to 1978 in McHenry County, Illinois, farmland prices increased five–fold as development expanded into McHenry from nearby Chicago and Rockford. Vandalism increased, farm markets moved out, soil eroded, and land owners absented their property—all changing the character of the county.

Toward the end of this period, the county hired Stephen Aradas as the new director of the planning department. He and his staff revised the simple land–use plan of 1971 with its 5–acre minimum lot zoning and created a new "Year 2000 Land Use Plan." It set goals for protecting natural areas, encouraging preservation of open space for recreation and for agricultural use. Notably, it created two kinds of agricultural districts: A–1, with a 160–acre minimum residential lot size, and A–2, with a 1–acre minimum. A–1, comprised of the best soils, covered about 75% of the active farmland in McHenry County, more than 200,000 acres. The remaining land was zoned A–2, but only on request.

Land rezoned to A–2 could be "parcelled off if it met a Plat Act exception." A–2 does not allow subdivision of property. Therefore, farmers could realize the economic advantages of development while retaining much of the overall acreage in farmland because of the large amount of land zoned A–1. In 1986, land sold for $2,600 per acre, slightly more than it did in adjacent counties with similar soils but fewer restrictions.

The zoning ordinance included another innovation: it allowed farmers who conduct a form of agriculture with features that neighbors might find offensive—e.g., feedlots, dairies, raising poultry—to fill out an intensive–use affidavit and file it with the county. Once filed, purchasers of neighboring property cannot complain that they did not know what types of agricultural business activities their neighboring farmers conducted.

In 1994, McHenry County reduced the 160–acre requirement to 40 acres in the A–1 district. (*Case History Source*: Samuel N. Stokes, et al., "McHenry County, Illinois: An Ambitious Agricultural Zoning Ordinance," *Saving America's Countryside: A Guide to Rural Conservation* [Baltimore, MD: Johns Hopkins University Press, 1989] 138-141; revised September 15, 1999, by SuzAnne Ehardt, Planning & Development Department, McHenry County, IL.)

CASE HISTORY #2: In 1965, only one of twelve townships in Preble County, Ohio, had any zoning. In this largely agrarian county, zoning was difficult to promote. In 1966, the other eleven townships quickly accepted a county–wide zoning ordinance, and in 1995 the twelfth, Jefferson County, joined the rest. The ordinance described about 30 zoning districts, such as "urban–residential, rural–residential, restricted–rural–residential," with *agricultural zoning* limiting farmland division to a 20–acre minimum.

However, over time the rural areas were being split into many 20–acre lots. Then, through a three–month appeal process, those lots were split into even smaller subdivisions.

To reduce the 20–acre farm lots into smaller residential lots, the landowners request rezoning from one zoning district to another through a three–step hearing. First, they appeal to a Planning Commission (11 members, including the county commissioners), which is not a published hearing, though the public may ask to be heard. Second, they present their case, accompanied by the minutes and recommendations of the first Planning Commission, to the Rural Planning Commission, comprised of five members and, again, including the county commissioners. This is a publicized hearing that is announced to neighbors of the applicant. Third, this second Commission forwards its recommendations to the Preble County commissioners, who have attended the prior hearings and have the minutes and recommendations as well as their own notes as a basis for making a final judgement to approve or reject the request for rezoning. After two public hearings, the Commissioners make their ruling and allow 30 days for any objections. All of these procedures strictly follow the provisions of the Ohio Revised Code.

To limit rezoning, in 1997 Preble County adopted a new 40–acre minimum for *agricultural districts*. This means that a farmer must have at least 81 or more acres (which excludes the road right of way) to split a parcel without the three–step rezoning process, which, incidentally, includes a $150 fee. Thus, a 170–acre farm can be split into four parcels without going through the appeal procedures.

Nonetheless, there is some confusion about the residential building lot size. Many people believe they must have 40 acres on which to build, but that is true for agricultural land division without rezoning. In Preble County, each parcel that is separately deeded is entitled to one home, regardless of its acreage. (*Case History Source:* Peggy A. Crabtree, Dir., Preble County Department of Building Inspection and Rural Zoning, Courthouse, 101 East Main St., Eaton, Ohio 45320. Tel: 937-456-8171; Fax: 937-456-8114.)

ACTION STEPS: SuzAnne Ehardt, Dir. & Code Enforcement Officer, Planning & Development Dept., McHenry County, Annex A Bldg., 2200 North Seminary Ave., Woodstock, IL 60098; Tel: 815-334-4560; Fax: 815-337-3720. Obtain a copy of *Farms and Farmland* and *History of Land Use Planning in McHenry County* from the McHenry County Planning & Development Department at the above address. Contact Jennifer Dempsey or Don Buckloh at American Farmland Trust's Farmland Information Center, Herrick Mill 1, Short St., Northampton, MA 01060; Tel: 800-370-4879 or 413-386-9330; Fax: 413-586-9332. In addition, contact the American Farmland Trust for further information on *agricultural zoning* at the national office at 1200 18th St., NW, Ste. 800, Washington, DC 20036; Tel: 202-331-7300; Fax: 202-659-8339; E-mail: <<info@farmland.org>>; Web Site: <<http://www.farmland. org>>, as well as their Ohio office: Jill Buckovac, Ohio Office Dir., 200 North High Street, Room 522 Columbus, OH 43215; Tel: 614-

469-9877; Fax: 614-469-2083; Web Site: <<http://www.farmland. org/Farmland/files/states/oh/htm>>. And, contact your local Farm Bureau via the national office at American Farm Bureau Federation, 225 Touhy Ave., Park Ridge, IL 60068; Tel: 847-685-8600; Web Site: <<http://www.fb.com>>, and via the Ohio Farm Bureau Federation, Inc., P.O. Box 479, Columbus, Ohio 43216; Tel: 614-249-2400; Fax: 614-249-2200; E-mail: <<webmaster.ofbf. org>>; Web Site: <<http://www.ofbf.org>>.

NOTES

[1] Stephen J. Hudkins, Ohio State University Extension, *Agricultural Zoning*, Fact Sheet CDFS–1266–99, 1-2. Contact Ohio State University Extension, Community Development, 700 Ackerman Rd., Ste. 235, Columbus, OH 43202-1578, or download from Web Site: <<http://ohioline.ag.ohio-state.edu/ cd-fact>>.

[2] Ibid., 1-2.

[3] Telephone conversation between a Lancaster County Planning Commission representative, Lancaster, PA, and J. Chadbourne, September 24, 1999; Tel: 717-299-8333.

CLUSTER DEVELOPMENT ZONING

OBJECTIVE: *Cluster development zoning,* or cluster development, one form of open space planning authorized under *planned unit development* regulations, "concentrates houses on smaller parcels of land, while the additional land that would have been allocated to individual lots becomes shared open space for use by all of the subdivision's residents."[1]

WHO ENACTS IT: A local jurisdiction with the project developer.

HOW IT WORKS: Conventional zoning specifies the number of dwellings per acre, say, one dwelling per 2 acres; or, 25 houses could be constructed on 50 acres, each on two acres of land. *Cluster development zoning* would allow all 25 houses to be located together, on perhaps 30 acres. This would leave 20 acres undeveloped, 40% of the original 50 acres, which could then be used to protect natural features, sensitive areas, historical structures, or open space modified for residential enjoyment and / or recreation. Such a distribution of residences is also made possible by new, smaller wastewater management systems, as opposed to leach field septic systems (see *conservation development zoning* case histories). These new systems may not require the large–lot zoning minimums for waste disposal specified under conventional zoning.

Usually, the open space is restricted from development by placing it in a *conservation easement* in perpetuity. The easement is stronger if it is assigned to two organizations, such as a land conservancy and the subdivision's homeowners association.

Most zoned communities in Ohio enable *planned unit development (PUD) zoning*, which allows zoning and subdivision flexibility well beyond the bounds of conventional subdivisions. While *PUDs* allow a mix of residential, industrial, commercial, and agricultural uses, *cluster development zoning* generally applies only to single–family residential dwellings.

Clustered housing offers both environmental and economic opportunities beyond traditional subdivisions. A greater amount of open space and sensitive lands can be preserved because less cleared land, rough grades, cut roads, fine grade, and planted lawns are needed. In addition, shorter utility and sewer hookups are possible, and some common walls on attached or semi–attached homes can reduce additional building materials.

Altogether, natural amenities and lower construction costs can be realized, benefitting both the the developer and the homeowners.[2]

ADVANTAGES: This type of conservation planning can help maintain a more rural character while allowing land to be developed. And, it has been documented that more attractive subdivisions sell more rapidly (see *conservation development zoning* case histories) and require less expense in continuing maintenance. Finally, clustered housing lowers potential contamination of water recharge areas and the downstream portion of the watershed.

DISADVANTAGES: Many early clustered subdivisions did not allow much open space, earning this type of development a poor reputation that was passed on to more recent proponents of *cluster development zoning.* "Clustering" emphasizes compactness of dwelling sites, rather than encompassing the environmental issues such as those highlighted in *conservation development zoning.* If a local government does not have *PUD* enabling zoning, the developer may have to expend considerable time and expense to work with a township's zoning commission and the county's commissioners to build a case for approval of a *cluster development zoning* plan.

CASE HISTORY: Sue and Russell Davis purchased about 170 acres of land at a sheriff's sale in 1983. The parcel is located on Bainbridge Road in Bainbridge Township, Ohio, where local zoning designates the land as R–5A, or land zoned for single–family, detached homes on lots no smaller than 5 acres.[3]

The Davises, with architect Dan Meehan, planned "Hawksmoor" in two Phases. Phase I included: (1) saving 15 acres for the Davises, (2) selling 15 acres to a single owner, and, (3) building 5 houses on 25 acres, leaving an additional 5 acres as open space. All but two of the five have been sold as of September 1999. This leaves 110 acres for Phase II. The Davises sold that acreage to another developer who will build about 20 units, complying with the original subdivision plan approved by Bainbridge Township, except that while the houses in the Phase I development shared wells, each house in Phase II will have its own well. In both Phases, the sewage systems are connected to the nearby McFarland Sewage Treatment Plant.

The 25 units are on 1.5– to 3.5–acre lots, which leaves about 45% of the total acreage as open space.

Mrs. Davis, a former Bainbridge zoning commissioner herself, favored the township's 5–acre zoning regulation. She wanted to preserve the natural features of the tract as much as possible. She believed that a cluster subdivision in Hawksmoor would demonstrate to the community how both goals could be met.

Ms. Davis reports that the Bainbridge Township zoning commission is pleased, too. The development complies with zoning regulations and the infrastructure cost is held down because the total roadway is significantly less than it would have been to serve 25 separate 5–acre residential lots scattered throughout the entire area. (**Case History Source:** Sue Davis, Smyth Cramer Realty, 8537 East Washington St., Chagrin Falls, Ohio 44023. Tel: 440-543-4404.)

ACTION STEPS: For a copy of the open space requirements from the Bainbridge Township Zoning Ordinance, contact Sue Angelino, Clerk, Bainbridge Township Hall, 17826 Chillicothe Rd., Chagrin Falls, OH 44023; Tel: 440-543-9872. Obtain a copy of the PEARL document, which describes a cluster development requiring 50% or more open space, from the Livingston County Planning Commission, 304 East Grand River, Howell, MI 48843; Tel. 517-546-7555. A copy of *Dealing with Change in the Connecticut River Valley: A Design Manual for Conservation and Development* can be ordered from the Lincoln Institute of Land Policy (see **Action Center Resources**). Also see The American Planning Association's 1980 pamphlet, *The Cluster Subdivision*, which discusses the actual structuring of a *cluster development* ordinance.

NOTES

[1] Thomas W. Blaine & Peggy Schear, Ohio State University Extension, *Cluster Development*, Fact Sheet CDFS–1270–99, 1-3. Contact Ohio State University Extension, Community Development, 700 Ackerman Rd., Ste. 235, Columbus, OH 43202-1578, or download from Web Site: <<http://ohioline.ag. ohio-state.edu/cd-fact/0301html>>.

[2] Richard Lasnier, All County Appraisal Services, *Clustered Housing Development*, Real Estate Information Network, 1. Tel: 516-941-3455; Fax: 516-941-3461; download from Web Site: <<http://www.reinet.com/library/ general/file3.htm>>.

[3] "Regulations and Standards for Cluster Development as a Conditional Use," Chapter 135.04, *Bainbridge Township, Ohio, Zoning Resolution* (Bainbridge Township, OH: Bainbridge Township Zoning Commission).

CONSERVATION DEVELOPMENT ZONING

OBJECTIVE: To implement a type of *cluster development zoning* that emphasizes conservation of specific, sensitive attributes potentially impacted by a development project—such as rural character, visual quality, trails, flood plains, storm water and wastewater management, roads, slopes, groundwater, wells, buffers, wetlands, farmlands, habitats, natural landscaping, woodlands, stream channels, viewscapes, and other features of community priority—and to protect those areas by directing or clustering development away from those resources.

WHO ENACTS IT: Local governments in conjunction with developers, counties, municipalities, and townships.

HOW IT WORKS: This is a relatively new term to describe a development plan that gives special emphasis to natural resources. It is authorized by *planned unit development* legislation, and it is similar to *cluster development zoning* and *limited development zoning*. *Conservation development zoning* was created by the principal sponsor of this guide, the Western Reserve Resource Conservation and Development Council. *Conservation development zoning* is broader in managing open space and land and water features within the area to be developed than other development zoning. For example, *cluster development zoning* focuses more on concentrating dwelling units together, rather than on the natural features of the site. To start a *conservation development* plan, a community first conducts a detailed inventory and evaluation of its resources, such as those sensitive attributes listed above. Next, it sets long- and short-term goals guided by the relative value of each resource and the feasibility of its conservation. Then, the open space plan can be developed with the appropriate "tools," including many in this guide, for each specific priority to be protected. To ensure effectiveness, many communities include a citizens' survey as part of the planning process and, thereafter, include a program for management—a combination of public and private partnerships and community volunteers can form an effective management team.[1]

The Ohio Revised Code, Section 303.022, states that "a township zoning resolution or amendment adopted in accordance with this chapter may establish or modify *planned-unit developments* [*PUDs*]. Planned-unit developments [of which *conservation development zoning* is a form] regulations shall apply to property only at the election of the property owner and shall include standards to be used by the board of township trustees or, if the board so chooses, by the township zoning commission, in determining whether to approve or disapprove any proposed development within a planned–unit development."

Under this authority, *conservation development zoning* may be included in the township's zoning regulation by several means: (1) the township creates a separate *conservation development zoning* district; then, a property owner may request rezoning of his or her land to the new classification; (2) the township, at the property owner's request, creates a *conservation development zoning* district for that property alone; (3) the township adds *conservation development zoning* to the list of permitted uses in a residential district; (4) the township creates a *conservation development zoning* district and applies it as an overlay district (see *overlay zoning*), making it an option in those areas with the overlay designation; or (5) *conservation development zoning* may be established as a conditional use in some or all residential districts.[2]

ADVANTAGES: Dwellings are built to existing permitted density levels. *Conservation development zoning* generally provides development income comparable or superior to conventional development due to the desirability, and therefore marketability, of the property: it emphasizes a rural form of development, treats land as unique, provides flexibility to property owners, requires common open space—usually 40% or more of the total parcel—reduces site disturbance, and preserves historic and / or cultural structures and landscape features. In addition, it reduces storm water runoff, thereby increasing the retention rate of surface waters. Finally, *conservation development zoning* may preserve the potential for farming of the land held in open space.

DISADVANTAGES: Open space planning is a concept practiced for many years, as the 1978 coding in Richfield Township indicates in the case history below. The *planned unit development zoning* enabling legislation allows *conservation development zoning* and *cluster development zoning*, but these last two terms are often used interchangeably, leading to confusion. Some may even erroneously equate the two with high–density "condominium" type development. In addition, the *PUD* concept has been abused in many communities, where developers have used it to *increase* densities in areas where wetlands or steep slopes would have prohibited development at permitted densities.

CASE HISTORY: Joe Scaletta in Avon, Lorain County, Ohio, developed "Devonshire Meadows." He built homes around wetlands, constructed boardwalks, benches, bird houses, nature signage—all of which were popular with prospective buyers. They ranked his lakes, catch–and–release fishing, trails, and other amenities preferentially to tennis courts, playgrounds, and other such constructs in the development. As a result, when he planned "Avenbury Lakes" nearby, he incorporated those preferred features into an open space development, under *planned unit development zoning* code from 1973. This time, he left about 45% of the total area as open space with adjoining wetlands, lakes, ponds, and trees—and he proved the advantage of doing so by his brisk sales for the units. (*Case History Source:* Joe Scaletta, Pres., Scaletta Development Corporation, 35290 Detroit Road, Avon, Ohio 44011. Tel: 440-937-9402, Fax: 440-937-9403.)

ACTION STEPS: Contact Kirby Date, Coord., The Countryside Program, a project of the Western Reserve Resource Conservation and Development Council, P.O. Box 24825, Lyndhurst, OH 44124; Tel: 216-295-0511; Fax: 216-295-0527; E-mail: <<ninmile@en. com>>. Copies of the *Conservation Development Resource Manual* may be purchased from her. The manual contains a full discussion of the concept, and includes model regulations for *conservation development zoning*. Also, for results of a state–wide survey of Ohio counties for *planned unit development zoning* ordinances, contact Thomas W. Blaine, Ph.D., District Specialist, Community Development, Ohio State University Extension, Northeast District, OARDC Bldg., 1680 Madison Ave., Wooster, OH 44691-4096; Tel: 330-263-3831; Fax: 330-263-3832; E-mail: <<blaine.17@osu. edu>>; Web Site: <<http://ohioline.ag.ohio-state.edu.>>.

NOTES

[1] Kirby Date, "Conservation Development: Tools for Open Space Preservation and Watershed Protection in Subdivisions, The Countryside Program," a presentation at OSU Extension's "Better Ways to Develop Ohio" conference on June 24-25, 1999, at the Columbus Athenaeum, Columbus, OH.

[2] Kirby Date et al., *The Countryside Program: Conservation Development Resource Manual* (Lyndhurst, OH, 1998), 2B-2. Copies are available from Kirby Date, Coord., The Countryside Program, P.O. Box 24825, Lyndhurst, OH 44124; Tel: 216-295-0511; Fax: 216-295-0527; E-mail: <<ninmile@en. com>>.

LARGE–LOT ZONING

OBJECTIVE: To minimize the detrimental impacts of development by limiting the number of dwelling units that can be placed on a parcel of land.

WHO ENACTS IT: The local government through its zoning ordinance.

HOW IT WORKS: *Large–lot zoning*, or low density zoning, establishes ratios of dwellings to parcel size that are "low," such as one dwelling per 10 acres, or 80 acres, or 160 acres. Sometimes this ratio is based upon the amount of land required to support one cattle or crop on farmland (see *agricultural zoning*). At other times, it is based upon available groundwater for human or agricultural needs, or the percolation rates of soils to manage sewage disposed on the site. By limiting the numbers of dwellings per acre, the local government can preclude the provision of public water and sewage to those sites, as well as additional schooling and safety forces and other public services which would be required with significant increased development.

On the contrary, the argument is made that low density zoning is an inefficient use of land. It asserts that public services, such as fire and police; utilities, such as electricity; and infrastructure costs, such as road construction and maintenance, all increase the cost of those services by adding to the raw materials necessary to build them and the distance and time required to deliver them. Therefore, opponents argue, it is more efficient to use small lot, or high density, development.

Discussed earlier in Section II, the Farmland Information Center urges overriding this issue of comparative costs. It states that "One type of land use is not intrinsically better than another, and COCS (costs of community services) do not judge the overall public good or long–term merits of any land use or taxing structure. Communities must balance goals such as maintaining affordable housing, creating jobs, and conserving land and resources. With good planning, these goals can complement rather than compete with each other. COCS studies give communities another tool to make decisions about their futures."[2]

Some of the methods for using *large–lot zoning* are presented in *agricultural zoning, conservation development zoning, cluster development zoning*, and other tools featured in this guide. Generally, they allow the local government to assign both low– and high–density zoning to different areas to take advantage of existing resources, such as prime soils in the former case and available infrastructure in the latter case. In these exchanges, the total numbers of dwellings allowed over an area remain the same as they were under prior zoning. To achieve the goal of an overall comprehensive plan, a community can pick and choose the appropriate tool for the goals of the community and the resources of its lands. *Large–lot zoning* does have a place among those tools.

ADVANTAGES: *Large–lot zoning* can be used to protect community resources, such as open space, agriculture, sensitive areas, scenic views, water recharge areas, and other prioritized interests of the community, when appropriately selected for the circumstances. It can also save the community costs that normally accompany small–lot zoning and its higher density development.

DISADVANTAGES: Conventional *large–lot zoning*, when applied in cookie–cutter practice, may prevent the preservation of large regions of open space or other natural resources by taking large blocks of land for residential development. And, in many communities, "large lots" have been reduced to the extent that they are neither large enough for farming nor small enough for development, which questions the very meaning of "large lot."

CASE HISTORY: Chardon Township in Geauga County, Ohio, 99% of which is zoned residential, permits 5–acre minimum lots in its R–1 Residential District and 3–acre lots in its R–2 Residential District. Both allow single–family detached dwellings, including industrialized units and manufactured homes (other than mobile homes).

Similarly, setbacks from roads to streets, minimum side and rear yard clearance, and lot widths also progressively increased. From 1957 to 1967, zoning required 1–acre minimums for all residences. R–1 zoning started in 1907 and increased the minimum to 3 acres. In 1979, following returns from a community–wide survey in which residents expressed strong desires to protect the rural nature of the township, the minimum was raised again to a 5–acre lot size.

R–2 zoning was initiated in 1957 with 1–acre minimums, increasing to 2 acres in 1980, and then to 3 acres in 1989.

During this interval of changes to large–lot zoning, the R–1 minimum lot width increased from 100 to 250 feet. Setbacks went from 80 feet from the center of any road or street to 100 feet, while side and rear yard clearance was increased from 20 to 50 feet. Changes paralleling these occurred with R–2 permitted distances.

The township's zoning inspector, Frank Holy, said that 1–acre lots did not work well for the septic systems. Five–acre minimums helped solve the problem. There were no further changes in lot sizes from 1979 to 1999."[3]

Residents interviewed report that the increased minimum lot size has, in contrast to other nearby towns, helped to foster good feelings about the Chardon community. (*Case History Source:* "Article V, R–1 Residential District," *Chardon Township, Ohio, Zoning Code* [Chardon, OH: Chardon Township, 1992], 30–38.)

ACTION STEPS: Contact Rose Woods, Clerk, Chardon Township, P.O. Box 0829, Chardon, OH 44024; Tel: 440-286-3711. Contact your local planning commission (see list in **Action Center Resources**). For two comprehensive summaries of the issues in groundwater and surface water protection associated with the control of storm water runoff in *large–lot* and other zoning, see *Groundwater & Surface Water: Understanding the Interaction: A Guide to Watershed Partners*, Conservation Technology Information Center, 1220 Potter Dr., Ste. 170, W. Lafayette, IN 47906; Tel: 765-494-9555; Fax: 765-494-5969; download from Web Site: <<http://www.ctic.purdue.edu/CTIC/CTIC.html>>; and "Chapter 5—Storm Water Strategies: Findings from the Case Studies," *Storm Water Strategies: Community Responses to Runoff Pollution*, Natural Resources Defense Council, 40 West 20th St., New York, NY 10111; Tel: 212-727-2700. Download from Web Site: <<http://www.nrdc.org/comm/nrdclist.html>>. To compare *large–lot zoning* and *cluster development zoning*, see the Lincoln Institute for Land Policy's *Dealing with Change in the Connecticut River Valley: A Design Manual for Conservation and Development*, 113 Brattle St., Cambridge, MA 02138-3400; Tel: 800-526-3873; Fax: 800-526-3944; Web Site: <<http://www.lincolninst.edu>>.

NOTES

[1] Farmland Information Center, American Farmland Trust, *Cost of Community Services*, Fact Sheet, June 1999, 1. American Farmland Trust, 1200 18th St., NW, Ste. 800, Washington, DC 20036; Tel: 202-331-7300; Fax: 202-659-8339; E-mail: <<info@farmland.org>>; download from Web Site: <<http://www.farm.fic.niu.edu/fic-ta/tafs-cocs.html>>.

[2] Ibid., 1.

[3] Telephone conversation on September 14, 1999, between Frank Holy, Zoning Inspector, Chardon Township, and J. Chadbourne.

OVERLAY ZONING

OBJECTIVE: To provide protection for specific natural or cultural resources that are not explicitly safeguarded under existing zoning regulations.

WHO ENACTS IT: Local governments.

HOW IT WORKS: As the name implies, *overlay zones* are generally laid on top of existing zoning regulations. The first step in developing an *overlay zoning* ordinance is to inventory the natural and cultural features of the community. Many planning commissions will have completed this task. With an inventory in hand, local planners can then map out the environmentally sensitive or culturally significant areas that require additional protection. Common examples of *overlay zones* include flood plains and historic districts.

ADVANTAGES: *Overlay zoning* allows communities to isolate and protect specific resources that are not covered in existing zoning regulations.

DISADVANTAGES: Like other zoning regulations, *overlay zones* can be circumvented or repealed, depending on the political climate in the community.

CASE HISTORY: The City of Columbus, Ohio, Franklin County Board of Commissioners and the Metropolitan Park District of Columbus and Franklin County, initiated and funded "The Model Watercourse Protection Ordinance Project." The project was recommended for implementation in Franklin County's comprehensive plan to protect its watercourses—"any natural, perennial or intermittent, stream, river or creek with a defined bed and bank that is contained within, flows through or borders a community."[1]

The Project's Model Ordinance Task Force recommended a Watercourse Protection Zoning Overlay.[2] And, under the management of the Mid–Ohio Regional Planning Commission, the Task Force prepared a model policy titled Model Watercourse & Scenic Byway Protections on February 19, 1999.

The model *zoning overlay* creates a natural buffer along watercourses that provides wildlife habitat and minimizes land use and development impacts within the immediate environs of a watercourse. The complete overlay has three sub–areas:

(1) streambank buffer, (2) transition area, and (3) disturbance area. Preferred activities include forestry, agriculture, passive recreation, and recreational trail use; all development activities are prohibited.[3]

The concluding point in a summary of the Model Ordinance Task Force Report integrates comprehensive planning ("a set of clear public purposes"), zoning, and the use of selected land management tools, to achieve the watercourse protection goals. We quote the Columbus Task Force Report directly:

> Adopting a Scenic Byway Zoning Overlay must be carefully based upon a set of clear public purposes outlined in the report. The model presented is a starting point for communities that may consider adopting zoning provisions to protect a given scenic byway. The district can stand alone as a local protection tool or can be adopted as a complement to state designation of a scenic byway. The model is intended to be modified by each community to reflect locally defined priorities and issues. The characteristics that make a corridor appropriate as a scenic byway will serve as the basis for drafting the details of the *Zoning Overlay*. A community's planning staff, Planning Commission and legal representatives should work together to prepare an acceptable zoning district before submitting it to the community's zoning process.[4]

ACTION STEPS: Information on historic *overlay districts* in Ohio is available from Amos Loveday, Ohio Historic Preservation Office, 567 East Hudson St., Columbus, OH 43211-1030; Tel: 614-297-2470; Fax: 614-297-2496. For setting up a "Sensitive Area Protection Ordinance," see pages 33-39 in *Protecting Coastal and Wetland Resources: A Guide for Local Governments*, 1992, U.S. EPA Document #842-R-002. For a free copy, write: U.S. EPA, 11029 Kenwood Rd., Bldg. 5, Cincinnati, OH 45242.

NOTES

[1] City of Columbus, et al., *Model Watercourse & Scenic Byway Protection* (Columbus, OH: City of Columbus, February 19, 1999), 1.

[2] Memorandum on June 8, 1999, from Frances Beasley, Sr. Proj. Coord., Franklin County Greenways, to J. Chadbourne on the "Summary of Watercourse Protection / Scenic Byways Model Ordinance Task Force Report," 1-2.

[3] Ibid., 1-2.

[4] Ibid., 2.

PERFORMANCE ZONING

OBJECTIVE: To provide protection for specific natural resources that are not explicitly safeguarded under existing land–use regulations.

WHO ENACTS IT: Local governments.

HOW IT WORKS: This technique is also known as impact zoning because it evaluates prospective developments based upon their projected impact on the local region. *Performance zoning* standards may govern traffic flow, storm water runoff, impacts on wetlands, steep slopes, groundwater, visual impact (viewsheds), and numerous other criteria, depending on the concerns of the community.

In contrast to the blanket restrictions on siting often established under traditional zoning regulations, *performance zoning* reviews new developments based on how they will "perform," regardless of where they are located. This gives developers greater flexibility in drafting their site plans, since they are not told how to do it, but stipulates only that their final creation must meet certain performance standards. In each case, the developer is given a chance to minimize harmful impacts in the design. In this way, *performance zoning* holds the individual creating a problem responsible for addressing it, not the local government. If the developer fails to mitigate the detrimental impacts, the local government can reject the application.

In some cases, *performance zoning* is implemented using a point system, with points assigned on the basis of how the proposed development is projected to impact each community resource cited in the zoning ordinance. Once all the impacts have been assessed, the points are added up. If the project falls within a certain range, it is approved. If it falls outside of the range, it is either conditionally approved, postponed pending revision, or rejected outright.

ADVANTAGES: Adding a *performance zoning* ordinance to existing land–use regulations provides greater flexibility than traditional zoning measures, since the land can be put to a wider range of uses as long as the specified performance standards are met. The technique also distributes the cost of protecting community resources among the parties that directly impact them.

DISADVANTAGES: *Performance zoning* requires more time and greater expertise to develop and administer than other zoning regulations, adding to the cost of local government. In establishing performance controls for natural systems, communities seek to translate the conditions needed for the continued functioning of the system into a numerical standard. While some processes like storm water runoff, erosion, and aquifer recharge are relatively easy to quantify, others—such as aesthetics—are not. As a result, *performance zoning* is often best used to supplement existing land–use regulations, not to replace them.[1]

CASE HISTORY: In January 1996, the Bucks County Planning Commission in Bucks County, Pennsylvania, amended the county's Subdivision and Land Development Ordinance with a "Performance Zoning Model Ordinance." They stated that performance zoning has the primary objective of protecting natural resources and a secondary objective of providing flexibility in the design of residential developments. It limits the amount of development intrusion on various natural resources, and it contains three performance criteria: minimum open space, maximum density, and maximum impervious surface.

In Bucks County, the predominant application of *performance zoning* by municipalities is in development districts. These are areas the municipality's comprehensive plan has identified for higher density residential development. *Performance zoning* is implemented in municipal zoning ordinances as a permitted use, and these uses are called a performance standard subdivision. A few townships in the county permit performance standard subdivisions in rural and *agricultural districts.* In those cases, the ordinance requires high open space ratio and a maximum density consistent with that for a single–family cluster in that district.

Performance standard subdivisions allow the grouping of dwelling units, a variety of housing types, and more flexible designs, while as a whole meeting the standards for open space, density, and impervious surfaces. The dwelling unit mix is specified in the model ordinance under Article III, Section 300, A. General Requirements. (*Case History Source:* Performance Zoning Model Ordinance, Bucks County, Pennsylvania; downloadable from Web Site: <<http://www.sustainable.doe.gov/codes/bucks.htm>>.)

ACTION STEPS: You may wish to obtain a copy of *Performance Zoning Model Ordinance* by the Bucks County Planning Commission, Bucks County, PA, 1996 (downloadable from Web Site: <<http://www.sustainable.doe.gov/codes/bucks.htm>>) and

Performance Controls for Sensitive Lands by the American Planning Association, 1975, both available from the Planners Press (see **Action Center Resources**). See also pages 19-20 in *Creating Successful Communities: A Guidebook to Growth Management Strategies* by Michael A. Mantell, et al., Island Press, 1990 (see **Action Center Resources**).

NOTES

[1] Charles Thurow and Duncan Erley, "Performance Controls for Sensitive Lands" in *A Planner's Guide to Land Use Law* (Washington, DC: American Planning Association, 1984), 286.

PLANNED UNIT DEVELOPMENT ZONING

OBJECTIVE: *Planned unit development (PUD)* allows property owners to rezone their property to *PUD* standards and no longer be subject to any previously applicable zoning regulations. This provides opportunities for more flexible site design, housing locations, localized commercial outlets, open space, and generally greater creativity than possible under conventional zoning.

WHO ENACTS IT: A property owner voluntarily applies to the local government for *PUD* rezoning.

HOW IT WORKS: Effective October 21, 1997, Ohio HB 280 amends ORC Sections 519.021 for townships and 303.022 for counties, essentially identically, to allow county commissioners and township trustees to establish *planned unit developments (PUDs)* by three options. And, as a fourth alternative, it contains language that does not prohibit a county or township from authorizing *PUDs* as a conditional use. The County Commissioners Association of Ohio has published Bulletin 97-8 titled "Optional Approaches to Planned Unit Development Zoning," which provides the background leading to these alternatives and a description of their similarities and differences.[1] The main features are summarized below.

Option A: Trustees or commissioners amend the zoning resolution to provide one or more types of *PUD* districts, e.g., *PUD*–residential, *PUD*–commercial, *PUD*–office, *PUD*–mixed use, etc. Each type of district would be established as part of the zoning resolution, but none of them would be place automatically on the zoning map in order to meet the requirement that *PUD* regulations apply to property "only at the election of the property owners." The resolution also contains standards for guiding subsequent approval of *PUD* plans, and these could be both general for all types of districts and separate for each individual type of district. The amendment is subject to a referendum. After passage, a property owner may request rezoning to one of the new *PUD* districts. Following regular zoning amendment procedures, trustees and commissioners would submit the rezoning to a referendum. Upon approval, the former zoning district designation is changed on the map to the new *PUD* district designation.

Upon amending the map, the property owner applies for approval of a *PUD* plan, complying with the new standards and regulations in the amended zoning resolution. The trustees and commissioners approve or disapprove the plan, unless that responsibility is delegated to the zoning commission. This decision is an administrative act, not an amendment, and is, therefore, not subject to a referendum; it may be appealed to the common pleas court.

Option B: A landowner may initiate the *PUD* district by applying for an amendment to the zoning resolution and, simultaneously, a change to the zoning map. Regular zoning amendment procedures are followed to designate the property as a *PUD* on the map and to adopt regulations that apply just to that one property. The zoning map and text are subject to a referendum.

Upon majority passage of the referendum, the owner applies for a *PUD* plan, again complying with the standards and regulations approved. Trustees or commissioners approve or disapprove the plan, or delegate that choice to the zoning commission. It is not an amendment, and thus not subject to a referendum.

Uniquely, the landowner establishes the regulations upon applying for the amendment. This is usually a broad authority based upon the terms and regulations the owner wishes, providing flexibility and creativity in plan design without the obstructions of regulations. Option B discloses the plan to the public and includes a right to referendum both on the property and on the regulations that will apply to the development.

Option C: Trustees and commissioners may enact a new *PUD* classification as an *overlay district* so that, unlike Option A, which upon rezoning eliminates the original, or base, zoning, both the existing non–*PUD* zoning and regulations continue to apply unless or until the owner exercises the option to develop under *PUD* regulations. This means the owner has two choices: (1) develop with the regular non–*PUD* zoning that was in existence before the *PUD* zoning was changed or (2) develop in compliance with the new *PUD* regulations. The owner cannot be forced to develop a *PUD* plan. The *overlay district* is subject to a referendum, but when the owner applies for administrative approval of a *PUD* plan, the approval or disapproval is, again, not an amendment and not subject to a referendum.

Conditionally Permitted Uses: This alternative authorizes the listing of *planned unit development* as a conditional use in a particular zoning district, along with adoption of conditions or criteria for their approval by amendment and, therefore, to a referendum. Under the conditional use approach, the application goes to the board of zoning appeals for approval or disapproval.

This decision, however, is an administrative act and is not subject to a referendum.

This choice does not provide the flexibility of the other options since district standards cannot be relaxed through conditional use approval. An administrative hearing is required to ensure no significant impact will result with the approval, and the board of zoning appeals may place conditions on the plan to guarantee district standards are maintained.

In all cases, upon receiving approval of a *PUD* designation, the owner or developer meets with the pertinent planning commission members to discuss the general development plan application. This pre–submission meeting helps to ensure compliance with the community's comprehensive plan, and in the case of a township plan, anticipates meshing with the county's subdivision regulations, while allowing the planning commission to make suggestions beyond zoning restrictions that will enhance the development. The planning commission should, and often does, seek (1) to limit development in and adjacent to environmentally sensitive lands; (2) to encourage preservation of agricultural lands, woodlands, and open spaces; and (3) to reduce the number of roads and utilities, from those that might be required in a conventional zone, to lower future public service costs. These, collectively, are the elements of *conservation development zoning.*

ADVANTAGES: *PUD's* aesthetic and design regulations can create more interesting developments than some conventional zoning, in turn attracting and creating economic development, jobs, and preserving individual community character. Unlike *cluster development zoning, PUD* permits mixed building types and uses, such as offices and convenience stores.

DISADVANTAGES: If overly complex, the planning commission oversight can extend the development period and construction efforts for *PUDs,* and there have been concerns that the planning commission may exert undue discretionary pressure on the development, possibly beyond the goal of the comprehensive plan. And, as mentioned earlier in the section on under *conservation development zoning,* in certain areas *PUDs* have been used to *increase* densities by taking the total number of acres—from which wetlands, steep slopes, and other sensitive areas would have been subtracted under conventional zoning—and allocating dwelling units to that total acreage.

CASE HISTORY: The City of Troy, Ohio, in Miami County includes *planned unit development* in its zoning guidelines. Troy distinguishes *PUD* by stating that the purpose "is to provide a means for encouraging ingenuity, imagination, and flexibility on the part of engineers, architects, site planners, and developers in the planning and design of development within the City of Troy."[2]

Troy is situated on very flat terrain, some of which is floodplain with drainage problems of an extraordinary nature. The planning commission looked toward means other than the "cookie–cutter" development plan to resolve these problems. Their *PUD* guidelines allow a "variety of housing and building types and permitting variations in lot dimensions, yards, building setbacks and area requirements."[3] And they work toward "a more efficient use of land than is generally achieved through conventional developments."[4]

The governing provisions of the *PUD* chapter note that subdivision regulations specified in other chapters of the planning and zoning code are not mandatory[5] under the *PUD* designation. The restrictions may, however, become even tighter than the zoning regulation. A more desirable and more diverse environment than required in non–*PUD* districts is one of the criteria for approval of *PUD* projects, too. This is accomplished by encouraging natural features, such as topography, trees, and drainageways to be left undisturbed in the development plan.

In each stage of approval, the planning commission takes part, recommending its findings to council. Because of the planning commission's active role in *PUD* projects, it exercises authorities it would not normally have, such as granting minor exceptions and variances to the plan as the project nears completion.

Troy's *PUD* describes one means of applying this technique to both residential and nonresidential development.[6, 7] Three *PUDs* have been constructed, and two others are under consideration. The stimulus to develop creative solutions has encouraged interest from designers in other regions who have worked with topography such as that found in Troy. Their involvement has added considerable value to the effectiveness of the *PUD* in this community. (*Case History Source:* Frank B. Davis, Asst. Development Dir., Troy, OH; contact details below.)

ACTION STEPS: Contact Frank B. Davis, Asst. Development Dir., City of Troy, 100 South Market St., Troy, OH 45373; Tel: 937-339-9481; Fax: 937-332-0300. See Colleen Grogan Moore's *PUDs in*

Practice, published by the Urban Land Institute (see **Action Center Resources**).To learn more about development in general, see Richard Klein's *Everybody Wins!: A Citizen's Guide to Development*, American Planning Association (see **Action Center Resources**).

NOTES

[1] County Commissioners Association of Ohio, "Optional Approaches to Planned Unit Development Zoning," *County Advisory Bulletin 97-8*, October 1997, 1-10. Available from the County Commissioners Association of Ohio, 37 W. Borad St., Suite 650, Columbus, OH 43215-4132; Tel: 614-221-5627; Fax: 614-221-6986; E-mail: <<webmaster@ccao.org>>; or may be downloaded from Web Site: <<http://www.ccao.org>>.

[2] "Chapter 1157—Planned Unit Development," page 113. Attachment to a February 8, 1993 letter from Frank B. Davis, Assistant Development Dir., City of Troy, Ohio, to J. Chadbourne.

[3] Ibid., 114.

[4] Ibid., 114.

[5] Ibid., 114.

[6] Herbert H. Smith, *The Citizen's Guide to Zoning* (Washington, DC: Planner's Press, American Planning Association, 1983), 227-228.

[7] Michael A. Mantell, Stephen F. Harper, and Luther Propst, *Creating Successful Communities: A Guidebook to Growth Management Strategies* (Washington, DC: Island Press, 1990), 181-182.

QUARTER / QUARTER ZONING

OBJECTIVE: To protect farming activities from urban sprawl by limiting the amount of nonfarm development.

WHO ENACTS IT: Local governments.

HOW IT WORKS: As the name suggests, *quarter / quarter zoning* limits nonfarm development to one house lot of one acre in size for every 40 acres of farmland. This number is derived from taking one fourth of the typical, original 640–acre tract, or 160 acres, and then one fourth of that quarter, or 40 acres. Thus, a farmer who owns 80 acres can build two houses on a total of two acres. Once these lots have been developed, no more nonfarm construction is allowed, preserving the rest of the land for agriculture.

Quarter /quarter zoning generally works best in rural regions that have large stretches of farmland.[1] In addition, prime farmland can be insulated from approaching residential development by creating buffer zones that only permit *limited development.*

ADVANTAGES: Compared to other zoning regulations, *quarter / quarter zoning* is relatively easy to administer. As a result, it can help to protect valuable farmland at a minimum of expense to the local government.

DISADVANTAGES: Like most zoning ordinances, it can be altered, repealed, or not enforced. As a result, it works best when used in conjunction with other land preservation techniques and when there is considerable community support for the measure.

CASE HISTORY: The Sparta Township Land Use Plan of 1992 in Kent County, Michigan, emphasizes the priority of active agricultural preservation. Agriculture is seen as the highest and best use of the land. Most of the land in the township's western, northern, and southern portions and all existing orchardlands within those areas are classified as prime soil under the USDA Soil Conservation Service criteria and, as such, are grouped as an Ag–1 zoning district. This USDA Soil Conservation Service designation is based on field analysis of the soil's qualities and capabilities.

Residential dwellings and nonagricultural uses of Ag–1 lands are restricted. For a proposed housing site to become eligible for construction on Ag–1 lands, a special use permit is required and the site must be located in a quarter of a quarter of the original 640–acre tract, or within a 40–acre lot where there are not more than two nonagricultural units now located. The planning commission may consider allowing a maximum of four nonagricultural dwellings per quarter where the soil conditions, slope, or wetlands limit farming opportunities and a septic permit can be secured.

Private roads are permitted in the Ag–1 zone only if allowed as a "special land use" by the planning commission and if the private road meets these standards: (1) it is not on prime farmland; (2) it is not on active farmland; (3) the road must be set back 150 feet from active farmland; (4) the road must not have an adverse effect on farm operations.[2] (*Case History Source*: Timothy J. Johnson, AICP, Community Planner, MainStreet Planning Co., Grand Rapids, MI; see contact information below.)

Quarter / quarter zoning **can help protect valuable farmland at a minimum of expense to local government.**

Nonfarm Development Permitted Under Quarter / Quarter Zoning		
○ ○ ○ ○ ☐ **160 Acres**	☐ ○ **40 Acres** ○ ☐ **40 Acres**	○ ○ **80 Acres** ☐
☐ ○ ○ ○ **320 Acres** ○ ○ ○ ○		

☐ = Farm Residence   **○ = Nonfarm Residence**

ACTION STEPS: Contact Timothy J. Johnson, AICP, Community Planner, MainStreet Planning Co., 77 Monroe Center NW, Ste. 406, Grand Rapids, MI 49503; Tel: 616-458-3449; Fax: 616-222-0281. Obtain a copy of *Planning and Zoning for Farmland Protection: A Community Based Approach* by the American Farmland Trust, 1987 (see **Action Center Resources**), and

Ecological Planning for Farmlands Preservation by Frederick Steiner, American Planning Association, 1981 (see **Action Center Resources**).

NOTES

[1] American Farmland Trust, *Planning and Zoning for Farmland Protection: A Community Based Approach* (Washington, DC: American Farmland Trust, 1987), 16.

[2] Telephone conversation on September 27, 1999 between Timothy J. Johnson and J. Chadbourne.

SLIDING SCALE ZONING

OBJECTIVE: To protect large tracts of farmland or open space from fragmentation by urban sprawl.

WHO ENACTS IT: Local governments.

HOW IT WORKS: Like *cluster development zoning, sliding scale zoning* seeks to concentrate development, thereby preserving large tracts of land for farming or open space. As the name implies, *sliding scale zoning* imposes different restrictions on development depending on the size of the parcel. As the size of the parcel increases, the number of houses allowed in relation to the total acreage decreases. For example, a community might permit one house lot on parcels ranging from 1.0 to 3.0 acres in size, two house lots on parcels ranging from 3.1 to 30 acres, three house lots on parcels ranging from 30.1 to 90 acres and so on.

ADVANTAGES: *Sliding scale zoning* concentrates development where it already exists, on smaller lots. *Sliding scale zoning* generally works best in communities that have a variety of different parcel sizes.[1]

DISADVANTAGES: For the technique to work smoothly, area residents have to participate in determining the scale. Otherwise, the technique will appear to favor some residents at the expense of others, even if this was not the intent.

CASE HISTORY: In Kent County, Michigan, northwest of Grand Rapids, lies Alpine Charter Township, a rural / agricultural community. Its soils, climate, and terrain are ideally suited for growing apples, a major part of the township's economy and, Kent County encompasses 20% of all acreage in Michigan that is used for growing apples.

Between 1980 and 1990, the population increased by 10.4%, whereas the state's average population growth was 0.36%. It was clear that the 5–acre minimum lot size in the agricultural zone did not discourage nonfarm residential construction. Farmland was being taken out of production.

In May 1988 the planning commission updated its 1977 Master Plan. The commission took three years and held exhaustive interactions with the community's residents, 90% of whom agreed that agricultural land should be preserved. In August 1992, the zoning ordinance was updated to limit the size and number of lot splits for single–family dwelling units. The number of splits allowed is based on the amount of acreage of the original parcel, with a maximum of four splits.

Each split for a single family dwelling has a minimum lot size of two acres, with a required lot width of 330 feet. The township's sliding scale is shown below:

Acreage of Parent Parcel	Number of Splits Allowed
10 acres or less	0
10.1 to 20 acres	1
20.1 to 40 acres	2
40.1 to 80 acres	3
80.1 acres and up	4

The Township maintains an official map with all existing lot splits and parcel owners. New splits are recorded onto a separate map. The town clerk reports that there has been limited lot splitting since the new regulation went into effect.[2] Private roads are prohibited in the Ag zone, which has helped to limit the opportunities for new lot splits.[3] (***Case History Source***: Timothy J. Johnson, Community Planner, MainStreet Planning Co., Grand Rapids, MI; **see** contact information below.)

ACTION STEPS: Contact Timothy J. Johnson, AICP, Community Planner, MainStreet Planning Co., 77 Monroe Center NW, Ste. 406, Grand Rapids, MI 49503; Tel: 616-458-3449; Fax: 616-222-0281. Obtain a copy of *Planning and Zoning for Farmland Protection: A Community Based Approach* by the American Farmland Trust (see **Action Center Resources**), and Frederick Steiner's *Ecological Planning for Farmlands Preservation*, American Planning Association (see **Action Center Resources**).

NOTES

[1] American Farmland Trust, *Planning and Zoning for Farmland Protection: A Community Based Approach* (Washington, DC: American Farmland Trust, 1987), 15.

[2] Barbara Moore, "Farmland Protection Using Sliding Scale Zoning," Planning and Zoning News (February 1991), 18-19.

[3] Telephone conversation on September 27, 1999 between Timothy J. Johnson and J. Chadbourne.

●

IV. LAND MANAGEMENT TOOLS

IV–B–3: Public Initiatives — Special Protection & Conservation Regulations

Capital Improvement Programming

Cooperative Agreement

Environmental Impact Ordinance

Growth Management

Impact Fees and Exactions

Moratoria

Special Designation (Government)

Transfer of Development Rights

CAPITAL IMPROVEMENT PROGRAMMING

OBJECTIVE: *Capital improvement programming (CIP)* is first and foremost an important tool tor budget planning for capital improvements and replacement and maintenance costs. Secondarily, by controlling investment, the community can guide not only when but also where development occurs, thereby providing the mechanism for protecting sensitive lands.

WHO ENACTS IT: Local government.

HOW IT WORKS: Usually part of the comprehensive plan, *capital improvement programming* provides a timetable for financing the extension of public facilities throughout the community. The process starts with the preparation of a 5 to 10–year budget based on the economics of the community and a projection of improvements it can afford.

After the public services or "utilities extension" policy has been generated, developers will know when and where a community is going to extend its infrastructure, helping them to make informed decisions and saving time and money. Bond issues are more likely to be approved since they now correlate with comprehensive plan priorities.

Many states now require the preparation and adoption of a capital budget by statute. However, this is often overlooked. Nevertheless, it is a part of the planning function to insist that careful *capital improvement programming* and budgeting are worked out and that both have the support of the public.

ADVANTAGES: *CIP* is less subject to legal challenges than zoning techniques because the authority to draft budgets is an accepted function of local government. The courts have generally ruled that making infrastructure improvements in an orderly and cost–effective manner protects the health, safety, and welfare of a community's residents and thus is a legitimate use of the police power exercised by local governments.

CIP can also be cost competitive. By protecting environmentally sensitive areas, it prevents subsequent mitigation costs that often accompany irresponsible development. Infrastructure costs can be held down by building incrementally and logically rather than haphazardly or by emergency.

CIP establishes a procedure for tracking the receipt and expenditure of *impact fees* charged to development projects and *exaction* commitments for specific facilities to be constructed later. To avoid legal challenges, local governments must use these funds for the precise purpose for which they were collected.

DISADVANTAGES: *CIP* may have little or no impact on controlling development if developers finance improvements themselves or if government agencies subsidize improvements. *CIP* should meet the procedural and substantive requirements of the state enabling legislation to minimize constitutional challenges. If, for example, *CIP* restricts growth unfairly by setting differential utility rates, it may be revoked by the courts.

CASE HISTORY: The City of Antioch, California, implements the long–range community goals of its General Plan (comprehensive plan) with a five–year *capital improvement program* and a one–year Capital Budget. The former guides the construction or acquisition of capital improvements, whereas the latter authorizes funding for only the first year of the five–year *capital improvement program.* The remaining four years are unfunded and the cost estimates are subject to change.

The *capital improvement program* covers the City's entire range of public facilities in these eight numbered categories:

1.   100—Major Projects: these are constructions by other agencies to which Antioch contributes, such as CALTRANS and BART transit systems

2.   200—Parks & Open Space: improvements and renovations for large and small parks in town

3.   300—Streets: new streets, widening and rehabilitation, grade separations, bridges, sidewalks and pavement management

4.   400—Traffic Signals: new signals and modifications

5.   500—Public Buildings and Facilities: new and renovated public buildings and the marina; the majority of projects are in the City's redevelopment areas

6.   600—Water Systems: water treatment plant, new lines, and repairs to existing ones

7.   700—Wastewater Collection: extensions, replacements, and reroutes of sewer lines

8.   800—Storm Drainage: new storm drains and repair of old drains

The succeeding year's cost estimates are reviewed and adjusted annually. Acquisitions and construction by neighboring jurisdictions as well as private developers are considered. Antioch cites the following advantages in using a five–year *capital improvement program*:

1.   Focusing attention on community plans, goals, needs, and capabilities. By prioritizing projects, those that are needed or desired the most will be constructed first.

2.   Achieving optimum use of the taxpayer's dollar. The *capital improvement program* assists the Council in making annual budget decisions. And, a listing of future constructions encourages advance selection of needed land.

3.   Serving wider community interests. The program keeps the community informed and citizens involved in decision making.

4.   Provides more efficient planning. Coordination required to produce the program reduces scheduling and conflict problems, such as paving a street one year and tearing it up the next.

5.   Improving intergovernmental and regional coordination. The planning process includes public officials from the city, county, and special districts in projecting timing and financing of improvements for the whole community.

6.   Maintaining a sound and stable financial program. With ample planning time, the most economical means of financing can be coordinated in advance, which helps the City's credit rating, an attraction to business and industry.

7.   Enhancing opportunities for participation in federal and state grants–in–aid programs. The *capital improvement program* improves the chances of winning that aid.

City Council updates the *capital improvement program* annually to maintain a current and comprehensive assessment of the City's capital needs. (*Case History Source:* "City of Antioch: Capital Improvement Planning—Introduction"; contact Steve Scudero, Dir. of Capital Improvements, P.O. Box 5007, Antioch, CA 94531-5007; Tel: 925-779-7050; downloaded September 3, 1999 from Web Site: <<http://www.ci.antioch.ca.us/puiblicwk/97%20cip/97cipint.htm>>.)

ACTION STEPS: Baltimore, County, Maryland, has an extensive description of its *capital improvement program* online. Its *CIP* program "is one means of implementing Baltimore County's goals for community conservation, commercial revitalization, environmental protection, education, public safety as well as a host of other issues." For details, contact C. A. ("Dutch") Ruppersberger, County Executive, 400 Washington Ave., Old Courthouse Mezzanine, Towson, MD 21204; Tel: 410-887-2450; E-mail: <<dutch@co.ba.md.us>>, or download the six–page description, *Capital Improvement Planning in Baltimore County*, (downloaded September 3, 1999) from Web Site: <<http://www.co.ba.md.us/bacoweb/services/planning/html/capimprv.htm>>. Another Web site worth visiting is that of King County, Washington, where the four–page document, *Capital Improvement Program Plan—Physical Environment and Resource Management Program*, can be downloaded from Web Site: <<http://www.metrokc.gov/budget/budget97/capital/physical/htm>>. For a guide on how communities can make informed infrastructure decisions, see the Government Finance Officers Association's *Building Together: Investing in Community Infrastructure*, American Planning Association, 1990. For a general reference on infrastructure issues, see the Urban Land Institute's Project Infrastructure Development Handbook by Donna Hanousek et al., 1989. For a critique of the methods used for planning capital improvements and a description of an alternative system, see Joseph H. Brevard's 1985 work, *Capital Facilities Planning*, APA Planners Press. Obtain a copy of Kristina Ford's book, *Planning Small Town America*, American Planning Association; it outlines a variation of *capital improvement programming* known as "committed lands analysis." Obtain copies of these American Farmland Trust's publications that show the impact of farmland loss to residential development on capital improvement budgets—all are available from the American Farmland Trust, 1200 18th St., NW, Ste. 800, Washington, DC 20036; Tel: 202-331-7300; Fax: 202-659-8339; Web Site: <<http://

www.farmland.org>>: *Cost of Community Services in Frederick County, Maryland.* This study, produced by AFT for the Frederick County AgriFuture Roundtable, analyzes the cost of community services in Frederick County and three of its towns (1997, 36 pages, $12.95, PFREDCOCS). *The Cost of Community Services in Madison Village and Township, Lake County, Ohio*—this first–of–its–kind study in the midwest compares service costs in two Cleveland–area municipalities (1993, 32 pages, $5, POHCOCS); *Does Farmland Protection Pay? The Cost of Community Services in Three Massachusetts Towns*—Done under contract to the Massachusetts Department of Food and Agriculture, a study of the cost of community services in three Connecticut River Valley towns (1992, 38 pages, $10, PPROTPAY). *Duchess County Cost of Community Services Study*, a study of development pressuring farmlands in Duchess County, N.Y., evaluates the cost of community services in two Duchess County towns (1989, 11 pages, $5, PDTHCOCS). *Farmland and the Tax Bill: The Cost of Community Services in Three Minnesota Cities*—AFT and the *Land Stewardship Project* analyze the cost of services in three Twin Cities metro–areas (1994, 20 pages, $10, PFARMTAX). *Is Farmland Protection a Community Investment? How to Do a Cost of Community Services Study*—To respond to the considerable interest in cost of community services studies, AFT developed this handbook to help communities undertake such analyses (1993, 26 pages, $10, PHOWTO). See also David Brower, et al., "Public Spending," *Managing Development in Small Towns* (Washington, DC: American Planning Association, 1984).

COOPERATIVE AGREEMENT

OBJECTIVE: To protect lands through cooperation with another organization or organizations.

WHO ENACTS IT: Public conservation organizations in conjunction with other government agencies or private conservation groups.

HOW IT WORKS: *Cooperative agreements* operate on the assumption that different organizations possess different resources and different areas of expertise. Like a joint venture in private enterprise, *cooperative agreements* seek to pool talents and resources for the benefit of the cooperating parties and their commonly held goals.

Cooperative agreements can take a variety of different forms, from management agreements that allow one organization to operate a facility owned by another, to exchanges or outright transfers of land from one owner to another. This latter scenario often takes place in the public sector when one government agency holds a property that ought to be administered by another. For example, the U.S. Department of Defense might discover that it controls land containing a rare natural habitat that could be managed more effectively by the Fish & Wildlife Service or the National Park Service.

Increasingly, partnerships are being encouraged not only in the public sector by government agencies but also in the private sector by charitable foundations. Often, grant applicants must demonstrate collaboration with other organizations to be eligible for funds or *special designation*.

ADVANTAGES: *Cooperative agreements* provide organizations with a mechanism for pooling their resources.

DISADVANTAGES: In the process of sharing resources, jurisdictional problems may arise. To alleviate any confusion about who is responsible for what, cooperating organizations should be careful to spell out the details of their agreement.

CASE HISTORY: When the Lake Metroparks Board of Park Commissioners requested a *Lake Metroparks Western Lake County Site Acquisition Analysis* in 1988, the expressed goal of the

project was to "determine the most favorable location or locations
for new parks in the western half of Lake County." By the time the
report was finished, however, it was clear that Lake Metroparks not
only had opportunities to acquire new land, but also to work with
communities to upgrade existing parks. With careful improvements,
several local parks could be transformed into a regional resource.
This realization led to a *cooperative agreement* now in effect
between Lake Metroparks and the City of Mentor for the
improvement and on–going management of Veteran's Park.

Located on 62.6 acres in the City of Mentor, Veteran's Park had
received minimal attention in the last 20 years. The city simply did
not have the money to make major capital improvements. The park
land, however, did contain several important natural assets. One
was Granger Pond, over 30 acres in size, and the other was one of
the few remaining examples of a lake–plain forest habitat in Lake
County.

Upgrading the park's facilities would improve access to one of the
few publicly owned inland lakes in the county. In addition, the park
lay adjacent to the Mentor Shore Junior High School, providing a
unique educational resource for the students. With its staff of park
professionals and with special funding from a park levy, Lake
Metroparks was well equipped to manage a natural resource–
based area such as Veteran's Park.

Following the release of the *Lake Metroparks Western Lake County
Site Acquisition Analysis*, the mayor of Mentor, James Struna,
assembled a citizens' committee to examine the issue of improving
Veteran's Park and to look into the possibility of cooperating with
Lake Metroparks. Meanwhile, Lake Metroparks hired a firm to
develop a concept plan for upgrading the park facilities. In
December of 1990, after a series of public meetings, Lake
Metroparks and the City of Mentor signed a *cooperative
agreement*. In return for a 20–year lease, Lake Metroparks agreed
to make $400,000 worth of improvements to Veteran's Park within
three years. The City of Mentor retained ownership of the land but
transferred all maintenance and management responsibility to the
Park District for the duration of the lease.

With the agreement in hand, Lake Metroparks began to assess
ways to ensure the protection of the park's natural assets. It started
by conducting a wetlands delineation to determine the most
sensitive areas of the park. In addition, it had its special Natural

Resources Advisory Council review the park's educational and recreational potential.

In 1994, Lake Metroparks dredged Granger's Pond with the intention of creating diverse wetland habitats. These habitat types were designed to support emergent, submergent, and sand–flat plant and animal communities.

Lake Metroparks has now monitored the wetland areas for five years. A fine vegetative community, including two "listed" species, continues to flourish. The site also provides important habitat for migratory and resting wildlife.

The numbers of human visitors to the park continue to climb from an estimated 94,000 in 1995 to more than 112,000 in 1998. Improvements made to the park include a paved parking area, trails, restrooms, picnic shelter, playground, fishing piers, and an observation deck.

The goal of the project, according to Metroparks Assistant Director of Natural Resource Management and Planning, Steve Madewell, is to achieve "a higher level of natural resource management and stewardship, while affording an appropriate level of public use." In so doing, the Park District helps to meet its goal of expanding recreational opportunities in the western half of Lake County. As for the City of Mentor, it gets a better park without spending a dime. (*Case History Source:* Stephen Madewell, Asst. Dir. of Natural Resource Management and Planning, Lake Metroparks, 11211 Spear Road, Concord Township, OH 44077; Tel: 440-639-7275; Fax: 440-639-9126; *Lake Metroparks Western Lake County Site Acquisition Analysis*, Lake County Planning Commission, 1989; *Concept Plan for Veteran's Park*, CT Consultants, 1990; Lake Metroparks update in September 1999.)

ACTION STEPS: Obtain a copy of the five-page description of a *cooperative agreement* among the states of Wyoming, Colorado, and Wyoming and the U.S. Department of the Interior to "develop and implement a 'recovery implementation program' to improve and conserve habitat for four threatened and endangered species: whooping crane, piping plover, least tern, and pallid sturgeon"; write: Dale Strickland, Exec. Dir., Cooperative Agreement Governance Committee, 2003 Central Ave., Cheyenne, WY 82001; Tel: 307-634-1756; Fax: 307-637-6981; E-mail: <<dstrickland@ west-inc.com>>; or download the document from Web Site:

<<http://www.ianr.uni.edu/pubs/wildlife/NF375.htm>>.Write for or
download a copy of the Water Environment Federation's report,
Funding Mechanisms for a Watershed Management Program,
which exemplifies the kinds of water quality protection possible
when organizations cooperate for common goals; write: 601 Wythe
St., Alexandria, VA 23314-1994; Tel: 800-666-0206; Fax: 703-684-
2492; or download the 7–page article from its Web Site: <<http://
www.wef.org>>. Obtain a copy of the *cooperative agreement*
between the U.S. Forest Service and Southern Utah University,
USDA Dixie National Forest Cooperative Agreement, the data from
which can be used for land management purposes; see Web Site:
<<http://www.gis.suu.ed/cops/fscoops>>. See also the *cooperative
agreement* between an educational institution (University of Hawaii)
and research organization (Oceanic Institute at Makapuu) at Web
Site: <<http://www.lava.net/~oi/i2c6.htm>>. Network with other
organizations both locally and nationally that have similar land
preservation interests (see **Action Center Resources**) to learn
what assets parties could bring to a *cooperative agreement* on a
preservation project.

ENVIRONMENTAL IMPACT ORDINANCE

OBJECTIVE: To minimize the detrimental impact of new development by providing for an environmental review of proposed projects. Some ordinances require developers to incorporate specific design features into their projects.

WHO ENACTS IT: State or local government.

HOW IT WORKS: First implemented at the federal level through the National Environmental Policy Act (NEPA) of 1969, the *environmental impact ordinance* concept has been adopted by a number of state and local governments. In its standard form, it provides for an environmental review of all government construction projects. Detrimental impacts must be identified, and all measures taken to alleviate them must be outlined.

In some cases, this process is incorporated into the existing *planned unit development zoning* or subdivision regulations (see Section III, Implementation—Zoning and Subdivision Regulations for Open Space and Farmland Preservation). In other cases, it takes the form of a community–wide ordinance that regulates a particular impact of development activity, such as storm water runoff. Jurisdictions may also designate "Critical Environmental Areas" throughout the community and require an environmental review before any development can occur in these locations. A more structured means of enactment is to establish special districts, or *overlay zoning*, to authorize low–impact uses such as passive recreation, e.g., hiking, bird–watching; to prohibit damaging uses, such as dredging or construction; and to issue permits after a formal environmental review of medium–impact activities, such as selective timber cutting.

ADVANTAGES: By establishing an institutionalized process for examining the impacts of new development, *environmental impact ordinances* can help to identify problems before they are created.

DISADVANTAGES: An environmental review program requires a substantial degree of expertise on the part of the community planning staff, which may increase the cost of local government. In addition, such a program often applies only to government–funded projects and may not provide for enforcement to ensure that harmful impacts have in fact been minimized in the final design of a project.

CASE HISTORY: As outlying communities in Cuyahoga County experience rapid growth, residents downstream from new development projects have suffered an increased incidence of flooding. To address this problem, the City of North Royalton passed an ordinance in 1989 to manage storm water and control sediment pollution from construction sites.

As a result of the ordinance, all developers must now have a Clearing and Sediment Control Plan approved by the city before beginning construction. In addition, retention basins are required on any property where over one acre of land is disturbed.

The ordinance also establishes specific standards for sites once development is complete. To minimize stream channel erosion, control sediment pollution, and protect against flooding downstream, the peak flow (rate, or velocity) of runoff from a site following development must be reduced in proportion to the increased volume of storm water leaving the site. If the volume of runoff does not exceed the predevelopment amount, then peak flows of runoff need only be held to the predevelopment rate.

In this way, the ordinance sets a standard for runoff based on the natural capacity of the land to handle storm water. Instead of trying to maintain the predevelopment rate of infiltration into the ground, which is difficult to accomplish once a substantial portion of the watershed has been paved over, the ordinance controls the maximum flow of runoff from a given site.

The ordinance implied that any major repair to the now 150 retention basins would be assumed by the city, while minor repairs and general maintenance would be the responsibility of each development's Home Owners' Association. Unfortunately, the city code was never amended to make the Association's responsibilities mandatory, and now the city has lost communications with the Home Owners Association. Often authorities can not even locate the Associations or their directors by name and / or address. This leaves the city with heavy maintenance bills and only marginal control of soil erosion and water runoff.

Though finally amended in 1998, the effect of the ordinance may become moot as the *storm water management—NPDES Phase II* regulations go into effect in early 2000. These will mandate best management practices and a comprehensive storm water management plan for small municipalities, which will make obsolete the present Clearing and Sediment Control Plan.

The advice offered by the city engineer to new ordinance writers is "to be sure that *all* areas of the City Code are amended to reinforce the intended new regulation." (*Case History Source:* Charles T. Althoff, PE, City Engineer, City of North Royalton, 11545 Royalton Rd., North Royalton, OH 44133; Tel: 440-582-3000; Fax: 440-582-3089.)

ACTION STEPS: Obtain a copy of *Performance Controls for Sensitive Lands* from the American Planning Association (see **Action Center Resources**), and a copy of *Rainwater and Land Development: Ohio's Standards for Storm water Management, Land Development and Urban Stream Protection*, Second Edition, 1996, from the Ohio Department of Natural Resources, Division of Soil and Water Conservation, Fountain Square Ct., Columbus, OH 43224; Tel: 614-265-6610; Fax: 614-262-2064 (see **Action Center Resources**). It describes erosion and sediment control plans, defines key terms, and provides standards for compliance. Information on the Ohio EPA's Nonpoint Source Program is available from its Division of Surface Water in Columbus, with contacts Julio Perez or Dale Eicher, Tel: 614-644-2001. For information on how to set up a "Sensitive Area Protection Ordinance," see pages 33-39 in *Protecting Coastal and Wetlands Resources: A Guide for Local Governments*, 1992, U.S. EPA Document #842-R-002. For a free copy, write U.S. EPA, 11029 Kenwood Rd., Bldg. 5, Cincinnati, OH 45242. For information at the federal level, obtain a copy of *The Environmental Impact Statement Process: A Guide to Citizen Action* by Neil Orloff (Washington, DC: Information Resources Press, 1978) and *Environmental Impact Statements: A Guide to Preparation and Review* by Martin S. Baker et al. (New York, NY: Practicing Law Institute, 1977).

GROWTH MANAGEMENT

OBJECTIVE: *Growth management* laws control the timing, phasing, and location of urban development.

WHO ENACTS IT: States, counties, and municipalities.

HOW IT WORKS: *Growth management* programs may originate at the state level and apply to the entire state or to high–growth counties or to a particular region. Also known as urban growth programs, they engage local governments in identifying lands with natural resource, economic, and environmental value and protect them from development. These programs help in implementing a comprehensive plan on a predictable, controlled basis. The justification for them originates from the fact that new development requires infrastructure improvements that are too expensive for the developers alone. Therefore, the improvements depend upon the community to finance a substantial portion of them. This dependence enables the community to exert significant influence on the rate and location of development.[1]

Some laws require local governments to make decisions that fit the comprehensive plans of neighboring governments. Others prescribe public services, such as water and sewer lines, roads, schools be in place before new development is approved.

Several examples from the American Farmland Trust's Farmland Information Center indicate the variations possible with growth management regulations to curtail, pace, or specify the location of development. Twelve states control development or set planning standards for local governments; seven of these also address agricultural land conversion.[2] The following illustrate possibilities:

1   Hawaii, in 1961, first experimented with statewide land–use planning, creating four zones covering all of the state. One of the zones was designated for farmland.

2.   Vermont passed Act 250 in 1970 and another in 1988 requiring state review of commercial, industrial, and residential projects to meet its criteria.

3.   Oregon, in 1972, enacted one of the country's strongest growth management laws. City governments were required to establish urban growth boundaries (limiting the extension of urban services), while county governments

enacted exclusive agricultural zoning and other farmland protection policies.

4.   Washington adopted and strengthened its Growth Management Act in 1990 and 1991. The Act compelled fast–growing counties and cities to prepare comprehensive plans to protect natural resource areas. In addition, counties have to designate urban growth areas projected over 20 years. It included restriction of land uses to those which did not interfere with farm and ranch operations.

5.   In 1992, the New Jersey State Development and Redevelopment Plan directed urban growth to defined urban areas. It provides a statewide framework to guide the investment policies of its state agencies.

6.   In that same year, the Maryland Economic Growth, Resource Protection, and Planning Act required local governments to adopt new comprehensive plans and revise their zoning and subdivision ordinances to protect natural resources, including agricultural land, and to direct growth to existing population centers. In 1997, the state's "Smart Growth Areas" bill now directs state funding to areas targeted for development.

7.   In 1997, Minnesota's Community–Based Planning Act set 11 goals to encourage, not require, local governments to develop comprehensive plans, again to protect, preserve, and enhance the state's resources.

ADVANTAGES: State–initiated and county *growth management* laws exceed local boundaries and can encourage jurisdictions to work together toward common goals. For example, they can provide *incentives* for areas already urban, and *disincentives* for open space and farmland. By joining regional efforts, local governments can save infrastructure costs by guiding development and protecting natural resources. Many city managers feel that *growth management* is the desired way of programming improvements, and it is the best way to avoid undue pressure from vested interest groups. Also, developers learn well in advance where development will be permitted or encouraged and what type of development will be allowed, thus saving them time and money.

DISADVANTAGES: *Growth management* regulations can be politically difficult, complex, and time consuming to produce. They are still controversial in some states and legally challenged, though cases in Ramapo Township, New York, and Petaluma, California, have been upheld by the Supreme Court.[3]

CASE HISTORY #1: Wayne County, Ohio, published its new comprehensive plan on April 23, 1997. The Steering Committee's first major recommendation was:

Redirect and Concentrate Development—The Plan seeks to redirect future development to cities, villages and hamlets, and to encourage higher densities to reduce the overall amount of land consumed by development. The result would be a savings in land otherwise developed (estimated at 15,000 acres of lost agricultural land and greenspace), reduced sprawl and reduced public expenditures for infrastructure.[4]

(*Case History Source:* Betsy Sparr, Planning Dir., Wayne County, Wooster, Ohio; Tel: 330-287-5420.)

CASE HISTORY #2: The City of Hudson, Ohio, in May 1996, passed Chapter 1207, "Growth Management Residential Development Allocation System," which regulates the rate at which the city issues zoning certificates for certain residential dwelling units and subdivisions.[5, 6]

Chapter 1207 implements the policies and goals of the preceding year's "City of Hudson Comprehensive Plan Relating to Growth Management Strategy, Transportation, Community Facilities and Infrastructure, Economic Development, and Community Character." The Hudson city council found that "the sustained high rate of residential development and associated population growth in the city (over the past decade greatly exceeding the growth rate of the region, Ohio, and the U.S.) has and continues to cause a deterioration in the level and quality of public services and infrastructure." And, the cost of municipal services were greater than tax revenues from a typical residential unit. Therefore, it recommended the residential development allotment system.

Since May 1996, the City has halted zoning certificates for construction of a residential dwelling unit until an applicant is awarded a residential development allotment, or is exempt from the ordinance. In 1996 to 1997 and again in 1998 to 1999, the City approved 100 allotments, with 80 for "priority development" and 20 for nonpriority status, while nonresidential (civic, commercial, industrial, and institutional) development and remodeling or replacement of existing dwellings are exempt from the ordinance.

"Priority developments" are housing that is (1) affordable—persons earning not more than 50% of the median family income of Hudson; (2) restricted to persons over 62 and disabled; (3) units to be constructed on a legal, buildable lot with approval granted prior to the ordinance; (4) new and of five acres or more with access to public streets and water and sewer within 1,000 feet.

One half of the allotments are awarded semi–annually, and the city council establishes the number of allotments for the following year at each year's end. In this manner Hudson has created its slow–growth ordinance and withstood the legal challenges to it. (*Case History Source:* Arlene Egan, Zoning Inspector, City of Hudson, Department of Community Development, 46 Ravenna Street, Ste. D–3, Hudson, Ohio 44236-3099; Tel: 330-342-1790; Fax: 330-342-1880.)

ACTION STEPS: Obtain a copy of the City of Hudson, OH, *Growth Management Residential Development Allocation System* and its amendments from the City's Department of Community Development, 46 Ravenna St., Ste. D–3, Hudson, OH 44236-3099; Tel: 216-342-1790; 216-656-1753; Fax: 216-342-1880. Visit numerous Web sites for a number of excellent sources on *growth management.* They include: The SmartGrowth Network, Web Site: <<http://www.smartgrowth.org>>; it is a partner of the Sustainable Communities Network (SCN) at Web Site: <<http://www. sustainable.org>>. E-mail contacts for two staff at SCN are Susanna MacKenzie Euston, Community Sustainability Resource Institute Co–Director & Webmaster at <<sustain@primeline.com>> and Susan Boyd, CONCERN, Inc., Co–Director at E-Mail: <<concern@igc.apc.org>>. Download a copy of Larry Kipp's 16–page article, *SmartGrowth,* a description of *growth management* in Douglas County, Kansas, at Web Site: <<http:// www.ixks.com/~larryvil/smartgro.htm>>. Write or call for copies of King County, Washington's *growth management* initiatives by contacting Ron Sims, Executive, King County Court House, 516 Third Avenue, Room 400, Seattle WA 98104; Tel: 206-296-4040; Fax: 206-296-0200; Web Site: <<http://www.metrokc.gov>>. Subjects available online include *growth management* practices for brownfields, recreation, and parks, and a host of other subjects. In addition, Washington's Department of Community, Trade, and Economic Development (CTED) has available on line and through mail inquiry its *Vision 2003—Growth Management Program,* downloadable at Web Site: <<http://www.cted.wa.gov/lgd/growth/ vision.html>>, or address inquiries to: Growth Management Program, 906 Columbus St. SW, P.O. Box 48300, Olympia, WA 98504-8300; Tel: 360-586-1274; Fax: 360-753-2950; E-mail:

<<juliek@cted.wa.gov>>. Four other sources of online information on *growth management* include Oregon's "Metro" Web Site's "At a Glance" page: <<http://www.multnomah.lib.or.us/metro/glance/ glance.html>>. California's Association of Bay Area Governments has compiled a downloadable list, *Regional Councils of Governments and Metropilitan Planning Organizations—United States and World Wide*, that is useful for state–by–state and foreign country contacts about managing growth. At the Munisource Web Site, described as the "largest collection of municipal government related information on the Web, with direct links to over 3,500 Official Muncipal Sites in 44 countries . . . , " one can search the database or send e-mail with inquiries about *growth management* issues at Web Site: <<http://www.munisource.org>>. Finally, information on *growth management* as a part of sustainable communities is available at the Indigo Development site, RPP International's "Industrial Ecology Research Center" Web Site: <<http://www.indigodev.com>>. Numerous hyperlinks with kindred organizations covering topics such as ecology; industrial ecology; materials flow analysis; eco-industrial parks; sustainable communities; architecture, community metabolism; design for environment; construction, and urban planing; and sustainable agriculture are available at Web Site: <<http://www.indigodev.com/ Links.html>>.

NOTES

[1] Herbert H. Smith, *A Citizens's Guide to Planning* (Washington, DC: American Planning Association, 1979), 92.

[2][3] Farmland Information Center, American Farmland Trust, *Growth Management Laws Fact Sheet*,1-3. Downloaded May 4, 1999 from Web Site: <<http://farm.fic.niu.edu/tic-ta/tats-gml.html>>.

[3] Michael A. Mantell, et al., *Creating Successful Communities: A Guidebook to Growth Management Strategies* (Washington, DC: Island Press, 1909), 103.

[4] Wayne County, Ohio, *Tomorrow Together—Honoring Our Past . . . Shaping Our Future: Comprehensive Plan, Wayne County, Ohio*, Executive Summary (Wooster, OH: April 23, 1997), ii.

[5] City of Hudson, Ohio, *Chapter 1207—Growth Management Residential Development Allocation System* (Hudson, OH: May 1996), 1-16.

[6] City of Hudson, Ohio, *An Ordinance Establishing the Residential Development Allocation for the 1998-99 Annual Allocation Period Under Section 1207.07 of the Codified Ordinances* (Hudson, OH: June 4, 1998), 1-2.

IMPACT FEES AND EXACTIONS

OBJECTIVE: To require new development to pay for the added burden that it places on public facilities, including parks.

WHO ENACTS IT: Local governments.

HOW IT WORKS: As a community grows, new residents increase the demand for public services. Everything from roadways to parks to water and sewage treatment plants becomes more heavily used. To maintain the established level of services and preserve the health of the local community, local governments must expand these facilities.

In the past, state and federal government contributed heavily to infrastructure improvements. Now, as these funding sources dry up, elected officials have been forced either to raise taxes on existing residents or to shift some of the financial burden to developers. *Impact fees* and *exactions* provide two means of doing this.

Impact fees, established through local ordinances, require developers to pay a calculated charge based on the type of development that they plan to build and the projected impact that it will have on local public facilities. If a community determines that 10 acres of new parkland must be acquired for every 1,000 new residents, then it might charge developers a parks and recreation fee based on the cost of acquiring this land.

Exactions are generally negotiated on a case–by–case basis with the developer. In return for rezonings, permits, or other development approval, the local government may require the developer to contribute land, improvements, or money to the community—or to underwrite new traffic signals, dedicate land for a park or a school, or help upgrade the local sewage treatment plant.

In general, *impact fees* and *exactions* are legal if a correlation exists between the impact of new development and the improvements financed or exacted using these techniques.[1] They must meet this test: those who pay are the ones who benefit. This so–called "rational nexus" test also considers whether the amount charged is proportional to the degree of impact caused by the development and whether the new residents of the development will derive any benefit from the improvements made. And, normally, the *impact fees* and *exactions* must be for initial costs and not maintenance expenses.

Another issue is whether the government using an *impact fee* or an *exaction* is legally empowered to do so. A handful of states that have passed *impact fees* and *exactions* have justified these charges based on their powers of home rule and, more generally, through the police power entrusted to local government to protect the health, safety, and welfare of its residents. *Impact fees* established by municipalities, if set up correctly, have generally been upheld in Ohio. The use of this technique by unincorporated areas, however, remains largely untested in the courts.

ADVANTAGES: *Impact fees* and *exactions* shift some or all of the costs of new development from the taxpayers to developers. By forcing new development to help pay for itself, these techniques encourage more compact design and help to ensure that adequate public facilities will be provided for community residents.

DISADVANTAGES: If set too high or used inappropriately, *impact fees* and *exactions* may be challenged on legal grounds. Communities that do not base their use of *impact fees* and *exactions* on a comprehensive plan and a capital improvements program will have trouble defending them in court.[2] Finally, the municipality must be extremely careful that its calculation of charges reflect the actual added development costs, that the funds are received and expended to offset those costs, and that, again, those who pay are the ones who receive the benefit.

Because *exactions* are often negotiated on a case–by–case basis, they represent an unknown cost for the developer and an unknown contribution to the municipal budget. *Impact fees* remove this uncertainty through the use of a calculated schedule of charges.

While *impact fees* have been most commonly used to fund water and sewer improvements (as in this case history, below, from Chardon, Ohio), some communities have employed them to protect open space and sensitive lands. Martin County, Florida, uses an *impact fee* to fund the acquisition of recreational beach lands. Parts of Riverside County, California, collect a fee to mitigate the impact of development on the endangered Stevens kangaroo rat. The City of Westlake, Ohio, in Cuyahoga County, has enacted an *impact fee* for parks and recreation.

CASE HISTORY: In Geauga County, Ohio, on March 22, 1993, the Village of Chardon passed Ordinance No. 1439, adding Chapter

924, "Development Impact Fees Regulation." The Ordinance was an emergency measure ". . . to assure proper and immediate payment for the wastewater treatment plant addition due to new development and so as to comply with EPA mandates."[3]

The Development Impact Fees Regulation imposes a charge at the time development permits are issued. The dollar amount is based upon the number of residential dwelling units, or equivalent units in a nonresidential subarea, which connect to the municipal sanitary sewer system. Thus, the fees are charged to those who benefit from an expanded and improved wastewater treatment facility.

Chardon's *impact fee*, now called a "System Development Charge," adds to other requirements of the comprehensive plan, the capital improvements plan, and other municipal policies, ordinances, and resolutions which are intended to provide added public facilities as a result of land development. The development area for the Wastewater Treatment Plant *impact fee* includes all of the land within the Village of Chardon.

The fees become a lien against the proposed development, and they must be paid before a permit is issued. If the fees are not paid within 30 days after they come due, the County Auditor places them on the tax duplicate at the highest interest rate allowable and they are collected in the same manner as a municipal tax. The Ordinance is now in effect, but in 1999 it is being challenged by the Home Builders Association.[4] (*Case History Source:* Jeff Smock, Finance Department, Village of Chardon; see contact details below.)

ACTION STEPS: Contact Jeff Smock, Finance Department, Village of Chardon, l08 South Ambden St., Chardon, Ohio, 44024, Tel. 440-286-2470; Fax: 440-286-2658. A seven–page review of *impact fees, Impact Fees Overview*, available at the Bozeman, MT, Web site offers an excellent summary of the issues of costs of service, fee collection, and other matters: download from Web Site: <<http://www.bozeman.net/planning/1F101.htm>>, and actual fees collected at Web Site: <<http://www.bozeman.net/planning/fees. htm>>. Information about imposing school *impact fees* within a school district's boundaries is available from Bill Sharp, Dir. of Maintenance and Operations, Sequoia Union High School District, 480 James Ave., Redwood City, CA 94062; Tel: 415-369-1411, ext. 2290; download from Web Site: <<http://198.31.87.75/schimp. htm>>. Santa Barbara, California's imposition of traffic *impact fees* is documented in *Traffic Impact Fees—Survey Results*, downloadable from Web Site: <<http://www.rain.org/~calapa/calapa/planners/tifsurv.htm>>. The State of Maryland's *Issue Brief: Impact Fees* explains some of the issues involved with one–time fees and lower–priced housing, downloadable at Web Site: <<http://www.mccd.org/ifees.htm>>. And these sources also explore how communities are coping with development with *impact fees*: Peter Colwell, "Impact Fees: Some Further Ruminations," *The Illinois Real Estate Letter*, Winter/Spring, 1996, 7; David Eades, "Impact Fees: They're Not All Bad," *The Illinois Real Estate Letter*, Winter, 1997, 2. And, for background on the subject see *A Practitioner's Guide to Development Impact Fees* by James C. Nicholas, Arthur C. Nelson, and Julian Conrad Juergensmeyer (1991) and *Development Exactions*, edited by James E. Frank and Robert M. Rhodes (1987). Both books are available through the American Planning Association (see **Action Center Resources**).

NOTES

[1] James C. Nicholas, Arthur C. Nelson, and Julian Conrad Juergensmeyer, *Development Impact Fees* (Chicago: American Planning Association, 1991) 14.

[2] Ibid., 19.

[3] Ordinance No. 1439, "An Ordinance Adding Chapter 924, Development Impact Fees Regulation, to the Codified Ordinances of the Village of Chardon, and Declaring an Emergency," Section 3, March 22, 1993.

[4] Jeff Smock, Village of Chardon, and Jim Gilette, Chardon Law Director, telephone conversations with J. Chadbourne, September 8, 1999.

MORATORIA

OBJECTIVE: To stop community development temporarily in order to plan for growth. This includes identifying and protecting sensitive lands and other community resources.

WHO ENACTS IT: Local government.

HOW IT WORKS: For the most part, *moratoria* are used to control the rate of a particular type of development, not the location. Sometimes they are used as a last–ditch measure to prevent the destruction of a valuable community resource until a comprehensive plan can be prepared. They are often enacted in areas where development outstrips the local government's ability to provide public services.

To maintain the legality of *moratoria*, communities must provide adequate justification for the implementation of these measures. Communities must also decide what kind of development they want to freeze, whether residential, commercial, or industrial, and for how long.

ADVANTAGES: *Moratoria* can bring rampant development under control and allow local governments sufficient time to plan for growth.

DISADVANTAGES: *Moratoria* should be used primarily by communities that have considerable experience in managing growth.[1] If used excessively or without adequate justification, the technique is vulnerable to legal challenges. Such challenges are generally filed on the basis of the right to travel, guaranteed in Article Four of the Constitution, or on the takings issue discussed in the Fifth and Fourteenth Amendments.

CASE HISTORY: In 1998 the City of Aurora, Ohio, found itself in a predicament. It had recently adopted a master plan to guide the city's development. One of the key recommendations in the plan was to update the city's existing zoning code so that Aurora "could take advantage of the most effective contemporary standards for managing growth." The city had contracted with Northstar Planning and Design, Inc. to "review and update the zoning code," with a contract finish date of 1999. Their dilemma was what to do about development during the period of time when Northstar was researching and then proposing changes to the existing zoning code.[2]

Aurora's planning commission proposed a *moratorium* on the following specific projects for a 12–month period while Northstar proceeded with its work: (1) applications for preliminary plat approval or new applications for residential subdivisions; (2) applications for conditional zoning certificates for cluster/group housing development; and (3) applications to amend the zoning code, zoning map, or zoning districts for property currently residentially zoned or to place property not currently zoned as residential into a residential zone. At the same time, the commission proposed that the following projects be permitted during the 12–month period: (1) commercial and industrial site plans, (2) subdivision phases, condominium site plans, and recreation site plans "within a *Planned Unit Development* where an overall general development plan has been approved by the city," (3) and four other categories of projects.[3] In Aurora's new master plan, conflicts between the plan and the old zoning code lay in several areas, including cluster home zoning and provision for sufficient open space in future developments.

The *moratorium* did have opposition in the community. Dick Anter, Executive Vice President of the Homebuilders Association of Greater Cleveland, stated that "a whole year is too long," while Aurora businessman, Ed Gray, owner of Creative Windows, believed that passage of the planning commission's proposal would "have a detrimental effect on my business and my employees." And, Aurora Chamber of Commerce President Alan Shorr urged members to attend the public hearing and oppose the move. Those in favor of the move pointed out that recent *moratoria* in the nearby communities of Hudson, Macedonia, and Twinsburg had no detrimental effects.[4]

On January 25, 1999, the Aurora City Council passed Ordinance 1998–200, "An Emergency Ordinance Declaring a Deferral of One (1) Year with Respect to Submission of Plans and Applications for Residential Subdivisions and Any Requests for Use Variances and Rezoning." Aurora mayor Peggy L. Duncan approved the *moratorium* on February 2, 1999, and made its effective dates March 4, 1999 to March 4, 2000.

Subsequently, in 1999, Northstar completed its contract work. Proposed as "Zoning Code Amendments—Revision to the Zoning Code, City of Aurora, Ordinance 1999–156," the revisions went as a referendum to Aurora's voters in November 1999.[5] Revision updates include such topics as "residential conservation development," "development agreements," "residential density standards," "development and site planning," "wetlands," "floodways," and other development issues. On November 2, 1999,

Aurora residents approved the zoning code amendments by a vote of 1,705 to 696.[6] (*Case History Source:* Planning Commission, City of Aurora, Ohio, Building Dept., 199 S. Chillicothe Rd., Aurora, OH 44202-8830; Tel: 330-562-9564; Fax: 330-562-9719; and Barry Kawa, "Aurora Halting New Development: One–year Moratorium to Allow Code Review," *The Plain Dealer*, January 26, 1999, 1–B — 2–B.)

ACTION STEPS: See the *Newsweek* article on sprawl in Atlanta, GA, "Sprawling, Sprawling . . . Move to a Suburb and the World Moves Out with You—A Case Study in Hypergrowth," by D. Pedersen, et al., July 19, 1999, 26, downloadable at Web Site: <<http://www.newsweek.com/nw-srv/issue/03_99b/printed/us/na/na0103_1.htm>>. See also the Dover, New Hampshire, *moratorium* legislation contained in the *Resource Guide for Creating Successful Communities*, 1990, available from Island Press, 1718 Connecticut Ave., NW, Ste. 300, Washington, DC 20009-1148; Tel; 202-232-7933; Fax: 202-234-1328; E-mail: <<info@islandpress.org>>; Web Site: <<http://www.islandpress. org>>. See also *Managing Development in Small Towns* by David Brower et al., published by the APA Planners Press, Planners Press (of American Planning Association), 122 S. Michigan Ave., Ste. 1600, Chicago, IL 60603-6107; Tel: 312-786-6344; Fax: 312-431-9985; E-mail: <<bookorder@planning.org>>. And, *Creating Successful Communities: A Guidebook to Growth Management Strategies*, 1990, by Michael Mantell et al., Island Press.

NOTES

[1] David Brower, et al., *Managing Development in Small Towns* (Washington, DC: American Planning Association, 1984) 60-61.

[2] City of Aurora, "Ordinance 1998-263—An Emergency Ordinance Declaring a Deferral of One (1) Year with Respect to Submission of Plans and Applications for Residential Subdivisions and Any Requests for Use Variances and Rezoning," adopted January 25, 1999, approved February 25, 1999, effective March 4, 1999, 1-3. Fax on September 8, 1999 from City of Aurora, Ohio, Building Department, to M. Chadbourne.

[3] Ibid., 1-3.

[4] Barry Kawa, "Aurora Halting New Development: One -year Moratorium to Allow Code Review," *The Plain Dealer*, January 26, 1999, 1–B — 2–B.

[5] City of Aurora, "Ordinance 1999-156—Zoning Code Amendments: Revision to the Zoning Code," 1-28. Downloaded September 8, 1999 from Web Site: <<http://www.auroraoh.com/newcode.html>>.

[6] "Election '99," *The Plain Dealer* (November 3, 1999), 5–B.

SPECIAL DESIGNATION

OBJECTIVE: To draw attention to resources of exceptional natural and cultural value by providing them with special recognition and, in some cases, legal protection, technical and financial assistance, and management support to the resource owners, depending on the characteristics of the resource.

WHO ENACTS IT: State or federal legislation establishes *special designation* programs. Government agencies then work with local communities to designate and manage the areas selected. Additionally, individuals may request a *special designation* of the state or federal government. Usually, the individual retains ownership of the property.

HOW IT WORKS: Below are five examples of how this tool can be used. The first two examples were initiated by a government agency, while individuals undertook *special designation* status in the other three examples.

A. Initiated by a Government Agency

1. Ohio Scenic Rivers Program

Enacted in 1968, the program includes three designation categories: wild, scenic, and recreational. Following a suitability study conducted by the Ohio Department of Natural Resources and a series of public meetings, the Director of the ODNR then determines whether the watercourse in question possesses "water conservation, scenic, fish, wildlife, historic, or outdoor recreation values which should be preserved."[1] If it does, a legal notice of "intent to designate" is issued and, following a 30–day comment period, the river or stream is entered into the program.

Once designated, a watercourse benefits from a variety of program components. These include an environmental review of public projects affecting designated streams, assistance and education for landowners within each designated area, a water quality monitoring program using local volunteers, and a plan for managing nonpoint source water pollution. As of September 1999, 20 river segments containing 679 river miles have been designated throughout the State of Ohio.[2]

2. National Heritage Corridor Program

National Heritage Corridor (NHC) designation promotes four kinds of activities: natural resource protection, historic preservation, public recreation, and economic growth. Designation provides no statutory regulations. Instead, it is intended as a nominal umbrella that raises community awareness about a special collection of resources. Created by Acts of Congress, NHCs become "affiliated areas" within the National Park System. This makes them eligible for limited technical and financial assistance from the federal government. A special Corridor Commission of public and private interests is assembled to oversee management of each NHC.

NHC status focuses local resources on protecting a corridor's assets. Designation may then lead to more concrete protection measures such as the donation or purchase of scenic easements. The National Park Service is presently considering incorporating the NHC concept into a broader designation program entitled the "National Heritage Partnerships Program" that would include a variety of significant areas across the country that are not appropriate for national park status.

B. Initiated by an Individual

1. Ohio Natural Areas Program

Enacted in 1970, the program is administered by the Ohio Department of Natural Resources (ODNR), Division of Natural Areas & Preserves. Through the program, ODNR purchases land or accepts donations of property and easements from landowners in an effort to develop a statewide system of nature preserves. Landowners can also negotiate with ODNR to have their land dedicated as a preserve. The Ohio Historical Society has a similar program for significant archaeological sites.

2. National Historic Landmark (NHL) Program

Administered by the National Park Service, the program works to "identify, designate, recognize, and protect buildings, structures, sites, and objects of national significance." After a formal review process, selected sites are registered and the owners are awarded a certificate of designation and a plaque. In addition to public recognition, the site also receives limited protection from federal projects that might adversely affect it. The owner forfeits none of the rights to the property and does not have to allow public access.

At the present time, more than 2,100 sites have been designated nationally.[3]

3. National Register of Historic Places

Administered by the National Park Service, the program functions as a planning tool for the federal government. More encompassing than the NHL Program, the *National Register Program* includes sites of local or regional significance as well as those of national importance. Sites are evaluated based on their age, significance, and integrity. Nationwide, almost 65,000 historic places have been designated.[4]

ADVANTAGES: *Special designation* publicizes valuable resources. In so doing, it paves the way for funding, tourism, management, and long–term protection. Additionally, the Ohio Natural Areas Program often provides legal protection and management support on dedicated preserves.

DISADVANTAGES: Disadvantages vary with the program. Like all government programs, *special designations* require paperwork, and the designation process is often time–consuming. In addition, designation generally provides little or no legal protection in and of itself. In some cases, some designations may require a legal agreement that limits the owner's use of the land in order to maintain the property's natural or cultural integrity.

CASE HISTORY #1: The Ohio & Erie Canal is an example of a National Heritage Corridor Program. Completed in 1832 and seven years in the building, the Ohio & Erie Canal was the first inland waterway to connect the Great Lakes with the Gulf of Mexico via the Ohio and Mississippi Rivers. From Cleveland to Zoar, Ohio, an 87–mile section of the original canal was designated by Congress in 1996 as the Ohio & Erie Canal National Heritage Corridor (NHC). As it winds through Cleveland, Akron, and near Canton, the historic corridor links natural, cultural, and recreational resources. One clear benefit from the designation is the impetus it has given surrounding communities along its path to set aside recreational and natural areas that might otherwise succumb to development. Some 5,000,000 people live within a one–hour drive of the corridor, and their leisure time and recreation dollars will help to support not only the corridor but also those projects that extend or otherwise enhance the natural, cultural, and recreational values of the urban, rural, and parkland areas through which the corridor runs.

The Ohio & Erie Canal National Heritage Corridor designation is the culmination of many years of cooperative work by government agencies, nonprofit organizations, and individuals. To assess the Ohio & Erie Canal's potential to be the fourteenth National Heritage Corridor in the country under a program administered by the Department of the Interior, Congress initially appropriated $175,000 in 1991 for a study. The Rivers, Trails, and Conservation Assistance Program of the National Park Service conducted the work, coordinating efforts closely with local interest groups, but with two key organizations in particular: the North Cuyahoga Valley Corridor, Inc., which has now become the Ohio Canal Corridor, and the Ohio & Erie Canal Corridor Coalition. These two groups were given the charge of preparing a management plan for the Heritage Corridor. They have since jointly formed the Ohio & Erie Canal Association (OECA) to undertake that work, with the U.S. Secretary of the Interior recognizing it as the "management entity" responsible for this enormous task. The management plan includes: (1) an inventory of corridor resources "to be conserved, restored, managed, developed, or maintained because of natural, cultural, or historic significance"; (2) policy recommendations for resource management "with appropriate and compatible economic viability"; (3) a six–year plan for restoration and construction activities; (4) a plan for coordinating federal, state, and local programs for corridor promotion; (5) and an interpretive plan for corridor visitors.[5]

In its management capacity the OECA receives and disburses federal funds for projects in the corridor, both small, community–based projects and those larger in scope: e.g., (1) Corridor—Byway Management Plan, Corridor Visitors Guide, and Byway Enhancements; (2) Cuyahoga County—Hulett Wayside Exhibit, Cleveland Neighborhoods, Millcreek Waterfall, Canal Reservation, and Thornburg Station; (3) Summit County—Township Hall, Mustill House/Store, Howe House, Akron Historic Landmarks, H & C Canal Cleanup, and Youth Outreach; (4) Stark County—St. Helena III Canalboat, Stark County Trail, and Massillon Trail; and (5) Tuscarawas County—Zoarville Bridge and the Lawrence Township Towpath. These activities demonstrate that the corridor not only links resources but also constituencies. Together, local governments, state agencies, small businesses, historical societies, community groups, industrial neighbors, private landowners, recreation organizations, and environmental groups are operating effectively as a public / private partnership to ensure the success of projects in these areas of priority: tourism development, recreation facility development, education programs, historic preservation, natural resources conservation, and economic development.[6] (*Case History Source*: For further information, contact Tim Donovan, Dir., Ohio Canal Corridor, P.O. Box 609420, Cleveland, OH 44109; Tel: 216-348-1825; Fax: 216-348-1832; Web Site: <<http://www.ohiocanal.org>>; and the Ohio & Erie Canal Corridor Coalition, 520 South Main St., #2541–F, Akron, OH 44311; Tel: 330-434-5657; Fax: 330-434-5688; Web Site: <<http://www.uakron.edu/bustech/canal/oeccc>>.)

CASE HISTORY #2: Ladd Natural Bridge in Washington County, Ohio, is a natural stone arch that was formed when the ceiling of a dry cave collapsed. All that remained was a 40–foot span of sandstone 15 feet thick.

In 1983, the Ohio Department of Natural Resources' (ODNR) Division of Natural Areas & Preserves recognized this "bridge" as an Ohio Natural Landmark. In 1984, the owners of the property, the Ladds—Alice Ladd and her son, Ben, who lend their surname to the Landmark—agreed to dedicate the structure and 35 acres of surrounding woodland as a state nature preserve. The site is now legally protected by the State of Ohio as "an area having outstanding geologic and floral characteristics."

Under the articles of dedication drafted between the landowners and ODNR, the Ladds retained ownership of the property, while ODNR received access and preservation rights. This agreement placed the property under the rules and regulations of ODNR natural preserves, so that inappropriate uses such as mineral extraction and hunting are forbidden. The Ladds reserved the right to harvest fallen trees for firewood and to use several springs on the property for agricultural purposes. The articles of dedication provide for an annual site visit by ODNR staff to assure that the conditions of the agreement are being upheld.

Visitors must obtain a permit from ODNR or the landowners before walking the property because of the site's sensitive resources and because the principal access route passes directly by the owner's house.

A major benefit for the landowners is peace of mind: the dedication runs in perpetuity and cannot be broken unless a determination is made that the land must be used due to some "imperative and unavoidable public necessity" (usually issues of national security). The Ladds also receive a 100% exemption from real estate taxes, while ODNR assumes management responsibility of the land, including trail and parking facility maintenance, and liability from visitor use of the property.

Through this *special designation*, ODNR has assured that a valuable piece of Ohio's natural heritage remains protected, without having to purchase the land outright. (*Case History Source*: Stephen W. Goodwin, Administrator, Preservation Services, Ohio Department of Natural Resources, Division of Natural Areas & Preserves, 1889 Fountain Square, Bldg. F, Columbus, OH 43224; Tel: 614-265-6456; Fax: 614-267-3096; Web Site: <<http://www. dnr.state.oh.us/odnr/dnap/dnap.html>>.)

ACTION STEPS: Contact the National Park Service, National and Midwest Region Offices for more information about the National Heritage Corridor designation: Robert Stanton, Dir., National Park Service, 1849 C St., NW, Washington, DC 20240; Tel: 202-208-6843; Web Site: <<http://www.nps.gov>>; and William W. Schenk, Regional Dir., Midwest Region, National Park Service, 1709 Jackson St., Omaha, NE 68102; Tel: 402-221-3471; Fax: 402-221-3480; Web Site: <<http://www.nps.gov/pub_aff/mwfa.htm>>. Contact the Ohio DNR's Division of Natural Areas and Preserves (see second case history, above) for more information about its Scenic Rivers Program. Contact the Rivers, Trails, and Conservation Assistance Program, Midwest Region, of the National Park Service: Paul Labovitz, Program Leader, 4570 Akron–Peninsula Rd., Peninsula, OH 44264; Tel: 330-657-2950; Fax: 330-657–2955; E-mail: <<paul_labovitz@nps.gov>>. Obtain a copy of the National Natural Landmarks Program brochure from the National Park Service, 1849 C. St., NW, Washington, DC 20240; E-mail: <<nnl@nps.gov>>. Contact the Ohio Historic Preservation Office for information on state and national preservation efforts: Ohio Historic Preservation Office, 567 East Hudson St., Columbus, OH 43211-1030; Tel: 614-297-2470; Fax: 614-297-2496; Web Site: <<www.ohiohistory.org/resource/ histpres/>>.

NOTES

[1] Ohio Wild, Scenic and Recreational River Law, Section 1501.16.

[2] Telephone conversation September 15, 1999, between Beth Wilson, Ohio Department of Natural Resources, Division of Natural Areas and Preserves, and M. Chadbourne.

[3] Historic Preservation Services, National Park Service, *Common Questions and Answers*, 4. Download this nine-page list of questions & answers about historic preservation from Web Site: <<http://www2.cr.nps.gov/nhl/quanda. htm>>.

[4] Ibid., 4.

[5] Ohio Canal Corridor, *How Was the Heritage Corridor Designated?*, 1-2. Downloaded September 14, 1999 from Web Site: <<http://www.ohiocanal.org/ designated.html>>.

[6] Ohio & Erie Canal Association, *Application for Ohio & Erie Canal Corridor Implementation Funds*, 1. Downloaded September 14, 1999 from Web Site: <<http://www.ohiocanal.org/grantapplication.html>>.

TRANSFER OF DEVELOPMENT RIGHTS

OBJECTIVE: To guide development away from threatened resources, such as farmland, environmentally sensitive areas, scenic views, forests, coastal areas, reservoir watersheds, wetlands, and historic sites and toward areas that can accommodate growth.

WHO ENACTS IT: Predominantly counties, municipalities, and townships with private landowners, developers, and realtors. By 1999, some 40 local jurisdictions in the U.S. have *TDR* enabling legislation. Ohio does not.

HOW IT WORKS: *TDR* programs accomplish the same purpose as an *agricultural conservation easement*: they prevent nonagricultural development of farmland, reduce the market value of the protected farms, and provide landowners with capital that can be used to enhance farm viability. They differ from *agricultural easements* because they involve the private market. Most *TDR* transactions are between private landowners and developers. In this way, local governments do not have to raise taxes or borrow funds to protect land. A few jurisdictions, however, do buy *development rights* with public funds and then sell the rights to private owners.[1]

Like other easement programs, *TDR* is based on an owner's bundle of rights to use, sell, and lease those rights separately. Each parcel of land in a region is assigned a specific number of *development rights* based on the market value or acreage of the land. The rights, in turn, can then be bought or sold, just like the deed to the property, and if they are *development rights*, then the property no longer can be developed.

TDR programs result from comprehensive planning and, therefore, differ from one another due to local variations. The common elements are: (1) a "Sending Area"—an area where a resource is to be protected; (2) a "Receiving Area"—the place to which development is transferred; (3) "Credits"—the transferable and marketable *development rights*; and (4) a procedure by which the development credit is actually transferred. This requires a developer in a receiving zone to purchase *development rights* if he wishes to exceed the base density zoning. The landowner selling the *development rights* receives income and the developer buying the rights can construct more housing to increase his profitability.[2]

ADVANTAGES: Unlike *cluster development zoning*, which protects land parcel by parcel, *TDR* can help to preserve large tracts of open space in a community. This program provides financial incentives both to the sending and to the receiving land owners, without the requirement of the local jurisdiction to raise the funds for that transaction.

DISADVANTAGES: *TDR* programs are very complex and can be difficult to administer. They should first be part of an overall growth management plan within a comprehensive plan with tight zoning ordinances to support the stakeholders. Then, landowners in the sending area should be able to understand the implications for their property, i.e., that it is under threat of development, so that they have a motivation to sell. And, the public within the receiving areas must welcome the potential for increased development where they live.

CASE HISTORY: In Montgomery County, Maryland, rapid development around Washington, DC, has strained the county's roads and other public facilities. Between 1979 and 1987, this pressure forced the loss of almost 20% of its agricultural land to urban development.

As a result, the county instituted a *TDR* program in 1983, with the goal of maintaining the viability of farming as a livelihood. The program severely restricts development in preferential agricultural areas, called the "rural density transfer zone," or "sending area." Encompassing two–thirds of the 93,000 acres of active farmland, *development rights* from this sending zone can be purchased for use in undeveloped sites within "growth centers," or "receiving areas." The other one–third of the farmland is close to developed areas and zoned to make room for continued commercial and residential expansion.

Development rights are bought and sold on an open market. Every five acres of land in the sending area equals one *development right* in the receiving area. One *development right* allows the buyer to build one additional residential unit over the maximum permitted by the base zone. At the present time, *development rights* are sold for between $7,000 to $8,000 each by real estate brokers for the sales commission. Others besides the real estate brokers may also make transactions.

The results? Since 1983, thousands of transactions have taken place; a total of 40,583 acres of active farmland are permanently preserved in deed restrictions.

Altogether, the *TDR* Program in Montgomery County works to protect agricultural land and open space, while encouraging growth in the areas that can best support it. (*Case History Source*: Jeremy V. Criss, Agricultural Services Mgr., Montgomery County Department of Economic Development, Ste. 1500, 101 Monroe St., Rockville, MD 20850; Tel: 301-590-2823; Fax: 301-590-2839.)

ACTION STEPS: A variety of hardcopy and online and publications are available on *transfer of development rights*. Obtain a copy of Tom Daniels' and Deborah Bowers' *Holding Our Own: Protecting America's Farms and Farmlands*, published in April 1997 by Island Press, Tel: 202-234-1328; E-mail: <<info@islandpress.org>>; Web Site: <<http://www.islandpress.com>>. Also, contact the American Planning Association for a copy of its Planning Advisory Service report No. 401, *Transferable Development Rights Programs*, Tel: 202-872-0611; Fax: 202-872-0643; Web Site: <<http://www. planning.org>>. Obtain a copy of, "Making Transferable Development Credits Work: A Study of Program Implementation," *Journal of the American Planning Association*, Vol. 52, No. 2, Spring 1982, 203-211; Tel: the APA at 312-431-9100; Fax: 312-431-9985. Obtain a copy of New Jersey's handbook on *TDR*, available from the Lincoln Institute of Land Policy at 113 Brattle St., Cambridge, MA 02138-3400; Tel: 617-661-3016; Fax: 617-661-7235; Web Site: <<http://www.lincolninst.edu>>; also, download the Institute's *Transfer of Development Rights for Balanced Development* published in the March 1998 issue of *Land Lines*, downloadable from Web Site: <<http://www.lincolninst.edu/landline/1998/march/march4.html>>. And, see the State of Maryland's 33–page *Maryland Agricultural Land Preservation Foundation, Annual Report 1997*, downloadable from Web Site: <<http://www. mda.md.us/agland.annual97.htm>>. See as well Richard James' article, *Transferable Development Rights: A Market Approach to Preserving Farmland and Open Space*, downloadable from Web Site: <<http://www.islandnet.com/~rajames/ite/NO94_DR.html>>.

Other information on *TDR* include these sources: The *Journal of the APA's* "From Landmarks to Landscapes: A Review of Current Practices in the Transfer of Development Rights," Summer 1997, 365-378; J. Stinson et al., *Transfer of Development Rights*, downloadable at Web Site: <<http://www.law.pace.edu/landuse/tdr>>.

html>>; also available from this source is an article titled *Transfer of Development Rights*, downloadable from <<http://www.law.pace. edu/landuse.btdr.html>>; and, the American Farmland Trust's *Transfer of Development Rights Fact Sheet*, downloadable at Web Site: <<http://www.farm.fic.niu.edu/fic-ta/tafs-tdr.html>>. Finally, King County, Washington, has its *TDR* policies and progress reports available at TDR Program, King County Department of Natural Resources, Resource Lands, 506 Second Ave., Ste. 720, Seattle, WA 98104; downloadable reports are available at Web Site: <<http://www.splash.metrokc.gov/wlr/lands/tdrinfo.htm>>. Also, see Michael A. Mantell, Stephen F. Harper, and Luther Propst, *Creating Successful Communities: A Guidebook to Growth Management Strategies* (Washington, DC: Island Press, 1990), 25-27.

NOTES

[1] Farmland Information Center, American Farmland Trust, *Transfer of Development Rights—Fact Sheet*, 1-6. Downloaded August 2, 1999 from AFT Web Site: <<http://www.farm.fic.niu.edu/fic-ta/tafs-tdr.html>>

[2] Amanda Jones Gottsegen, PP, et al., *Planning for Transfer of Development Rights: A Handbook for New Jersey Municipalities* (Mount Holly, NJ: 1992), 9.

V. How Your Local Government Works with Respect to Land Use

I. Some Background on the Kinds of Local Government

There are five kinds of local government in Ohio. Counties, municipalities, and townships are political units of the state. School districts are separate units of government through which the state fulfills its mandated responsibilities for education, with school boards elected locally. Finally, "special districts" are distinct purpose governing bodies independent of any other government unit.[1,2]

- Counties: There are 88 in Ohio.

- Municipalities: These are incorporated cities and villages.

- Townships: Unincorporated areas—there are 1,373 in Ohio.

- School districts: As of 1998, city districts (192 total) exempted village districts (49 total), local districts (371 total); two or more districts may also form a district for vocational education called a joint vocational school district (49 total); educational service centers (formerly called county school districts) provide special services and oversight to local districts in a county or multi-county area.[3]

- Special districts: These include park districts, river watershed districts, regional water and sewer districts, soil and water conservation districts, and conservancy districts (e.g., for flood control, sewage disposal, etc.).

Everyone in Ohio lives in a county. Counties themselves have land–use powers granted by the state. Within counties, municipalities (cities and villages) and townships have powers that affect land use as well.

How Does Government Work in a County, a Municipality, a Township, a School District, or a Special District?

❐ Counties are the major subdivision of the state for administering state laws. They were created by the state, without the consent of the people living within their borders. There are currently three categories of county government available:

- General Law: Used by all counties in Ohio except Summit.
- Home Rule Charter: Only Summit County has elected this method.
- A Form of Government Approved Under the Alternate Forms Law: Currently, no Ohio counties have elected this method.

Under the General Law, three County Commissioners are elected to make and administer county policies about many matters, but land–use issues include annexations, rural zoning, and incorporating cities and villages.

County officers include an auditor, prosecuting attorney, coroner, engineer, clerk of courts, treasurer, sheriff, and recorder. Nearly all of them may be involved in some phase of land use.

❑ Municipalities, also known as "municipal corporations" as well as cities and villages under the Ohio Constitution and the Ohio Revised Code (ORC), are—in contrast to counties—created by their residents who ask the state to recognize an area as incorporated. If approved, people living within them are governed by their elected officials in one of three ways which the voters choose:

- General Plan Law: Mayor–council form of government.
- Home Rule Authority: Cities and villages can elect rules for governing themselves that differ from those under the general law; people elect a "charter" government whose terms are approved by a majority of the voters.
- Optional or Alternative Plan Laws: Three options of governance are available—city manager, commission, and federal forms of government.

Finally, cities have populations over 5,000; villages are under 5,000 inhabitants, both based on the federal census done every 10 years (*Ohio Revised Code*, 703.01).

In some cases, municipalities may undertake *annexation* (adding other land to an existing municipality) and *detachment* (removing an area from a municipality's boundaries). Sections 709.01 through 709.47 describe the legal procedures necessary for either action.

❐ Townships include any land areas within a county that lie outside the boundaries of a city or a village. They govern by two different means:

- *General Law:* Governed by a three–member board of trustees and a clerk elected for four–years, township government responsibilities include fire protection, lighting, roads, zoning, and cemetery care and management.

- *Limited Home Rule Authority for Townships:* On September 17, 1991 through Substitute House Bill No. 77, this form of township government became an option for townships. And, effective September 20, 1999, House Bill 187 modified the procedure for certain townships to adopt limited home rule authority. The latter requires a minimum population of 5,000 in the unincorporated area of the township to adopt the measure. With a 5,000 to 15,000 population, a township's majority of trustees may pass a resolution for a referendum, which, if approved by a majority of voters, commences home rule beginning January 1 of the following year. If the population is greater than 15,000, the trustees may alternatively hold at least one public hearing and then unanimously pass a resolution establishing home rule. This resolution would go into effect within 30 days of passage unless a petition is filed requesting a referendum. Then, with voters' majority approval, home rule begins the next January 1st. This limited home rule township, with more than 15,000 in an unincorporated area, will be called an "Urban Township."[4]

A township under home rule must (1) appoint a lawyer as a part– or full–time township law director (Section 504.15) and (2) establish its own township police district, or a joint police district, or contract for police protection services (Section 504.16). The new HB 187 now allows a home rule township to hire an independent professional engineer to be in charge of or to assist the county engineer with the supervision of, construction, surfacing, or improvement of township roads. Traditionally, the county engineer has been responsible for not only county but also township roads. Also, HB 187 balances the role that home rule townships can take to provide water and sewer services. Before this act, townships could provide water but not sewer services. HB 187 requires the adoption of a general service plan, then notification of the board of county commissioners, or a municipal corporation, or a regional water and sewer district if any or all presently serve the township's planned service area. A comment, objection, and mediation process is stipulated in the bill to determine if the township has grounds on which to justify its provision of water and sewer services. HB 187 allows a home rule township contract for water and sewer services with relatively unlimited authority.[5]

❒ School districts are governmental units created by the state legislature to deliver public education. They are governed under the State Department of Education as well as by a locally elected board of education. The local school board levies taxes and issues bonds, both of which have to be approved by voters, to finance the schools in the district.

❒ Special districts are established to serve a distinct purpose in the communities where created. And, they are created in many different ways, depending on the kind of district: for example, petition by landowners to common pleas court (sanitary district, conservancy district), petition by one or more municipalities or counties to common pleas court (regional water & sewer districts), petition by citizens or governing units to the probate judge. One is even mandatory in each county under Ohio law: soil and water conservation districts. How they are administered and financed is as various as how they are created. For example, the local probate judge appoints a park district's board. It can then levy bond issues, ask voters to approve property tax levies, and make assessments.

II. Planning Commissions

Planning commissions exist at three levels of government: regional, county, and city. An example of one regional planning commission is the Northeast Ohio Areawide Coordinating Agency (NOACA). NOACA serves Cuyahoga, Geauga, Lake, Lorain, and Medina Counties. It is a clearinghouse for the review and processing of federal funding applications on water quality, transportation, and transportation related air quality, seating three commissioners from each of the five member counties. Generally, county planning commissions are responsible for planning studies, mapping, land–use studies, and other zoning–related activities at the county level and for rural areas in the county. County commissioners, who were empowered with zoning authority by the Ohio legislature in 1947, must establish a county zoning commission and a county board of zoning appeals to submit zoning plans and to hear zoning appeals, respectively.[6] Similar provisions apply to townships under ORC 519. Even under county zoning, however, a vote by the residents of the unincorporated area of each township is required before zoning can be instituted.

In municipalities, planning commissions are responsible for coordinating the development of the city. In the case of a city such as Cleveland, if the city planning commission turns down an ordinance or other proposals affecting zoning and public property generally, a two–thirds vote of the Cleveland city council is required to override the item's rejection.[7]

III. Historic & Legislative Basis for Land–Use Decisions in Ohio

Land–use decisions made by governing bodies are of four major kinds, (1) eminent domain, (2) zoning, (3) annexation, detachment, and merger, and (4) ordinances and / or resolutions promulgated under the specific legislative authority of a unit of government—county, municipality, or township.

- Eminent domain: Approved under the Ohio Constitution of 1851. Article I, Section 19 says that the state has the right to take private property for the public welfare, but compensation in money must be made to the owner.[8] Title 3, Section 307.08 of the Ohio Revised Code describes counties' rights to appropriate land for public purposes, while Article XVIII on Municipal Corporations gives municipalities the power of eminent domain in Sections 10 and 11.
- Zoning: Zoning is a legal method to control the use of land.[9] Approved under various sections of the Ohio Revised Code, zoning is "locally enacted law that regulates and controls the use of private property."[10]

  - County zoning: In 1947 the Ohio General Assembly passed legislation allowing counties to zone.[11] The Board of County Commissioners are responsible for county zoning, assisted by a zoning inspector, a zoning commission, and a board of zoning appeals.[12] Under Ohio law, counties and townships may zone rural areas. Enactment of county zoning requires submission of a question for zoning the unincorporated area of each township. It must be approved by a majority in each township.
  - Municipal zoning: Historically, Ohio municipal corporations (cities and villages) were first granted the right to zone within their boundaries by enactment in 1919 (House Bill No. 697 passed

by the Eighty–third General Assembly). It
provided for the city planning commission to
frame and adopt plans to specify, limit, and
regulate uses, building dimensions, and set
backs. It also gave village councils the power to
create a planning commission with the powers set
forth in this act. Various sections allow the
municipality's regulations to prevail over the said
limitation provided by the state statute. Later, the
federal government's 1924 Standard State Zoning
Enabling Act became the basis for zoning
enabling legislation in Ohio and all the states.[13]
Municipal zoning must be approved by a majority
of the residents.

■   Township zoning (rural zoning, zoning in
unincorporated areas): The same legislation
(1947) enabling counties to zone also applied to
townships. Townships, governed by three
township trustees and a clerk, have their own
zoning resolution, zoning inspector, zoning
commission, and board of zoning appeals.[14, 15] As
in counties, zoning resolutions must be approved
through a referendum.

●   Annexation, Detachment, and Merger: Detachment is
removal of land from a municipality and placement back in
the township. Ohio law also allows for the merger of an
existing municipality (city or village) to the remaining
unincorporated area of the township. Chapter 709 of the
Ohio Revised Code addresses how land in a township can
be joined with (annexed into) an existing municipality. The
process requires a petition for annexation signed by a
majority of the property owners within the area to be
annexed. Sponsors then file the petition with the clerk of
the county commissioners who notify the clerk of the
township(s) involved. Next come plat and survey
verification, public hearings, and a vote of the county
commissioners on the action. The general standard for
action by the county commissioners is on the basis of the
"general good of the territory proposed for annexation"
(Section 709.033). Commissioners currently can not
consider the impact on the remainder of the township.
Finally, the county commissioners send notice of their
decision to the annexed area, the township, and the
municipality, with the municipality's own council accepting

or rejecting the measure. If they pass it, notice is sent on to the county auditor and the secretary of state's office.[16]

● Ordinances, resolutions, petitions, contracts and other legislative authorities: Granted under various Articles in the Ohio Constitution or by state law, counties, municipalities, and townships have various powers that affect land use. Whether a municipal zoning ordinance, a joint resolution of county commissioners to form a regional water and sewer district, or the petitioning of the common pleas court by the citizens via their township trustees to set up a township park district—all are authorized under the state constitution and further specified at the local level. Landowners themselves may petition the common pleas court directly to establish conservancy districts for flood control, sewage disposal, or water supplies. Such legislative authorities, or powers, are diverse and have far-reaching consequences for how land is used currently and in the future. (In particular, see the Ohio Constitution, Article II, Sections 1f [municipalities] and 36 [conservation, including forest reserves and other natural resources; and development and regulation of mining, and weighing of coal, oil, gas, and all other minerals]; and Article X, Sections 1 through 4, apply to county, municipal, and township government authorities; Article XIII, Section 6 [organization of cities and villages], and Article XVIII [Municipal Corporations], especially Sections 3 through 11 [powers, public utilities, local self-government, city charters and amendments, and eminent domain])[17]

IV. Zoning Commissions, Zoning Inspectors, Zoning Boards of Appeal

County Zoning: County commissioners are responsible for county zoning. Its administration, too, must comply with the ORC, and its units are a county zoning commission, a county zoning inspector, and a county board of appeals. A county may also have a planning commission to create a county comprehensive plan.[18]

Municipal Zoning: Villages and cities are authorized to administer zoning under the ORC unless they have adopted a home rule charter (i.e, cities and villages can elect rules for governing themselves that differ from those under the general law of the ORC; voters elect a charter government—the terms of which are approved by a majority of the voters—in Ohio, the majority has elected home rule). While township zoning regulations are contained in a resolution and are administered by a township zoning commission, municipal zoning regulations are adopted as a zoning code (or planning and zoning code, or a zoning ordinance), and are administered by a planning commission.[19]

Township Zoning: Township trustees are responsible for township zoning through zoning resolutions. Townships must administer zoning according to the Ohio Revised Code (ORC), unless the township has voted to let the county administer it (ORC 519.01-519.99). The administrative units are a township zoning commission, a township zoning inspector, and a township board of appeals—each with its own resolution.[20]

❐ County Level

- **Planning Commission:** With the passage of Ohio HB 187, effective September 20, 1999, county planning commissions now consist of three county commissioners; three representatives from municipalities (if the population of a city within the county exceeds 50% of the county population, that city shall have at least three representatives selected from city planning commission nominees); three from the unincorporated area of the county, selected from township nominees, with at least one from a limited home rule township—if there are any; two citizens of the county, one in the unincorporated area representing townships and one in the incorporated area representing municipalities, selected by the board of county commissioners. Primary tasks include:

  - Researching and preparing a comprehensive plan
  - Providing the Zoning Commission with a zoning plan, text, and maps for the unincorporated areas of the county

- **Zoning Commission:** It is comprised of five members who reside in the unincorporated area of the county to be zoned, appointed by the board of commissioners. If there is a county planning commission, its members may be selected to serve on the zoning commission. The major responsibilities are:

  - Preparing a zoning plan, with text and maps, for unincorporated areas in the county
  - Holding public hearings in each of the townships affected by the plan

■   Submitting the plan after public hearings to the county planning commission, if there is one, or the regional planning commission for comments. Then, certifying its recommendations to the board of county commissioners for adoption, and after a second hearing for possible changes, submission to a public referendum.

■   Initiating amendments to the zoning text and map, as needed

■   Making formal recommendations on all amendments (text and map) after a public hearing and after receiving the advice of the county or regional planing commission

●   **Board of Zoning Appeals:** The board of county commissioners appoints five residents of the county's unincorporated area with these powers:

■   Hearing and deciding appeals of error in compliance with the resolution

■   Authorizing a variance from the resolution when enforcement would create a "hardship"

■   Granting conditional zoning certificates for specific uses, if they are provided in the zoning resolution's conditions and standards

■   Revoking variances or conditional zoning permits if the condition of the variance or conditional certificate is violated[21]

⬚ **Municipal Level:**

●   **Planning Commission:** City and village planning commissions carry out a range of tasks, such as:

■   Writing zoning ordinances
■   Developing zoning maps
■   Reporting to the public on zoning matters

●   **Zoning Commission:** At this level, commissions may be given assignments including:

■   Conducting development research and other investigations that precede the actual writing of ordinances

■   Holding public hearings before zoning ordinances can become law

- ■ Making recommendations to city or village councils on zoning text and map amendments

- **Zoning Inspector:** Once the zoning code becomes law, the inspector is responsible for the following:

  - ■ Enforcing the current code through inspections Investigation zoning violations
  - ■ Recording violations
  - ■ Reviewing subdivision plats
  - ■ Updating tax records on new permits

- **Board of Zoning Appeals:** The city or village council usually appoints five to this municipal board. Their jobs involve:

  - ■ Hearing appeals from those whose building permits were rejected
  - ■ Holding public meetings for petitions, witnesses, testimony, and other information regarding the appeal
  - ■ Granting variance permits when enforcement would create "unfair hardship"
  - ■ Granting conditional zoning permits for uses specified in the resolution, if standards and conditions are included in the resolution

❐ **Township Level:**

- **Zoning Commission:** Consists of five residents of the unincorporated area appointed for five years, initially in staggered terms so that a new commissioner comes on board each year. Service is unpaid. Responsibilities include:

  - ■ Advising township trustees on zoning matters
  - ■ Preparing zoning resolutions
  - ■ Initiating amendments to the zoning text and map, as needed
  - ■ Making formal recommendations on all amendments (text and map) after hearing and holding a public hearing and receiving the advice of the county or regional planning commission

- **Zoning Inspector:** The zoning inspector, appointed by either the county commissioners or the township trustees, enforces the current zoning resolution. The position is paid, and the inspector, who need not be a resident of the township or county, may inspect zoning for more than one governmental unit (city, township). Duties include:

  - Reviewing zoning permit applications
  - Conducting site inspections
  - Investigating zoning violations
  - Keeping a record of nonconforming uses, i.e., uses that violate the current zoning resolution (they are allowed if they existed before the resolution was adopted, but not if created afterward)
  - Keeping an updated zoning map and zoning resolution text
  - Proposing amendments
  - Reviewing subdivision plats
  - Cooperating with the county auditor so that tax records are updated regularly on the basis of new permits granted

- **Board of Zoning Appeals:** Administered by five members who must be residents of the township (and also appointed in staggered terms so that one is replaced each year), the Ohio Revised Code grants them powers to include:

  - Reviewing appeals of a zoning inspector's decision
  - Granting variances from the zoning resolution in cases of "hardship"
  - Granting conditional zoning permits for uses specified in the resolution, if standards and conditions are included in the resolution
  - Board actions may be appealed in the Common Pleas Court[22]

V. Enforcement and Penalties for Zoning Violations

Enforcing zoning codes is not only the responsibility of appointed and elected officials, but also of citizens. A zoning inspector may find violations at a site visit, but identifying violations has also become the activity of many citizen groups concerned with maintaining property values and the characteristics of the community. Problems may include malodorous septic outfalls into ditches, a garage or fence built too close to a neighbor's property line, junk vehicles lining a driveway, illegal dumping of garbage—all are reportable, some to the health department, some to the police. Some problems are not zoning matters: for example, deed restriction violations do not fall under the purview of a city's zoning ordinance.[23] (Rather, these are civil suits, contractual violations.) Residents should acquaint themselves with their local zoning ordinances, purchasing copies through the township, village, city, or county.

Civil penalties normally run between $25 to $100 per offense, varying by state. Criminal fines may be much larger, with amounts, jail sentences, "community service" requirements, and other punishments determined by the courts. For an excellent overview of civil and criminal penalties for zoning violations, the issues involved, and the importance of enforcement actions by private citizens in resolving zoning or land–use violations, see Eric D. Kelly's book, *Enforcing Zoning and Land–Use Controls* (American Planning Association, **Action Center Resources**).

NOTES

[1] Damaine Vonada, ed., *The Ohio Almanac* (Wilmington, OH: Orange Frazer Press, 1992) 52-55.

[2] League of Women Voters of Ohio, *Know Your Ohio Government* (Columbus, OH: League of Women Voters of Ohio Education Fund, 1987) 68-95.

[3] Telephone conversation October 1, 1999, between Jack Gleason, Ohio Department of Education, and M. Chadbourne.

[4] Ohio Revised Code, 504.01 and 504.02. Available at Web Site: <<http://www.orc.avv.com>> and from *County Advisory Bulletin 99-10*; for a copy, contact the County Commissioners Association of Ohio, 37 W. Broad St., Suite 650, Columbus, OH 43215-4132; Tel: 614-221-5627; Fax: 614-221-6986;
E-mail: <<webmaster@ccao.org>>; or may be downloaded from Web Site: <<http://www.ccao.org>>.

[5] Ibid.

[6] See planning commission functions in Titles 3, 5, and 7 of the Ohio Revised Code, using ORC search engine at Web Site: <<http://www.orc.avv.com>>.

[7] Leslie Kay, ed., *A Citizen's Guide to Cleveland*, (Cleveland, OH: League of Women Voters Educational Fund of Cleveland, Inc., 1992), 50-58.

[8] See Article 1, Section 19 of the Ohio Constitution at Web Site: <<http://www.legislature.state.oh.us/constitution.cfm?Part=1&Section=19>>.

[9] Ibid., 8.

[10] Ibid., 2.

[11] Ibid., 2.

[12] Ibid., 8.

[13] Ibid., 1.

[14] Ibid., 8.

[15] Ohio Revised Code, Section 713.23, 1-2. Downloaded September 30, 1999 from Web Site: <<http://www.orc.avv.com>>.

[16] Ohio Revised Code, Title 7, 1-31. Downloaded September 30, 1999 from Web Site <<http://www.orc.avv.com>>.

[17] Ohio Constitution, Articles 2, 13, and 18. Downloaded September 30, 1999 from Web Site: <<http://www.legislature.state.oh.us/constitution.cfm?Part= 2>>; << . . . Part=13>>; and <<. . . Part=18>>.

[18] Terry Jacobs, ed., *Ohio Rural Zoning Handbook* (Columbus, OH: Ohio Department of Development, 1991), 8.

[19] Ohio State University Extension (J. Stamm), *Zoning*, CDFS-1265-99 (April 1999), 1-3. Available from the "Land Use Series" of Fact Sheets, Ohio State University Extension, Community Development, 700 Ackerman Road, Columbus, OH 43202-1578; Web Site: <<http://ohioline.ag.ohio-state.edu>>.

[20] Ibid.

[21] Ibid.

[22] Jacobs, 8.

[23] Eric D. Kelly, *Enforcing Zoning and Land-use Controls* (Chicago, IL: American Planning Association, 1988), 19-20.

VI. ACTION CENTER RESOURCES

VI–A: Funding Sources for Protecting Rural and Urban Land

VI–B: Agencies, Organizations, Publications, and Internet Start–up & Use

Community Supported Agriculture Programs
Computer–Based Resources: The Internet & World Wide Web
Conservancy Districts
Farm Bureaus
Farmers' Markets in Ohio
Historic Preservation Resources
Land Trusts
Metropolitan Planning Organizations
Ohio's Forests
Ohio's Nature Preserves
Ohio's Scenic Rivers
Ohio State University Extension Offices
Organizations & Publications Interested in Land–Use Issues
Park Districts
Parks
Planning Commissions & Councils—County & Regional
Resource Conservation & Development Councils
Soil and Water Conservation Districts and Natural Resources
        Conservation Service Offices
Watershed Protection Organizations

VI–C: Glossary of Land–Use Terms

VI–D: Map of Ohio Counties

VI–A: FUNDING SOURCES FOR PROTECTING RURAL AND URBAN LAND

(**Authors' Note:** In the earlier Section IV, a number of the tools have funding or tax benefits associated with them. Though some are also mentioned below, Section IV provides additional details and contact information about them.)

OBJECTIVE: To preserve land for farming, open space, its cultural or natural history value, or to manage sensitive areas for their contribution to the quality of water, soil, and air resources, and overall ecosystem health.

WHO ENACTS IT: Individual citizens, government entities (such as townships, villages, cities, and counties), nonprofit organizations and others (also known as NGOs, nongovernmental organizations), educational institutions, businesses, and consortiums composed of combinations of the above.

HOW IT WORKS: Funding can come from many sources, such as an individual donor, a community, a company, a government agency, a foundation, a university, or citizens sponsoring a referendum on a ballot that passes successfully and funds a project with bonds or millage.

Those wishing to fund projects successfully will usually find they must answer these questions about the project: (1) what the project is, its description; (2) why it is needed; (3) what work must be done; (4) who will do the work, their qualifying credentials, and what person or group will manage the project's financial accounting and, if required, report writing, (5) who will benefit from the project; (6) what the project will cost and in what cost categories, by percentage, the funds will be spent, (7) what other sources of funding have been secured.

With these questions answered, it is possible to look at many different sources for financial support. Although some funding agencies will make grants to individuals, often the applicant must be a public agency or a nonprofit organization. So, an individual may come up with a land preservation idea, but to fund it he or she may have to find an organization willing to take on the project and to apply for the funds, such as a local land trust or park district.

Direct Donations of Land: What's in It for the Donor?

Land owners, such as individuals or companies or government agencies, all can make donations of land. The job of the project champion is to convince the potential givers that something they value will be achieved. A donor's motivations may not always be environmental. A company may make a donation "to be a good citizen of the community," e.g., by donating land for play fields. A township might donate a few acres of land for a park in an adjacent community with the understanding that the township will receive a benefit in exchange, e.g., the adjacent community might grant access for traffic right–of–way. Individual donors may value the recognition of their gift as a matching contribution to the grant requirement. In addition, private donations may be eligible for tax write–offs, depending on the donor's financial situation and filing status. Qualified tax lawyers or accountants can determine these benefits for individuals and companies. Overall, it is helpful to explore the feasibility of the many benefits possible before approaching the potential donor.

Grants: Foundations, such as the George Gund Foundation in Cleveland and the Lake Erie Protection Fund in Ohio (which provided a grant for this book revision); state agencies, such as the Ohio Environmental Protection Agency; and granting agents of multi–government agencies, such as the Great Lakes Protection Fund, usually publish "guidelines" for grant applicants. Guidelines tell who may and may not apply, what activities are eligible for grants and which are not, what the cap is on individual projects, what the project duration is, reporting requirements, deadlines for applications, specific formats for writing the proposal, as well as any pre–proposal requirements and, if so, a prescribed format for them. Preproposals typically consist of a letter and a brief one– to three–page proposal summary. Submitters of favorably reviewed preproposals will be invited to submit a full proposal. This screening process saves both the applicant and the granting agency time and resources.

Sources of Funding:

The following organizations offer lists of funding sources, including Web–site "hyperlinks" (see Part VI–B, "Computer–Based Resources: The Internet & World Wide Web," below) to many of the foundations' and agencies' own Web sites:

Council on Foundations. 1828 L St., NW, Washington, DC 20038; Tel: 202-466-6512; Web Site: <<http://www.cof.org>>. A nonprofit membership association of grantmaking foundations and corporations. Its Web site includes a map for finding grant money sources in one's community, including: community foundations, corporate foundations / giving programs, family foundations, private operating foundations, private independent foundations, public foundations, and international programs.

The Foundation Center. 79 Fifth Ave., New York, NY 10003; Tel: 212-620-4230; Fax: 212-691-1821; Web Site: http://www. fdncenter.org>>. A library of hardcopy and computer–based records on grantmaking organizations, including records of past giving, guidelines of foundations, etc. Has access to over 200 libraries nationwide, with computer access available in its regional centers, listed below:

> **Atlanta.** 50 Hurt Plaza, Ste. 150, Atlanta, GA 30303; Tel: 404-880-0094; Fax: 404-880-0097; Web Site: <<http:// www.fdncenter.org/atlanta>>.

> **Cleveland.** 1422 Euclid Ave., Ste. 1356, Cleveland, OH 44115-2001; Tel: 216-861-1933; Fax: 216-861-1936; Web Site: <<http://www.fdncenter.org/cleveland>>.

> **New York.** (See address above)

> **San Francisco.** 312 Sutter St., San Francisco, CA 94108-4314; Tel: 415-397-0902; Fax: 415-397-7670; Web Site: <<http://www.fdncenter.org/sanfrancisco>>.

> **Washington, DC** 1001 Connecticut Ave. at K St., Ste. 938, Washington, DC 20036; Tel: 202-331-1400; Fax: 202-331-1739; Web Site: <<http://www.fdncenter.org/ washington>>.

Great Lakes / Big Rivers, Region 3, U.S. Fish & Wildlife Service. 1 Federal Dr., BHW Federal Bldg., Fort Snelling, MN 55111; Tel: 612-713-5360; E-mail: <<r3_pao@fws.gov>>; Web Site: <<http://www.Fws.gov/r3pao/level1/fed-aid.htm>>. The Federal Aid Division grant programs focus on habitat and species management, and the Division typically works with state fish and wildlife agencies on projects.

Great Lakes Information Network. Michael J. Donahue, Exec. Dir., 400 Fourth St., Ann Arbor, MI 48103-4816; Tel: 734-665-9135; Fax: 734-665-4370; E-mail: <<glc@great-lakes.net>>; Web Site: <<http://www.glc.org/>>. The Great Lakes Information Network, a project of the Great Lakes Commission, is a valuable source of funding leads for the Great Lakes area in these categories: academic sources, foundations, government sources, fellowships, and scholarships. Its listings for most sources in the first three categories appear below, after the contact information for the GLIN. (The complete listing may be downloaded directly from the Internet at Web Site: <<http://www.great-lakes.net/research/ funding.html>>.) We have added some other Great Lakes–based sources to this list as well.

Academic Sources

• **Michigan Sea Grant**. Russell Moll, Dir., University of Michigan, 2200 Bonisteel Blvd., Ann Arbor, MI 48109-2099; Tel: 734-763-1437; Fax: 734-647-0768; Web Site: <<www.engin.umich.edu/seagrant/>>.

• **University of Wisconsin Sea Grant Institute**. Anders W. Andren, Dir., Sea Grant Institute, University of Wisconsin—Madison, 1975 Willow Dr., 2nd Floor, Madison, WI 53706-1177; Tel: 608-262-0905; Fax: 608-262-0591; Web Site: <<http://www.seagrant.wisc.edu>>.

Foundations

• **Center for Field Research**. 680 Mt. Auburn St., P.O. Box 9104, Watertown, MA 02471; Tel: 617-926-8200; Fax: 617-926-8532; E-mail: cfr@ earthwatch.org; Web Site: <<http://www.earthwatch.org/cfr>>.

• **Charles Stewart Mott Foundation**. 1200 Mott Foundation Bldg., Flint, MI 48502-1851; Tel: 810-238-5651; Fax: 810-766-1753; Web Site: <<http://www.mott. org>>.

• **The Cleveland Foundation**. 1422 Euclid Ave., Ste. 1400, Cleveland, OH 44115-2001; Tel: 216-861-3810; E-mail: <<askcf@clevefdn.org>>; Web Site: <<http://www. clevelandfoundation.org>>. A community–based foundation that serves the Greater Cleveland area.

• **Community of Science**. 1629 Thames St., Ste. 200, Baltimore, MD 21231; Tel: 410-563-2378; Fax: 410-563-5389; Web Site: <<http://www.cos.com>>.

• **Council of Michigan Foundations**. One South Harbor Ave., Ste. 3, Grand Haven, MI 49417; Tel: 616-842-7080; Web Site: <<http://www.cmif.org>>.

• **Donors Forum of Chicago & Donors Forum Library**. 208 LaSalle St., Ste. 740 (Library, Ste. 735), Chicago, IL 60604; Tel: 312-578-0175; Fax: 312-578-0158; Web Site: <<http://www.donorsforum.org>>.

• **German Marshall Fund of the United States**. 11 DuPont Circle, NW, Ste. 750, Washington, DC 20036; Tel: 202-745-3950; Fax: 202-265-1662; E-mail: <<info@gmfus.org>>; Web Site: <<http://www.gmfus/org>>. To date, environmental grants have been to projects that address global warming.

• **Great Lakes Aquatic Habitat Network & Fund**. Tip of the Mitt Watershed Council, P.O. Box 300, Conway, MI 49722; Tel: 616-347-1181; Fax: 616-347-5928; E-mail: <<water@freeway.net>>; Web Site: <<http://www.glhabitat.org>>. For grassroots citizens' initiatives to protect and restore Great Lakes shorelines, inland lakes, rivers, wetlands, and other aquatic habitats in the Great Lakes Basin.

• **Great Lakes Protection Fund**. 35 E. Wacker Dr., Ste. 1880, Chicago, IL 60601; Tel: 312-201-0660; Web Site: <<http://wwwglpf.org>>. For projects that enhance the health of the Great Lakes ecosystem.

• **The George Gund Foundation**. 1845 Guildhall Bldg., 45 Prospect Ave., West, Cleveland, OH 44115; Tel: 216-241-3114; Fax: 216-241-6560; E-mail: <<info@gundfdn.org>>; Web Site: <<http://www.gundfdn.org>>. Historically has given to local and national environmental projects. Its primary grantmaking emphasis is in the Cleveland bioregion for the protection of ecosystems and natural features.

• **Illinois Humanities Council**. 203 N. Wabash Ave., Ste. 2020, Chicago, IL 60601-2417; Tel: 313-422-5580; Web Site: <<http://www.prairie.org>>.

• **The Joyce Foundation**. Three First National Plaza, 70 West Madison St., Ste. 2750, Chicago, IL 60602; Tel: 312-782-2464; Fax: 312-782-4160; Web Site: <<http://www.joycefdn.org>>. Supports efforts to strengthen public policies in ways that improve the quality of life in the Great Lakes region.

• **Lake Erie Protection Fund**. Ohio Lake Erie Office, One Maritime Plaza, Toledo, OH 43604-1866; Tel: 419-245-2514; Web Site: <<http://www.epa.state.oh.us/oleo/lepf1. htm>>. Awards small and large grants to help the state of Ohio protect and enhance Lake Erie.

• **John D. & Catherine T. MacArthur Foundation**. Office of Grants Management, 140 S. Dearborn St., Chicago, IL 60603; Tel: 312-726-8000; Fax: 312-920-6285; Web Site: <<http://www.macfdn.org>>.

• **National Environmental Education and Training Foundation**. 734 15th St., NW, Ste. 420, Washington, DC 20005; Tel: 202-628-8200; Fax: 202-628-8204; E-mail: <<neetf@neetf.org>>; Web Site: <<http://www. conservenow.org/environmental_education.html>>. Authorized by the U.S. Congress in 1990, the Foundation's mission is the attainment of essential environmental knowledge by all Americans to ensure a prosperous, healthy, and sustainable future.

• **National Fish and Wildlife Foundation**. National Program Partnership Office, 1120 Connecticut Ave, NW, Ste. 900, Washington, DC 20036; Tel: 202-857-0166; Fax: 202-857-0162; Web Site: <<http://www.nfwf.org>>. Promotes conservation and sustainable use of our natural resources through environmental education, natural resources management, habitat protection, ecosystem restoration, and public policy development.

• **Northwest Area Foundation**. 332 Minnesota St., Ste. E-1201, St. Paul, MN 55101-1373; Tel: 651-224-9635; Fax: 651-225-3881; E-mail: <<info@nwaf.org>>; Web Site: <<http://www.nwaf.org>>. Seeks to help communities most in need of creating positive futures—economically, ecologically, and socially.

• **Pew Charitable Trusts**. 2005 Market St., Ste. 1700, Philadelphia, PA 19103-7070; Tel: 215-575-9050; E-mail: <<webmaster@pewtrusts.org>>; Web Site: <<http://www. pewtrusts.org>>.

Government–Based Funding Sources

• **Federal Information Exchange**. 555 Quince Orchard Rd., Ste. 360, Gaithersburg, MD 20878; Tel: 800-875-2562 or 301-975-0103; Fax: 301-975-0109; Web Site: <<http://www.fie.com>.

• **EcoAction 2000—Ontario Region**. Environment Canada, 4905 Dufferin St., Downsview, Ontario M3H 5T4 CANADA; Tel: 800-661-7785 or 416-739-4734; Fax: 416-739-4781; E-mail: <<ecoaction2000@ec.gc.ca>>; Web Site: <<http://www.cciw.ca/ecoaction>>.

• **National Science Foundation**. 4201 Wilson Blvd., Arlington, VA 22230; Tel: 703-306-1234; Web Site: <<http://www.nst.gov/home/grants.htm>>.

Independent Sector. 1200 Eighteenth St., Ste. 200, Washington, DC 20036; Tel: 202-467-6100; Fax: 202-467-6101; Web Site: <<http://www.indepsec.org>>. A membership organization that brings together foundations, nonprofit groups, and corporate giving programs to support philanthropy, volunteering, and citizen action.

Nonpoint Source Pollution & Conservation Project Funding Sources. (**Source:** Ohio EPA's Division of Surface Water's *A Guide to Developing Local Watershed Action Plans in Ohio*, Ohio DNR's *Ohio Department of Natural Resources—Grant Opportunities*, available at Web Site: <<http://www.dnr.state.oh.us/odnr/grant.htm>>; and Internet searches)

• **Agricultural Pollution Abatement Cost Sharing Program**. Kevin Elder, ODNR, Division of Soil and Water Conservation, 1939 Fountain Square Ct., Bldg. E-2, Columbus, OH 43224-1336; Tel. 614-265-6617.

• **Conservation Reserve Program**. See program details in Section IV–A–2, above.

• **Environmental Quality Incentives Program**. USDA Farm Service Agency (FSA), Ohio Office, Federal Bldg., 200 N. High St., Room 540, Columbus, OH 43215; Tel: 614-469-6735; or Natural Resources Conservation Services (NRCS), Ohio Office, 200 N. High St., Rm. 522, Columbus, OH 43215-2478; Tel: 614-469-6932. Financial assistance for erosion control and sedimentation, promotion of nutrient management.

• **NatureWorks (State Bond Issue 1).** Mike Cook, ODNR, Division of Real Estate & Land Management, Building C, 1952 Belcher Dr., Columbus, OH 43224-1386; Tel: 614-265-6395; Fax: 614-267-4764. Watershed management, streambanking, precision farming, manure brokerages.

• **Nonpoint Source Education Grants.** ODNR, Division of Soil and Water Conservation, E-2, Fountain Square Ct., Columbus, OH 43224; Tel: 614-265-6610. Nonpoint source education.

• **Nonpoint Source Watershed Grants Program.** ODNR, Division of Soil and Water Conservation, E-2, Fountain Square Ct., Columbus, OH 43224; Tel: 614-265-6610.

• **Ohio Water Pollution Control Loan Fund.** OEPA, Division of Environmental and Financial Assistance, P.O. Box 1049, Columbus, OH 43216-1049; Tel: 614-644-2798. Landfill closure, wellhead protection, upgrading on–site water treatment systems, etc.

• **Ohio Water Pollution Control Loan Fund, Linked Deposit Program.** OEPA, Division of Environmental and Financial Assistance, P.O. Box 1049, Columbus, OH 43216-1049; Tel: 614-644-2798. Nonpoint source pollution control, agricultural best management practices and other projects on private land.

• **PL–566 Small Watershed Program.** Natural Resources Conservation Service, Ohio Office, 200 N. High St., Rm. 522, Columbus, OH 43215-2478; Tel: 614-469-6962. Planning and implementing improvement, protection, development, and use of land and water resources in small watersheds.

• **Research and Development Grant.** Ohio Water Development Authority, 88 East Broad St., Ste. 1300, Columbus, OH 43215-3516; Tel: 614-466-5822; Fax: 614-644-9964.

• **Section 314 (Clean Lakes).** Ohio EPA, Division of Surface Water, P.O. Box 1049, Columbus, OH 43216-1049; Tel: 614-644-2001. Lake water quality assessment, sampling, diagnostic studies, implementation, and monitoring projects.

• **Section 319 Nonpoint Source**. Ohio EPA, Division of Surface Water, P.O. Box 1049, Columbus, OH 43216-1049; Tel: 614-644-2001. Watershed–wide nonpoint source pollution projects.

• **State Cost Share Program (House Bill 88)**. ODNR, Division of Soil and Water Conservation, E-2, Fountain Square Ct., Columbus, OH 43224; Tel: 614-265-6610. Grants to individual farmers for erosion and animal waste using best management practices.

• **Stewardship Incentives Program**. Contacts: A joint project of the Ohio Department of Natural Resources, Division of Forestry; Tel: 614-265-6694; Ohio EPA, Division of Surface Water; Tel: 614-644-2001; and the Farm Service Agency, Tel: 614-469-6735. Tree planting for windbreaks, soil erosion control, riparian corridors, and wildlife habitat.

• **Sustainable Development Challenge Grants**. Lynn Desaulels, Office of Administration, U.S. EPA, 401 M St., SW, Washington, DC 20460-0003; Tel: 202-260-6995; Web Site: <<http://www.aspe/hhs.gov/cfda/p66651.htm>>. Objectives are (1) to catalyze community–based and regional projects that promote sustainable development, thereby improving environmental quality and economic prosperity; (2) to leverage significant private and public investments to enhance environmental quality by enabling community sustainability efforts to continue past EPA funding; (3) to build partnerships that increase a community's long–term capacity to protect the environment through sustainable development; and (4) to enhance EPA's ability to provide assistance to communities and promote sustainable development through lessons learned. Eligible applicants include community groups and other nonprofit organizations, local governments, universities, tribes, and States.

• **Wetland Reserve Program**. See program details in Section IV–A–2, above.

Ohio Department of Natural Resources. Publications Center, 1952 Belcher Dr., Bldg. C-1, Columbus, OH 43224; Tel: 614-265-6565; Fax: 614-268-1943; Web Site: <<http://www.dnr.state.oh.us>>.

Ohio Environmental Education Fund, Ohio EPA. Carolyn Watkins, Chief, 122 South Front St., 6th Floor, P.O. Box 1049, Columbus, OH 43216-1049; Tel: 614-644-2873; Fax: 614-644-3687; E-mail: <<carolyn.watkins@epa.state.oh. us>> Web Site: <<http://www.epa.state.oh.us/other/oeemain.html>>.

Ohio Environmental Protection Agency. Mailing address: Lazarus Government Center, P.O. Box 1049, Columbus, OH 43216-1049; Street address: Lazarus Government Center, 122 South Front St., Columbus, OH 43215; Tel: 614-644-3020; Fax: 614-644-2329; Web Site: <<http://www.epa.ohio.gov>>. Consult its "topics" page under "G" for grants for programs available at Web Site: <<http://www.epa.ohio.gov/new/topics.html>>.

Program Guide to Federally Funded Environment and Natural Resources R&D. c/o Exec. Secretary, Committee on Environment and Natural Resources, National Oceanic and Atmospheric Administration (NOAA), Office of Policy and Strategic Planning, U. S. Department of Commerce, Washington, DC 20230; Tel: 202-482-5917; Fax: 202-482-1156; Web Site: <<http://wwwgcrio.org/ USCRP/CENR/proguide96/toc.html>>. Listing of programs by federal departments that are supported by those agencies in environmental and natural resources areas. Provides hyperlinks to: National Science Foundation, Environmental Protection Agency, Department of the Interior, Department of Commerce/NOAA, Department of Agriculture, Department of Energy, and others.

USDA Nonprofit Gateway. U.S. Department of Agriculture, 14th & Independence Ave., SW, Washington, DC 20250; Tel: 202-720-2791; Web Site: <<http://wwwusda.gov/nonprofit.htm>>. Includes grant monies available in business, community development, research & education, and the volunteer sector.

U.S. EPA, Great Lakes Program Funding. EPA Headquarters: 401 M St., SW, Washington, DC 20460-0003; Tel: 202-260-2090; Web Site: <<http://www.epa.gov/epahome/postal.htm>>. The site lists requests for proposals (RFPs), Great Lakes project requirements, etc. The 10 EPA Regions are listed at the Web site, along with the states they represent. Contact information for the eight states in the Great Lakes Basin (IL, IN, MI, MN, OH, PA, NY, WI) is provided below:

> **Region 2 (NJ, NY, PR, VI).** 290 Broadway, New York, NY 10007-1866; Tel: 212-637-3000; Fax: 212-637-3526; Web Site: <<http://www.epa.gov/region02>>.

Region 3 (DC, DE, MD, PA, VA, WV). 1650 Arch St., Philadelphia, PA 19103-2029; Tel: 800-438-2474 or 215-814-5000; Fax: 215-814-5103; Web Site: <<http://www.epa.gov/region03>>.

Region 5 (IL, IN, MI, MN, OH, WI). 77 West Jackson Blvd., Chicago, IL 60604-3507; Tel: 312-353-2000; Fax: 312-353-4135; Web Site: <<http:// www.epa.gov/ Region05>>.

VI–B: AGENCIES, ORGANIZATIONS, PUBLICATIONS, AND INTERNET START–UP & USE

COMMUNITY SUPPORTED AGRICULTURE PROGRAMS

Farmers who are committed to keeping their land in farming have struggled with ways to make their businesses economically viable. At the same time, people who value the taste and health benefits of fresh produce, much of it organically grown, have been looking for ways to buy fresh foods and to support the farmers who produce it. A solution for both farmers and consumers, "community sustained agriculture" (CSA) programs, allow people to become shareholders in a farm's production, their share investments providing them with fresh fruits, vegetables, and in some cases dairy products, eggs, honey, and organically grown meats.

This economic relationship between the farmer and shareholder also holds the potential for building important social relationships among the farmer, the shareholder families, and the "drop off group" where shares are delivered for pick up by those who cannot "pick their own."

Depending on a particular program's requirements, some levels of shareholders perform farm work, such as weeding, harvesting, and preparing share bundles for delivery. Ultimately, the social and economic relationships and the benefits of hands–on, direct experience on the farm by children and adults of all ages, helps to build value in and commitment to keeping farmland in production and to providing people with the fresh, healthful food sources.

Share prices vary from program to program, but they may range from $90 to $600 a season, with many options in between. CSA program farmers normally have literature they will provide upon request about their programs rates, products available, work requirements, and drop–off sites, and other program details.

The U.S. Department of Agriculture's Sustainable Agriculture Research and Education (SARE) Program works to distribute information about CSAs and other economically viable farming programs: Sustainable Agriculture Research and Education Program. Jill Auburn, Dir., National Office, USDA, Room 3868 South Bldg., Ag Box 2223, Washington, DC 20250-2223; tel; 202-720-5203; Fax: 202-720-6071; E-mail: <<jauburn@reeusda.

gov>>; Web Site: <<http://www.sare.org>>). A list of Ohio CSA's follows below. Those interested in becoming shareholders should contact the farm owners directly (county locations follow each entry in parenthesis). In addition, see "Organizations & Publications with Land-Use Interests," below, for further references on sustainable agriculture.

Ashbrook Bio–Dynamic Farm. Elbert P. Crary, 10089 Bartholomew Rd., Chagrin Falls, OH 44023; Tel: 440-543-8369. (Geauga)

Autumn Harvest Farm. Beth & Marcus Ladrach, 4959 Rice Hill Rd., Wooster, OH 44691; Tel: 330-264-8708. (Wayne)

Beam Road Berry Farm CSA Project. Lyn & Ken Chapis, 5493 Beam Rd., Crestline, OH 44827; Tel: 419-683-2139. (Richland)

Boulder Belt Gardens. Eugene Goodman & Lucy Goodman–Owsley, 4526 Crubaugh Rd., New Paris, OH 45347; Tel: 937-273-3502; E-mail: <<goodows@mailexcite.com>>. (Preble)

Crown Point Ecology Learning Center. David Irvine, 3220 Ira Rd., P.O. Box 484, Bath, OH 44210; Tel: 330-666-9200. (Summit)

Far Corner Farm. Elise McMath and Kevin Smyth, 12788 New England Rd., Amesville, OH 45711; Tel: 740-448-2228; E-mail: <<ab210@seorf.ohiou.edu>>. (Athens)

Fox Run CSA. Ame Vanorio, P.O. Box 457, Kendall Rd., Winchester, OH 45697; Tel: 937-695-1483; E-mail: <<foxrun1@bright.net>>. (Brown)

Grailville Organic Gardens / CSA. Susie Rench or Mary Lu Lageman, 932 O'Bannonville Rd., Loveland, OH 45140; Tel: 513-677-3241. (Clermont)

Hamper Homestead Farm–CSA. Mike & Margaret Hamper, 1507 Lenox–New Lyme Rd., Jefferson, OH 44047; Tel: 440-576-4281. (Ashtabula)

Herb Connection CSA. Don Tarlton, 200 Main St., Springboro, OH 45066; Tel: 513-748-0172 (home); 513-748-4877 (store). (Warren)

Hickory Hollow. Janine Welsby, 42211 Glasgow Rd., Wellsville, OH 43968; Tel: 330-532-9625. (Columbiana)

Katona's Country Garden. Dennis & Jennifer McEndree, 9273 Black Diamond Rd., Marshallville, OH 44645; Tel: 330-855-5811. (Wayne)

Larksong Farm CSA. David & Elsie Kline & family, 8940 County Rd. 235, Fredricksburg, OH 44627. (Holmes)

Mayflag Farms. Fred & Julia Rhoades, 2080 Lombard–Chuckery Rd., Plain City, OH 43064; Tel: 740-857-1596. (Madison)

Meadowlark Farm. Jeff & Jan Goodland Metz, 5144 S. Princeton Rd., Berlin Center, OH 44401; Tel: 330-547-9316; E-mail: <<metzjg @hiram.edu>>. (Mahoning)

Oberlin Sustainable Agriculture Project. Kenneth Sloane, Pres., or Brad Masi, MPO Box 357, Oberlin, OH 44074; Tel: 440-775-4158; E-mail: <<osap@aol.com>>. (Lorain)

Silver Creek Farm. Molly & Ted Bartlett, 7097 Allyn Rd., P.O. Box 254, Hiram, OH 44234-0254; Tel: 330-569-3487; Fax: 330-569-7076; E-mail: <<silvrcf@aol.com>>. (Geauga)

Spruce Hill Farm. Joyce & Greg Studen, 7675 Squires Lane, Novelty, OH 44072; Tel: 440-338-1325. (Geauga)

Sweetbriar Farm. Roy 7 Janet Hahn, 11213 Parkman Rd., Garrettsville, OH 44231; Tel: 330-527-5813; Fax: 330-527-5396. (Portage)

The Farmer Is Adele. Adele Straub, 36089 Neff Rd., Grafton, OH 44044; Tel: 440-926-3316; E-mail: <<FarmerAdele@prodigy. net>>. (Lorain)

Turner Farm CSA. Bonnie Mitsui, 7400 Given Rd., Cincinnati, OH 54243; Tel: 513-561-8482. (Hamilton)

(Sources: *The Many Faces of Community Supported Agriculuture [CSA]: A Guide to Community Supported Agriculture in Indiana, Michigan, and Ohio,* by the Michigan Organic Food and Farm Alliance, Hartland, MI, 1999, 107 pages; ISBN 0-9656980-1-7; Molly & Ted Bartlett, Silver Creek Farm, 7097 Allyn Rd., Hiram, OH 44234-0126; Tel: 3300-569-3487; E-mail: <<silvrcf@aol.com>>.)

COMPUTER–BASED RESOURCES: THE INTERNET & WORLD WIDE WEB

The Internet is a superb, timely source of information about land–use practices, whether the subject is land preservation, farming, smart growth, land banking, reinvestment in our urban centers, or hundreds of other topics of local, national, and international interest. The focus here, briefly, is on (1) what the Internet and World Wide Web are, (2) what's needed to use them, (3) what kind of information one can find on the Internet, and (4) how to get rapid responses to questions. Finally, a list of Web sites related to land–use follows the introduction.

First, if you know nothing about computers but are ready to learn and want practical help written in very simple layman's language, you might try *Computer Friendly*, a brief beginner's handbook / self–taught course that contains what any user needs to know (and no more) about computer hardware; software; the Windows operating system; printers; scanners; the basics of desktop publishing, spreadsheets, and bookkeeping; the Internet, Web browsers, and search engines; plus some simple "projects" ($12.95 plus $3 shipping/handling, Green Tree Press, 3603 West 12th St., Erie, PA 16505, Tel: 800-834-3888; Fax: 814-838-3094). There are many other fine books for beginners available at your local bookstore, but this one is so simple and straightforward that even the most computer–shy will find it helpful.

Once you have a computer, or if you already own one, you may want a complete but easy–to–understand guide to using the Internet. Of use to anyone is *The Farmer's Guide to the Internet, Third Edition*, 1997, by Henry James and Kyna Estes (published by TVA Rural Studies, 400 Agriculture Engineering Building, The University of Kentucky, Lexington, KY 40546-0276 or call 606-257-1872 or e–mail <<tvars@rural.org>>, $19.95 plus $3.95 shipping & handling). It has a simple introduction describing the Internet and the World Wide Web, as well as the computer hardware, software, and phone connections needed to use the Internet. In addition, for farmers and others interested in agricultural issues, there are over 150 pages of Internet addresses for such subjects as "crop resources," "entomology," "farmers online," "forestry," "management and marketing," "market price information," precision farming," "soil and water," and a host of others.

One other online resource is Ohio State University's "Farming the Net" Web site that lists downloadable publications about the Internet, terms and definitions, equipment and software recommendations, and even the basics of constructing a Web page. Its Web site is <<http://www2.ag.ohio-state.edu/~farmnet>>.

Finally, we have used both of these books to guide the discussion that follows about getting, exchanging, and applying online information for making informed decisions about land use.

The Internet and the World Wide Web

The Internet started out as separate collections of information on computers about many subjects, much like separate shelves at a library—math books in one place, history in another. Computers made it possible to wire a single huge computer, which stored all the information, with many small computers in a building, making a *network*. But when people outside the building *also* wanted access for their computers, in another state, for example, a phone line was needed to create an *internet*, or a network of networks.

Over the years, government–sponsored research had generated vast amounts of information, much of it scientific and mathematical, at universities and other research organizations. Because many people outside of these institutions felt this publicly funded information was valuable and wanted to have it at their fingertips, and because computers had become powerful enough to make sharing of the information possible—state to state and around the world—the "Internet," the network of networks, became available to the public.

Once people saw what a fast and comprehensive source of information the Internet could be, they also saw the advantages of being able to have more than just text—words and numbers—on the computer screen. What if you could actually show a photograph of a housing development layout that conserved land and allowed farming of open space to continue? This desire for "graphics" or pictures, and now moving pictures with sound, led computer programmers to create a "web" of graphical computer programs that would allow people simply to "point and click" with their mouse button to move around the Internet. This overlay on the Internet that makes it possible to view graphics and not just text is known as the *World Wide Web*, or the "Web."

What's Needed to Use the Internet and the Web

To use the Internet, you need a computer, a telephone line, a modem—a device that hooks the computer to the telephone line—a software program that communicates between your computer's modem and your telephone line, a subscription to an

"Internet service provider" (ISP), which provides the phone connection from your home telephone line to the ISP phone lines into the Internet, and a "browser," software on your computer that the ISP may also provide. You use the browser once you are connected to the Internet and ready to move about in search of information, to read mail, etc. The browser you use—e.g., Netscape Communicator or Internet Explorer—will allow you to send and receive e–mail, receive newsletters to which you wish to subscribe, and navigate around the Internet.

Web Addresses or "Uniform Resource Locators," URLs

Addresses on the Web are made up of several parts. Let's use the example of the American Farmland Trust's address, <<http://www. farmland.org>>. The << . . . >> enclose the proper form, including any punctuation such as slashes, periods, hyphens, and tilde signs—all these and precise spelling are critical or the address will not be recognized. The first group of letters before the colon and two slashes tell how the files will be transferred, usually by "HyperText Transmission Protocol," or "http." As cited earlier, the "www" stands for World Wide Web; "farmland" is the shortened name, or domain name, of the American Farmland Trust, and "org" indicates that it is not a commercial business but a nonprofit organization. Altogether, "www.farmland.org" is the identity of the server where the AFT Web page resides. (Note: In the early Internet days ".org" was used exclusively by nonprofits, while ".com" was for businesses. Today, you may find nonprofits or commercial entities using ".org," ".com," or even ".net.")

If an organization is a commercial business, its suffix will usually be <<.com>>; if a governmental organization, <<.gov>>; and if an educational entity, <<.edu>>. Addresses may be much longer, with the additional information telling precisely where the page is located. The last item in a long, specific address typically ends with <<.htm>>.

Some National Internet Service Providers:

America On Line, Tel: 800-827-6364; Web Site: <<http://www.aol.com>>
AT&TWorldnet, Tel: 800-967-5363; Web Site: <<http://www.att.net>>
CompuServe, Tel: 800-848-8990; Web Site: <<http:// www.compuserve.com>>
IBM Internet Connection, Tel: 800-821-4612; Web Site: <<http://www.ibm.net>>
Internet MCI, Tel: 800-955-5210; Web Site:

<<http://www.internetmci.com>>
Microsoft Network, Tel: 800-373-3676; Web Site:
<<http://www.msn.com>>
Netcom On-line Comunications, Tel: 800-638-2661;
Web Site: <<http://www.netcom.com>>

An extensive list of Internet service providers, "The List," can be
found at Web Site: <<http://www.thelist.internet.com>>.

Internet Browsers:

Microsoft Internet Explorer, Tel: 425-882-8080; Web
Site: <<http://www.microsoft.com>>
Netscape Communicator, Tel: 650-937-2555; Web Site:
<<http://www.netscape.com>>

Internet Search Engines:

Alltheweb, Web Site: <<http://www.alltheweb.com>>
Alta Vista, Web Site: <<http://www.altavista.com>>
AOLNetFind, Web Site: <<http://www.aolnetfind.com>>
Ask Jeeves, Web Site: <<http://www.askjeeves.com>>
Excite, Web Site: <<http://www.excite.com>>
Hotbot, Web Site: <<http://www.hotbot.com>>
InfoSeek, Web Site: <<http://www.infoseek.com>>
Lycos, Web Site: <<http://www.lycos.com>>
Northernlight, Web Site: <<http://www.northernlignt.
com>>
Snap, Web Site: <<http://www.snap.com>>
Webcrawler, Web Site: <<http://www.webcrawler.com>>
Yahoo, Web Site: <<http://www.yahoo.com>>

A list of several other search engines can be found at Web Site:
<<http://www.theinternetdirectories.com>> or at the "Ask Jeeves"
Web site (above), which featured nearly 70 in a September 1999
query. It also can list engines by their major focus, such as
environmentally related sites, computing, etc.

Once at a Web site you found through a search engine, you are
likely to find underlined and/or different colored text called
"hyperlinks" within the regular text of the Web page. Clicking your
mouse button on these activates the link and will take you directly
to that place at the Web site or to some other Web site altogether,
which is the target of the link you clicked.

There are many sources of computers already packaged for
Internet use, and some of the most dependable and economical

systems are available by mail–order from Dell, Gateway, Micron, and many others. A quick source of such information can be found in standard computer magazines such as *PC Magazine* or *PC World*, available on the newsstand. Generally, because the Internet is so dependent on graphics, computers need both speed and memory to run well. This is also true of the graphics card itself—it should be speedy and have lots of memory. Finally, the modem you buy will run no faster than the telephone line to which you are connected. You need to know how fast your local phone line runs, as well as what speed is available on the Internet service provider lines in your area. Very fast ISDN (i.e., Integrated Service Digital Network) lines are available in some telephone areas, but they'll cost $30 to $60 more per monthly phone bill plus initial setup and installation charges. Cable companies have Internet access available in some areas as well, and the demand for faster connections grows daily. It makes sense to do some initial research to find out what your telephone or cable company can provide right now and in the foreseeable future—and at what likely cost.

As an example of a system with Internet capability, consider the specifications for the system used to search the Internet and to desktop publish this guide, *Common Groundowrk*:

Computer: 400 megahertz Pentium II chip with 512k of cache & 128 megabytes of memory
Graphics card: 66 megahertz chip with 8 megabytes of memory
Modem: originally, a 56k modem; upgraded to an ISDN modem (approximately 128k)
Phone line: Alltel ISDN line (serves modem and fax)
Internet service provider: CoreComm/CompuServe
Browser: CompuServe
Operating system: Windows 98

Conventional systems in late 1999 feature 600 megahertz Pentium III processors.

What You Can Do on the Internet

You can carry out research on virtually any subject via search engines, e–mail, chat rooms, and subscriptions to subject–specific newsletters; view electronic news, have your own Web site. A good source for learning more about the Internet as a tool is the Web Site: <<http://www.internet.com>>.

For anyone interested in land preservation tools, land–use decision–making, and related areas, including preservation of farmland and open space, there are superb resources available online. Some of them can be found in this "Resource Center" as well as in the "Case History" and "Notes" sections of the individual tools featured in this guide in Section IV.

CONSERVANCY DISTRICTS

Citizens or their governmental representatives may petition the Common Pleas Court to establish a conservancy district. Upon court approval, these special districts are then financed through voter–approved bonds and property taxes, with each district setting rates and assessments in its own area of jurisdiction. The 19 regional agencies in Ohio oversee water issues—such as flood control, sewage disposal, and water supply—that affect the health, property, economic viability, and overall quality of life of the region's citizens.

Black Brook Conservancy District. Marianne Berzinskas, Pres., 12012 Mantua Center Rd., Mantua, OH 44255-9303; Tel: 330-562-4574 (Berzinskas residence).

Celeryville Conservancy District. Kenneth Thornton, Secy. & Legal Counsel, 111 Myrtle Ave., P.O. Box 207, Willard, OH 44890; Tel: 419-935-0171 (Thornton office).

East Fork Buck Creek Conservancy District. Daniel Bline, Secy.–Treas., 4820 Allison Road, Mechanicsburg, OH 43044; 513-834-3487 (Bline residence).

Hocking Conservancy District. Terry Courtney, Secy.–Treas., 560 West Union St., Athens, OH 45701; Tel: 614-592-1792 (District office).

Hunter's Run Conservancy District. Edward Rowles, Secy. Treas., 4890 Richland Rd., Pleasantville, OH 43148-9722; Tel: 614-468-3270 (Rowles residence).

Leading Creek Conservancy District. Brent Bolin, Gen. Mgr., 34481 Corn Hollow Rd., Rutland, OH 45775; Tel: 614-742-2411 (District office).

Maumee Watershed Conservancy District. Geraldine M. Landon, Exec. Officer & Secy.–Treas., 1464 Pinehurst Dr., Defiance, OH 43512; Tel: 419-782-8746.

Miami Conservancy District. P. Michael Robinette, Gen. Mgr., 38 East Monument Ave., Dayton, OH 45402; Tel: 937-223-1271 (District office); Web Site: <<http://www.conservancy.com/index. asp>>.

Millcreek Valley Conservancy District. James W. Johns, PE, Chief Engineer Secy., 105 East Fourth St., Ste. 1104-B, Cincinnati, OH 45202; Tel: 513-721-8173 (District office).

Muskingum Watershed Conservancy District. John Hoopingarner, Gen. Mgr. & Secy.–Treas., 1319 Third St. NW, New Philadelphia, OH 44663-0349; Tel: 330-343-6647 (District office).

Reno Beach–Howard Farms Conservancy District. Joretta Warner, Secy.–Treas., 12373 Lagoon Dr., Curtice, OH 43412; Tel: 419-836-7401 (Warner residence).

Rushcreek Conservancy District. James Young, Contracting Officer, 160 Carter St., Bremen, OH 43107; Tel: 614-569-4500 (District office).

Sand Beach Conservancy District. Jane Ruch, Secy.–Treas., 8661 West Sand Beach Rd., Oak Harbor, OH 43449; Tel: 419-898-6752 (Ruch residence).

Shortcreek Watershed Conservancy District. Martin McKim, P.O. Box 488, Adena, OH 43901; Tel: 614-546-3536 (McKim residence).

South Licking Watershed Conservancy District. Gordon Postle, Secy.–Treas., 771 E. Main St., Ste. 100, Newark, OH 43055; Tel: 614-349-6920 (Licking SW District office).

Springfield Conservancy District. Stanley N. Husted II, Secy.–Treas., Ste. 906 BancOhio Bldg., Springfield, OH 45502; Tel: 937-325-7648 (Husted office).

Upper Scioto Drainage and Conservancy District. Gary Oates, Pres., Board of Directors, Number One Courthouse Square, Ste. 338, Kenton, OH 43326; Tel: 419-674-2259.

Wabash River Conservancy District. Cyril Fortkanys, Treas., 14574 St. Rt. 49, Fort Recovery, OH 45846.

Wightman's Grove Conservancy District. Jim Vollmer, Pres., 2158 County Rd. 259, Fremont, OH 43420; Tel: 419-332-5864 (Vollmer residence).

(**Source:** Ohio Division of Natural Resources, Division of Water, Tel: 614-265-6722, June 1999, & Internet Web sites)

FARM BUREAUS

Farm Bureaus at the state and federal levels offer extensive online information for farmers and other interested parties, including many hyperlinks to other Web sites. Some Ohio Farm Bureau hyperlinks by topic include grain / crops, livestock / poultry, fruit / vegetable growers, county extension offices, family, special interests (tractors, pesticides, etc.), universities with agricultural departments, Ohio agriculture commodity facts, and hyperlinks to major search engines for finding topics not covered at the site or for locating additional information on available topics.

The American Farm Bureau Web site has even more subject matter with national and international hyperlinks to serve its state members, including such topics as associations, weather, market information, government and politics, extension service, publications and information, commodity production, conservation & environment, crop protection, forestry, livestock, machinery and equipment, specialty agriculture, financial and insurance services, international agricultural sites, consumer/commodity information, family topics, youth and student topics, gardening, rural life, and additional agricultural hyperlinks. These Include information on ordering *A Farmer's Guide to the Internet* (call toll free, 1-888-885-9800, IVA Rural Studies, 1998 Edition FG, University of Kentucky, 408 Agricultural Engineering Bldg., Lexington, KY 40546-0276, $19.95 plus $3.95 shipping & handling) and a hyperlink to the national collection of agronomic links. This last site, "Agronomic Links Across the Globe," is a project of Bob Nielsen, Department of Agronomy, Purdue University; Web Site: <<http://www.agry. purdue.edu/agronomy/links/national.htm>>.

State

Ohio Farm Bureau Federation, Inc. Linda Mossbarger, P.O. Box 479, 2 Nationwide Plaza, Floor 6, Columbus, Ohio 43216; Tel: 614-249-2400; Fax: 614-249- 2200; E-mail: <<webmaster.ofbf.org>>; Web Site: <<http://www.ofbf.org>>.

National

American Farm Bureau Federation, 225 Touhy Ave., Park Ridge, IL 60068; Tel: 847-685-8600. Web Site: <<http://www.fb.com>>.

FARMERS' MARKETS IN OHIO

Local markets for farm produce are an important part of the farming industry. They offer citizens a fresh, local food source and, in the process, increase people's understanding of the importance of local agriculture as a major contributor to the state's economy. Of all the industries in Ohio, farming is the largest. This list of farmers' markets comes from the Agricultural Marketing Service (AMS) of the U.S. Department of Agriculture (USDA). The AMS maintains a current list of markets for all fifty states. It provides the names in alphabetical order, a description of the kind of market it is (seasonal or year 'round), its days of business, and whether the market accepts entitlement coupons, such as those for the Women–Infants–Children (WIC) Program (a supplemental nutrition program for pregnant, breastfeeding, and postpartum women and their infants and children).

Other markets not on the AMS list are included, with location, hours, a contact number, and the kinds of produce available, where known.

The Web site address for the U.S. map allows one to click on a state to drill down to the local listing: <<http://www.ams.usda. gov/farmersmarkets/states>>. The state list may also be accessed through a link with the American Farmland Trust Web Site: <<http://www.farmland.org>>.

Local

Apple Cabin. 7665 Lafayette Rd., Lodi, OH; Tel: 330-948-1476; 10 a.m. to 5 p.m. weekdays & Saturday; noon to 4 p.m. Sunday (fruits, vegetables, cider, jams, jellies, homemade ice cream).

Athens County Farmers' Market. Dave Gutkneckt, 733 East State St., Athens, OH 45701; Tel: 614-538-1912; open–air / year 'round – Wednesday, Saturday; WIC Coupons.

Athens Farmers' Market. Dave Gutknecht, 270 Highland Ave., Athens, OH 45701; Tel: 740-594-4990; year 'round – Wednesday, Saturday.

Aufdenkampe Family Farm. 3275 So. Ridge Rd, Vermillion, OH; Tel: 440-984-3844; hours vary, but open June through October (melons, peaches, raspberries, rhubarb, strawberries, watermelon, cut flowers, asparagus, green beans, cabbage, Indian corn, sweet corn, popping corn, cucumbers, gourds, green / hot peppers, pickles, pumpkins, squash, tomatoes, zucchini; pick–your–own and prepicked).

Auglaize Farmers' Market. John Smith, 208 South Blackhoof St. Wapakoneta, OH 45895; Tel: 419-738-2219; seasonal – Saturday.

Barnersville Farmers' Market. John Echradel, 300 East Church St., Barnersville, OH 43713; Tel: 614-425-3043; open–air / seasonal – Tuesday, Friday; WIC Coupons.

Bauer's Honor Stand. Ryan Rd. & Ohio 162, Medina, OH; 9 a.m. to dusk daily (vegetables).

Berry Farm. ½ mile south of Ohio 2 on Baumhart Rd., Avon, OH; Tel: 440-246-7983; hours vary, but open Tuesday through Saturday, August only (blueberries only; pick–your–own and prepicked).

Bessemer Farm Market. 1410 St. Michaels Ave., Akron, OH 43320; Tel: 330-864-8333; seasonal.

Bexley Farmers' Market. Frank Musson, 2570 E. Main St. Columbus, OH 43209; Tel: 419-674-4719; seasonal – Thursday.

Bowling Green Farmers' Market. Jennifer Buskey, 121 E. Wooster, State Route 258, Bowling Green, OH 44233; Tel: 419-354-4332; seasonal – Saturday.

Bowman Market. Allen Bowman, 2397 Center Rd., Hinckley, OH 44233; Tel: 330-225-4748; seasonal – Monday, Friday.

Butternut Farm. 36433 Butternut Ridge Rd., Elyria, OH 44035; Tel: 440-784-2081; mid–July – October (apples, melons, green beans, sweet corn, onions, green peppers, potatoes, pumpkins, tomatoes).

Carrolton Weekly Farmers' Market. Mike Hogan, 119 Public Square, Carrolton, OH 44615; Tel: 330-627-4310; open–air / seasonal – Saturday.

Champaign County Farmers' Market. Jill Michael, 5200 Prairie Rd., Urbana, OH 43078; Tel: 937-484-3727; seasonal – Saturday.

Christ United Methodist Church. Mike Neuendorf, 1140 Claremont Ave., Ashland, OH 44805; Tel: 419-289-0507; seasonal – Saturday.

Frank Cigona. 4336 N. Bend Rd., Ashtabula, OH; Tel: 440-998-2637; 8 a.m. to 5 p.m. weekdays only (fruits, including blueberries).

Cincinnati Court Street Market. Viola Napeer, Court & Vine Sts., Cincinnati, OH 45202; Tel: 513-241-8934; seasonal – Wednesday, Friday; WIC Coupons.

City of Wooster Farmers' Market. Larry Miller, 241 S. Bever St., Wooster, OH 44691; 330-263-5207; seasonal – Thursday.

Cold Springs Orchard. 878 Mechanicsville Rd., Rock Creek, OH; Tel: 440-466-0474; 8 a.m. to 6 p.m. daily (apples, other fruit).

Columbia Berry Farm. 19060 West River Rd., Columbia Station, OH 44028; Tel: 440-236-8416; July - September (fruits, honey, & maple syrup).

Community Market. Scott Santangelo, Location 1: Alms Park Location; 2: French Park Location; 3: Devon Park; 4027 Allston St., Cincinnati, OH 45209; seasonal – Saturday.

Daniel Ray Byler. 15658 Burton–Windsor Rd., Middlefield, OH (vegetables).

Dayton Court House Square. Shane Conley, 3rd & Main Sts., Dayton, OH 45402; Tel: 937-275-1206; seasonal – Monday.

Dayton Mall Farmers' Market. Shane Conley, State Routes 741 & 725, Miamisburg, OH 45342; Tel: 937-275-1206; seasonal – Wednesday.

Dechant's Greenhouse, Inc. 5464 Detroit Rd., Elyria, OH 44035; Tel: 440-934-6419; February – July (cucumbers, tomatoes).

Delaware Co. Farmers' Market. County Fairgrounds, off Pennsylvania Ave., Delaware, OH 43015; 614-368-1925; open–air / seasonal.

Downtown Fremont Farm Market. Gerald Gonya, 134 South Front, Fremont, OH 43420; Tel: 419-332-0481; seasonal – Saturday.

Downtown Sidney Farmers' Market. Sharon Wysong, Court Square, State Routes 47 & 29, Sidney, OH 45365; Tel: 937-497-7111; seasonal – Saturday.

Downtown Wooster Farmers' Market. Beth Ladrach, 4959 Rice Hill Rd., Wooster, OH 44691; Tel: 330-264-8708; seasonal – Saturday.

East Cleveland Farmer's Market. Colt & Woodworth Rds., East Cleveland, OH; 8 a.m. to noon, Saturdays (fruits and vegetables).

East 37th Market. Len Forthofer, East 37th, Cleveland, OH 44114; Tel: 216-647-3227; seasonal – Saturday, WIC Coupons.

Eastgate Farmers' Market. Tractor Supply Co. parking lot, State Route 32, Batavia, OH 45103; Tel: 513-753-3883; seasonal – Thursday.

Eddy Fruit Farm. 12079 Caves Rd., Chester Township, OH; Tel: 440-729-7842; 9 a.m. to 6 p.m. daily (fruits, vegetables).

Farmers Produce Auction. Jim Mullett, 7701 State Route 241, Millersburg, OH 44654; Tel: 330-674-7661; seasonal – Monday, Tuesday, Thursday, Friday.

Fenik Farms. 6413 Lake Ave., Elyria, OH; 440-324-2507; mid–July to mid–October (sweet corn, pumpkins).

Findlay Market. Tom Jackson, Elder St., Cincinnati, OH 45227; Tel: 513-352-4638; year 'round - Monday, Tuesday, Thursday, WIC Coupons.

Fitch's Farm Market. 4413 Center Rd. (Ohio 83), Avon, OH 44011; Tel: 440-934-6125; hours vary, but open through October (fruits, vegetables, bedding plants, & honey).

Foote Farms. 5860 Canal Rd., Valley View, OH; Tel: 216-524-3712; 9 a.m to 8 p.m., Mon. through Sat., 9 a.m. to 6 p.m.; Sundays (fruits and vegetables; Amish goods and bakery).

Fremont Farmers' Market. Mark Koeing, 440 E. Poe Rd., Ste. 201, Bowling, Green, OH 43402; Tel: 800-858-4678; seasonal; WIC Coupons.

Garden Isle Farm. Ohio 83, 1½ miles south of Lodi), Lodi, OH; Tel: 330-948-2444; 11 a.m. to 6 p.m. daily (sweet corn, vegetables, melons, & other fruit).

Garden State Produce. 8847 N. Girdle Rd., Middlefield, OH (vegetables).

Geig's Orchard. 8468 Wooster Pike, Seville, OH; Tel: 330-769-3276; 9 a.m. to 7 p.m. weekdays; noon to 5 p.m.; Sunday (fruits, vegetables, sweet corn, squash).

John Gerlica/Mike Gerlica. 4860 Lockwood Rd., Perry, OH; Tel: 440-259-3444; 5 a.m. to dark, weekdays; 9 a.m. to dark, weekends (fruits, vegetables, grapes, red potatoes, black & red raspberries, pumpkins in autumn).

Granville Farmers' Market. Ruth Owen, Box 135, Granville, OH 43023; Tel: 740-587-4490; seasonal – Saturday.

Greater New Lexington Farmers' Market. Deb Hutmire, McDougal Park at Main Street, New Lexington, OH 43764; Tel: 740-342-4121; seasonal – Friday.

Greene County Farmers' Market I. Keith Manor, Location 1: Fairborn, 5 Points Shopping Center, Location 2: Beavercreek, K-Mart; 2239 Tarbox Cemetery Rd., Cedarville, OH 45314; Tel: 513-766-2754; seasonal – Thursday, Saturday.

Greene County Farmers' Market. Robert Irving, Sr., 4087 Route 35, Jamestown, OH 45335; Tel: 937-675-4071; seasonal – Tuesday; WIC Coupons.

Grove City Farmers' Market. Clair Beglen, Town Center, Grove City, OH 43123; Tel: 614-871-0382; open-air / seasonal – Saturday; WIC Coupons.

Hahn's Sweet Corn Farm. 804 Bogart Rd., Huron, OH; 10 a.m. to 5 p.m. daily (sweet corn, vegetables, melons).

Hawks. 2810 North Ridge Rd., Elyria, OH 44035; July – September (green beans, cabbage, green peppers, tomatoes).

Hayes Road Orchard. 12995 N. Hayes Rd., Middlefield, OH (apples).

Haymaker Farmers' Market. Fritz Seefeldt, Franklin Avenue & Summit St., Kent, OH 44240; Tel: 330-678-5748; open–air / seasonal – Saturday.

Henry County Farmers' Market. Sue Westendorf, 611 North Perry St., Napoleon, OH 43545; Tel: 419-592-1786; seasonal – Saturday.

Hillard Farmers' Market. Downtown Hillard, Hillard, OH 43026; seasonal – Saturday.

Hillcrest Orchards, Inc. 50336 State Route 113, Amherst, OH 44001; Tel: 440-965-8884; July - April (cider, apples, peaches, pears, Indian corn, sweet corn, potatoes, pumpkins, squash, tomatoes; tours, hayrides).

Hillsboro Farmers' Market. Brad Bergeford, Governor Foaker Place, Hillsboro, OH 45133; Tel: 800-628-7722; open-air / seasonal – Saturday.

Hillside Orchard. 2397 Center Rd., Hinckley, OH; Tel: 330-225-4748; 10 a.m. to 6 p.m., Tuesday through Saturday; noon to 5 p.m. Sunday (fruits, vegetables, sweet corn, melons, squash).

Hisey's Homestead. 18314 State Route 83, Grafton, OH 44044; Tel: 440-926-1295; small back porch market, pick–your–own by appointment (apples, currants, gooseberries, raspberries, honey).

Holmes County Senior Center. State Route 83, Millersburg, OH 44654; seasonal – Tuesday.

Homerville Produce Auction. Fred Owen, 9430 Spencer Rd., Homerville, OH 44235; Tel: 330-625-2369; seasonal – Monday, Wednesday, & Friday.

Howard's Apples. 9554 Bainbridge Rd., Bainbridge Township, OH; Tel: 440-543-7587 (fruits, vegetables, maple syrup).

Huffman's Produce. Paul Huffman, 4645 E. U.S. 6, Pemberville, OH 43450; Tel: 419-287-3388; seasonal daily.

I-70/I-77 Farmers' Market. Bill Bertram, Guernsey County Fairgrounds, Old Washington, OH 43768; Tel: 740 658 3150; open–air / seasonal – Thursday.

Jamie's Flea & Produce Market. Lorna Ward, ½ mile west of Route 58, Amherst, OH 44001: Tel: 440-986-4402; year 'round – Wednesday, Sunday.

Jay Fowl Farm. 9256 West Ridge Rd., Elyria, OH 44035; Tel: 440-322-4413; late July - September (melons, nectarines, watermelon, hay, sweet corn).

Karey's. 34742 Lorain Rd., North Ridgeville, OH 44039; Tel: 440-327-9302; June (hay, green beans, sweet corn, green peppers, potatoes, tomatoes).

Klingshirn Winery. 33050 Webber Rd., Avon lake, OH 44012; Tel: 440-933-6666; year 'round (grape juice, wine, tours, hayrides).

Lancaster Farmers' Market. P.O. Box 2530, Lancaster, OH 43130; 740-653-2322; open–air / seasonal – Saturday.

Rex Lees Orchards. 50586 State Route 113, Amherst, OH 44001; Tel: 440-965-7761; year 'round (cider, apples, sweet & tart cherries, peaches, pears, plums, honey, Indian corn, popping corn, gourds, pumpkins).

Lodi Farmers' Market. On the Square, Lodi, OH; 8 a.m. to 12:30 p.m. Saturdays through October 16 (fruits, vegetables, flowers, vinegars, honey, baked and canned goods, eggs, maple syrup, organic produce).

Logan County Farmers' Market. Jan Dawson, 3624 Township Rd., 136 Bellefontaine, OH 43311; Tel: 937- 468-2853; open–air / seasonal – Saturday.

Mapleside Farms. 294 Pearl Rd., Brunswick, OH; Tel: 330-225-5577; 9 a.m. to 8 p.m. Monday through Thursday; 9 a.m. to 9 p.m. Friday & Saturday; 9 a.m. to 6 p.m., Sunday (bag–your–own apples any time of the year; large selection of other fruits and vegetables).

Bill Mayton Farm. 3815 Center Rd. (Ohio 83), Avon, OH; Tel: 440-934-5600; 11 a.m. to 5 p.m. daily (fruits & vegetables; raspberries in September).

McCaskey Farms. 5515 Stoney Ridge Rd., North Ridgeville, OH 44039; Tel: 440-327-6958; July - October (sweet corn, green peppers, potatoes, tomatoes).

McDowell Orchards. 50603 State Route 113, Amherst, OH 44001; Tel: 440-965-7762; July - November, December - April (cider, apples, peaches, pears, plums, prunes, honey, popping corn, potatoes, pumpkins, squash).

McLaughlin's Greenhouse & Market. Jan McLaughlin, 22867 Kellogg Rd., Grand Rapids, OH 43522; Tel: 419-832-3053; seasonal – Sunday, Monday.

Milford Farmers' Market. 825 Main Street (Big Lots parking lot), Milford, OH 45150; seasonal – Wednesday, Saturday; WIC Coupons.

Miller Orchards. 8763 Vermilion Rd., Amherst, OH 44001; Tel: 440-988-8405; late June & August – January (cider, apples, sweet cherries, grapes, peaches, pears, plums, raspberries, hay, honey, Indian corn, sweet corn, gourds, pumpkins).

Miller's Blacksmith & Produce Shop. 15478 Madison Rd., Middlefield, OH (vegetables).

Modroo Farm Market. 15571 Hemlock Rd., Chagrin Falls, OH; Tel: 440-247-7994; 10 a.m. to 6 p.m. daily (fruits & vegetables).

Monroe County Farmers' Market. Becky Devier, 42900 Reef Rd., Sardis, OH 43946; Tel: 740-483-1528; open–air / seasonal – Friday.

Nagel Farms. 2282 Nagel Rd., Avon, OH 44011; Tel: 440-937-6759; August - January (apples, grapes, nectarines, peaches, cut flowers, hay, sweet corn).

North Market. Anne Leonard-Palmer, 59 Spruce St., Columbus, OH 43215; Tel: 614-463-9664; Web Site: <<http://www.northmarket.com>>; seasonal – Saturday; WIC Coupons.

North Union Farmers' Market. Donita Anderson, Shaker Square, Cleveland, OH 44120; Arthur & Detroit Avenues, Lakewood, OH; Tel: 216-751-3712; 8 a.m. to noon, Saturday at Shaker Square (fresh produce, heirloom vegetables, herbs, cheeses, eggs, maple syrup, organically grown meats, cut and dried flowers) and 3 to 7 p.m. Wednesdays in Lakewood (fresh produce, heirloom vegetables).

Novotny Farms. 1809 State Route 60, Vermilion, OH 44089; Tel: 440-967-5757; year 'round (cider, apples, grapes, nectarines, peaches, plums, raspberries, strawberries, broccoli, cabbage, cauliflower, sweet corn, cucumbers, lettuce, onions, green peppers, potatoes, pumpkins, tomatoes, zucchini).

Fred Owen. 9430 Spencer Rd., Homerville, OH; Tel: 330-625-2369; Produce auction at 10:30 a.m. Monday, Wednesday, & Friday (fruits & vegetables).

Oxford Farmers' Market. Sarah James, 5184 Garver Elliott Rd., Oxford, OH 45056; Tel: 513-756-9186; seasonal – Saturday.

Patterson Fruit Farm. 11414 Caves Rd., Chester Township, OH; Tel: 440-729-1964; 9 a.m. to 6 p.m. daily (fruits & vegetables).

Pearl Alley Farmers' Market I. Frank Musson, Pearl Alley at Broad St., Columbus, OH 43215; Tel: 419- 674-4719; open–air / seasonal – Tuesday, Friday; WIC Coupons.

Pearl Alley Growers' Market. Frank Musson, Corner of West Bridge & North High Sts., Dublin, OH 43017; Tel: 419-674-4719; seasonal – Saturday; WIC Coupons.

Pearl Alley Upper Arlington Market. Frank Musson, The Mallway, 2100 Arlington Ave., Upper Arlington, OH 43221; Tel: 419-674-4719; seasonal – Wednesday; WIC Coupons.

Penton's Farm Market. 44905 North Ridge Rd., Amherst, OH 44001; Tel: 440-282-5486; year 'round (green beans, Indian corn, sweet corn, pumpkins, squash, tomatoes).

Pickering Hill Farms. 35699 Detroit Rd., Avon, OH 44011; Tel: 440-937-5155; June – December (cider, apples, blueberries, grapes, grape juice, melons, nectarines, peaches, plums, raspberries, strawberries, honey, maple syrup, asparagus, green beans, cabbage, cauliflower, Indian corn, sweet corn, cucumbers, gourds, green onions, herbs, lettuce, onions, peas, green peppers, hot peppers, pickles, potatoes, pumpkins, radishes, squash, tomatoes, zucchini).

Rainbow Farms. 2464 Townline Rd., Perry, OH; Tel: 440-259-4942; 9 a.m. to dark, weekdays only (fruits & vegetables).

Red Wagon Farm. 16081 East River Rd., Columbia Township, OH; Tel: 440-236-3007; 9 a.m. to 6 p.m. weekdays; 9 a.m. to 5 p.m. weekends, July - October (apples, grapes, melons, peaches, watermelon, Indian corn, sweet corn, cucumbers, gourds, green peppers, pickles, potatoes, pumpkins, squash, tomatoes, tours, hayrides).

Roberts Fruit Farm/Cider Mill. 10000 Sherman Rd., Chester Township, OH; Tel: 440-729-1148 (fruits, apples, cider products).

Rock Bottom Farms. 7767 Parkman–Mesopotamia Rd, Middlefield, OH; Tel: 440-693-4126; 8 a.m. to 5 p.m., Monday through Saturday (blueberries).

Rosby Brothers Greenhouse. 42 E. Schaaf Rd., Brooklyn Hts., OH; Tel: 216-351-0850; 9 a.m. to 8 p.m. Monday through Friday; 9

a.m. to 5 p.m. Saturday & Sunday (pick–your–own raspberries–
may begin late August and run through October).

Ross County Farmers' Market. Tom Wall, 78 West Main St.,
Chillicothe, OH 45601; Tel: 614-775-3200; seasonal – Saturday;
WIC Coupons.

Sages Apples. 1135 Chardon Rd., Chardon, OH; Tel: 440-286-
3416; 9 a.m. to 5:30 p.m., Monday – Saturday and noon to 5 p.m.
Sunday (fruits & vegetables).

Donald A. Schuster Greenhouse, Inc. 8638 Murray Ridge Rd.,
Elyria, OH 44035; September 25 - October (pumpkins); May
(greenhouse plants).

Secor's Nursery. 4940 North Ridge Rd. East, Perry, OH; Tel: 440-
259-3487; 8 a.m. to 5:30 p.m., Monday through Friday; 8 a.m. to 5
p.m. Saturday & Sunday (tomatoes & sweet corn).

Silver Creek Farm. 7097 Allyn Rd., Hiram, OH 44234-0126; Tel:
330-569-3487; Fax: 330-569-3487; E-mail: <<silvrcf@aol.com>>;
May – October, Wednesday – Saturday, 10 a.m. to 5 p.m.;
November – April, Saturday, 10 a.m. to 5 p.m. (spring: certified
organic heirloom seedlings, herb plants, organic gardening aids,
and seed books; summer: blueberries, squash, kale, chard, peas,
heirloom tomatoes, sweet corn, peppers, herbs, eggplant, beets,
broccoli, and garlic; fall: turkeys, winter squash, root crops,
pumpkins, and potatoes; all year: pottery, yarn, sheepskins,
certified Ohio organic beef, farm—raised chicken & lamb, and
maple syrup).

Solomon's Strawberry Farm. 5150 Avon–Belden Rd., North
Ridgeville, OH 44039; Tel: 440-327-4961; May – October (apples,
currants, raspberries, strawberries, sweet corn, cucumbers,
eggplant, gourds, herbs, lettuce, green peppers, pumpkins,
tomatoes, zucchini, tours, hayrides).

Spiegelberg Orchards. 6161 Middle Ridge Rd., Lorain, OH; Tel:
440-233-6083; 8 a.m. to 6 p.m. weekdays; Saturday, year 'round
(sweet corn, vegetables, and fruits).

Springhill Orchard Market & Farm. Tom Swank, 6062 South
Ridge, West Geneva, OH 44041; Tel: 440-466-7480; seasonal –
Friday, Saturday.

Springhill Orchards. 6192 So. Ridge Rd. West, Geneva, OH; Tel:
440-466-7480; 9 a.m. to 6 p.m. Monday through Saturday; noon to

6 p.m. Sunday (fruits, strawberries, raspberries, cherries, plums, peaches, and apples).

Starr Farm. 14030 Mayfield Rd., Huntsburg, OH; Tel: 440-635-4371; 10 a.m. to 6 p.m. Tuesday through Friday, 10 a.m. to 4 p.m. Saturday & Sunday (fruits & vegetables).

Steubenville Farmers' Market. Joe Walkosky, Fourth & Market St. Steubenville, OH 43952; Tel: 740-283-4935; open–air / seasonal – Thursday.

Stock Exchange Market. 453 Cincinnati Batavia Pike, Mt. Carmel, OH 45244; seasonal – Tuesday.

Sunrise Farm Market & Cider Mill. Ohio 87 (1 mile west of Burton), Burton, OH; Tel: 440-834-1298; 9 a.m. to 7 p.m., Monday through Friday; 9 a.m. to 5 p.m. Saturday & Sunday (fruits & vegetables).

Sweetbriar Farm. 11213 Parkman Rd., Garrettsville, OH (vegetables).

Tailgate Market. Carol Lynn, Ridge Rd., Cincinnati, OH 45237; Tel: 513-251-0990; open–air / seasonal – Monday

Toledo Farmers' Market. Luis Mikesell, P.O. Box 9294, Toledo, OH 43697; Tel: 419-255-6765; year 'round – Monday – Saturday; WIC Coupons.

Union County Farmers' Market. Kathy Custer, South Main St., Marysville, OH 43040; open–air / seasonal – Saturday.

Voytko Blueberry Farm. 11391 Frank Rd., Burton, OH (fruits & vegetables).

Waynesville Farmers' Market. Milton Cook, P.O. Box 731, Waynesville, OH 45068; Tel: 513-897-5946; seasonal – Saturday.

Wegerzyn Horticultural Assoc. Farmers' Market. Shane Conley, 1301 East Siebenthaler Ave., Dayton, OH 45414; Tel: 937-277-9028; seasonal – Saturday.

West Side Market. George A. Bradac, 1979 West 25th St., Cleveland, OH 44113; Tel: 216-664-3386; Web Site: <<http://www.westsidemarket.com>>; year 'round.

West Union Farmers' Market. Robin Stephenson, 110 West Main, West Union, OH 45693; Tel: 937-544-2339; seasonal – Wednesday, Saturday; WIC Coupons.

Westerville Farmers' Market. Main & Home Sts., Westerville, OH 43081; Tel: 614-262-5638; open–air / seasonal – Wednesday; WIC Coupons.

West's Orchard & Fruit Market. 3096 North Ridge Rd., Perry, OH; Tel: 440-259-3192; 9 a.m. to 6 p.m., Monday – Friday; 9 a.m. to 5 p.m., Saturday & Sunday (fruits, vegetables, apples, peaches, & corn).

Williams County Farmers' Market I. Donald R. Knepper, Courthouse Square, Bryan, OH 43506; Tel: 419- 924-5130; open–air / seasonal – Tuesday, Friday; WIC Coupons.

Williams County Farmers' Market II. East Main St., Williams County Fairgrounds, Montpelier, OH 43543; seasonal – Thursday; WIC Coupons.

Windmill Farm Market. 454 East State Route 73, Springsboro, OH 45066, Tel: 513-885-3065; seasonal.

Woodsfield Farmers' Market. Becky Devier, 47029 Moore Ridge Rd., Woodsfield, OH 43793; Tel: 740-483-1528; seasonal – Friday; WIC Coupons.

Woodworth Market. 6401 Middle Ridge Rd , Madison, OH 44057; Tel: 216-428-1385; seasonal – Wednesday, Saturday.

Worthington Farmers' Market. Julian Larson, 187 Desantis Dr., Columbus, OH 43214; Tel: 614-262-5638; open air / seasonal – Saturday.

Wyandot County Farmers' Market. Daniel Debolt, 5742 C H 43, Upper Sandusky, OH 43351; Tel: 419-927-4733; open–air / seasonal – Saturday.

Zanesville Farmers' Market. Karen Brown, 2620 Ford Rd., Mt. Perry, OH 43760; Tel: 614-849-9743; seasonal – Saturday; WIC Coupons.

State

State Farmers' Market Representative: Tim Sword, Ohio Dept. of Agriculture, 8995 East Main St., Reynoldsburg, OH 43068; Tel:

614-752-9816; Fax: 614-644-5017; E-mail: <<sword@odant.agri. state.oh.us>>.

National

American Farmland Trust's FRESHFARM Market. 1200 18th St. NW, Ste. 800, Washington, DC 20036; Tel: 202-331-7300; Fax: 202-659-8339; Web Site: <<http://www.farmland.org/Farmland/ files/states/local.htm>>.

Agricultural Marketing Services, U.S. Department of Agriculture. Kathleen A. Merrigan, 14th & Independence Ave., SW, Washington, DC 20250; Tel: 202-720-5115; Web Site: <<http:// www.ams.usda.gov>>.

(**Sources:** Internet searches, June through July 1999; "Finding It Farm Fresh," *The Plain Dealer*, August 4, 1999, 4-F; James Skeeles, OSU Extension Office, Lorain County.)

HISTORIC PRESERVATION RESOURCES

At its Web site, the Ohio Historical Society (OHS) offers a variety of resources for those interested in historic preservation, including hyperlinks to the National Register of Historic Places, the Ohio Historic Inventory, and the Ohio Archaeological Inventory. The Web site also features searchable databases, a catalogue of OHS's online collections, as well as educational and research services (e.g., geneology, books, birth / death / marriage records, etc.). The National Register of Historic Places is a program of the National Park Service. It has a cultural resources area called "Links to the Past," which is extensive. Web Sites: <<http://www.nps. gov>> and <<http://www.cr.nps.gov>>.

Local

Cleveland Restoration Society & Preservation Resource Center of Northeastern Ohio. Sarah Benedict House, 3751 Prospect Ave., Cleveland, OH 44115-2705; Tel: 216-426-1000.

State

Ohio Historical Society, Ohio Historical Center, 1982 Velma Ave., Columbus, OH 43211-2497; Tel: 614-297-2300 & 614-297-2300; Fax: 614-297-2546; E-mail: <<ohsref@ohiohistory.org>>; Web Site: <<http://www.ohiohistory.org/>>.

Ohio Historic Preservation Office, 567 East Hudson St., Columbus, OH 43211-1030; Tel: 614-297-2470; Fax: 614-297-2496; Web Site: <<www.ohiohistory.org/resource/histpres>>.

National

National Register of Historic Places, National Park Service, Carol Shull, Keeper of the Register, 1849 C St., NW, NC 400, Washington, DC 20240; Tel: 202-343-9504; Fax: 202-343-1836; E-mail: <<Carol_Shull@nps.gov>>; Web Site: <<http://www.cr.nps.gov/nr>>.

LAND TRUSTS

Land trusts hold in common an active interest in protecting and preserving the rural character, natural resources, cultural and historic features, and the overall environmental quality of their communities. In addition, some national groups set aside lands for public use, still others, for preservation of plant and animal species or unusual land formations. As of November 1999, there are 33 land trusts in Ohio. Increasingly, citizens are looking to them as a means for managing growth in their communities, in particular protecting open spaces, unique areas and land forms, and species diversity.

Beaver Creek Wetlands Association. Bob Limbered, Admin. Coord., P. O. Box 42, Alpha, OH 45301; Tel: 937-320-9042; E-mail: <<bcwa@erinet.com>>.

Black Swamp Conservancy. John Wright, Dir., P. O. Box 332, Perrysburg, OH 43552-0332; Tel: 419-872-5263; Fax: 419-872-8197; E-mail: <<bsc@wcnet.org>>.

Buckeye Trail Association. Herb Hulls, Pres., P.O. Box 254, Worthington, OH 43085; Tel: 800-881-3002, E-mail: <<hhulls@frognet.net>>; Web Site: <<http://www.buckeyetrail.org>>.

Chagrin River Land Conservancy. Rich Cochran, Exec. Dir., P.O. Box 148, Chagrin Falls, OH 44022; Tel: 440-247-0880; Fax: 440-247-0881. E-mail: <<crlc148@aol.com>>. **Purpose:** To preserve open space, habitat, and the rural character of the Chagrin River Valley (holdings are approximately 2000 acres).

Cleveland Museum of Natural History. James Bissell, Coord. of Natural Areas, Wade Oval, University Circle, Cleveland, OH 44106;

Tel: 216-231-4600. **Purpose:** To acquire materials (and land) from the natural world, protect them, and interpret the collections to the public.

Darby Creek Land Conservancy. Pam Sayre, Pres., P.O. Box 114, Amlin, OH 43002; Tel:614-470-1115; Web Site: <<http://www.infinet.com/~jmartin/dclc>>.

Firelands Land Conservancy. Carl Kudrna, 24331 E. Oakland Rd., Bay Village, OH 44140; Tel (toll free): 877-281-8485 or Tel/Fax: 440-835-0222. E-mail: <<sitesmart@aol.com>>. **Purpose:** To preserve lands for aesthetic, scenic, conservation, and educational value.

Four Mile Valley Conservation Trust. James E. Reid, Chmn., Box 234, Oxford, OH 45056; Tel: 513-524-1874; Fax: 513-524-1874; E-mail: <<reidyou@aol.com>>. **Purpose:** To protect the open, natural, and historic places in Four Mile Valley, starting at Acton Lake and 18 miles south of it.

Gates Mills Land Conservancy. Rob Galloway, Pres., P.O. Box 13, Gates Mills, OH 44040; Tel: 440-423-0421 or 216-861-7423; E-mail: <<rgalloway@bakerlaw.com>>. **Purpose:** To preserve and maintain open areas within the village for outdoor recreation and scenic enjoyment and to plan for use of land which will protect and preserve the natural resources and open spaces of the village along the Chagrin River and its tributaries.

Grand River Watershed Partners. Chuck Ashcroft, Exec. Dir., Lake Erie College, Austin Hall, Room 314-Box M25, 391 West Washington St., Painesville, OH 44077; Tel/Fax: 440-639-4773; E-mail: <<grandriver@ncweb.com>>. **Purpose:** To protect the Grand River and its watershed by working with private land owners and public agencies.

Granville Land Conservancy. Don Wiper, Chmn., P.O. Box 196, Granville, OH 43023; Tel: 614-365-2751 or 740-587-3934; Fax: 614-365-2499.

Headwaters Land Trust. Stan Fischer, Pres., P.O. Box 171, Hiram, OH 44234; Voice Mail: 330-569-0091 + 271; Tel/Fax: 330-569-7863. **Purpose:** Dedicated to helping people protect fields, streams, forests, and farms through preservation and wise land use. Active in the Headwaters Region of the Cuyahoga and Grand Rivers and Eagle Creek Branch of the Mahoning River.

Hillside Trust. William Cherry, Dir., Alms Park, P.O. Box 8625, Cincinnati, OH 45208-0625; Tel: 513-321-3886; Web Site: <<http:// www.fullservice.net/~cincynature/enviroscan/orgs/HillsideTrust>>.

The Holden Arboretum. Roger Gettig, Landscape Consultant, 9500 Sperry Rd., Mentor, OH 44094-5172; Tel: 440-256-1110; Fax: 440-256-1655; E-mail: <<rgettig@holdenarb.org>>. **Purpose:** To promote the knowledge and appreciation of plants for personal enjoyment, inspiration, recreation, scientific research, education, and aesthetic purposes.

Hudson Land Conservancy. Donna Studniarz, Pres., P.O. Box 1381, Hudson, OH 44236; Tel: 330-528-0688.

IMAGO. R. James Schenk, Co-Dir., 553 Enright Ave., Cincinnati, OH 45205; Tel/Fax: 513-921-5124; Fax: 513-921-5136; E-mail: <<IMAGO@one.net>>.

Little Beaver Creek Land Foundation. Carol F. Bretz, Chair, P.O. Box 60, East Liverpool, OH 43920; Tel: 330-424-7221; Fax: 330-424-3731.

Little Miami. Eric Partee, Exec. Dir., 6040 Price Rd., Milford, OH 45150; Tel/Fax: 513-965-9344; E-mail: <<partee@littlemiami. com>>; Web Site: <<http://www.littlemiami.com>>.

Medina County Land Conservancy. Jeff Holland or Cynthia Szunyog, Pres., P.O. Box 141, Medina, OH 44258; Tel: 330-666-1994; 330-239-4480; Fax: 330-239-4479; E-mail: <<jjholland@aol. com>>. **Purpose:** A private, nonprofit organization dedicated to preserving open space, natural areas, and the rural atmosphere of Medina County.

Natural Areas Stewardship. Michelle Grigore, Exec. Dir., P.O. Box 351262, Toledo, OH 43635; Tel/Fax: 419-829-6226; E-mail: <<firebug@glasscity.net>>.

North Central Ohio Land Conservancy. Eric Miller, Trustee, 24 West Third St., Ste. 300, Mansfield, OH 44902; Tel: 419-522-6262; Fax: 419-522-4315.

Northside Greenspace. Stephen Albert, Pres., 1674 Pullan Ave., Cincinnati, OH 45223; Tel/Fax: 513-541-9119; E-mail: <<salbert@ iac.net>>.

Oxbow, Inc. Norma L. Flannery, Pres., P.O. Box 43391, Cincinnati, OH 45243; Tel: 513-471-8801; Fax: 513-471-8001-51;

E-mail: <<Steve.Pelikan@UC.edu>>; Web Site: <<http://math.uc. edu/~pelican/OXBOW/wm.html>>. **Purpose:** Protecting and improving a 2,500 acre wetland ecosystem in the floodplain surrounding the confluence of the Great Miami and Ohio Rivers through land purchases and conservation easements.

PLACE (Portage Land Association for Conservation and Education). Romi Fox, P.O. Box 3286, Kent, OH 44240; Tel: 330-673-2488.

Quail Hollow Land Conservancy. Judy Semroc, Pres., 13340 Congress Lake Ave., Hartville, OH 44632; Tel/Fax: 330-699-6213.

Revere Land Conservancy. Bruce Merchant, Pres., P.O. Box 484, Bath, OH 44210; Tel: 330-659-3137; Fax: 330-659-4247; E-mail: <<bmerchant@cisco.com>>.

Tecumseh Land Trust. Julia Cady, Pres., P.O. Box 417, Yellow Springs, OH 45387; Tel: 937-767-1586; E-mail (Al Deneman): <<adenemen@antiochcollege.com>>.

The Nature Conservancy, Ohio Chapter. Jan Burkey; Scott Davis, Assoc. Dir., Jeff Newberg, Dir. of Acquisitions, 6375 Riverside Drive, Ste. 50, Dublin, OH; 43017; Tel: 614-717-2770; Fax: 614-717-2777. Web Site: <<http://www.tnc.org/Infield/State/ Ohio>>.

Tinkers Creek Land Conservancy. Marion Olson, Pres., PMB #271, 9224 Darrow Rd., Twinsburg, OH 44087-1891; Tel: 330-425-4159.

Trust for Public Land. Christopher Knopf, Ohio Field Office Dir., 1836 Euclid Ave., Ste. 800, Cleveland, OH 44115; Tel: 216-694-4416; Fax: 216-696-2326.

Upper Cuyahoga Association. Charles P. English, 4129 Dudley Rd., Mantua, OH 44155; Tel: 330-274-2746. **Purpose:** To promote quiet enjoyment of the upper Cuyahoga River.

Wilderness Center. Gordon Maupin, Exec. Dir., P.O. Box 202, 9877 Alabama Ave., SW, Wilmot, OH 44689-0202; Tel: 330-359-5235; Fax: 330-359-7898; E-mail: <<two@assnet.com>>. **Purpose:** Nature education, wildlife conservation, natural history research, community service.

Willoughby Natural Areas Conservancy. Dale Cook or Joe Bole, 37639 Second St., Willoughby, OH 44094; Tel: 440-951-6169 (Dale Cook), 440-951-5649 (J. Bole).

National

The following organizations have lists of land trusts available by state:

Land Trust Alliance. 1319 F St. NW, Ste. 501, Washington, DC 20004; Tel: 202-638-4725; Fax 202-638-4730; Web Site: <<http://www.lta.org>>.

Mayo Law Firm. Mayo Law Firm P.C., 92 Boston Post Rd., P.O. Box 23, Amherst, New Hampshire 03031-0023; Tel: 603-673-6607; Fax: 603-672-9394; E-mail: <<tmayo@mayolawfirm.com>>; Web Site: <<http://www.mayolawfirm.com>>.

(**Source:** August 1998 Land Trust Alliance list; Roger Gettig, The Holden Arboretum, June 1999 list; Chris Craycroft, Portage County Park District, July 1999 list; Internet searches, June through September 1999)

METROPOLITAN PLANNING ORGANIZATIONS

In Ohio, the state's 1999 Transportation Equity Act (TEA-21) allocation was given to 16 Metropolitan Planning Organizations, MPOs. These are "urbanized" centers defined by the latest population census. Nonurbanized areas are overseen by the Ohio Department of Transportation (ODOT). Most MPOs are hosted by Regional Planning Organizations (see "Planning Commissions and Councils—Regional & County," below), like the Northeast Ohio Area Coordinating Agency; others are separately housed but coordinate planning with their local Planning Organization. Each MPO received the additional 10% for "enhancements," and they can apply for a share of $5,000,000 "taken off the top of the federal award," which is open to competitive bidding from all MPOs and nonurbanized areas. Eligible activities include the following:

Transportation Enhancements

- Safety and educational activities for pedestrians and bicyclists

- Acquisition of scenic easements and scenic or historic sites, including provision of tourist and welcome center facilities
- Environmental mitigation to address water pollution due to highway runoff or reduce vehicle–caused wildlife mortality while maintaining habitat connectivity
- Transportation museums
- Historic preservation
- Preservation of abandoned railway corridors, including conversion to hike/bike trails
- Control and removal of outdoor advertising
- Archaeological planning and research, landscaping, and other scenic beautification.

Transit Enhancements

A 1% set aside provides new funds of $20,840,000 in FY 1998 up to $32,610,000 in FY 2003 for transit enhancements. The nine eligible categories are:

- Historic preservation, rehabilitation, and operation of mass transportation buildings, structures, and facilities, including historic bus and railroad facilities
- Bus shelters
- Landscaping and other scenic beautification, including, tables, benches, trash receptacles, and street lights
- Public art
- Pedestrian access and walkways
- Bicycle access, including bicycle storage facilities and installation equipment for transporting bicycles on mass transportation vehicles
- Transit connections to parks within the recipients' transit service areas
- Signage
- Enhanced access for persons with disabilities to mass transportation.

Ohio's MPOs are listed below.

Akron—Akron Metropolitan Area Transportation Study (AMATS). Warren Woolford, Study Dir., City of Akron, Policy Committee of the Akron Metropolitan Area Study, 146 South High St., Citicenter Bldg., Room 806, Akron, OH 44308-1423; Tel: 330-375-2436; Fax: 330-375-2275; E-mail: <<hansoke@ci.akron.oh. us>>.

Canton—Stark County Area Transportation Study (SCATS).
Gerald Bixler, Exec. Dir., Stark County Regional Planning
Commission, 201 3rd St., NE, Ste. 201, Canton, OH 44702-1231;
Tel: 330-438-0389; Fax: 330-438-0990; E-mail: <<starkpc@aol.
com>>.

**Cincinnati—Ohio–Kentucky–Indiana Regional Council of
Governments (OKI).** James Duane, Exec. Dir., 801-B West 8th St.,
Ste. 400, Cincinnati, OH 45203; Tel: 513-621-7060; Fax: 513-621-
9325; E-mail: <<plan@oki.org>>.

**Cleveland—Northeast Ohio Areawide Coordinating Agency
Policy Board (NOACA).** Howard Maior, Exec. Dir., 1299 Superior
Ave., Cleveland, OH 44114-3204; Tel: 216-241-2414; Fax: 216-
621-3024; E-mail: <<jhosek@mpo.noaca.org>>.

**Columbus—Policy Committee of the Columbus Area
Transportation Study, Mid–Ohio Regional Planning
Commission (MORPC).** William Habig, Exec. Dir., 285 E. Main
St., Columbus, OH 43215; Tel: 614-228-2663; 614-621-2401; E-
mail: <<rlawler@mail.morpc.org>>.

**Dayton—Miami Valley Regional Planning Commission,
Transportation Committee (TC).** Nora Lake, Exec. Dir., 40 W.
Centre, Ste. 400, Dayton, OH 45402; Tel: 937-223-6323; Fax: 937-
223-9750; E-mail: <<firstinitial.lastname@mvrpc.org>>.

**Huntington—HIATS Coordinating Committee, KYOVA
Interstate Planning Commission.** Michele Craig, Exec. Dir., 1221
6th Ave., P.O. Box 939, Huntington, West Virginia 25712; Tel: 304-
523-7434; Fax: 304-529-7229; E-mail: <<ssalemeb@citynet.
net>>.

**Lima—Coordinating Committee of the Lima Area
Transportation Study, Lima–Allen County Regional Planning
Commission.** Tom Mazur, Exec. Dir., 130 W. North St., Lima, OH
45801; Tel: 419-228-1836; Fax: 419-228-3891; E-mail:
<<lacrpc@bright.net>>.

**Mansfield—Coordinating Committee of the Mansfield Area
Transportation Study, Richland County Regional Planning
Commission.** Richard Adair, Exec. Dir., 35 North Park St.,
Mansfield, OH 44902; Tel: 419-774-5684; Fax: 419-774-5685; E-
mail: <<rcrpc@richnet.net>>.

**Newark–Heath—Policy Committee of the Licking County Area
Transportation Study (LCATS).** Jerry Brems, Exec. Dir., 20 South

2nd St., Newark, OH 43055; Tel: 740-349-6930; Fax: 740-349-6567; E-mail: <<lcats@infinet.net>>.

Parkersburg–Belpre—Wood–Washington–Wirt Interstate Planning Commission (WWW), Mid–Ohio Valley Regional Planning and Development Council. James Mylott, Exec. Dir., 531 Market St., P.O. Box 247, Parkersburg, WV 26101; Tel: 304-422-4993; Fax: 304-422-4998; E-mail: <<randy.durst @movrc. org>>.

Springfield—Coordinating Committee of the Clark County– Springfield Transportation Study. Larry Himes, Exec. Dir., 76 E. High St., Springfield, OH 45502; Tel: 937-324-7751; Fax: 937-328-3940; E-mail: <<clark_springtcc@compuserve.com>>.

Steubenville–Weirton Brooke–Hancock–Jefferson Transpor– tation Study (BHJTS) Policy Committee. Dr. John Brown, Exec. Dir., 814 Adams St., Steubenville, OH 43952; Tel: 740-282-3685; Fax: 740-282-1821; E-mail: <<bhjmpc@bhjmpc.org>>.

Toledo—Executive Committee of the Toledo Metropolitan Area Council of Governments (TMACOG), Transportation and Land Use Committee. William Knight, Exec. Dir., 300 Central Union Terminal, P.O. Box 9508, Toledo, OH 43697-9508; Tel: 419-241-9155; Fax: 419-241-9116; E-mail: <<last name up to 8 letters@tmacog.org>>.

Wheeling–Bridgeport—Bel–O–Mar Regional Council and Interstate Planning Commission (BOMTS). Williams Phipps, Exec. Dir., 105 Bridge St. Plaza, P.O. Box 2086, Wheeling, WV 26003; Tel: 304-242-1800; Fax: 304-242-2437; E-mail: <<belomar @ovnet.com>>.

Youngstown—General Policy Board of the Eastgate Development and Transportation Agency (EDATA). John R. Getchey, Exec. Dir., 25 E. Boardman St., Ste. 400, Youngstown, OH 44503-1805; Tel: 330-746-7601; Fax: 330-746-8509; E-mail: <<edata@cisnet.com>>.

OHIO'S FORESTS

State

Ohio's 19 state forests are administered by the Ohio Department of Natural Resources' Division of Forestry, Bldg. H, 1855 Fountain

Square Dr., Columbus, OH 43224-1327, Tel: 614-265-6694. Contact information for each appears below. Web Site: <<http://www.hcs.ohio-state.edu/ODNR/Forestry.htm>>.

Blue Rock State Forest, 6665 Cutler Lake Road, Blue Rock, OH 43720-9740; Tel: 740-674-4035.
Brush Creek State Forest, Route 3, Box 156, Peebles, OH 45660-9592; Tel: 740-372-3194.
Dean State Forest, Route 1, Pedro, OH 45659; Tel: 740-532-7228.
Fernwood State Forest, Division of Forestry, 1888 E. High Ave., New Philadelphia, OH 44663-7232; Tel: 330-339-2205.
Gifford State Forest, 17221 State Rte. 377, Chesterhill, OH 43728-9604; Tel: 740-554-3177.
Harrison State Forest, Division of Forestry, 1888 E. High Ave., New Philadelphia, OH 44663; Tel: 330-339-2205.
Hocking State Forest, 19275 SR 374, Rockbridge, OH 43149; Tel: 740-385-4402.
Maumee State Forest, 3390 County Road D, Swanton, OH 43558; Tel: 419-822-3052.
Mohican–Memorial State Forest, Rte. 2, 3060 CR 939, Perrysville, OH 44864-9791; Tel: 419-938-6222.
Perry State Forest, 6665 Cutler Lake Road, Blue Rock, OH 43558; Tel: 740-674-4035.
Pike State Forest, 334 Lapperell, Latham, OH 45646-9722; Tel: 740-493-2441.
Richland Furnace State Forest, P.O. Box 330, SR 278, Zaleski, OH 45698-0330; Tel: 740-596-5781.
Scioto Trail State Forest, 124 North Ridge Road, Waverly, OH 44690-9513; Tel: 740-663-2523.
Shade River State Forest, 17221 SR 377, Chesterhill, OH 43728-9604; Tel: 740-554-3177.
Shawnee State Forest, 13291 U.S. 52, West Portsmouth, OH 45663-8906; Tel: 740-858-6685.
Sunfish Creek State Forest, 360 E. State St., Athens, OH 45701; Tel: 740-593-3341.
Tar Hollow State Forest, 124 Norh Ridge Road, Waverly, OH 45690-9513, Tel: 740-663-2523.
Yellow Creek State Forest, 1888 E. High Ave., New Philadelphia, OH 44663-3272; Tel: 330-339-2205.
Zaleski State Forest, P.O. Box 330, SR 278, Zaleski, OH 45698-0330; Tel: 740-596-5781.

National

National forest areas are administered by the U.S. Department of Agriculture's Forest Service, P.O. Box 96090, Washington, DC 20090-6090, Mike Dombeck, Chief, Forest Service, Tel: 202-205-1661. Web Site: <<http://www.fs.fed.us>>.

Wayne National Forest: Wayne is Ohio's only national forest, served by three district ranger stations. Its Web Site is: <<http://www.gorp.com/gorp/resource/US_National_Forest/OH_Wayne.htm>>.

> Athens Ranger District, 219 Columbus Rd., Athens, OH 45701; Tel: 614-592-6644.
>
> Ironton Ranger District, 6518 St. Rt.93, Pedro, OH 45659; Tel: 614-532-3223.
>
> Marietta Ranger District, Rte. 1, Box 132, Marietta, OH 45750; Tel: 614-373-9055.

OHIO'S NATURE PRESERVES

The Ohio Department of Natural Resources' Division of Natural Areas and Preserves as well as other managing agencies (e.g., The Nature Conservancy or local park systems) oversee 115 state nature preserves. Established in 1970 under the Ohio Natural Areas Act, this statewide system totaling over 26,000 acres is open to the public. However, some preserves require a permit for access because of their fragile nature, lack of public use facilities, or limited accessibility.

Acreage is in parenthesis. The preserve manager is ODNR's Natural Areas and Preserves unless otherwise indicated. An "*" indicates a permit is required; a "♦" indicates that a brochure is available. County names appear in boldface.

For further information, contact ODNR, Ohio Division of Natural Areas and Preserves, 1889 Fountain Square Ct., Columbus, OH 43224; Tel: 614-265-6456; Fax: 614-267-3096; Web Site: <<http://www.dnr.state.oh.us/odnr/dnap/dnap.html>>.

COUNTY/PRESERVE	PRESERVE MANAGER

Adams County
Adams Lake Prairie♦ (22.37)

Chaparral Prairie* (66.7)
Davis Memorial (87.48)
Strait Ck Prairie Bluff♦ (266)   The Nature Conservancy
Johnson Ridge (200.37)
Whipple (187.29)
Allen County
Kendrick Woods (159.20)   Johnny Appleseed Park District
Ashland County
Clear Fork Gorge (28.77)
Ashtabula County
Pallister* (84.7)
Pymatuning* Creek (194)
Athens County
Acadia Cliffs (277.35)   Ohio Division of Wildlife
Desonier (490.89)
Belmont County
Emerald Hills* (73.58)
Butler County
Hueston Woods ♦ (200)
Champaign County
Cedar Bog (426.50)   Ohio Historical Society
Davey Woods (103.17)
Klser Lake Wetlands* (50.7)
Siegenthaler-Kaestner♦ (36.88)
Clark County
Crabill Fen* (31.66)
Gallagher/Springfield Fen* (213.3)
Prairie Road Fen*♦ (94.49)
Clermont County
Crooked Run (77.51)   Clermont County Parks
Clinton County
Culberson Woods (238.49)
Columbiana County
Sheepskin Hollow (456.69)
Crawford County
Carmean Woods (39.16)   Crawford Park District
Sears Woods (98.57)   Crawford Park District
Darke County
Drew Woods (14.57)
Delaware County
Highbanks (206.48)   Metro. Park Dist. of Columbus &
                                       Franklin County

Seymour Woods (106)
Stratford Woods* (740)   Stratford Ecological Center
Erie County
Erie Sand Barrens ♦ (31.85)
DuPont Marsh (113.94)   Erie MetroParks

North Pond (30)
North Shore Alvar (0.7)
Old Woman Creek♦ (570.8)
Sheldon Marsh♦ (462.63)
Fairfield County
Clear Creek (3,361.26)   Metro. Park Dist. of Columbus &
                                Franklin County
Christmas Rocks* (414.92)
Pickerington Ponds (405.98)   Metro. Park Dist. of Columbus &
                                Franklin County
Rhododendron Cove* (69.78)
Shallenberger♦ (87.57)
Tucker, Walter (54.67)   Metro. Park Dist. of Columbus &
                                Franklin County
Franklin County
Gahanna Woods (53.89)   Gahanna City Parks
Pickerington Ponds (405.98)   Metro. Park Dist. of
                                Columbus & Franklin County
Thomas, Edward (319)   Metro. Park Dist. of Columbus &
                                Franklin County
Fulton County
Goll Woods♦ (320.64)
Greene County
Clifton Gorge♦ (268.72)
Travertine Fen* (21.19)   Greene County Park District
Zimmerman Prairie (3.48)
Hamilton County
Greenbelt* (97.29)   Hamilton County Park District
Newberry * (50.03)   Hamilton County Park District
Sharon Woods Gorge (20.86)   Hamilton County Park District
Spring Beauty* Dell (41.26)   Hamilton County Park District
Trillium Trails* (22.91)   Hamilton County Park District
Warder-Perkins* (25.66)   Audubon Society of Ohio
Hardin County
Lawrence Woods (1058)
Highland County
Etawah Woods* (47.48)   Highlands Nature Sanctuary
Miller*♦ (88.46)
Hocking County
Clear Creek (3,261)   Metro. Park Dist. of Columbus &
                                Franklin County
Conkles Hollow ♦ (86.88)
Crane Hollow* (1,112.22)   Crane Hollow, Inc.
Little Rocky Hollow* (259)
Rockbridge♦ (99.29)
Sheick Hollow* (151)
Huron County

Olsen (132)
Jackson County
Lake Katharine♦ (1,850.37)
Knox County
Knox Woods (29.83)
Lake County
Hach-Otis♦ (80.25)
Headlands Dunes♦ (25)
Mentor Marsh♦ (646.55)
Lawrence County
Compass Plant Prairie (15.5)
Licking County
Blackhand Gorge♦ (980.87)
Cranberry Bog*♦ (19.54)
Morris Woods (104)
Logan County
McCracken Fen* (82)
Owens/Liberty Fen* (18.59)
Lucas County
Audubon Islands (170)   Metropolitan Park District of the
                                         Toledo Area

Campbell, Lou* (169.94)
Irwin Prairie♦ (223.49)
Kitty Todd* (672   The Nature Conservancy
Madison County
Bigelow Cemetery♦ (0.5)
Smith Cemetery♦ (0.63)
Mahoning County
Kyle Woods♦ (81.86)
Medina County
Swamp Cottonwood (20.52)
Mercer County
Baker Woods* (47.3)
Miami County
Goode Prairie* (28.43)   Miami County Park District
Greenville Falls (79.45)
Monroe County
Rothenbuhler Woods* (44.33)   The Nature Conservancy
Ottawa County
Lakeside Daisy*♦ (19.09)
Pickaway County
Stage's Pond♦ (177.99)
Pike County
Strait Creek Prairie* (266)   The Nature Conservancy
Portage County
Beck, Evans Memorial* (10.1)   The Nature Conservancy
Eagle Creek♦ (441.33)

Flatiron Lake Bog* (126)	The Nature Conservancy
Frame Lake Fen (137)	The Nature Conservancy
Gott Fen* (44.92)	
Cooperrider-Kent Bog♦ (43.45)	
Mantua Bog* (99)	
Marsh Wetlands (152.28)	Ohio Division of Wildlife
Tinker's Creek♦ (786)	
Triangle Lake Bog* (61.13)	
Tummonds (85.67)	
Preble County	
Hueston Woods♦ (200)	
Richland County	
Fowler Woods♦ (148.37)	
Ross County	
Betsch Fen* (34.7)	The Nature Conservancy
Scioto County	
Raven Rock* (95.27)	
Seneca County	
Collier, Howard (200)	
Springville Marsh♦ (201.37)	
Shelby County	
Gross Memorial Woods (48.54)	
Stark County	
Jackson Bog (40)	
Summit County	
Karlo Fen* (14.6)	
Portage Lakes Wetland* (5.86)	
Tinker's Creek♦ (786)	
Union County	
Milford Railroad Prairie (6.7)	
Warren County	
Caesar Creek Gorge♦ (460.84)	
Halls Creek Woods (278.05)	
Washington County	
Acadia Cliffs (277.35)	Ohio Division of Wildlife
Boord (89.24)	
Ladd Natural Bridge* (34.98)	
Wayne County	
Brown's Lake Bog (119)	The Nature Conservancy
Johnson Woods♦ (205.79)	
Williams County	
Mud Lake Bog* (74)	

Contact Information for Other Managing Agencies:

Audubon Society of Ohio, 3398 W. Galbraith Road, Cincinnati, Ohio 45239, Tel: 513-741-7926.

Clermont County Parks, P. O. Box 234, Batavia, Ohio 45103, Tel: 513-732-2977.
Crane Hollow Inc.: Please contact ODNR's Division of Natural Areas Preserves.
Crawford Park District, 117 East Mansfield St., Bucyrus, Ohio 44820; Tel: 419-562-8394.
Erie MetroParks, 3910 East Perkins Ave., Huron, Ohio 44839, Tel: 419-625-7783.
Gahanna City Parks, Gahanna, Ohio, Tel: 614-471-2563.
Greene County Park District, 651 Dayton-Xenia Road, Xenia, Ohio 45385-2698, Tel: 937-376-7440.
Hamilton County Park District, 10245 Winton Road, Cincinnati, Ohio 45231, Tel: 513-521-7275.
Highlands Nature Sanctuary, Inc., P. O. Box 457, Bainbridge, Ohio 45612, Tel: 937-365-1363.
Johnny Appleseed Park District, 2355 Ada Road, Lima, Ohio 45801, tel: 419-221-1232.
Metropolitan Park District of Columbus & Franklin Co., P. O. Box 29169, Columbus, Ohio 43229, Tel: 614-891-0700.
Miami County Park District, 2535 E. Ross Road, Tipp City, Ohio 45371-9213, Tel: 937-667-1086.
Metropolitan Park District of the Toledo Area, 5100 Central Avenue, Toledo, Ohio 43615, Tel: 419-535-3050.
Ohio Division of Wildlife, 1840 Belcher Drive, Columbus, Ohio 43224, Tel: 614-265-6300.
Ohio Historical Society/Cedar Bog, 980 Woodburn Road, Urbana, Ohio 43078-9417, Tel: 937 484 3744 or 800-860-0147.
Stratford Ecological Center, 3083 Liberty Road, Delaware, Ohio 43015, Tel: 740-363-2548.
The Nature Conservancy-Ohio Chapter, 6375 Riverside Drive, Ste. 50, Dublin, Ohio 43017, Tel: 614-717-2770.

OHIO'S SCENIC RIVERS

The Ohio Department of Natural Resources' Division of Natural Areas and Preserves oversees the 11 Ohio rivers designated as "scenic" under the Scenic Rivers Act of 1986. Information about conservation easements on these rivers is available from the Division. Contact Stuart Lewis, Administrator, Ohio Scenic Rivers Program, Ohio Department of Natural Resources, Division of Natural Areas and Preserves, 1889 Fountain Square, Bldg. F–1, Columbus, OH 43224; Tel: 614-265-6453. Web Site: <<http://www.dnr.state.oh.us/odnr/dnap/dnap.html>>.

Northeast Region: Steve Roloson, 11027 Hopkins Rd., Garrettsville, OH 44231; Tel: 330-527-4184; **Rivers:** Chagrin River, Grand River, Little Beaver Creek, Upper Cuyahoga River.

Northwest Region: Bob Vargo, 1435 Township Rd., 38 West, Tiffin, OH 44883; Tel: 419-981-6319; **Rivers:** Maumee River, Sandusky River.

Southwest Region: Don Rostefer, Sycamore State Park, 4675 Diamond Mill, Trotwood, OH 45426; Tel: 937-854-0350; **Rivers:** Stillwater & Greenville Creek Rivers, Little Miami River.

Central Ohio Region: Bob Gable, 1889 Fountain Square, Bldg. F-1, Columbus, OH 43224; Tel: 614-265-6814; **Rivers:** Big & Little Darby Creek, Olentangy River, Kokosing River.

Headquarters: Stuart Lewis, Administrator, Ohio Scenic Rivers Program, Ohio Department of Natural Resources, Division of Natural Areas and Preserves, 1889 Fountain Square, Bldg. F–1, Columbus, OH 43224; Tel: 614-265-6453.

OHIO STATE UNIVERSITY EXTENSION OFFICES

The Ohio State University Extension Offices (formerly the Ohio Cooperative Extension Service Offices) offer expertise on agricultural and horticultural practices to prevent erosion, restore nutrients to soils, establish habitat for birds and other animals, and develop natural resources generally. Additionally, they provide educational materials and technical help on such subjects as economic development, agribusiness, and a host of other subjects of value to large and small landowners. The offices are listed below alphabetically by county name. Where available, the fax number and Web site addresses are included. The main administrative contact for the state-wide program is Dr. Keith L. Smith, Dir., Ohio State University Extension, Room 3, Agricultural Administration Building, 2120 Fyffe Rd., Columbus, OH 43210-1084, Tel: 614-292-4067, Fax: 614-688-3807; E–mail: <<smith.150 @osu.edu>>; Web Site: <<http://www.ag.ohio-state.edu>>.

Adams County OSU Extension Office, 215 North Cross St., West Union, OH 45693; Tel: 937-544-2339; Fax: 937-544-8125; Web Site: <<http://www.ag.ohio-state.edu/~adam/index.html>>.

Allen County OSU Extension Office, 3900 Campus Dr., Ste. B, Lima, OH 45804-3596; Tel: 419-222-9946; Fax: 419-228-3601; Web Site: <<http://www.ag.ohio-state.edu/~alle/index.html>>.

Ashland County OSU Extension Office, 804 U.S. 250 East, Ashland, OH 44805-9750; Tel: 419-281-8242; Fax 419-281-7431; Web Site: <<http://www.ag.ohio-state.edu/~ash/index.html>>.

Ashtabula County OSU Extension Office, 39 Wall St., Extension Bldg., Jefferson, OH 44047-1137; Tel: 440-576-9008; Fax: 440-576-5821; Web Site: <<http://www.ag.ohio-state.edu/~asht/index. html>>.

Athens County OSU Extension Office, 280 W. Union St., Athens, OH 45701-2394; Tel: 740-593-8555; Fax: 740-592-1113; Web Site: <<http://www.ag.ohio-state.edu/~athe/index.html>>.

Auglaize County OSU Extension Office, 208 S. Blackhoof St., Wapakoneta, OH 45895-1902; Tel: 419-738-2219; Fax: 419-738-8262; Web Site: <<http://www.ag.ohio-state.edu/~augl/index. html>>.

Belmont County OSU Extension Office, 410 Fox Shannon Place, St. Clairsville, OH 43950-9772; Tel: 740-695-1455; Fax: 740-695-5614; Web Site: <<http://www.ag.ohio-state.edu/~belm/ index.html>>.

Brown County OSU Extension Office, 740 Mt. Orab Pike, Georgetown, OH 45121-1124; Tel: 937-378-6716; Fax: 937-378-6646; Web Site: <<http://www.ag.ohio-state.edu/~brow/index. html>>

Butler County OSU Extension Office, 1810 Princeton Rd., Hamilton, OH 45011-4797; Tel: 513-887-3722; Fax: 513-887-3726; Web Site: <<http://www.ag.ohio-state.edu/~butl/index.html>>.

Carroll County OSU Extension Office, Courthouse, 119 Public Square, Carrollton, OH 44615-1498; Tel: 330-627-4310; Fax: 330-667-6656; Web Site: <<http://www.ag.ohio-state.edu/~carr/index. html>>.

Champaign County OSU Extension Office, 1512 S. U.S. 68, Ste. B100, Urbana, OH 43078; Tel: 937-652-2204; Fax: 937-652-3935; Web Site: <<http://www.ag.ohio-state.edu/~cham/index. html>>.

Clark County OSU Extension Office, Ste. 104, 4400 Gateway Blvd., Prime Ohio Corp. Park, Springfield, OH 45502-9337; Tel:

937-328-4607; Fax: 937-328-4609; Web Site: <<http://www.ag.ohio-state.edu/~clar/index.html>>.

Clermont County OSU Extension Office, 1000 Locust St., P.O. Box 670, Owensville, OH 45160-0670; Tel: 513-732-7070; Fax: 513-732-7060; Web Site: <<http://www.ag.ohio-state.edu/~cler/index.html>>.

Clinton County OSU Extension Office, 111 S. Nelson Ave., Ste. 2, Wilmington, OH 45177-2099; Tel: 937-382-0901; Fax: 937-382-4995; Web Site: <<http://www.ag.ohio-state.edu/~clin/ndex.html>>.

Columbiana County OSU Extension Office, 330½ S. Lincoln Ave., Lisbon, OH 44432; Tel: 330-424-7291; Fax: 330-424-7292; Web Site: <<http://www.ag.ohio-state.edu/~cler/index.html>>.

Coshocton County OSU Extension Office, 724 S. 7th St., Coshocton, OH 43812-2392; Tel: 740-622-2265; Fax: 740-622-2197; Web Site: <<http://www.ag.ohio-state.edu/~cosh/index.html>>.

Crawford County OSU Extension Office, 117 E. Mansfield, Bucyrus, OH 44820-2389; Tel: 419-562-8731; Fax: 419-562-3677; Web Site: <<http://www.ag.ohio-state.edu/~cosh/index.html>>.

Cuyahoga County OSU Extension Office, 2490 Lee Blvd., Ste. 108, Cleveland Hts., OH 44118-1255; Tel: 216-397-6000; Fax: 216-397-3980; Web Site: <<http://www.ag.ohio-state.edu/~cuya/index.html>>.

Darke County OSU Extension Office, 700 Wayne St., Greenville, OH 45331-2267; Tel: 937-548-5215; Fax: 937-548-5215; Web Site: <<http://www.ag.ohio-state.edu/~dark/index.html>>.

Defiance County OSU Extension Office, 197-A Island Park Ave., Defiance, OH 43512-2551; Tel: 419-782-4771; Fax: 419-784-3883; Web Site: <<http://www.ag.ohio-state.edu/~defi/index.html>>.

Delaware County OSU Extension Office, 560 Sunbury Rd., Ste. 5, Delaware, OH 43015-8692; Tel: 740-368-1925; Fax: 740-363-9143.; Web Site: <<http://www.ag.ohio-state.edu/~dela/index.html>>.

Erie County OSU Extension Office, 2900 S. Columbus Ave., Sandusky, OH 44870-5554; Tel: 419-627-7631; Fax: 419-627-7692; Web Site: <<http://www.ag.ohio-state.edu/~erie/index/html>>.

Fairfield County OSU Extension Office, Ste. D, 831 College Ave., Lancaster, OH 43130-1081; Tel: 740-653-5419; Fax: 740-687-7010; Web Site: <<http://www.ag.ohio-state.edu/~fair/index. html>>.

Fayette County OSU Extension Office, 1415 U.S. Rt. 22 SW, Washington CH, OH 43160-9557; Tel: 740-335-1150: Fax: 740-335-2757; Web Site: <<http://www.ag.ohio-state.edu/~faye/index. html>>.

Franklin County OSU Extension Office, 1945 Frebis Ave., Columbus, OH 43206-3793; Tel: 614-462-6700; Fax: 614-462-6745; Web Site: <<http://www.ag.ohio-state.edu/~fran/index. html>>.

Fulton County OSU Extension Office, 135 Courthouse Plaza, Wauseon, OH 43567-1300; Tel: 419-337-9210; Fax: 419-335-0813; Web Site: <<http://www.ag.ohio-state.edu/~full/index. html>>.

Gallia County OSU Extension Office, 111 Jackson Pike, Gallipolis, OH 45631-1572; Tel: 740-446-7007; Fax: 740-441-2038; Web Site: <<http://www.ag.ohio-state.edu/~gall/index.html>>.

Geauga County OSU Extension Office, 14269 Claridon–Troy Rd., P.O. Box 387, Burton, OH 44021-0387; Tel: 440-834-4656; Fax: 440 834 0057; Web Site: <<http://www.ag.ohio-state.edu/ geau/index.html>>.

Greene County OSU Extension Office, 100 Fairgrounds Rd., Xenia, OH 45385-9543; Tel: 937-372-9971; Fax: 937-372-4070; Web Site: <<http://www.ag.ohio-state.edu/~gree/index.html>>.

Guernsey County OSU Extension Office, 9711 E. Pike, Room 200, Cambridge, OH 43725-9642, Tel. 740-432-9300, Fax. 740-439-1817; Web Site: <<http://www.ag.ohio-state.edu/~guer/index. html>>.

Hamilton County OSU Extension Office, 11100 Winton Rd., Cincinnati, OH 45218-1199; Tel: 513-825-6000; Fax: 513-825-6276; Web Site: <<http://www.ag.ohio-state.edu/~hami/index. html>>.

Hancock County OSU Extension Office, 7708 C.R. 140, Findlay, OH 45840-1817; Tel: 419-422-3851; Fax: 419-422-3866; Web Site: <<http://www.ag.ohio-state.edu/~hanc/index.html>>.

Hardin County OSU Extension Office, Ste. 40, 1 Courthouse Square, Kenton, OH 43326-2399; Tel: 419-674-2297; Fax: 419-674-2268; Web Site: <<http://www.ag.ohio-state.edu/~hard/index. html>>.

Harrison County OSU Extension Office, 104 West Market St., Courthouse, Cadiz, OH 43907-1132; Tel: 740-942-8823; Fax: 740-942-4693; Web Site: <<http://www.ag.ohio-state.edu/~harr/index. html>>.

Henry County OSU Extension Office, 104 E. Washington St., Ste. 107, Hahn Center, Napoleon, OH 43545-1646; Tel: 419-592-0806: Fax: 419-592-8750; Web Site: <<http://www.ag.ohio-state. edu/~henr/index.html>>.

Highland County OSU Extension Office, 119 Gov. Foraker Pl., Hillsboro, OH 45133-1092; Tel: 937-393-1918.

Hocking County OSU Extension Office, 150 N. Homer Ave., Logan, OH 43138-1730; Tel: 740-385-3222.

Holmes County OSU Extension Office, 165 N. Washington St., Millersburg, OH 44654-1105; Tel: 330-674-3015; Fax: 330-674-1908.

Huron County OSU Extension Office, 180 Milan Ave., Norwalk, OH 44857-1192; Tel: 419-668-8219.

Jackson County OSU Extension Office, 275 Portsmouth St., P.O. Box 110, Jackson, OH 45640-0110; Tel: 740-286-5044.

Jefferson County OSU Extension Office, Ste. A, 135 Main St., Wintersville, OH 43952-3733; Tel: 740-264-2212.

Knox County OSU Extension Office, 1025 Harcourt Rd., P.O. Box 1268, Mt. Vernon, OH 43050-8268; Tel: 740-397-0401; Fax: 740-393-0126; Web Site: <<http://www.ag.ohio-state.edu/~knox/ index.html>>.

Lake County OSU Extension Office, 99 E. Erie St., Painesville, OH 44077-3907; Tel: 440-350-2582; Fax: 440-350-5928; Web Site: <<http://www.ag.ohio-state.edu/~lake/index.html>>.

Lawrence County OSU Extension Office, Courthouse, Ironton, OH 45638-1592; Tel: 740-533-4322; Fax: 740-533-4416; Web Site: <<http://www.ag.ohio-state.edu/~lawr/index.html>>.

Licking County OSU Extension Office, Ste. 103, 771 E. Main St., Newark, OH 43055-6974; Tel: 740-349-6900; Fax: 740-349-6909; Web Site: <<http://www.ag.ohio-state.edu/~lick/index. html>>.

Logan County OSU Extension Office, 117 E. Columbus Ave., Ste. 100, Bellefontaine, OH 43311-2053; Tel: 937-599-4227; Fax: 937-592-6404; Web Site: <<http://www.ag.ohio-state.edu/~loga/ index.html>>.

Lorain County OSU Extension Office, 42110 Russia Rd., Elyria, OH 44035-6813; Tel: 440-322-0127; Fax: 440-329-5351; Web Site: <<http://www.ag.ohio-state.edu/~lora/index.html>>.

Lucas County OSU Extension Office, Room 550, One Government Center, Toledo, OH 43604-2245; Tel: 419-245-4254; Fax: 419-213-4241; Web Site: <<http://www.ag.ohio-state.edu/~luca/index.html>>.

Madison County OSU Extension Office, 217 Elm St., P.O. Box 230, London, OH 43140-1185; Tel: 740-852-0975; Fax: 740-852-0744; Web Site: <<http://www.ag.ohio-state.edu/~madi/index. html>>.

Mahoning County OSU Extension Office, 490 S. Broad St., Canfield, OH 44406-1604; Tel: 330-533-5538; Fax: 330-533-2424; Web Site: <<http://www.ag.ohio-state.edu/~maho/index.html>>.

Marion County OSU Extension Office, 1100 E. Center St., Marion, OH 43302-4496; Tel: 740-387-2260; Web Site: <<http:// www.ag.ohio-state.edu/~mari/index.html>>.

Medina County OSU Extension Office, 120 Washington St., Medina, OH 44256-2269; Tel: 330-725-4911; Fax: 330-754-8453; Web Site: <<http://www.ag.ohio-state.edu/~medi/index.html>>.

Meigs County OSU Extension Office, Mulberry Hts., P.O. Box 32, Pomeroy, OH 45769-0032; Tel: 740-992-6696; Fax: 740-992-7931; Web Site: <<http://www.ag.ohio-state.edu/~meig/index. html>>.

Mercer County OSU Extension Office, 220 W. Livingston St., Ste. 6, Celina, OH 45822-1632; Tel: 419-586-2179; Fax: 419-586-3367; Web Site: <<http://www.ag.ohio-state.edu/~merc/index. html>>.

Miami County OSU Extension Office, Courthouse, 201 W. Main St., Troy, OH 45373-3263; Tel: 937-332-6829; Fax: 937-339-9883; Web Site: <<http://www.ag.ohio-state.edu/~miami/index.html>>.

Monroe County OSU Extension Office, Room 17, 101 N. Main St., Woodsfield, OH 43793-1070; Tel: 740-472-0810; Fax: 740-472-2510; Web Site: <<http://www.ag.ohio-state.edu/~monr/index. html>>.

Montgomery County OSU Extension Office, 1001 S. Main St., Dayton, OH 45409-2799; Tel: 937-224-9654; Fax: 937-224-5110; Web Site: <<http://www.ag.ohio-state.edu/~mont/index.html>>.

Morgan County OSU Extension Office, 6A W. Main St., P.O. Box 179, McConnelsville, OH 43756-0179; Tel: 740-962-4854; Fax: 740-962-6508; Web Site: <<http://www.ag.ohio-state.edu/ ~morg/index.html>>.

Morrow County OSU Extension Office, 871 Marion Rd., Mt. Gilead, OH 43338-1088; Tel: 419-947-1070; Fax: 946-1950; Web Site: <<http://www.ag.ohio-state.edu/~morr/index.html>>.

Muskingum County OSU Extension Office, 225 Underwood St., Room 6, Zanesville, OH 43701-3789; Tel: 740-454-0144; Fax: 740-454-0154; Web Site: <<http://www.ag.ohio-state.edu/~musk/index. html>>.

Noble County OSU Extension Office, 150 Courthouse, Caldwell, OH 43724-1245; Tel: 740-732-5681; Fax: 740-732-5434; Web Site: <<http://www.ag.ohio-state.edu/~nobl/index.html>>.

Ottawa County OSU Extension Office, 240 W. Lake St., Unit C, Oak Harbor, OH 43449-1056; Tel: 419-898-1618; Fax: 419-898-3232; Web Site: <<http://www.ag.ohio-state.edu/~otta/index. html>>.

Paulding County OSU Extension Office, Fairground Dr., P.O. Box 87, Paulding, OH 45879-0087; Tel: 419-399-8225; Fax 419-399-5590; Web Site: <<http://www.ag.ohio-state.edu/~paul/index. html>>.

Perry County OSU Extension Office, 104 S. Columbus St., P.O. Box 279, Somerset, OH 43783-0279; Tel: 740-743-1602; Fax: 740-743-1215; Web Site: <<http://www.ag.ohio-state.edu/~perr/index. html>>.

Pickaway County OSU Extension Office, Ste. B, 110 Island Rd., P.O. Box 29, Circleville, OH 43113-0029; Tel: 740-474-7534; Fax: 740-474-7967; Web Site: <<http://www.ag.ohio-state.edu/~pick/index.html>>.

Pike County OSU Extension Office, 120 S. Market St., Waverly, OH 45690-1317; Tel: 740-947-2121; Fax: 740-947-4413; Web Site: <<http://www.ag.ohio-state.edu/~pike/index.html>>.

Portage County OSU Extension Office, 6970 S.R. 88, Ravenna, OH 44266-9150; Tel: 330-296-6432; Fax: 330-296-7737; Web Site: <<http://www.ag.ohio-state.edu/~port/index.html>>.

Preble County OSU Extension Office, 119 S. Barron St., Eaton, OH 45320-2394; Tel: 937-456-8174; Fax: 937-456-8180; Web Site: <<http://www.ag.ohio-state.edu/~preb/index.html>>.

Putnam County OSU Extension Office, 219 S. Oak St., P.O. Box 189, Ottawa, OH 45875-0189; Tel: 419-523-6294; Fax: 419-523-3192; Web Site: <<http://www.ag.ohio-state.edu/~putn/index.html>>.

Richland County OSU Extension Office, 1495 Longview Ave., 206, Mansfield, OH 449056; Tel: 419-747-8755; Fax: 419-747-8770; Web Site: <<http://www.ag.ohio-state.edu/~rich/index.html>>.

Ross County OSU Extension Office, 475 Western Ave., Ste. F, Chillicothe, OH 45601; Tel: 740-702-3200; Fax: 740-702-3209; Web Site: <<http://www.ag.ohio-state.edu/~ross/index.html>>.

Sandusky County OSU Extension Office, 2000 Countryside Dr., Fremont, OH 43420-9574; Tel: 419-334-6340; Fax: 419-334-6344; Web Site: <<http://www.ag.ohio-state.edu/~sand/index.html>>.

Scioto County OSU Extension Office, Courthouse, 602 Seventh St., Portsmouth, OH 45662-3948; Tel: 740-354-7879; Fax: 740-355-8338; Web Site: <<http://www.ag.ohio-state.edu/~scio/index.html>>.

Seneca County OSU Extension Office, 155½ E. Perry St., Tiffin, OH 44883-2389; Tel: 419-447-9722; Fax: 419-447-7677; Web Site: <<http://www.ag.ohio-state.edu/~sene/index.html>>.

Shelby County OSU Extension Office, 810 Fair Rd., Sidney, OH 45365-2949; Tel: 937-498-7239; Fax: 937-498-7241; Web Site: <<http://www.ag.ohio-state.edu/~shel/index.html>>.

Stark / Summit County OSU Extension Office, Regional Extension Education Center, 5119 Lauby Rd., No. Canton, OH 44720-1544; Tel: 330-497-1611; Fax: 330-497-2807; Web Site: <<http://www.ag.ohio-state.edu/~star/index.html>>.

Trumbull County OSU Extension Office, 303 Mahoning NW, Warren, OH 44483-4698; Tel: 330-675-2595; Fax: 330-675-2594; Web Site: <<http://www.ag.ohio-state.edu/~trum/index.html>>.

Tuscarawas County OSU Extension Office, 219 Stonecreek Rd. NW, New Philadelphia, OH 44663-6902; Tel: 330-364-8811, ext. 230; Fax: 330-339-7442; Web Site: <<http://www.ag.ohio-state. edu/~tusc/index.html>>.

Union County OSU Extension Office, 246 W. Fifth St., Marysville, OH 43040-1195; Tel: 937-644-8117; Fax: 937-644-3062; Web Site: <<http://www.ag.ohio-state.edu/~unio/index. html>>.

Van Wert County OSU Extension Office, 1055 S. Washington, Van Wert, OH 45891-2499; Tel: 419-238-1214; Fax: 419-238-3276; Web Site: <<http://www.ag.ohio-state.edu/~vanw/index. html>>.

Vinton County OSU Extension Office, P.O. Box 473, County Community Bldg., McArthur, OH 45651-0473; Tel: 740-596-5212; Fax: 740-596-4734; Web Site: <<http://www.ag.ohio-state.edu/~ vint/index.html>>.

Warren County OSU Extension Office, 1054 Monroe Rd., Ste. 102, Lebanon, OH 45036-1415; Tel: 513-932-1891; Fax: 513-695-1111; Web Site: <<http://www.ag.ohio-state.edu/~warr/index. html>>.

Washington County OSU Extension Office, 206 Davis Ave., Marietta, OH 45750-7431; Tel: 740-376-7431; Fax: 740-376-7085; Web Site: <<http://www.ag.ohio-state.edu/~wash/index.html>>.

Wayne County OSU Extension Office, 428 W. Liberty St., Wooster, OH 44691-5092; Tel: 330-264-8722; Fax: 330-263-7696; Web Site: <<http://www.ag.ohio-state.edu/~wayn/index.html>>.

Williams County OSU Extension Office, 1122 W. High St., Bryan, OH 43506-1599; Tel: 419-636-5608; Fax: 419-636-0595; Web Site: <<http://www.ag.ohio-state.edu/~will/index.html>>.

Wood County OSU Extension Office, 440 E. Poe Rd., Ste. A, Bowling Green, OH 43402-1351; Tel: 419-354-9050; Fax: 419-352-7413; Web Site: <<http://www.ag.ohio-state.edu/~wood/index. html>>.

Wyandot County OSU Extension Office, 109 S. Sandusky Ave., Room 16, Upper Sandusky, OH 43351-1423; Tel: 419-294-4931; Fax: 419-294-6415; Web Site: <<http://www.ag.ohio-state.edu/ ~wyan/index.html>>.

District Offices

East District, 16714 S.R. 215, Caldwell, OH 43724-9506; Tel: 740-732-2381; Fax: 740-732-5992; Web Site: <<http://www.ag. ohio-state.edu/county/maps/east.html>>.

Northeast District, Ohio Agricultural Research & Development Center (OARDC), 1680 Madison Ave., Wooster, OH 44691-4096; Tel: 330-263-3831; 330-263-3832; Fax: 330-263-3667; Web Site: <<http://www.ag.ohio-state.edu/county/maps/neast.html>>.

Northwest District, 952 Lima Ave., Box C, Findlay, OH 45840; Tel: 419-422-6106; Fax: 419-422-7595; Web Site: <<http://www. ag.ohio-state.edu/county/maps/nwest.html>>.

South District, 17 Standpipe Rd., P.O. Box 958, Jackson, OH 45640-0958; Tel: 740-286-2177; Fax: 740-286-1578; Web Site: <<http://www.ag.ohio-state.edu/county/maps/south.html>>.

Southwest District, 303 Corporate Center Dr., Ste. 208, Vandalia, OH 45377-1171; Tel: 937-454-5002; Fax: 937-454-1237; Web Site: <<http://www.ag.ohio-state.edu/county/maps/swest.html>>.

Specialty Centers for Business Enhancement, Enterprise, & Economic Development

Agricultural Business Enhancement Center, 440 E. Poe Rd., Ste. D, Bowling Green, OH 43402-1351; Tel: 419-354-6916; 800-358-4678; Fax: 419-354-6416; Web Site: <<http://www.ag.ohio-state. edu/~abe>>.

Alber Enterprise Center, 1465 Mt. Vernon Ave., #122, Marion, OH 43302-5695; Tel: 740-389-6786 & 614-292-9133.

Enterprise Center for Economic Development, 1864 Shyville Rd., Piketon, OH 45661-9749; Tel: 740-289-3727.

ORGANIZATIONS & PUBLICATIONS WITH LAND–USE INTERESTS

The names of publications in the list below appear in italics.

Local

Audubon Society of Greater Cleveland. Daniel H. Melcher, Pres., The Park Building, 140 Public Square, Cleveland, OH 44114-2213; Tel: 216-861-5093; E-mail: <<71634.140@ compuserve.com>>.

Blackbrook Audubon Society. Mary Hoffman, Pres., 3920 Princeton Blvd., South Euclid, OH 44121; Tel: 216-382-8053; E-mail: <<mvhoff@en.com>>.

Chagrin River Watershed Partners. Thomas J. Denbow, Exec. Dir., 2705 River Rd., Willoughby Hills, OH 4094-9445; Tel: 440-975-3840; Fax: 440-975-3865; Web Site: <<http://www.crwp. org>>.

Chagrin Watershed Institute. Reini Friebertshauser, University School, 2785 SOM Center Rd., Hunting Valley, OH 44022; Tel: 216-831-2200 or 216-831-1984 ext. 329; Fax: 216-292-7809; Web Site: <<http://cwi.us.edu>>.

Cleveland Community Development Network. Web Site: <<http://www.little.nhlink.net/nhlink/cdc>>.

Cleveland Neighborhood Development Corporation. 540 E. 105th St., Ste. 330, Cleveland, OH 44108; Tel: 216-3130.

Cleveland Restoration Society & Preservation Resource Center of Northeastern Ohio. Sarah Benedict House, 3751 Prospect Ave., Cleveland, OH 44115-2705; Tel: 216-426-1000.

The Countryside Program. Contact; Kirby Date, Coord., P.O. Box 24825, Lyndhurst, OH 44124; Tel: 216-295-0511; Fax: 216-295-0527; Fax: 216-295-0527; E-mail: <<ninmile@en.com>>.

Cuyahoga River Remedial Action Program. Kelvin Rogers, RAP Coord., Ohio EPA, Northeast District Office, 2110 E. Aurora Rd., Twinsburg, OH 44087; Tel: 330-963-1117; Fax: 330-487-0769; E-mail: <<kelvin.rogers@epa.state.oh.us>>;Web Site: <<http:// www.chagrin.epa.Ohio.gov/programs/rap/cuyahoga.html>>.

Cuyahoga Valley Association. P.O. Box 222, Peninsula, OH 44264-0222; Tel: 330-657-2909; Web Site: <<http://www.nps.gov /cuva/cva>>.

Earth Day Coalition. 3606 Bridge Ave., Cleveland, OH 44113; Tel: 216-281-6468; Fax: 216-281-5112; E-mail: <<edc@ earthdaycoalition.org>>; Web Site: <<http://www. earthdaycoalition.org>>.

EcoCity Cleveland. David Beach, 2841 Scarborough Rd., Cleveland Hts., OH 44118; Tel: 216-932-3007; Web Site: <<http:// www.ecoclevelend.org>>.

EcoCity Cleveland Journal. Published by EcoCity Cleveland (see above).

Friends of the Crooked River. Elaine Marsh, 2390 Kensington Rd., Akron, OH 44333; Tel: 330-666-4026; Fax: 330-657-2955; E-mail: <<ohgreenway@aol.com>>.

Friends of Wetlands. P.O. Box 2016, Elyria, OH 44036; Tel: 440-324-7522.

Great Lakes Information Network (GLIN). Great Lakes Commission, 400 Fourth St., Argus II Bldg., Ann Arbor, MI 48103-4816; Tel: 734-665-9135; Fax: 734-665-4370; Web Site: <<http:// www.glc.org/>>.

Kent Environmental Council. P.O. Box 395, Kent, OH 44240, Tel: 330-673-6534.

Preservation Resource Center of Northeastern Ohio. See listing for Cleveland Restoration Society, above.

Sovonth Generation. George Espy, Exec. Dir., 25 Lake Ave., Elyria, OH 44035; Tel: 440-322-4187; Fax: 440-322-1785; E-mail: <<SevnGen@aol.com>>.

Sierra Club, Northeast Ohio Group. 13677 Old Pleasant Valley Rd., Middleburg Hts., OH 44130; Tel: 440-843-7272; Web Site: <<http://www.sierraclub.org/chapters/oh>>.

Trust for Public Land, Cleveland Field Office. 1836 Euclid Ave., Ste. 800, Cleveland, OH 44115; Tel: 216-694-4416; Fax: 216-696-2326; E-mail: <<info@tpl.org>>.

State

American Farmland Trust. Jill Buckovac, Dir., Ohio Office 200 North High St., Room 522, Columbus, OH 43215; Tel: 614-469-9877; Fax: 614-469-2083; Web Site: http://www.farmland.org/ Farmland/files/states/oh.htm>>.

Bureau of Land Management, Eastern States Office. 7450 Boston Blvd., Springfield, VA 22153; Tel: 703-440-1713; Web Site: <<http://www.blm.gov/nhp/state.html>>.

Community Service, Inc. Marianne MacQueen, Dir., P.O. Box 243, 114 E. Waterman St., Yellow Springs, OH 45387; Tel: 937-767-2161; Fax: 937-767-2826; E-mail: <<communityservice@ usa.net>>.

County Commissioners' Association of Ohio. 37 West Broad St., Ste. 650, Columbus, OH 43215-4132; Tel: 614-221-5627; Fax: 614-221-6986; Web Site: <<http://www.ccao.org>>.

Farm Service Agency of Ohio (USDA). Room 540, Federal Building, 200 North High St., Columbus, OH 43215; Tel: 614-469-6735; Web Site: <<http://www.fas.usda.gov/EDSO/oh/oh.htm>>.

League of Women Voters of Ohio. 17 South High St., Ste. 650, Columbus, OH 43215; Tel: 800-598-6446 or 614-469-1505; Fax: 614-469-7918; Web Site: <<http://www.lwvohio.org>>.

The Nature Conservancy, Ohio Chapter. Jan Burkey; Scott Davis, Assoc. Dir., Jeff Newberg, Dir. of Acquisitions, 6375 Riverside Drive, Ste. 50, Dublin, OH; 43017; Tel: 614-717-2770; Fax: 614-717-2777. Web Site: <<http://www.tnc.org/Infield/State/ Ohio>>.

National Audubon Society/Ohio. Stephen Sedam, Exec. Dir., 692 North High St., Ste. 208, Columbus, OH 43215-1585; Tel: 614-224-3303; Fax: 614-224-3305; Web Site: <<http://www.audubon. org/chapter/oh>>.

The Nature Conservancy, Ohio Field Office. David Weekes, Dir., 6375 Riverside Dr., Ste. 50, Dublin, OH 43017; Tel: 614-717-2770; Web Site: <<http://www.tnc.org>>.

Office of Farmland Preservation. Howard Wise, Exec. Dir., 8995 E. Main St., Reynoldsburg, OH 43068; Tel: 614-466-2732; Fax: 614-466-6124; E-mail: <<farmland@odant.agri.state.oh.us>>.

Ohio & Erie Canal National Heritage Corridor. Special designation of the National Park Service. Contact Ohio Canal Corridor, below.

Ohio & Erie Canal Corridor Coalition. 520 South Main St., #2541–F, Akron, OH 44311; Tel: 330-434-5657; Fax: 330-434-5688; Web Site: <<http://www.uakron.edu/bustech/canal/oeccc>>.

Ohio Canal Corridor. Tim Donovan, Dir., P.O. Box 609420, Cleveland, OH 44109; Tel: 216-348-1825; Fax: 216-348-1832; Web Site: <<http://www.ohiocanal.org>>.

Ohio Coastal Resource Management Project. Edith Chase, Box 3160, Kent, OH 44240; Tel: 330-673-1193.

Ohio Department of Agriculture. 8995 E. Main St., Reynoldsburg, OH 43068; Tel: 614-728-6200; Fax: 614-728-6226; Web Site: <<http://www.state.oh.us/agr/>>.

Ohio Department of Development. 24th - 29th Floors, 77 S. High St., Columbus, OH 43215-6108; Tel: 614-466-3379; Fax: 614-644 0754.

Ohio Department of Natural Resources. Administrative Offices, Building D, 1930 Belcher Dr., Columbus, OH 43224-1387; Tel: 614-265-6875; Fax: Web Site: <<http://www.dnr.state.oh.us>>.

> **Division of Civilian Conservation.** Building B., 4383 Fountain Square Dr., Columbus, OH 43224-1362; Tel: 614-265-6423; 614-447-8005.

> **Division of Computers & Communication.** Building I, 1894 Fountain Square Ct., Columbus, OH 43224-1360; Tel: 614-265-6852; Fax: 614-799-2512.

> **Division of Engineering.** Building F, 1889 Fountain Square Ct., Columbus, OH 43224-1331; Tel: 614-265-6948; Fax 614-262-2197.

> **Division of Forestry.** Building H, Fountain Square Ct., Columbus, OH 43224-1327; Tel: 614-265-6694; Fax: 614-447-9231.

> **Division of Geological Survey.** Building B, Fountain Square Dr., Columbus, OH 43224-1362; Tel: 614-265-6576; Fax: 614-268-3669.

Division of Mines & Reclamation. Building H, 1855 Fountain Square Ct., Columbus, OH 43224-1327; Tel: 614-265-6633; Fax: 614-265-7999.

Division of Natural Areas & Preserves. Building F, Fountain Square Ct., Columbus, Ohio 43224-1331; Tel: 614-265-6453; Fax: 614-256-3096.

Division of Oil & Gas. Building B, Fountain Square Dr., Columbus, OH 43224-1362; Tel: 614-265-6922; Fax: 614-268-4316.

Division of Parks & Recreation. Building C, 1952 Fountain Square Dr., Columbus, Ohio 43224-1386; Tel: 614-265-6561; Fax: 261-8407.

Division of Real Estate & Land Management. Building C, 1952 Belcher Dr., Columbus, OH 43224-1386; Tel: 614-265-6395; Fax: 614-267-4764.

Division of Recycling & Litter Prevention. Building F, 1889 Fountain Square Ct., Columbus, OH 43224-1331; Tel: 614-265-6333; Fax: 614-262-9387.

Division of Soil and Water Conservation. Building E, 1939 Fountain Square Ct., Columbus, OH 43224-1336; Tel: 614-265-6610; Fax: 614-262-2064.

Division of Water. Building E, 1939 Fountain Square Ct., Columbus, OH 43224-1336; Tel: 614-265-6717; Fax: 614-447-9503.

Division of Watercraft. Building A, 4435 Fountain Square Dr., Columbus, OH 43224-1300; Tel: 614-265-6480; Fax: 614-267-8883.

Division of Wildlife. Building G, 1840 Belcher Dr., Columbus, OH 43224-1329; Tel: 614-265-6300; Fax: 252-1143.

> ***Wildlife District One.*** 1500 Dublin Rd., Columbus, OH 43215; Tel: 614-644-3925.

> ***Wildlife District Two.*** 952 Lima Ave., Box A, Findlay, OH 45840; Tel: 419-424-5000.

Wildlife District Three. 912 Portage Lakes Dr.,
Akron, OH 44319; Tel: 614-644-2293.

Wildlife District Four. 360 E. State St., Athens,
OH 45701; Tel: 740-594-2211.

Wildlife District Five. 1076 Old Springfield Pike,
Xenia, OH 45385; Tel: 937-372-9261.

Office of Public Information & Communications.
Building D, 1930 Belcher Dr., Columbus, OH 43224-1387;
Tel: 614-265-6791; Fax: 614-267-9165.

Public Interest Center (Media & Public Involvement).
122 South Front St., P.O. Box 1049, Columbus, OH
43216-1049; Tel: 614-644-2160

Ohio Department of Transportation. 1180 W. Broad St.,
Columbus, OH 43223; Tel: 614-466-7170; Web Site: <<http://www.
dot.state.oh.us>>.

Divisions and Offices

Director. Tel: 614-466-2335.

Division of Multi–Modal Planning and Programs. Tel:
614-466-8969.

Division of Engineering Policy. Tel: 614-466-3598.

Division of Project Management. Tel: 614-728-9544.

Ohio Rail Development Commission. 614-644-0310

District Offices (counties in parentheses)

District #1. 1885 N. McCullough St., P.O. Box 40, Lima,
OH 45802-0040; Tel: 419-222-9055 (Allen, Defiance,
Hancock, Hardin, Paulding, Putnam, Van Wert, Wyandot)

District #2. 317 E. Poe Rd., Bowling Green, OH 43402;
Tel: 419-353-8131 (Defiance, Fulton, Henry, Lucas,
Ottawa, Sandusky, Seneca, Williams)

District #3. 906 N. Clark St., Ashland, OH 44805-1989;
Tel: 800-276-4188 or 419-283-0513 (Ashland, Crawford,
Erie, Huron, Lorain, Medina, Seneca, Wayne)

District #4. 705 Oakwood St., Ravenna, OH 44266; Tel: 330-297-0801 (Ashtabula, Mahoning, Portage, Stark, Summit, Trumbull)

District #5. 9600 Jacksontown Rd., SE, Jacksontown, OH 43030; Tel: 740-323-4400 (Coshocton, Fairfield, Guernsey, Knox, Licking, Muskingham, Perry)

District #6. 400 E. William St., Delaware, OH 43015; Tel: 800-372-7714 or 714-363-1252; Fax: 740-369-7437 (Delaware, Fayette, Franklin, Madison, Marion, Morrow, Pickaway, Union)

District #7. 1001 St. Mary's Ave., P.O. Box 969, Sidney, OH 45365-0969; Tel: 937-492-1141(Auglaize, Champagne, Clark, Darke, Logan, Mercer, Miami, Montgomery, Shelby)

District #8. 505 S. State Route 741, Lebanon, OH 45036-9518; Tel: 800-831-2142 or 513-932-3030 (Butler, Clermont, Clinton, Greene, Hamilton, Preble, Warren)

District #9. 650 Eastern Ave., P.O. Box 467, Chillicothe, OH 45601; Tel: 800-845-0226 or 740-773-2691 (Adams, Brown, Highland, Jackson, Lawrence, Pike, Ross, Scioto)

District 10. Muskingham Dr., P.O. Box 658, Marietta, OH 45750; Tel: 740-373-0212 (Athens, Gallia, Hocking, Meigs, Monroe, Morgan, Noble, Vinton, Washington)

District #11. 2201 Reiser Ave. SE, P.O. Box 1000, New Philadelphia, OH 44663; Tel: 330-339-6633 (Belmont, Carroll, Columbiana, Harrison, Holmes, Jefferson, Tuscarawas)

District #12. 5500 Transportation Blvd., Garfield Hts., OH 44125; Tel: 216-581-2100 (Cuyahoga, Geauga, Lake)

Ohio Ecological Food and Farm Association (OEFFA, certifier of organic farms). P.O. Box 82234, Columbus, OH 43202; Tel; 614-267-3663; or Lisa Ferguson, South West District Co-Representative, Ty Bryn Organic Farm, 3211 E. State Route 55, Troy, OH 45373-9785; Tel: 513-339-6514.

Ohio Environmental Council. 1207 Grandview Ave., Ste. 201, Columbus, OH 43212; Tel: 614-487-7506; Fax: 614-487-7510; Web Site: <<http://www.theoec.org>>.

Ohio Environmental Protection Agency. Mailing address: Lazarus Government Center, P.O. Box 1049, Columbus, OH 43216-1049; Street address: Lazarus Government Center, 122 South Front St., Columbus, OH 43215; Tel: 614-644-3020; Fax: 614-644-2329; Web Site: <<http://www.epa.ohio.gov>>.

Divisions and Offices

Division of Air Pollution Control. 122 South Front St., 6th Floor, Columbus, P.O. Box 1049, Columbus, OH 43216-1049; Tel: 614-644-2270; Fax: 614-644-3681.

Division of Drinking & Ground Waters. 122 South Front St., P.O. Box 1049, Columbus, OH 43216-1049; Tel: 614-644-2752; Fax: 614-644-2909.

Division of Emergency & Remedial Response. 122 South Front St., 6th Floor, Columbus, OH 43216-1049; Tel: 614-644-2924; Fax: 614-644-3146.

Division of Environmental & Financial Assistance. 122 South Front St., 6th Floor, Columbus, OH 43216-1049; Tel: 614-644-2798; Fax: 614-644-3687.

Division of Environmental Services. 1571 Perry St., Columbus, OH 43201-2670; Tel: 614-644-4247; Fax: 614-644-4272.

Division of Hazardous Waste Management. 122 South Front St., 6th Floor, P.O. Box 1049, Columbus, OH 43216-1049; Tel: 614-644-2917; Fax: 614-644-728-1245.

Division of Solid & Infectious Waste Management. 122 South Front St., 5A, P.O. Box 1049, Columbus, OH 43216-1049; Tel: 614-644-2621, Fax: 614-728-5316.

Division of Surface Water. 122 South Front St., 6th Floor, P.O. Box 1049, Columbus, OH 43216-1049; Tel: 614-644-2001; Fax: 614-644-2745.

Office of Environmental Education. 122 South Front St., P.O. Box 1049, Columbus, OH 43216-1049; Tel: 614-644-2873; Fax: 614-644-1275.

Office of Pollution Prevention. 122 South Front St., 5th Floor, P.O. Box 1049, Columbus, OH 43216-1049; Tel: 614-644-3469; Fax: 614-644-2807.

Ohio Environmental Education Fund. 122 South Front St., 6th Floor, P.O. Box 1049, Columbus, OH 43216-1049; Tel: 614-644-2873; Fax: 614-644-3687.

Districts: The five districts of OEPA follow below, with counties they represent in parenthesis.

Central District Office, 3232 Alum Creek Dr., Columbus, OH 43207-3417; Tel: 614-728-3778 or 800-686-2330; Fax: 614-728-3898. (Delaware, Fairfield, Fayette, Franklin, Knox, Licking, Madison, Morrow, Pickaway, and Union)

Northeast District Office, 2110 E. Aurora Rd., Twinsburg, OH 44087; Tel: 330-963-1200 or 800-686-6330; Fax: 330-487-0769. (Ashtabula, Carroll, Columbiana, Cuyahoga, Geauga, Holmes, Lake Lorain, Mahoning, Medina, Portage, Stark, Summit, Trumbull, and Wayne)

Northwest District Office, 347 North Dunbridge Rd., Bowling Green, OH 43402; Tel: 419-352-8461 or 800-686-6930; Fax: 419-352-8468. (Allen, Ashland, Auglaize, Crawford, Defiance, Erie, Fulton, Hancock, Hardin, Henry, Huron, Lucas, Marion, Mercer, Ottawa, Paulding, Putnam, Richland, Sandusky, Seneca, Van Wert, Williams, Wood, and Wyandot)

Southeast District Office, 2195 Front St., Logan, OH 43138; Tel: 740-385-8501 or 800-686-7330; Fax: 740-385-6490. (Adams, Athens, Belmont, Coshocton, Gallia, Guernsey, Harrison, Hocking, Jackson, Jefferson, Lawrence, Meigs, Monroe, Morgan, Muskingum, Noble, Perry, Pike, Ross, Scioto, Tuscarawas, Vinton, and Washington)

Southwest District Office, 40 S. Main St., Dayton, OH 45402; Tel: 937-285-6357 or 800-686-8930; Fax: 937-285-6249. (Brown, Butler, Champaign, Clark, Clermont, Clinton, Darke, Greene, Hamilton, Highland, Logan, Miami, Montgomery, Preble, Shelby, and Warren)

Ohio Fund for the Environment. 3821 North High St., Columbus, OH 43214-3526; Tel: 614-263-6367; Web Site: <<http://www. junior. apk.net>>.

Ohio Government Information and Services. Governor Bob Taft, 77 South High St., 30th Floor, Columbus, OH 43215; Tel: 614-466-3555; Web Site: <<http://www.state.oh.us>>.

Ohio Geographically Referenced Information Program (OGRIP). State of Ohio Computer Center, 1320 Arthur E. Adams Dr., 1st Floor, Columbus, OH 43221; Tel: 614-466-4747; Fax: 614-644-2133; Web Site: <<http://www.state.oh.us/ogrip>>.

Ohio River Valley Water Sanitation Commission. 5735 Kellogg Ave., Cincinnati, OH 45228; Tel: 513-231-7719; Fax: 513-231-7761; E-mail: (Kristi Rose), <<krose@orsanco. org>>; Web Site: <<http://www.orsanco.org>>.

Ohio Rural Zoning Handbook, Fourth Edition. Office of Local Government Services, Ohio Department of Development, 24th - 29th Floors, 77 S. High St., Columbus, OH 43215-6108; Tel: 614-466-3379; Fax: 614-644-0754.

The Ohio State University, Department of Agricultural Economics. Lawrence W. (Larry) Libby, Prof. and C. William Swank Chair in Rural–Urban Policy, Dept. of Agricultural Economics, OSU, 336 Agricultural Administration Bldg., 2120 Fyfe Rd., Columbus, OH 43210-1067; Tel: 614-688-4907; Fax: 614-292-4749; E-mail: <<libby.7@osu.edu>>; Web Site: <<http://www-agecon.ag.ohio-state.edu>>.

Ohio Township Association. Michael H. Cochran, Exec. Dir., 5969 East Livingston Ave., Ste. 110, Columbus, OH 43232-2970; Tel: 614-863-0045; Fax: 614-863-9751; E-mail: <<OTAOhio@ aol.com>>; Web Site: <<http://www.localgovt.muohio.edu>>.

Ohio Water Environment Association. Curtis Truss, Jr., Exec. Dir., OTCO, 3972 Indianola Ave., Columbus, OH 43214-3158; Tel: 614-268-4069; Fax: 614-268-3244; E-mail: <<owea@ohiowater. org>>; Web Site: <<http://www.ohiowater.org/owea>>.

Rivers, Trails, and Conservation Assistance Program, Midwest Region (National Park Service). Paul Labovitz, Prog. Leader, 4570 Akron–Peninsula Rd., Peninsula, OH 44264; Tel: 330-657-2950; Fax: 330-657-2955; E-mail: <<paul_labovitz@nps. gov>>.

Sierra Club. Marc Conte, State Program Coord., 145 N. High St., Ste. 409, Columbus, OH 43215; Tel: 614-461-0734; Fax: 614-461-0730; Web Site: <<http://www.sierraclub.org/chapters/oh>>.

State and Local Government Commission of Ohio. Scott W. Sigel, Exec. Dir., 77 S. High St., Ste. 714, Columbus, OH 43266-0535; Tel: 614-466-2108; Fax: 614-466-9150; Web Site: <<http://www.state.oh.us/slg/index.htm>>.

State of Ohio Board of Landscape Architect Examiners. 77 S. High St., 16th Floor, Columbus, OH 43266-0303; Tel: 614-466-2316; Fax: 614-644-9048; E-mail: <<cmharch@aol.com>>; Web Site: <<http://www.state.oh.us/arc/lae/contacts.htm>>.

National

Adding Value for Sustainability. Created by the Pennsylvania Association for Sustainable Agriculture Research and Education Program (SARE) and Cornell University's Farming Alternatives ($8.50 +$3 s/h from Cornell University, Farming Alternatives Program, 17 Warren Hall, Cornell University, Ithaca, NY 14853; Tel: 607-255-9832).

American Farmland Trust. 1200 18th St., NW, Ste. 800, Washington, DC 20036; Tel: 202-331-7300; Fax: 202-659-8339; E-mail: <<info@farmland.org>>; Web Site: <<http://www.farmland.org>>.

American Forests. P.O. Box 2000, Washington, DC 20013; Tel: 202-955-4500; Web Site: <<http://www.amfor.org>>.

American Littoral Society. Sandy Hook, Highlands, NJ 07732; Tel: 732-291-0055; Web Site: <<http://www.Americanlittoralsoc.org>>.

American Planning Association. Headquarters: 1776 Massachusetts Ave., NW, Washington, DC 20036; Tel: 202-872-0611; Fax: 202-872-0643; Memberships & Subscriptions: 1313 E. 60th St., Chicago, IL 60637; Tel: 312-955-9100; Fax: 312-955-8312; Fax–on–demand service: 800-800-1589; Web Site: <<http://www.planning.org>>. International Division: 55 West 44th St., 3rd Floor, New York, NY 10036; Tel: 212-730-5171; Fax: 212-768-9071; E-mail: <<webmaster@interplan. org>>; Web Site: <<http://www.interplan.org>>.

American Rivers. 11025 Vermont Ave., NW, Ste. 720, Washington, DC 20005; Tel: 202-347-7550; Fax: 202-347-9240; Web Site: <<http://wwwamrivers.org>>.

American Society for Environmental History. Web Site: <<http://h-net2.msu.edu/~aseh>>.

American Society of Landscape Architects. 636 Eye St., NW, Washington, DC 20001-3736; Tel: 202-898-2444; Fax: 202-898-1185; Web Site: <<http://www.asla.org>>.

Association for Conservation Information. Web Site: <<http://www.dfw.state.or.us/aci>>.

The Back Forty. The Hyperion Society, University of California's Hastings College of the Law, 200 McAllister St., San Francisco, CA 94102; Tel: 415-565-4857; Fax: 415- 565-4818.

Bureau of Land Management. BLM, Office of Public Affairs, 1849 C St., Room 406-LS, Washington, DC 20240; Tel: 202-452-5125; Web Site: <<http://www.blm.gov>>.

California Center for Land Recycling. 455 market St., Ste. 1100, San Francisco, CA 94105; Tel: 415-820-2080; Fax: 415-882-7666; E-mail: <<emily.rosenberg@cclr.org>>; Web Site: <<http://www.cclr>>.

California Environmental Resources Evaluation System (CERES). 900 N St., Ste. 250, State Library & Courts Building II, Sacramento, CA 95814; Tel: 916-654-9990; Fax: 916-654-5829; Web Site: <<http://www.ceres.ca.gov>>.

Center for Environmental Information & Statistics. U.S. Environmental Protection Agency, 401 M St., SW, Washington, DC 20460-0003; Tel: 202-260-2090; Web Site: <<http://www.epa.gov/ceis>>.

Center for Livable Communities. c/o Local Government Commission, 1414 K St., Ste. 250, Sacramento, CA 95014; Tel: 916-448-1198; Fax: 916-448-8246; Web Site: <<http:// www.lgc.org/clc>>.

Center for Neighborhood Technology. 2125 W. North Ave., Chicago, IL 60647; Tel: 773-278-4800; Fax: 773-278-3840; Web Site: <<http://www.cnt.org>>.

Center for Watershed Protection. 8391 Main St., Ellicott City, MD 21043; Tel: 410-461-8323; Fax: 410-461-8324; E-mail: <<mrrunoff @pipeline.com>>; Web Site: <<http://www.cwp.org>>.

Center of Excellence for Sustainable Development (a project of the U.S. Department of Energy). U.S. Dept. of Energy, Office of Energy Efficiency and Renewable Energy, Denver Regional Support Office, 1617 Cole Blvd., Golden, CO 80401; Tel: 800-363-3732; Fax: 303-275-4830; Web Site: <<http://www.sustainainable. doe.gov>>.

Citizens' Network for Sustainable Development (CitNet), P.O. Box 316, Bolinas, CA 94924; Tel: 415-868-9720; Fax: 415-868-2230; Web Site: <<http://www.igc.org/citizensnet>>.

Community Rights Council. 1726 M St., NW, Ste. 703, Washington, DC 20036-4524; Tel: 202-296-6889; Fax: 202-296-6895; Web Site: <<http://www.communityrights.org>>.

Concern, Inc. Susan Boyd, 1794 Columbia Rd., NW, Washington, DC 20009; Tel: 202-328-8160; Fax: 202-387-3378; E-mail: <<concern@igc.org>>.

Conservation Ecology. Ecological Society of America, Biology Department, Carleton University, 1125 Colonel By Drive, Ottawa, Ontario, Canada K1S 5B6; Tel: 613-520-3657; Fax: 613-520-4497; Web Site: <<http://www.consecol.org/Journal>>.

The Conservation Fund. National Office, 1800 North Kent St., Ste. 1120, Arlington, VA 22209-2156; Tel: 703-525-6300; Fax: 703-525-4610; Web Site: <<http://www.conservationfund.org>>.

Conservation Technology Information Center. 1220 Potter Dr., Ste. 170, W. Lafayette, IN 47906; Tel: 765-494-9555; Fax: 765-494-5969; download from Web Site: <<http://www.ctic.purdue. edu>>.

Earth Island Institute. 300 Broadway, Ste. 28, San Francisco, CA 94133; Tel: 415-788-3666; Fax: 415-788-7324; Web Site: <<http:// www.earthisland.org>>.

Earth Island Journal. See Earth Island Institute entry, above.

Ecotrust 1200 NW Naito Parkway, Ste. 470, Portland, OR 97209; Tel: 503-227-6225; Fax: 503-222-1517; Web Site: <<http://www. ecotrust.org>>.

Environmental Council of the States (ECOS). 444 N. Capitol St., NW, Ste. 305, Washington, DC 20001; Tel: 202-624-3660; Fax: 202-624-3666; Web Site: <<http://www.sso.org/ecos>>.

Environmental Defense Fund. 257 Park Avenue South, New York, NY 10010; Tel: 800-684-3322; Web Site: <<http://www.edf. org>>.

Environmental Law Foundation. 1736 Franklin St., Ninth Floor, Oakland, CA 94612; Tel: 510-208-4555; Fax: 510-208-4562; Web Site: <<http://www.envirolaw.org>>.

Environmental Organizations Web Directory. Web Site: <<http://www.foe.co.uk/pubsinfo/infosyst/other_services.html>>.

Farm*A*Syst. B142 Steenbock Library, 550 Babcock Dr., Madison, WI 53706-1293; Tel: 608-262-0024; Web Site: <<http:// www.wisc.edu/farmasyst>>.

The Farmer's Guide to the Internet, Third Edition, 1997. Henry James and Kyna Estes; published by and available from TVA Rural Studies, 400 Agriculture Engineering Building, The University of Kentucky, Lexington, KY 40546-0276 or call 606-257-1872 or e–mail <<tvars@ rural.org>>, $19.95 plus $3.95 shipping & handling.

Farmers' Market Directory, 1999 Edition. U.S. Department of Agriculture's Agricultural Marketing Service; Tel: 202-690-0531; download by state at Web Site: <<http://www.ams.usda.gov/ farmersmarkets/map.htm>>.

Gil Friend & Associates—Strategic Sustainability. 48 Shattuck Sq., Ste. 103, Berkeley, CA 94704; Tel: 510-548-7904 & 888-326-6771; Fax: 510-849-2341; E-mail: <<gfriend@eco-ops.com>>; Web Site: <<http://www.igc.apc.org/eco-ops>>.

Great Lakes Commission. Michael J. Donahue, Exec. Dir., 400 Fourth St., Ann Arbor, MI 48103-4816; Tel: 734-665-9135; Fax: 734-665-4370; E-mail: <<glc@great-lakes.net>>; Web Site. <<http://www.glc.org/>>.

Great Lakes United. 1300 Elmwood Ave., Cassety Hall, State University of New York at Buffalo, Buffalo, NY 14222; Tel: 716-886-0142; Faz: 716-882-0303; E-mail: <<glu@glu.org>>; Web Site: <<http://www.glu.org>>.

A Green Plan Primer. A 13-page downloadable publication from Web Site: <<http://www.rri.org/grenplans.html>>.

Guidebook of Financial Tools. Web Site: <<http://www.epa.gov/ definepage/guidebk>>.

Indigo Development—Industrial Ecology Research Center. RPP International, 6423 Oakwood Dr., Oakland, CA 94611; Tel: 510-339-1090; Fax: 510-339-9361; E-mail: <<kathy@rppintl. com>>; Web Site: <<http://www.indigodev.com>>.

Information Center for Economic Developers. Tel: 908-322-5123; Web Site: <<http://www.CEDinfo.com>>.

Institute for Conservation Leadership. 6930 Carroll Ave., Ste. 420, Tacoma Park, MD 20912; Tel: 301-270-0610; Fax: 301-270-0610; E-mail: <<toicl@aol.com>>; Web Site: <<http://www.sustain. web.net/keycont/icl.htm>>.

Island Press.1718 Connecticut Ave., NW, Ste. 300, Washington, DC 20009-1148; Tel; 202-232-7933; Fax: 202-234-1328; E-mail: <<info@islandpress.org>>; Web Site: <<http://www.islandpress. org>>.

Izaak Walton League of America. 707 Conservation Lane, Gaithersburg, MD 20878; Tel: 1-800-453-5463; Web Site: <<http:// www.iwla.org>>.

Journal of Conservation Ecology. Web Site: <<http://www. consecol.org/Journal>>.

Journal of Industrial Ecology. Massachusetts Institute of Technology Journals, Five Cambridge Ctr., Cambridge, MA 02142-1407; Tel: 617-253-2889; Fax: 617-577-1545; E-mail: <<journals-info@mit.edu>>; Web Site: <<http://www.mit.edu>>.

Land Trust Alliance. 1319 F St. NW, Ste. 501, Washington, DC 20004; Tel: 202-638-4725; Fax 202-638-4730; Web Site: <<http:// www.lta.org>>.

Land Use and Community Alliance Service (LUCAS). Pace University School of Law, 78 North Broadway, White Plains, NY 10603; Tel: 914-422-4262; Web Site: <<http://www.law.pace.edu/ landuse/homepage.htm>>.

Land Use Forum Network, Inc. (LUFNET). 84 Woodlawn Rd., Burlington, VT 05401; Tel: 908-625-0638; Fax: 908-459-4494; E-mail: <<karl@landuse.org>>; Web Site: <<http://www.landuse. org>>.

League of Conservation Voters. 1707 L St., NW, Ste. 750, Washington, DC 20036; Tel: 202-785-8683; Fax: 202-835-0491; web Site: <<http://www.lcv.org>>.

League of Women Voters. 1730 M St., NW, Ste. 1000, Washington, DC 20036-4508; Tel: 202-429-1965; Web Site: <<http://www.lwv.org>>.

LGC Reports. A monthly publication of the Local Government Commission (see above).

Lincoln Institute of Land Policy. 113 Brattle St., Cambridge, MA 02138-3400; Tel: 617-661-3016 or 800-526-3873; Fax: 617-661-7235 or 800-526-3944; Web Site: <<www.lincolninst.edu>>.

Livable Places Update. A monthly publication of the Local Government Commision (see above).

Local Government Commission. 1414 K St., Ste. 250, Sacramento, CA 95814; Tel: 916-448-1198; Fax: 916-448-8246; Web Site: <<http://www.lgc.org>>.

Local Government Environmental Assistance Network. A service managed and operated by the International City / County Management Association, 777 North Capitol Street, NE, Ste. 500, Washington, DC 20002-4201; Tel: 202-962-3531; E-mail: <<lgean@icma.org>>; Web Site: <<http://www.lgean.org>>.

The Many Faces of Community Supported Agriculture (CSA): A Guide to Community Supported Agriculture in Indiana, Michigan, and Ohio. Published by the Michigan Organic Food and Farm Alliance, P.O. Box 530, Hartland, MI 48353-0530; Tel: 810-632-7952. Funding provided by the North Central Sustainable Agriculture Research and Education (SARE) Program.

Mayo Law Firm. Todd Mayo, Mayo Law Firm P.C., 92 Boston Post Rd., P.O. Box 23, Amherst, New Hampshire 03031-0023; Tel: 603-673-6607; Fax: 603-672-9394; E-mail: <<tmayo@mayolawfirm.com>>; Web Site: <<http://www.mayolawfirm.com>>.

Michigan Organic Farm and Food Alliance (MOFFA). P.O. Box 530, Hartland, MI 48353-0530; Tel: 810-632-7952; Fax: 810-632-7620.

Munisource Web Site. <<http://www.munisource.org>>.

National Agricultural Library. Agricultural Research Service, U.S. Department of Agriculture, 10301 Baltimore Ave., Beltsville, MD 20705; Tel: 301-504-5755; Web Site: <<http://www.nal.usda.gov/wqic>>.

National Association of Conservation Districts. 509 Capitol Court, NE, Washington, DC 20002-4946; Tel: 202-547-6223; Fax: 202-547-6450; E-mail: <<washington@nacdnet.org>>; Web Site: <<http://www.nacdnet.org>>.

National Association of Counties. 440 First St., NW, Ste. 800, Washington, DC 20001; Tel: 202-393-6226; Fax: 202-393-2630; Web Site: <<http://www.naco.org>>.

National Association of State Park Directors. Glenn Alexander, Exec. Dir., 9894 E. Holden Place, Tucson, AZ 85748; Tel: 520-298-4924; Fax: 520-298-6515; Web Site: <<http://www.indiana.edu/~naspd>>.

National Association of Towns & Townships. 444 N. Capitol St., NW, Ste. 208, Washington, DC 20001; Tel: 202-624-3550; Fax: 202-624-3554; Web Site: <<http://www.natat.org>>.

National Audubon Society. 700 Broadway, New York, NY 10003; Tel: 212-979-3000; Fax: 212-979-3188; Web Site: <<http://www.audubon.org>>.

National Civic League. 1445 Market St., #300, Denver, CO 80202-1728; Tel: 303-571-4343; Fax: 303-571-4404; Web Site: <<http://www.ncl.org>>.

National Ground Water Association. 601 Dempsey Rd., Westerville, OH 43081; Tel: 800-551-7379 or 614-898-7791; Fax: 614-898-7786; E-mail: <<ngwa@ngwa.org>>; Web Site: <<http://www.ngwa.org>>.

National Library for the Environment. Committee for the National Institute for the Environment, 1725 K St., NW, Ste. 212, Washington, DC 20006; Tel: 202-530-5810; Fax: 202-628-4311; E-mail: <<cnieAcnie.org>>; Web Site: <<http://www.cnie.org/nle/crs_main.html>>.

National Park Trust. 415–2nd St., NW, Ste. 210, Washington, DC 20002; Tel: 202-548-0500; Fax: 202-548-0595; Web Site: <<http://www.parktrust.org>>.

National Parks and Conservation Association. 1776 Massachusetts Ave., NW, Washington DC 20036; Tel: 800-628-7275 or 202-223-6722; E-mail: <<npca@npca.org>>; Web Site: <<http://www.npca.org>>.

National Trust for Historic Preservation. 1785 Massachusetts Ave., NW, Washington, DC 20036; Tel: 800-944-6847 or 202-588-6000; Web Site: <<http://www.nthp.org>>.

National Wildlife Federation. 8925 Leesburg Pike, Vienna, VA 22184; Tel: 703-790-4000; Web Site: <<http://www.nwf.org>>.

Natural Areas Association. P.O. Box 1504, Bend, OR 97709; Tel: 541-317-0199; E-mail: <<naa@natarcas.org>>; Web Site: <<http://www.natareas.org>>.

Natural Resources Defense Council. 40 West 20th St., New York, NY 10111; Tel: 212-727-2700; E-mail: <<nrdcinfo@nrdc.org>>; download from Web Site: <<http://www.nrdc.org>>.

The Nature Conservancy. International Headquarters, 4245 North Fairfax Dr., Ste. 100, Arlington, VA 22203-1606; Tel: 703-841-5300; TNC Great Lakes Program, Helen Taylor, Prog. Dir., 8 South Michigan Ave., Ste. 2301, Chicago, IL 60603; Tel: 312-759-8017; Fax: 312-759-8409; Web Site: <<http://www.tnc.org>>.

Nonpoint Education for Municipal Officials (NEMO) Project. c/o Chester Arnold, University of Connecticut CES, 1066 Saybrook Rd., Haddam, CT 06438-0070; Tel: 860-345-4511; Fax: 860-345-3357; E-mail: <<carnold@canr1.cag.uconn.edu>>

Orion Afield. A quarterly publication of The Orion Society (see below).

The Orion Society. 195 Main St., Great Barrington, MA 01230; Tel: 413-528-4422; E-mail: <<orion@orionsociety.org>>; Web Site: http://www.orionsociety.org>>.

Planners Press (of American Planning Association). Planners Book Service, 122 S. Michigan Ave., Ste. 1600, Chicago, IL 60603-6107; Tel: 312-786-6344; Fax: 312-431-9985; E-mail: <<bookorder@planning.org>>.

Planning Commissioners Journal: News and Information for Citizen Planners. P.O. Box 4295, Burlington, VT 05406; Tel: 802-864-9083; Fax: 802-862-1882; Web Site: <<http://www.plannersweb.com>>.

Project for Public Spaces, Inc. 153 Waverly Place, 4th Floor, New York, NY 10014; Tel: 212-620-5660; Fax: 212-620-3821; E-mail: <<pps@pps.org>>; Web Site: <<http://www.pps.org>>.

Rails–to–Trails Conservancy. 1400 Sixteenth St., NW, Ste. 300, Washington, DC 20036; Tel: 202-797-5400; Web Site: <<http:// www.well.net/nomadics/345.trails.html>>.

Renew America, 1200 18th Street, NW, Ste. 1100, Washington, DC 20036; Tel: 202-721-1545; Fax: 202-467-5780; E-mail: <<renewamerica@counterpart.org>>; Web Site: <<http://www. crest.org/renew_america>>.

Resource Renewal Institute (RRI). In CA: Fort Mason Center, Pier 1, San Francisco, CA 94123; Tel: 415-928-3774; Fax: 415-928-6529; e-mail: <<info@rri.org>>; In NY: P.O. Box 381, Delmar, NY 12054; Tel: 518-768-8039; Fax: 518-768-8039; Web Site: <<http://www.rri.org>>.

River Network. P.O. Box 8787, Portland, OR 97207; Tel: 800-423-6747 or 503-241-3506; Fax: 503-241-9256; E-mail: <<rivernet@ igc.apc.org>>; Web Site: <<http://www.teleport.com/~rivernet>>.

Rocky Mountain Institute. 1739 Snowmass Creek Rd., Snowmass, CO 81654-9199; Tel: 907-927-3851; Fax: 970-927-3420; E-mail: <<simon@rmi.org>>; Web Site: <<http://www.rmi. org>>.

Scenic America. 801 Pennsylvania Ave., SE, Ste. 300, Washington, DC 20003; Tel: 202-543-6200; Fax: 202-543-9130; E-mail: <<webmaster@scenic.org>>; Web Site: <<http://www. scenic.org>>.

Sell What You Sow! The Grower's Guide to Successful Produce Marketing. New World Publishing, 3085 Sheridan St., Placerville, CA 95667; Tel: 916-622-2248 ($22.50 + $3 s/h).

Sharing the Harvest: A Guide to Community-Supported Agriculture. Elizabeth Henderson with Robyn Van En, Sustainable Agriculture Research and Education Program, Hills Bldg., University of Vermont, Burlington, VT 05405-0082; Tel: 802-656-0471; Fax: 802-656-4656; E-mail: <<nesare@zoo.uvm.edu>>.

Sierra Club. 85 second St., Second Floor, San Francisco, CA 94105-3441; Tel: 415-977-5500; Fax: 415-977-5799; Web Site: <<http://www.sierraclub.org>>.

Smart Growth Network. Noah A. Simon, Research Assistant, International City/County Management Association, 777 North Capitol Street, NE, Ste. 500, Washington, DC 20002-4201; Tel:

202-962-3591; Fax: 202-962-3500; E-mail: <<nsimon@isma.
org>>; Web Site: <<http://www.icma.org>>.

Society for Ecological Restoration. 1207 Seminole Highway,
Ste. B, Madison, WI 53711; Tel: 608-262-9547; Fax: 608-265-
8557; E-mail: <<ser@vms2.macc.wisc.edu>>; Web Site: <<http://
www.ser.org>>.

Soil and Water Conservation Society. 7515 NE Ankeny Rd.,
Ankeny, IA 50021; Tel: 515-289-2331; Fax: 515-289-1227; We
Site: <<http://www.swcs.org>>.

Surf Your Watershed. Web Site: <<http://www.epa.gov/surf>>.

**Sustainable Communities Resource Collaborative & the
Community Sustainability Resource Institute**. Susanna
Mackenzie Euston, P.O. Box 981, Arden, NC 28704; Tel: 828-681-
1955; Fax: 828-687-0441; E-mail: <<sme@SustainableResource.
org>>; Sustainable Communities Network Web Site: <<http://www.
sustainable.org>>.

Sustainable Conservation. 109 Stevenson St., Fourth Floor, San
Francisco, CA 94105; Tel: 415-977-0380; Fax: 415-977-0381;
E-mail: <<suscon@igc.org>> ; Web Site: <<http://www.suscon.
org>>.

Sustainable Earth, Inc. 100 Georgeton Ct., W. Lafayette, IN
47906; Tel: 765-463-9366; Fax: 765-497-0164; E-mail: <<sbonney
@iquest.net>>.

Terrene Institute. 4 Herbert St., Alexandria, VA 22305; Tel: 703-
548-5473; Fax: 703-548-6299; E-mail: <<terrinst@aol.com>>; Web
Site: <<http://www.terrene.org>>.

Trout Unlimited. 1500 Wilson Blvd., Ste. 310, Arlington, VA
22209-2404; Tel: 703-522-0200; Fax: 703-284-9400; Web Site:
<<http://www.tu.org>>.

Trust for Public Land. National Office, 116 New Montgomery St.,
4th Floor, San Francisco, CA 94105; Tel: 415-495-4014; Fax: 415-
4954103; E-mail: <<mailbox@tpl.org>>; Web Site: <<http://www.
tpl.org>>.

U.S. Department of Agriculture. 14th & Independence Ave. SW,
Washington, DC 20250; Tel: 202-720-2791; Web Site: << http://
www.usda.gov>>.

Sustainable Agriculture Research & Education Program. Jill Auburn, Dir., National Office, USDA, Room 3868 South Bldg., Ag Box 2223, Washington, DC 20250-2223; tel; 202-720-5203; Fax: 202-720-6071; E-mail: <<jauburn@reeusda.gov>>; Web Site: <<http://www.sare.org/san/tdocs/socs/DANandSARE.html>>. Valerie Burton, National Communications Specialist, 2121 Ag/Life Sciences Surge Bldg., University of Maryland, College Park, MD 20742-3358; Tel: 301-405-3186; Fax: 301-314-7373; E-mail: vberton@wam.umd.edu>>.

Regional SARE Offices

North Central. Steve Waller, Coord., University of Nebraska–Lincoln, 13–A Activities Bldg., Lincoln, NE 68583-0840; Tel: 402-472-7081; Fax: 402-472-0280; E-mail: <<sare001@unlvm.unl.edu>>.

Northeast. Fred Magdoff, Coord., University of Vermont, Hills Bldg., Burlington, VT 05405-0082; Tel: 802-656-0471; Fax: 802-656-4656; E-mail: <<fmagdoff@zoo.uvm.edu>>.

Southern. Regional Coord., University of Georgia, Agricultural Experiment Station, Griffin, GA 30223-1797; Tel: 770-412-4787; Fax: 770-412-4789.

Western. Phil Rasmussen, Coord., Utah State University, Plants, Soils, & Biomet. Dept., UMC 4820, Logan, UT 84322-4820; Tel: 801-797-3394; Fax: 801-797-3376; E-mail: <<soilcomp@cc.usu.edu>>

Sustainable Agriculture Network. Andy Clark, Coord., Sustainable Agriculture Network, Room 304, National Agricultural Library, 10301 Baltimore Ave., Beltsville, MD 20705-2351; Tel: 301-504-6425; Fax: 301-504-6409; E-mail: <<san@nal.usda.gov>>. SAN is the communications and outreach arm of SARE, which sponsors competitive grants for sustainable agriculture research and education in a regional process nationwide.

Urban Land Institute. 1025 Thomas Jefferson St., NW, Ste. 500 West, Washington, DC 20007; Tel: 800-321-5011 & 202-624-7000; Fax: 202-624-7140; Web Site: <<http://www.uli.org>>.

Water Environment Federation. 601 Wythe St., Alexandria, VA 23314-1994; Tel: 800-666-0206; Fax: 1-703-684-2492; Web Site: <<http://www.wef.org>>.

Wilderness Land Trust. 4060 Post Canyon Dr., Hood River, OR 97031-7724; Web Site: <<http://www.wildernesstrust.org>>.

The Wilderness Society. 900 17th St., NW, Washington, DC 20006; Tel: 800-843-9453; Web Site: <<http://www.wilderness. org>>.

Wildlife Habitat Council. 1010 Wayne Ave., Ste. 920, Silver Spring, MD 20910; Tel: 301-588-8994; Fax: 301-588-4629; E-mail: <<whc@wildlifehc.org>>; Web Site: <<http://www.wildlifehc.org>>.

International

Forum: Habitat on Developing Countries. (Virtual library on a range of environmental topics, including growth management) Dipartimento Interateneo Territorio, c/o Biblioteca Territorio Ambiente, Architettura-Politecnico di Torino, Viale Mattiolo 39, 10125 Torino, Italy; Tel: +39-11-5647469; Fax: +39-11-5647499; E-mail: <<forum@archi.politico.it>>; Web Site: <<http://www.obelix. polito.it/forum/links/home.htm>>.

International City / County Management Association (ICMA). Noah A. Simon, Asst. Project Mgr., ICMA's Smart Growth Program, 777 North Capitol St., NE, Ste. 500, Washington, DC 20002-4201; Tel: 202-962-3591; Fax: 202-962-3500; E-mail: <<nsimon@icma. org>>; Web Site: <<http://www.icma.org>>.

International Council for Local Environmental Initiatives (ICLEI). City Hall, East Tower, 8th floor 100 Queen Street West, Toronto, ON M5H 2N2, Tel: 416-392-1462, Fax: 416-392-1478, E-mail: <<iclei@iclei.org>>; Web Site: <<http://www.iclei.org>>.

International Joint Commission. Frank Bevacqua, U.S. Section, 1250 23rd St., NW, Ste. 100, Washington, DC 20440; Tel: 202-736-9000; Fax: 202-735; 9015; Fabien Lengellé, Canadian Section, 100 Metcalfe St., 18th Floor, Ottawa, ON K1P 5M1; Tel: 613-995-2984; Fax: 613-993-5583; U.S. Great Lakes Regional Office, P.O. Box 32868, Detroit, MI 48232; Tel: 313-226-2170, ext. 6733; Canadian Great Lakes Regional Office: Jennifer, Day, 100 Oullette Ave., 8th

Floor, Windsor, ON N9A 6T3; Tel: 519-257-6733; Fax: 519-257-6740; Web Site: <<http://www.ijc.org>>.

PARK DISTRICTS

Under Ohio law, park districts may be created either by voters or by public governing bodies petitioning the probate judge to set aside an area as parkland. If the probate judge approves, then a park district is created. Methods for financing park districts are issuing bonds and levying property taxes (voter approval required) and assessments. Like other special districts, they are separate political subdivisions and independent units of government.

Individual landowners may give land to park districts, just as they may give their land to land trusts for special uses.

County Park Districts (Ohio Revised Code 1545):

Ashtabula County Metropark District. Charles H. Kohli, Board Pres., 25 W. Jefferson St., Jefferson, OH 44047; Tel. 440-576-0717.

Auglaize County Park District. Kurt Kuffner, 201 Willipie St., Ste. G, Wapakoneta, OH 45895-1972; 419-738-3612.

Bellefontaine Joint Park District. William Roberts, Dir., 135 N. Detroit, Bellefontaine, OH 43311-1463; Tel: 937-592-3475.

Butler County Metro Parks. Michael Muska, 2200 Hancock Ave., Hamilton, OH 45011-4455; Tel: 513-867-5835.

Clark County Park District. Jim Campbell, Dir., 930 S. Tecumseh Rd., Springfield, OH 45506-4238; Tel: 937-882-6000.

Clermont County Park District. Dona Kohls, Dir., 2228 Highway 50, Batavia, OH 45103-0234; Tel: 513-732-2977.

Cleveland Metroparks. Vern Hartenberg, Dir.–Secy., 4101 Fulton Pkwy., Cleveland, OH 44144-1923; Tel: 216-351-6300.

Clinton County Park District. Bob Johnson, Park Board, 46 South St., Wilmington, OH 45177; Tel: 937-382-2103.

Columbiana County Park District. Charles Clark, 130 West Maple St., Lisbon, OH 44432-1222; Tel: 330-424-9078.

Columbus & Franklin County Metroparks. John O'Meara, Dir., 1069 W. Main St., Westerville, OH 43081; Tel: 614-891-0700.

Coshocton City & County Park District. Steve Miller, Dir., 23353 State Route 83, Coshocton, OH 43812-9601; Tel: 740-622-7528.

Crawford Park District. James Little, Dir., 117 E. Mansfield St., Bucyrus, OH 44820-2302; Tel: 419-562-8394.

Darke County Park District. Art Burke, 603 S. Broadway St., Greenville, OH 45331-0801; Tel: 937-548-0165.

Defiance County Park District. Michael McCann, Secy., 1927 Jefferson Ave., Defiance, OH 43512-3410; Tel: 419-784-5570.

Erie Metroparks. Jon Granville, Dir.–Secy., 3910 E. Perkins Ave., Bldg. C, Huron, OH 44839-1059; Tel: 419-625-7783; E-mail: <<EmetroPark@aol.com>>.

Fairfield County Park Board. Bill Huston, Exec. Secy., P.O. Box 1063, Lancaster, OH 43130-1063; Tel: 740-653-2005.

Five Rivers Metroparks District. Charles Shoemaker, Deputy, 1375 East Siebenthaler Ave., Dayton, OH 45414-5398; Tel: 937-278-8231.

Geauga Park District. Tom Curtin, Dir., 9160 Robinson Rd., Chardon, OH 44024-9148; Tel: 440-285-2222.

Greene County Park District. Tim Leiwig, Dir., 651 Dayton–Xenia Rd., Xenia, OH 45385-2699; Tel: 937-376-7440; E-mail: <<gcparkdir@dayton.net>>.

Guernsey County Park District. Ernest Rogers, Secy., 221 East Main St., Byesville, OH 43723-1338; Tel: 740-685-2263.

Hamilton County Park District. Jon Brady, Dir., 10245 Winton Rd., Cincinnati, OH 45231-2699; Tel: 513-521-7275.

Hancock Park District. Tim Brugeman, Dir., 819 Park St., Findlay, OH 45840-5018; Tel: 419-425-7275; E-mail: <<hpdparks@bright.net>>.

Hardin County Veteran's Memorial Park District. Judge James Rapp, Probate Court, Court of Common Pleas, Kenton, OH 43326-2392; Tel: 419-674-2230; E-mail: <<probjuv@bright.net>>.

Heritage Trails Park District. David Stillwell, Commissioner, 240 W. 5th St., Minster, OH 45865-0120; Tel: 419-628-2331.

Holmes County Park District. Linda Frenette, Dir., 10 S. Clay St., Millersburg, OH 44654-1309; Tel: 330-674-0266.

Huron County Park District. Glen Berhhardt, Dir., 603 U.S. Route 250 S., Norwalk, OH 44857-9572; Tel: 419-668-7288.

Jefferson County Park District. Joseph Hickle, Chmn., P.O. Box 336, Smithfield, OH 43948-0336; Tel: 216-576-9052.

Johnny Appleseed Metro Park District. Kevin Haver, Dir., 2355 Ada Rd., Lima, OH 45801-3343; Tel: 419-221-1232; E-mail: <<jampd@wcoil.com>>.

Knox County Park District. Doug McLarnan, P.O. Box 559, Gambier, OH 43022-0559.

Lake Metroparks. Dave Noble, Dir., 11211 Spear Rd., Concord, OH 44077-9542; Tel: 440-639-7275.

Lawrence County Park District. Clifford Langden, Box 697, Route #1, Southpoint, OH 45680-9743; Tel: 614-867-3689.

Licking Park District. Russell Edgington, P.O. Box 590, Granville, OH 43023-0590; Tel: 740-587-2535.

Lorain County Metropark District. James Martin, Dir., 12882 Diagonal Rd., LaGrange, OH 44050-9728; Tel: 440-458-5121.

Madison County Park District. Joe Yoder, Commissioner, 1 W. High St., Courthouse, London, OH 43140-1068; Tel: 740-852-2972.

Marion County Park District. Jack Telfer, Dir., 196 W. Center St., Marion, OH 43302-3706; Tel: 740-387-5343; E-mail: <<mcrpc@gte.net>>.

Medina County Park District. Thomas James, Dir., 6364 Deerview Ln., Medina, OH 44256-8008; Tel: 330-722-9364; E-mail: <<medcoparks@access.com>>.

Metro Park District Serving Summit County. Keith Shy, Dir., 975 Treaty Line Rd., Akron, OH 44313-5898; Tel: 330-867-5511; Web Site: <<http://wwwlocal-server.neo.lrun.com/MetroParks>>.

Miami County Park District. Jerry Eldred, 2535 E. Ross Rd., Tipp City, OH 45371-9231; Tel: 937-667-1086.

Mill Creek Park District. William Schollaert, P.O. Box 596, Canfield, OH 44406-0596; Tel: 330-702-3000.

Monroe County Park District. James Heimann, 105 W. Court St., Woodfield, OH 43793-1018; Tel: 740-472-1328.

Morrow County Park District. Nancy Strayer, 7479 CR 242, Bellville, OH 44813.

Muskingham County Park District. Bonnie Daily, P.O. Box 446, Zainesville, OH 43702-0446; Tel: 740-455-8237.

Muskingum Watershed Conservancy District. John Hoopingarner, P.O. Box 349, New Philadelphia, OH 44663-0349; Tel: 330-343-6647.

O. O. McIntyre Park District. Josette Baker, 18 Locust St., Room 1262, Gallipolis, OH 45631-1262, Tel. 740-446-4612.

Ottawa County Park District. Mark Mulligan, 315 Madison, Port Clinton, OH 43452; Tel: 419-734-3862.

Portage County Park District. Christine Craycroft, 449 South Meridian St., Ravenna, OH 44266-2963; Tel: 330-673-9404; E-mail: <<ccraycroft@earthlink.com>>.

Preservation Park District of Delaware. Rita Au, 40 N. Sandusky St., Ste. 201, Delaware, OH 43015-1901; Tel: 740-524-8600.

Richland County Park District. Steve McKee, 2295 Lexington Ave., Mansfield, OH 44907-3027, Tel. 419-884-3764.

Ross County Park District. Gary Merkamp, 15 N. Paint St., Chillicothe, OH 45601-3116; Tel: 740-773-8794.

Sandusky County Park District. Steve Gruner, 1970 Countryside Pl., Fremont, OH 43420-9574; Tel: 419-334-4495.

Seneca County Park District. Tom Bartlett, 1933 S. Winfield, Tiffin, OH 44883; Tel: 419-447-0005.

Shelby County Park District. Richard Millhouse, 9871 Fessler–Buxton Rd., Piqua, OH 45356-9602; Tel: 937-773-4818.

Stark County Park District. Robert Fonte, 5300 Tyner St. N.W., Canton, OH 44708-5041; Tel: 330-477-3552.

Toledo Area Metropark District. Jean Ward, 5100 W. Central Ave., Toledo, OH 43615-2100; Tel: 419-535-3050.

Trumbull County Metro Park District. Mitzi Sabella, 160 High St. NW, Planning Dept., Warren, OH 44481-1003; Tel: 330-841-0480.

Warren County Park District. Onlie Gulley, 312 W. Silver St., Lebanon, OH 45036-1800; Tel: 513-933-1109.

Wayne County Park District. Dale Kretchman, 428 West Liberty St., County Bldg., Wooster, OH 44691-4851; Tel: 330-287-5400.

Wood County Park District. Andrew Kalmar, 18729 Mercer Rd., Bowling Green, OH 43402; Tel: 419-353-1897; E-mail: <<wcpd@ wcnet.org>>.

Township Park Districts (Ohio Revised Code 511):

Anderson Township Park District. Molly McClure, Dir., 8249 Clough Pike, Cincinnati, OH 45224-2746; Tel: 513-474-0003.

Auglaize Township Park District. Jerry Mason, Secy.–Treas., P.O. Box 247, Harrod, OH 45850-0247.

Beavercreek Township Park District. Pat Cochran, Chmn., 1981 Dayton-Xenia Rd., Beavercreek, OH 45434; Tel: 937-427-5514; E-mail: <<IAMMOMOF3@aol.com>>.

Bellbrook–Sugarcreek Park District. Joan Lipot, Dir., 2751 Washington Mill Rd., Bellbrook, OH 45305; Tel: 937-848-3535.

Boardman Township Park District. Dale Slagle, Supt., 375 Boardman-Poland Rd., Boardman, OH 44512-4904; Tel: 330-726-8107.

Centerville–Washington Park District. Carol Kennard, Dir., 221 N. Main St., Centerville, OH 45459-4651; Tel: 937-433-5155; E-mail: <<cwpdmail@aol.com.>>

Chester Township Park District. Pam Anzells, 12701 Chillicothe Rd., Chesterland, OH 44026-3194.

Colrain Township Park District. 4200 Springdale Rd., Cincinnati, OH 45251-1419; Tel: 937-383-7500.

Conneaut Township Park District. Mary Reydak, Clerk, 480 Lake Rd., P.O. Box 373, Conneaut, OH 44030-0373; Tel: 440-599-7071.

Delhi Township Park District. Dan Hilvert, Clerk, 271 Sebastian Ct., Cincinnati, OH 45238; 513-4921-3744.

Geneva Township Park District. Judge Howard Warner, 5404 Lake Rd., Geneva–on–the–Lake, OH 44041.

Goshen Township Park District. Wait Keller, Mechanicsburg, OH 43044.

Howland Township Park District. Larry Wright, 169 Niles Cortland Rd. NE, Warren, OH 44484-1997; Tel: 330-856-1115.

Hubbard Township Free Park District. Barb Stoner, Clerk, P.O. Box 177, Hubbard, OH 44425-0177; Tel: 330-534-5907.

Jackson Township Park District. Donald Boyd, Clerk, 8450 Sandusky Rd., Lima, OH 45854; Tel: 330-832-2641.

Liberty Memorial Park District. Dir., Park District, 100 W. Main St., Girard, OH 44120-0390.

Painesville Township Park District. J. Thomas Dean, Clerk, P.O. Box 526, Painesville, OH 44077-0526; Tel: 440-639-4898.

Plain Township/New Albany Park District. Jay Bowe, 39 Second St., New Albany, OH 43054; Tel: 614-855-7770.

Russell Township Park District. Sandy Siegler, 14469 W. Ridge Rd., Novelty, OH 44072-9507; Tel: 440-338-3805.

Saybrook Township Park District. Mary Palmer, Clerk, 7247 Center Rd., Ashtabula, OH 44004-9505.

Spencer Township Park District. Jack Huber, Secy., R.R.#2, Spencerville, OH 45887-9802.

Springfield Township Park District. Mabel Myers, Treas., P.O. Box 271, Stryker, OH 43557-0271; Tel: 419-682-4441.

Sycamore Township Parks & Recreation. Mike McKeown, Dir., 8540 Kenwood, Cincinnati, OH 45236-2010; Tel: 513-791-8447.

Sylvania Township Park District. Mary Langenderfer, 6390 Sylvania Ave., Sylvania, OH 43560-3524; Tel: 419-885-4237.

Thompson Township Park District. Fred Green, Clerk, P.O. Box 24, 16027 Thompson Rd., Thompson, OH 44086-9769; Tel: 216-298-1315.

Tully Township-Convoy Corporation Park. Jerry Helm, Secy., 6412 Van Horn Rd., Convoy, OH 45832-9801.

Waldo Township Park District. Nancy Salyer, Clerk–Treas., P.O. Box 58, Waldo, OH 43356-0058; Tel: 614-726-2531.

Warren Township Park District. Myrna Bibbo, Secy.–Treas., 615 Maple Ave., Tiltonsville, OH 43963-1120; Tel: 513-695-1109.

Washington Township Park District. Dianne Wisniewski, Clerk–Treas., 5319 Hammond Dr., Toledo, OH 43611-1523; Tel: 614-876-9554; E-mail: <<dwisniewski@mco.ed>>.

(**Source:** Ohio Parks and Recreation Association, *Park Districts in the State of Ohio, 1545 & 511*, May 1999.)

PARKS

State

Ohio Department of Natural Resources, Division of Parks and Recreation, 1952 Belcher Dr., Columbus, OH 43224-1886; Tel: 614-261-8407; E-mail: <<jim.henahan@ohio.gov.usa>>; Web Site: <<http://www.dnr.state.oh.us/odnr/parks/>>.

Additional information on the 73 state parks in Ohio can be accessed through the internet at the following Web Site: <<http://www.dnr.state.oh.us/odnr/parks/directory/alphadir.htm>>.

Adams Lake, c/o Shawnee State Park, 4404 State Route 125, West Portsmouth, OH 45663-9003; Tel: 740-858-6652.

Alum Creek, 3615 S. Old State Road, Delaware, OH 43015-9673; Tel: 740-548-4631.

A.W. Marion, c/o Deer Creek State Park, 20635 Waterloo Road, Mt. Sterling, OH 43143-9501; Tel: 740-869-3124.

Barkcamp, 65330 Barkcamp Park Road, Belmont, OH 43718-9733; Tel: 740-484-4064.

Beaver Creek, 12021 Echo Dell Road, East Liverpool, OH 43920-9719; Tel: 330-385-3091.

Blue Rock, 7924 Cutler Lake Road, Blue Rock, OH 43720-9728; Tel: 740-674-4794.

Buck Creek, 1901 Buck Creek Lane, Springfield, OH 45502-8801; Tel: 937-322-5284.

Buckeye Lake, P.O. Box 488, Millersport, OH 43046-0488; Tel: 740-467-2690.

Burr Oak, 10220 Burr Oak Lodge Road, Glouster, OH 45732-9589; Tel: 740-767-3570.

Caesar Creek, 8570 E. State Route 73, Waynesville, OH 45068-9719; 513-897-3055.

Catawba Island, c/o Lake Erie Islands State Park, 4049 E. Moore's Dock Road, Port Clinton, OH 43452-9708; Tel: 419-797-4530.

Cleveland Lakefront, 8701 Lakeshore Blvd., NE, Cleveland, OH 44108-1069; Tel: 216-881-8141.

Cowan Lake, 729 Beechwood Road, Wilmington, OH 45177-9737; Tel: 937-289-2105.

Crane Creek, c/o Maumee Bay State Park, 1400 Park Road #1, Oregon, OH 43618-9713; Tel: 419-836-7758.

Deer Creek, 20635 Waterloo Road, Mt. Sterling, OH 43143-9501; Tel: 740-869-3124.

Delaware, 5202 U.S. 23 North, Delaware, OH 43015-9714; Tel: 740-369-2761.

Dillon, P.O. Box 126, Nashport, OH 43830-9568; Tel: 740-453-4377.

East Fork, P.O. Box 119, Bethel, OH 45106-0119; Tel: 513-734-4323.

East Harbor, 1169 N. Buck Road, Lakeside-Marblehead, OH 43440; Tel: 419-734-4424.

Findley, 25381 State Route 58, Wellington, OH 44090-9208; Tel: 440-647-4490.

Forked Run, P.O. Box 127, Reedsville, OH 45772-0127; Tel: 740-378-6206.

Geneva, P.O. Box 429, Padanarum Rd., Geneva, OH 44041-0429; Tel: 440-466-8400.

Grand Lake St. Marys, 834 Edgewater Drive, St. Marys, OH 45885-0308; Tel: 419-394-3611.

Great Seal, 825 Rocky Road, Chillicothe, OH 45601-9335; Tel: 740-773-2726.

Guilford Lake, 6835 E. Lake Road, Lisbon, OH 44432- 9444; Tel: 330-222-1712.

Harrison Lake, Route #1, Box 240, Fayette, OH 43521-9751; Tel: 419-237-2593.

Headlands Beach, 9601 Headlands Road, Mentor, OH 44060-1001; Tel: 216-881-8141.

Hocking Hills, 20160 State Route 664, Logan, OH 43138-9537; Tel: 740-385-6841.

Hueston Woods, Route #1, College Corner, OH 45003-9625; Tel: 513-523-6347.

Independence Dam, 27722 State Route 424, Defiance, OH 43512-9085; Tel: 419-784-3263.

Indian Lake, 12774 State Route 235 N., Lakeview, OH 43331; Tel: 937- 843-2717.

Jackson Lake, P.O. Box 174, Oak Hill, OH 45656-0174; Tel: 740-682-6197.

Jefferson Lake, R.D. # 1, Box 140, Richmond, OH 43944-9710; Tel: 740-765-4459.

John Bryan, 3790 State Route 370, Yellow Springs, OH 45387-9743; Tel: 937-767-1274.

Kelleys Island, c/o Lake Erie Islands State Park, 4049 E. Moore's Dock Road, Port Clinton, OH 43452-9708; Tel: 419-797-4530.

Kiser Lake, P.O. Box 55, Rosewood, OH 43070-0055: Tel: 937-362-3822.

Lake Alma, Route #1, Box 422, Wellston, OH 45692-9801; 740-384-4474.

Lake Erie Islands, 4049 E. Moore's Dock Road, Port Clinton, OH 43452-9708; Tel: 419-797-4530.

Lake Hope, 27331 State Route 278, McArthur, OH 45651-8220; Tel: 740-596-5253.

Lake Logan, 30443 Lake Logan Road, Logan, OH 43138-9546; Tel: 740-385-3444.

Lake Loramie, 11221 State Route 362, Minster, OH 45865-9311; Tel: 937-295-2011.

Lake Milton, 16801 Mahoning Avenue, Lake Milton, OH 44429-9998; Tel: 330-654-4989.

Lake White, 2767 State Route 551,Waverly, OH 45690-9126; Tel: 740-947-4059.

Little Miami, c/o Caesar Creek State Park, 8570 E. State Route 73, Waynesville, OH 45068-9719; 513-897-3055.

Madison Lake, c/o Deer Creek State Park, 20635 Waterloo Road, Mt. Sterling, OH 43143-9501; Tel: 740-869-3124.

Malabar Farm, 4050 Bromfield Road, Lucas, OH 44843-9745; Tel: 419-892-2784.

Marblehead Lighthouse, c/o Lake Erie Islands State Park, 4049 E. Moore's Dock Road, Port Clinton, OH 43452-9700; Tel: 419 797-4530.

Mary Jane Thurston, I-466, State Route 65, McClure, OH 43534; Tel: 419-832-7662.

Maumee Bay, 1400 Park Road #1, Oregon, OH 43618-9713; Tel: 419-836-7758.

Mohican, 3116 State Route 3, Loudonville, OH 44842-9526; Tel: 419-994-4290.

Mosquito Lake, 1439 State Route 305, Cortland, OH 44410-9303; Tel: 330-637-2856.

Mt. Gilead, 4119 State Route 95, Mt. Gilead, OH 43338-9586; Tel: 419-946-1961.

Muskingum River, P.O. Box 2806, Zanesville, OH 43702-2806; Tel: 740-452-3820.

Nelson Kennedy Ledges, c/o Punderson State Park, P.O. Box 338, Newbury, OH 44065-9684; Tel: 440-564-2279.

Paint Creek, 4265 U.S. Route 50, Bainbridge, OH 45612-9503; Tel: 937-365-1401.

Pike Lake, 1847 Pike Lake Road, Bainbridge, OH 45612-9640; Tel: 740-493-2212.

Portage Lakes, 5031 Manchester Road, Akron, OH 44319-3999; Tel: 330-644-2220.

Punderson, P.O. Box 338, Newbury, OH 44065-9684; Tel: 440-564-2279.

Pymatuning, P.O. Box 1000, Andover, OH 44003-1000; Tel: 440-293-6030.

Quail Hollow, 13340 Congress Lake Avenue, Hartville, OH 44632-0823; Tel: 330-877-6652.

Rocky Fork, 9800 N. Shore Drive, Hillsboro, OH 45133-9205; 937-393-4284.

Salt Fork, 14755 Cadiz Road, Lore City, OH 43755; Tel: 740-439-3521.

Scioto Trail, 144 Lake Road, Chillicothe, OH 45601-9478; Tel: 740-663-2125.

Shawnee, 4404 State Route 125, West Portsmouth, OH 45663-9003; Tel: 740-858-6652.

South Bass Island, c/o Lake Erie Islands State Park, 4049 E. Moore's Dock Road, Port Clinton, OH 43452-9708; Tel: 419-797-4530.

Stonelick, 2895 Lake Drive, Pleasant Plain, OH 45162-9613; Tel: 513-625-7544.

Strouds Run, 11661 State Park Road, Athens, OH 45701-9781; Tel: 740-592-2302.

Sycamore, 4675 N. Diamond Mill, Trotwood, OH 45426-2454; Tel: 937-854-4452.

Tar Hollow, 16396 Tar Hollow Road, Laurelville, OH 43135-9210; Tel: 740-887-4818.

Tinker's Creek, c/o West Branch State Park, 5708 Esworthy Road, Route #5, Ravenna, OH 44266-9659; Tel: 330-296-3239.

Van Buren, P.O. Box 117, Van Buren, OH 45889-0117; Tel: 419-299-3461.

West Branch, 5708 Esworthy Road, Route #5, Ravenna, OH 44266-9659; Tel: 330-296-3239.

Wolf Run, 16170 Wolf Run Road, Caldwell, OH 43724-9503; Tel: 740-732-5035.

National

Cuyahoga Valley National Recreation Area, 15610 Vaughan Rd., Brecksville, OH 44141; Tel: 216-524-1497; Web Site: <<http://www.nps.gov/htdocs1/cuva/home.htm>>.

National Park Service Headquarters, Robert Stanton, Supt. 1849 C St., NW, Washington, DC 20240; Tel. 202-208-6843; Fax: 202-219-0910; E-mail: <<Bob_Stanton@nps.gov>>; Web Site: <<http://www.nps.gov>>.

> **Alaska Regional Office,** Robert D. Barbee, Supt., National Park Service, 2525 Gambell St., Room 107, Anchorage, AK 99503; Tel: 907-257-2574; Fax: 907-257-2533; E-mail: <<AKRO_Regional_Director@nps.gov>>.

> **Midwest Regional Office,** William Schenk, Supt., National Park Service, 1709 Jackson St., Omaha, NE 68102; Tel: 402-221-3456; Fax: 402-221-3461; E-mail: <<Bill_Schenk@nps.gov>>.

> **Intermountain Regional Office,** John E. Cook, Supt., National Park Service, 12795 Alameda Pkwy., Denver, CO

80225; Tel: 303-969-2020; Fax: 303-969-2785; E-mail: <<IMFA_Field_Director@nps.gov>>.

Pacific West Regional Office, John Reynolds, Supt., National Park Service, 600 Harrison St., Ste. 600, San Francisco, CA 94101; Tel: 415-427-1343; Fax: 415-744-4043; E-mail: <<PWFA_Regional_Director@nps.gov>>.

Northeast Regional Office, Marie Rust, Supt., National Park Service, U.S. Custom House, 200 Chestnut St., Room 322, Philadelphia, PA 19106; Tel: 215-597-4971; Fax: 215-597-7013; E-mail: <<NEFA_Regional_Director @nps.gov>>.

National Capital Regional Office, Terry Calstrom, Supt., National Park Service, 1100 Ohio Dr., SW, Washington, DC, 20242; Tel: 202-619-7256; Fax: 202-269-7220; E-mail: <<Terry_Calstrom@nps.gov>>.

Southeast Regional Office, Jerry Belson, Supt., National Park Service, 75 Spring St., SW, Ste. 1130, Atlanta, GA 30303; Tel: 404-331-5711; Fax: 404-562-3263; E-mail: <<Jerry_Belson@nps.gov>>.

(**Sources:** Ohio Department of Natural Resources, Division of Real Estate and Land Management; Tel: 614-265-6395, and Internet Web site searches, June 1999.)

PLANNING COMMISSIONS & COUNCILS—COUNTY & REGIONAL

County and regional planning commissions are empowered under the *Ohio Revised Code* (ORC) to perform a number of duties, including preparation of plans, studies, maps, and recommendations on (we quote from ORC Section 713.23): "(a) Regional goals, objectives, opportunities, and needs, and standards priorities and policies to realize such goals and objectives; (b) Economic and social conditions; (c) The general pattern and intensity of land use and open space; (d) The general land, water, and air transportation systems, and utility and communication systems; (e) General locations and extent of public and private works, facilities, and services; (f) General locations and extent of areas for conservation and development of natural resources and the control of the environment; (g) Long–range programming and financing of capital projects and facilities."

Besides preparing documents on these land–use issues, county and regional planning bodies also are charged with: (1) promoting an understanding of what is necessary to administer and regulate the plans for these land uses; (2) synthesizing social and economic data; (3) initiating studies on natural and human resources and coordinating these efforts with government, educational, and private organizations; (4) contracting and cooperating with other planning entities in government at all levels and coordinating activities and programs in the region; (5) reviewing, evaluating, commenting on, and making recommendations on proposed and amended comprehensive land use, transportation, and other tasks detailed in the ORC.

Planning commissions and councils are housed in various offices throughout the state—departments of development, engineering, economic development, county commissioners. We have listed the regional planning commissions and councils of government, and included the Ohio counties under their purview (i.e., some cross state lines, such as in Ohio–West Virginia (Brooke–Hancock–Jefferson Metropolitan Planning Commission) and Ohio–Kentucky (Ohio Valley Regional Development Commission). Still other planning entities are city–county based, such as the Lima–Allen County Regional Planning Commission, and some county commissions are also represented in regional planning entities, such as the Northeast Ohio Areawide Coordinating Agency (NOACA), representing Cuyahoga, Geauga, Lake, Lorain, and Medina Counties. E–mail and Web site information is included where available.

Full *Ohio Revised Code* text is available at: <<http://orc.avv.com>>.

Adams County. See Ohio Valley Regional Development Commission, OVRDC.

Allen County. See Lima–Allen County Regional Planning Commission.

Ashland Regional Planning Commission. Michael Wolfson, Director. Courthouse, W. 2nd St., Ashland, OH 44805; Tel: 419-282-4209.

Ashtabula County Regional Planning Commission. Robert Kagler, Exec. Dir., 25 W. Jefferson St., Jefferson, OH 44047; Tel: 440-576-3772; Fax: 440-576-3775.

Athens County Planning Office. Robert Eichenberg, Planning Dir., 28 Curran Dr., Chauncy, OH 45701; Tel: 740-594-6069; Fax: 740-594-6343; E-mail: <<beichenberg@ci.athens.oh.us>>. (See also: Buckeye Hills–Hocking Valley Regional Development District.)

Auglaize County Regional Planning Commission. Doug Crawford, Secy., County Courthouse, 201 Willipie St., Ste. G16, Wapakoneta, OH 45895-0330; Tel: 419-738-9025; Fax: 419-738-4299; E-mail: <<augmap@bright.net>>.

Belmont County. See Bel-O-Mar Regional Council.

Bel–O–Mar Regional Council. William C. Phipps, Exec. Dir., P.O. Box 2086, Wheeling, WV 26003-0290; Tel: 304-242-1800; Fax: 304-242-2437. (Belmont)

Brooke–Hancock–Jefferson Metropolitan Planning Commission. Dr. John C. Brown, Exec. Dir., 814 Adams St., Steubenville, OH 43952; Tel: 740-282-3685; Fax: 740-282-1821. (Jefferson)

Brown County. See Ohio Valley Regional Development Commission, OVRDC.

Buckeye Hills–Hocking Valley Regional Development District. Boyer Simcox, Exec. Dir., Route 1, P.O. Box 299 D, Marietta, OH 45750; Tel: 740-374-9436; Fax: 740-374-8038. (Athens, Hocking, Meigs, Monroe, Morgan, Noble, Perry, and Washington)

Butler County Department of Development. Mike Juengling, Dir., 130 High St., Hamilton, OH 45011; Tel: 513-887-3413; Fax: 513-887-3505. (See also Ohio– Kentucky–Indiana Regional Council of Governments, OKI.)

Carroll County. See Ohio Mid–Eastern Governments Association, OMEGA.

Champaign County. See Logan–Union–Champaign Regional Planning Commission.

Clark County Planning Commission. Phil Tritle, Planning Dir., 25 W. Pleasant St., Springfield, OH 45506; Tel: 937-328-2498; Fax: 937-328-2621.

Clermont County Planning Commission. Contact David Spinney, Dir., 101 E. Main St., Batavia, OH 45103; Tel: 513-732-7230; Fax: 513-732-7310. (See also Ohio– Kentucky–Indiana Regional Council of Governments, OKI, and Ohio Valley Regional Development Commission, OVRDC.)

Clinton County Regional Planning Commission. Kenneth Schaublin II, 69 N. South St., Ste. 100, Wilmington, OH 45177-2211; Tel: 937-382-3852; Fax: 937-383-1175.

Columbiana County Planning Commission. John Goemple, Chmn., 130 West Maple St., Lisbon, OH 44432; Tel: 330-424-9078; Fax: 330-424-0577.

Coshocton County Regional Planning Commission. Dale Hartle, Dir., 349 W. Main St., Coshocton, OH 43812; Tel: 740-622-7776; Fax: 740-295-0023. (See also Ohio Mid–Eastern Governments Association, OMEGA.)

Crawford County Board of Commissioners. Barbara Blackford, Pres. of the Board, 112 East Mansfield St., Bucyrus, OH 44820; Tel: 419-562-5876; Fax: 419-562-3491.

Cuyahoga County Planning Commission. Paul Alsenas, Dir., 323 Lakeside Ave., Ste. 400, Cleveland, OH 44113-1010; Tel: 216-443-3700.; Fax: 216-443-3737. (See also Northeast Ohio Areawide Coordinating Agency, NOACA.)

Darke County Planning Commission. Linda Manus, 520 S. Broadway, 2nd Flr., Greenville, OH 45331; Tel: 937-547-7379; Fax: 937-547-7367. (See also Miami Valley Regional Planning Commission.)

Defiance County Planning Commission. Dennis Miller, Dir., 197-2B-2 Island Park Ave., Defiance, OH 43512; Tel: 419-784-3882; Fax: 419-784-2061. (See also Maumee Valley Planning Organization.)

Delaware County Regional Planning Commission. Philip Laurien, Exec. Dir., 50 Channing St., Delaware, OH 43015; Tel: 740-368-1960; Fax: 740-368-1958.

Eastgate Development and Transportation Agency. John R. Getchey, Exec. Dir., Ohio One Building, Ste. 400, 25 East Boardman St., Youngstown, OH 44503; Tel: 330-746-7601; Fax: 330-746-8509. (Mahoning & Trumbull)

Erie County Regional Planning Commission. Alex Macniclos, Dir., 2900 Columbus, Ave., Sandusky, OH 44870; Tel: 419-627-7792; Fax: 419-627-6670.

Fairfield County Regional Planning Commission. R. Brooks Davis, Exec. Dir., 210 E. Main St., Lancaster, OH 43130; Tel: 740-687-7110; Fax: 740-687-6048.

Fayette County Zoning Inspector. Dan Dean, 101 Country Side Dr., Washington, CH, OH 43160; Tel: 740-335-8912. (See also Ohio Valley Regional Development Commission, OVRDC.)

Franklin Country Development Department. George Kinney, Dir., 373 S. High St., 15th Flr., Columbus, OH 43215; Tel: 614-462-3094; Fax: 614-462-7155.

Fulton County Regional Planning Commission. Steven Brown, Dir., Courthouse, P.O. Box 69, Wauseon, OH 43567; Tel: 419-337-9214; Fax: 419-337-9297. (See also Maumee Valley Planning Organization.)

Gallia County. See Ohio Valley Regional Development Commission, OVRDC.

Geauga County Planning Commission. David Dietrich, Dir., Courthouse Annex, 215 Main St., Chardon, OH 44024-1243; Tel: 440-285-2222; Fax: 440-286-9177. (See also Northeast Ohio Areawide Coordinating Agency, NOACA.)

Greene County Regional Planning Comission. Robert Schroeder, Exec. Dir., 651 Dayton-Xenia Rd., Xenia, OH 45385. Tel: 937-376-7480; Fax: 937-376-7485. (See also Miami Valley Regional Planning Commission.)

Guernsey County. See Ohio Mid–Eastern Governments Association, OMEGA.

Hamilton County Regional Planning Commission. Ronald Miller, Exec. Dir., 138 E. Court St., Room 807, Cincinnati, OH 45202; Tel: 513-946-4500; Fax: 513-946-4475. See also Ohio–Kentucky–Indiana Regional Council of Governments, OKI.)

Hancock County Regional Planning Commission. John W. Anning, Dir., 115 Municipal Bldg., Findlay, OH 45840; Tel: 419-424-7094; Fax: 419-424-7245.

Hardin County Regional Planning Commission. Mark D. Doll, Dir., 1 Courthouse Square, Ste. 130, Kenton, OH 43326; Tel: 419-674-2215; Fax: 419-674-2272.

Harrison County Regional Planning Commission. Gordon McLean, Dir., CIC, P.O. Box 175, 133 E. Market St., Cadiz, OH 43907; Tel: 740-942-2027; Fax: 740-942-2000. (See also Ohio Mid–Eastern Governments Association, OMEGA.)

Henry County Regional Planning Commission. Tom Wiggins, Dir., 104 E. Washington Ave., Ste. 301, Napoleon, OH 43545; Tel: 419-599-7370; Fax: 419-599-9865. (See also Maumee Valley Planning Organization.)

Highland County. See Ohio Valley Regional Development Commission, OVRDC.

Hocking County. See Buckeye Hills–Hocking Valley Regional Development District.

Holmes County Planning Commission. Arnold Oliver, Dir., 2 Court St., Ste. 21, Millersburg, OH 44645; Tel: 330-674-8625; Fax: 330-674-1582. (See also Ohio Mid–Eastern Governments Association, OMEGA.)

Huron County Commissioners. Cheryl Nolan, 180 Milan Ave., Norwalk, OH 44857; Tel: 419-668-3092; Fax: 419-663-3370.

Jackson County. See Ohio Valley Regional Development Commission, OVRDC.

Jefferson County Regional Planning Commission. Barbara Wilson, Dir., 814 Adams St., Steubenville, OH 43952; Tel: 740-283-8568; Fax: 740-283-8656. (See also Brooke—Hancock—Jefferson Planning Commission.)

Kentucky–Ohio–Virginia Interstate Planning Commission (KYOVA). Michele Craig, Exec. Dir., P.O. Box 939, 1221 6th Ave., Huntington, WV 25712-0939; Tel: 304-523-7434; Fax: 304-529-7229. (Lawrence)

Knox County Office of Planning. Page Price, Dir., 110 E. High St., Mt. Vernon, OH 43050; Tel: 614-393-6718; Fax: 614-393-6806.

Lake County Planning Commission. Darrell C. Webster, Dir., 125 E. Erie St., Painesville, OH 44077; Tel: 440-350-2740; 440-350-2606. (See also Northeast Ohio Areawide Coordinating Agency, NOACA.)

Lawrence County Regional Planning Commission. Doug Kade, 305 N. Fifth St., Ironton, OH 45638; Tel: 740-533-2159; Fax: 740-532-4763. (See also Kentucky–Ohio–Virginia Interstate Planning Commission, KYOVA., and Ohio Valley Regional Development Commission, OVRDC.)

Licking County Planning Commission. Jerry Brems, Planning Dir., County Planning Dept., 20 S. Second St., Newark, OH 43055; Tel: 740-349-6555; Fax: 740-349-6552.

Lima–Allen County Regional Planning Commission. Thomas M. Mazur, Dir., 130 W. North St., Lima, OH 45801-4432; Tel: 419-228-1836; Fax: 419-228-3891.

Logan–Union–Champaign Regional Planning Commission. Greg Harris, Dir., P.O. Box 141, East Liberty, OH 43319; Tel: 937-645-3012; Fax: 937-666-6203. (Champaign, Logan, & Union)

Lorain County Planning Commission. Ronald Twining, Dir., 226 Middle Ave., Admin. Bldg., Elyria, OH 44035-5641; Tel: 440329-5544; Fax: 440-329-5199. (See also Northeast Ohio Areawide Coordinating Agency, NOACA.)

Lucas County. See Toledo-Lucas County Planning Commission and Toledo Metropolitan Area Council of Governments, TMACOG.

Madison County Regional Planning Commission, Building & Zoning. Bob Turvy, Chmn., 75 West St. SE, London, OH 43140; Tel: 740-852-2833; Fax: 740-852-7144.

Mahoning County Planning Commission. Mike O'Shaugnessy, Dir., 50 Westchester Dr., Ste. 203, Youngstown, OH 44515; Tel: 330-270-2890; Fax: 330-270-2893. (See also Eastgate Development and Transportation Agency.)

Marion County Regional Planning Commission. Kenneth J. Lengieza, Dir., 196 W. Center St., Marion, OH 43302; Tel: 740-387-6188; Fax: 740-387-1883.

Maumee Valley Planning Organization. Dennis Miller, Dir., 197-2B-2 Island Park Ave., Defiance, OH 43512; Tel: 419-784-3882; Fax: 419-784-2061. (Defiance, Fulton, Henry, Paulding, & Williams)

Medina County Planning Commission. Bruce Freeman, Planning Dir., 124 W. Washington St., Ste. B4, Medina, OH 44356; Tel: 330-722-9219. (See also Northeast Ohio Areawide Coordinating Agency, NOACA.)

Meigs County. See Buckeye Hills–Hocking Valley Regional Development District.

Mercer County Planning Commission. Ken Phares, Interim Dir., 101 N. Main St., Room 102, Celina, OH 45822; Tel: 419-586-2963; Fax: 419-586-1714. (Mercer)

Miami County Planning Commission. Daniel L. Brandewie, Planning Dir., 201 W. Main St., Troy, OH 45373; Tel: 937-332-6997; Fax: 937-339-9882.

Miami Valley Regional Planning Commission. Nora E. Lake, Dir., 40 W. Fourth St., Ste. 400, Dayton, OH 45402; Tel: 937-223-6323; Fax: 937-223-9750. (Darke, Greene, Montgomery, & Preble)

Mid–Ohio Regional Planning Commission. William Habig, Exec. Dir., 285 E. Main St., Columbus, OH 43215-5272; Tel: 614-228-2663; Fax: 614-621-2401; Web Site: <<http://www.morpc.org>>. (Delaware & Franklin)

Monroe County Regional Planning Commission. Nelson Potts, Chmn., 37411 Fifth St., Sardis, OH 43946; Tel: 740-472-1341; Fax: 740-472-5156. (See also Buckeye Hills–Hocking Valley Regional Development District.)

Montgomery County Planning Commission. Joe Klosterman, Planning Mgr., 451 W. 3rd, Dayton, OH 45422; Tel: 937-225-4354; Fax: 937-225-6327. (See also Miami Valley Regional Planning Commission.)

Morgan County. See Buckeye Hills–Hocking Valley Regional Development District.

Morrow County Planning & Development Office. Jean McClintock, County Planning Dir., 7 W. High St., Mt. Gilead, OH 43338; Tel: 419-947-7686; Fax: 419-947-7686.

Muskingham County Planning Commission. Dorothy Montgomery, Pres., 401 Main St., Zanesville, OH 43701-3519; Tel: 740-455-7100; Fax: 740-455-3785. (See also Ohio Mid–Eastern Governments Association, OMEGA.)

Noble County. See Buckeye Hills–Hocking Valley Regional Development District.

Northeast Ohio Areawide Coordinating Agency (NOACA). Howard R. Maior, Acting Exec. Dir., 1299 Superior Ave., Cleveland, OH 44114; Tel: 216-241-2414; Fax: 216-621-3024; Web Site: <<http://www.noaca.org>>. (Cuyahoga, Geauga, Lake, Lorain, and Medina)

Northeast Ohio Four County Regional Planning & Development Organization (NEFCO). Joseph Hadley Jr., Exec. Dir., 969 Copley Rd., Akron, OH 44320-2992; Tel: 330-836-5731; Fax:330-836-7703. (Portage, Stark, Summit, & Wayne)

Ohio–Kentucky–Indiana Regional Council of Governments, OKI). James Q. Duane, Exec. Dir., 801-B W. Eighth St., Ste. 400, Cincinnati, OH 45203-1607; Tel: 513-621-7060; Fax: 513-621-9325. (Butler, Clermont, Hamilton, & Warren)

Ohio Mid–Eastern Governments Association (OMEGA). Daniel Neff, Exec. Dir., P.O. Box 130, Cambridge, OH 43725; Tel: 740-439-4471; Fax: 740-439-7783; Web Site: <<http://www.omega.ldd.org>>. (Carroll, Coshocton, Guernsey, Harrison, Holmes, Muskingum, & Tuscarawas)

Ohio Valley Regional Development Commission (OVRDC). Jeffrey A. Spencer, Exec. Dir., P. O. Box 728, Waverly, OH 45690-0728; Tel: 740-947-2853;1-800-223-7491; Fax: 740-947-3468; Web Site: <<http://www.ovrdc.org>>. (Adams, Brown, Fayette, Gallia, Highland, Jackson, Pike, Ross, Scioto, & Vinton; optional review of Clermont and Lawrence)

Ottawa County Regional Planning Commission. Walter Wehenkel, Dir., 315 Madison St., Room 107, Port Clinton, OH 43452; Tel: 419-734-6780; Fax: 419-734-6898; E-mail: <<orpc@cross.net>>. (See also Toledo Metropolitan Area Council of Governments, TMACOG.)

Paulding County Planning Commission, Engineers Office.
Mark Stockman, Acting Exec. Dir., 115 N. Williams St., Room B2,
Paulding, OH 45879; Tel: 419-399-2366; Fax: 419-399-8246. (See
also Maumee Valley Planning Organization.)

Perry County Planning Commission. Chad Berginnis, Planning
Dir., 121 W. Brown St., P.O. Box 952, New Lexington, OH 43764;
Tel: 740-342-5519; Fax: 740-342-7203. (See also Buckeye
Hills–Hocking Valley Regional Development District.)

**Pickaway County Regional Planning Commission, Engineer's
Office.** Terry Frazier, Exec. Dir., County Courthouse, 207 S. Court
St., Circleville, OH 43113; Tel: 740-474-3360; Fax: 740-477-1245.

Pike County Planning Commission. John Cook, Chmn.,
Planning Board, 227 Valley View Dr., Waverly, OH 45690-9135;
Tel: 740-947-9573; Fax: 740-947-1109. (See also Ohio Valley
Regional Development Commission, OVRDC.)

Portage County Regional Planning Commission. Lynne
Erickson, Dir., 128 N. Prospect St., Ravenna, OH 44266; Tel: 330-
297-3613; Fax: 330-297-3617. (See also Northeast Ohio Four
County Regional Planning & Development Organization, NEFCO.)

Preble County Planning Commission. Peggy Crabtree, Planning
Dir., 101 E. Main St., Court House, Eaton, OH 45320; Tel: 937-
456-8171; Fax: 937-456-9438. (See also Miami Valley Regional
Planning Commission.)

Putnam County Planning Commission. Jack Betscher, Planning
Dir., 245 E. Main St., Ste. 101, Ottawa, OH 45875; Tel: 419-523-
3056; Fax: 419-523-5284.

Richland County Regional Planning Commission (RCRPC).
Dick Adair, Exec. Dir., 35 N. Park St., Mansfield, OH 44902; Tel:
419-755-5684; Fax: 419-774-5685; E-mail: <<rcrpc@richnet.net>>.

Ross County Planning Department. Tracy Hatmaker, County
Administrator, 15 N. Paint St., Ste. 200, Chillicothe, OH 45601; Tel:
740-702-3008; Fax 740-773-1668. (See also Ohio Valley Regional
Development Commission, OVRDC.)

Sandusky County. See Toledo Metropolitan Area Council of
Governments, TMACOG.

Scioto County Economic Development Office. Steve Carter,
Exec. Dir., 602 7th St., Room 301, Portsmouth, OH 45662; Tel:

740-354-5395; Fax: 740-353-7358. (See also Ohio Valley Regional Development Commission, OVRDC.)

Seneca Regional Planning Commission. Paul Hairston, Exec. Dir., 103 S. Washington St., Tiffin, OH 44883; Tel: 419-443-7936; Fax: 419-443-7948; E-mail: <<srpc@bpsom.com>>.

Shelby County Regional Planning Commission. David Waltz, Dir., 129 E. Court St., Sidney, OH 45365; Tel: 937-498-7273; Fax: 937-498-1293.

Stark County Regional Planning Commission. Gerald Bixler, Exec. Dir., 201 Third St., NE, Ste. 201, Canton, OH 44702; Tel: 330-438-0389; Fax: 330-438-0990. (See also Northeast Ohio Four County Regional Planning & Development Organization, NEFCO.)

Summit County Department of Development. Robert Cortlett, Planning Dir., Room 207, Ohio Bldg., 175 S. Main St., Akron, OH 44308; Tel: 330-643-2552; Fax: 330-643-2886. (See also Northeast Ohio Four County Regional Planning & Development Organization, NEFCO.)

Toledo-Lucas County Planning Commission. Stephen Herwat, Exec. Dir., 1 Government Center, Ste. 1620 Jackson St., Toledo, OH 43604; Tel: 419-245-1200; Fax: 419-936-3730. (Lucas)

Toledo Metropolitan Area Council of Governments (TMACOG). William L. Knight, Exec. Dir., P. O. Box 9508, 300 Central Union Plaza, Toledo, OH 43697-9508; Tel: 419-241-9155; Fax: 419-241-9116. (Lucas, Ottawa, Sandusky, & Wood)

Trumbull County Planning Commission. Gary Newbrough, PE, Exec. Dir., 347 North Park, Warren, OH 44481; Tel: 330-675-2480; Fax: 330-675-2790. (See also Eastgate Development and Transportation Agency.)

Tuscarawas County Regional Planning Commission. Robert Filkorn, Dir., 125 East High Ave., Room 210, New Philadelphia, OH 44663-2574; Tel: 330-364-8811, ext. 246; Fax: 330-364-8811 x 281. (See also Ohio Mid–Eastern Governments Association, OMEGA.)

Union County. See Logan–Union–Champaign Regional Planning Commission.

Van Wert County Regional Planning Commission. Nancy Blanke, Exec. Dir., 114 E. Main St., Van Wert, OH 45891; Tel: 419-238-4544; Fax: 419-238-4162.

Vinton County. See Ohio Valley Regional Development Commission, OVRDC.

Warren County Regional Planning Commission. Robert Price, Exec. Dir., 320 E. Silver St., Lebanon, OH 45036; Tel: 513-695-1223; Fax: 513-695-2933. (See also Ohio–Kentucky–Indiana Regional Council of Governments, OKI.)

Washington County. See Buckeye Hills–Hocking Valley Regional Development District.

Wayne County Planning Commission. Betsy Sparr, Dir., Wayne County Planning Department, 428 W. Liberty St., Wooster, OH 44691; Tel: 330-287-5420; Fax: 330-287-5425. (See also Northeast Ohio Four County Regional Planning & Development Organization, NEFCO.)

Williams County Regional Planning Commission. Dennis Miller, Dir., 197-2B-2 Island Park, Defiance, OH 43512; Tel: 419-784-3882; Fax: 419-784-2061. (See also Maumee Valley Planning Organization.)

Wood County Regional Planning Commission. David Miesmer, Dir., Courthouse Square, Bowling Green, OH 43402-2431; Tel: 419-354-9128; Fax: 419-354-1522. (See also Toledo Metropolitan Area Council of Governments, TMACOG.)

Wyandot County Board of Commissioners. M. Sue Shrider, Clerk & Review Coord., 109 S. Sandusky Ave., Room 10, Upper Sandusky, OH 43351-1497; Tel: 419-294-3836; Fax: 419-294-6427.

(**Source:** State of Ohio's Office of Management and Budget, 1996 list; Cuyahoga County Planning Commission, 10-25-96 list; John Stamm, OSU Extension, Franklin County, County Planning Directors, July 1999; Internet Web site searches and calls to offices, June & July 1999)

RESOURCE CONSERVATION & DEVELOPMENT COUNCILS

The U.S. Department of Agriculture's Ohio Natural Resources Conservation Service describes the purpose of the Resource Conservation & Development Councils (RC&Ds) as "to improve the general level of economic activity and to enhance the environment and standard of living in authorized RC&D areas by accelerating the conservation development and utilization of natural resources."

Local

Buckeye Hills RC&D. Contact Robert First, RC&D Coord. (Mark Forni, Pres. of Council), R.D. #2, Box 1D, Marietta, OH 45750-9614; Tel: 740-373-7926; Fax: 740-374-5340; E-mail: <<buckeyehills@ee.net>>.

Crossroads RC&D. Sandra Chenal, RC&D Coord. (Richard Houk, Pres. of Council), 10875 SR 212 NE, Ste. A, Bolivar, OH 44612-9568; Tel: 330-874-4692; Fax: 330-874-3539; Web Site: <<http://www.crossroadsrcd.org>>.

Erie Basin RC&D. Ed McConoughey, RC&D Coord. (Henry De Julia, Pres. of Council), 8 Fair Rd., Norwalk, OH 44857-1923; Tel: 419-668-4113; Fax: 419-663-0611.

Heart of Ohio RC&D. Wes Beery, RC&D Coord. (Jack McDowell, Pres. of Council), 200 N. High St., Room 522, Columbus, OH 43215; Tel: 614-469-6942; Fax: 614-469-2083.

Maumee Valley RC&D. Clifford Thornton, RC&D Coord. (Howard Skiles, Pres. of Council), 06825 SR 66 N, Ste. C, Defiance, OH 43512-9650; Tel: 419-784-3717; 419-782-3244.

Miami Valley RC&D. John Kellis, RC&D Coord. (Rick Record, Pres. of Council), 777 Columbus Ave., Ste. 5B, Lebanon, OH 45036-1684; Tel: 513-695-1336 or 513-695-1187; Fax: 513-695-2943.

Ohio Valley RC&D. Kurt Simon, RC&D Coord. (Deb Harsha, Pres. of Council), 12681 US Rt. 62, Sardinia, OH 45171; Tel: 937-695-1293; Fax: 937-695-8093.

Top of Ohio RC&D. Jim Rush, RC&D Coord. (Jerry Laffin, Pres. of Council), 1413 S. Main St., Ste. 102, Bellefontaine, OH 43311-1588; Tel: 937-592-2233; Fax: 937-592-9524.

Western Reserve RC&D. John Niedzialek, RC&D Coord. (Carol Thaler, Pres. of Council), 125 E. Erie St., Painesville, OH 44077-3948; Tel: 440-350-2034; Fax: 440-350-2601.

National

U.S. Department of Agriculture. 14th & Independence Ave., SW, Washington, DC 20250; Tel: 202-720-2791; Web Site: <<http://www.usda.gov>>.

(**Source:** Richard Burke, Ohio DNR, Division of Soil and Water Conservation, July 1999; Jon Warner, Program Mgr., Ohio Natural Resources Conservation Service, July 1999)

SOIL AND WATER CONSERVATION DISTRICTS AND NATURAL RESOURCES CONSERVATION SERVICE OFFICES

Organized by referendum in 1991 by local landowners, soil and water conservation districts (SWCDs) are governed by an elected board of supervisors comprised of local concerned citizens. SWCDs are assisted by the Natural Resources Conservation Service (NRCS, formerly USDA's Soil Conservation Service) and the Ohio Division of Soil and Water Conservation (Ohio Department of Natural Resources). Financed by county and state governments, SWCDs are autonomous entities free from control by other state government agencies. **NOTE:** Office addresses and phone numbers for the NRCS offices are the same, except where indicated.

Local

Adams SWCD, 508 E. Main St., W. Union, OH 45693; Tel: 937-544-5121; NRCS Office: Tel: 937-544-2033.

Allen SWCD, 3900 Campus Dr., Ste. A, Lima OH 45804-3596; Tel: 419-222-0967; NRCS Office: 419-223-0040.

Ashland SWCD, 804 U.S. Rte. 250 East, Ashland, OH 44805; Tel: 419-281-7645.

Ashtabula SWCD, 39 Wall St., Jefferson, OH 44047-1137; Tel: 440-576-4946; NRCS Office: 33 Grand Valley, Orwell, OH 44076; Tel: 440-437-5888.

Athens SWCD, Country Corners Shopping Center, 70 N. Plains Rd., Ste. 107, The Plains, OH 45780; Tel: 740-797-9686; Fax: 614-582-8890; Web site: <<http://www.seort.ohio.edu/~aswcd>>.

Auglaize SWCD, 110 Industrial Dr., Ste. F/G, Wapakoneta, OH 45895-9231; Tel: 419-738-4016.

Belmont SWCD, 1119 E. Main St., Ste. 2, Barnesville, OH 43713; Tel: 740-425-1100.

Brown SWCD, 706 S. Main St., Georgetown, OH 45121; Tel: 937-378-4424.

Butler SWCD, 1810 Princeton Rd., Hamilton, OH 45011; Tel: 513-887-3720.

Carroll SWCD, 613 N. High St., Carrollton, OH 44615; Tel: 330-627-5537.

Champaign SWCD, 11512 S. US Highway 68, Ste. 100, Urbana, OH 43078; Tel: 937-484-1507.

Clark SWCD, 4400 Gateway Blvd., Ste. 103, Springfield, OH 45502; Tel: 937-328-4600 or 937-328-4601.

Clermont SWCD, P.O. Box 549, 1000 Locust St., Owensville, OH 45160; Tel: 513-732-8882; Fax: 513-732-8884; E-mail: <<soil_water@fuse.net; Web Site: <<http://home.fuse.net/soil_water>>.

Clinton SWCD, 24 Randolph St., Wilmington, OH 45177; Tel: 937-382-2461.

Columbiana SWCD, 1834-B S. Lincoln Ave., Salem, OH 44460; Tel: 330-332-8732.

Coshocton SWCD, Coshocton County Service Bldg., 724 S. Seventh St., Coshocton, OH 43812; Tel: 740-622-8087.

Crawford SWCD, 3113 SR 98, Bucyrus, OH 44820; Tel: 419-562-9165.

Cuyahoga SWCD, 6100 W. Canal Rd., Valley View, OH 44125; Tel: 216-524-6580.

Darke SWCD, 1117 S. Towne Ct., Greenville, OH 45331; Tel: 937-548-1715.

Defiance SWCD, 06825 SR 66 N., Ste. F, Defiance, OH 43512; Tel: 419-782-8751; Fax: 419-782-3244; Web Site: <<http://www. defiance-online.com/commissioners/soil&water.html>>.

Delaware SWCD, 557 Sunbury Rd., Ste. A, Delaware, OH 43015; Tel: 740-368-1921 or 740-548-7313, ext. 1921; NRCS Office: Tel: 740-362-4011.

Erie SWCD, 2900 Columbus Ave., Sandusky, OH 44870; Tel: 419-626-5211; NRCS Office: Tel: 419-626-6419.

Fairfield SWCD, 831 College Ave., Ste. B, Lancaster, OH 43130; Tel: 740-653-8154 or 740-653-5320.

Fayette SWCD, 1415 US 22 SW, Ste. 500, Washington Court House, OH 43160-9566; Tel: 740-636-0279.

Franklin SWCD, 1945 Frebis Ave., Columbus, OH 43206; Tel: 614-443-9416 or 614-443-9417.

Fulton SWCD, 126 Clinton St., Wauseon, OH 43567; Tel: 419-335-5846 or 419-337-9112; Fax: 419-335-0802; Web Site: <<http://www.powersupply.net/users/fswcd>>.

Gallia SWCD, 111 Jackson Pk., Ste. 1569, Gallipolis, OH 45631-1569; 740-446-6173.

Geauga SWCD, P.O. Box 410, Burton, OH 44021; Tel: 440-834-1122; NRCS Office: 33 Grand Valley, Orwell, OH 44076.

Greene SWCD, 1363 Burnett Dr., Xenia, OH 45385; Tel: 937-372-4478.

Guernsey SWCD, Agricultural Service Center, 9711 E. Pike, Room 102, Cambridge, OH 43725; Tel: 740-432-5624 or 800-367-5702.

Hamilton SWCD, 29 Triangle Office Park, Ste. 2901, Cincinnati, OH 45246; Tel: 513-772-7645.

Hancock SWCD, 7710 Co. Rd. 140, Findlay, OH 45840; Tel: 419-422-6569; Fax: 419-422-2080; Web site: <<http://www.bright.net/ ~hanswcd>>; NRCS Office: 419-422-8347.

Hardin SWCD, P.O. Box 436, SR 309, Kenton, OH 43326-9474; Tel: 419-673-8621.

Harrison SWCD, 239 E. Warren St., Cadiz, OH 43907; Tel: 740-942-8837.

Henry SWCD, 2260 N. Scott St., Napoleon, OH 43545; Tel: 419-599-8171.

Highland SWCD, 1019 W. Main St., Ste. B, Hillsboro, OH 45133-8236; Tel: 937-393-1922.

Hocking SWCD, 88 S. Market St., Logan, OH 43138; Tel: 740-380-2517.

Holmes SWCD, 62 W. Clinton St., Millersburg, OH 44654-1148; Tel: 330-674-2811.

Huron SWCD, 8 Fair Rd., Norwalk, OH 44857; Tel: 419-668-7645.

Jackson SWCD, 2026 Fairgreens Rd., Jackson, OH 45640-9057; Tel: 740-286-5208.

Jefferson SWCD, 131 Main St., Lower Level, Wintersville, OH 43953; Tel: 740-264-9790 or 740-264-9792.

Knox SWCD, Box 270, 1025 Harcourt Rd., Mt. Vernon, OH 43050; Tel: 740-392-7806 or 740-393-6725; Fax: 740-392-5519; E-mail: SWCD@axom.com>>; Web site: <<http://www.axom.com/swcd/knoxhome.html>>.

Lake SWCD, 125 East Erie St., Painesville, OH 44077; Tel: 440-350-2730; Fax: 440-350-2601; E-mail: <<jps1@soil.co.lake.oh.us>>; Web site: <<http://soil.co.lake.oh.us>>; NRCS Office: 440-350-2034.

Lawrence SWCD, 5459 St. rt. 217, P.O. Box 144, Willow Wood, OH 45696; Tel; 740-867-4737.

Licking SWCD, 771 E. Main St., Ste. 100, Newark, OH 43055; Tel: 740-349-6920.

Logan SWCD, 324 Road 11, Bellefontaine, OH 43311; Tel: 937-593-2946.

Lorain SWCD, 42110 Russia Rd., Elyria, OH 44035-6813; Tel: 440-322-1228 or 440-329-5352.

Lucas SWCD, 130–A W. Dudley St., Maumee, OH 43537; Tel: 419-893-3131 or 419-893-1966.

Madison SWCD, 1375 U.S. Rte. 42 SE, London, OH 43140; Tel: 740-852-4004.

Mahoning SWCD, 490 S. Broad St., Canfield, OH 44406; Tel: 330-533-2231.

Marion SWCD, 1100 E. Center St., Marion, OH 43302; Tel: 740-387-1314.

Medina SWCD, 803 E. Washington St., Ste. 160, Medina, OH 44256; Tel: 330-722-2628.

Meigs SWCD, 33101 Hiland Rd., Pomeroy, OH 45769; Tel: 740-992-4282; NRCS Office: Tel: 740-992-6646.

Mercer SWCD, 220 W. Livingston, Celina, OH 45822; Tel: 419-586-2548.

Miami SWCD, 1330 N. County Rd. 25A, Troy, OH 45373; Tel: 937-335-7645.

Monroe SWCD, Courthouse, 101 N. Main St., Room 16, Woodsfield, OH 43793; Tel: 740-472-0833.

Montgomery SWCD, 10025 Amity Rd., Brookville, OH 45309; Tel: 937-854-7645.

Morgan SWCD, 55 S. Kennebec Ave., McConnelsville, OH 43756; Tel: 740-962-4234.

Morrow SWCD, 871 W. Marion Rd., Ste. 203, Mt. Gilead, OH 43338; Tel: 419-946-7923.

Muskingum SWCD, 225 Underwood St., Ste. 100, Zanesville, OH 43701; Tel: 740-454-2767, Fax. 740-454-1451; Web Site: <<http://oh.nacdnet.org/muskingum>>.

Noble SWCD, 18506 SR 78 E, Caldwell, OH 43724; Tel. 740-732-4318.

Ottawa SWCD, 240 W. Lake St., Unit B, Oak Harbor, OH 43449-1039; Tel: 419-898-6431 or 419-898-1595.

Paulding SWCD, 315 C N. Walnut St., Paulding, OH 45879; Tel: 419-399-4771.

Perry SWCD, E. Gay St., P.O. Box 337, Somerset, OH 43783; Tel: 740-743-1325.

Pickaway SWCD, 110 Island Rd., Ste. D, Circleville, OH 43113-9575; Tel: 740-477-1693; NRCS Office: Tel: 740-477-1641.

Pike SWCD, 11752 SR 104, Waverly, OH 45690; Tel: 740-947-5353.

Portage SWCD, 6970 SR 88, Ravenna, OH 44266; Tel: 330-297-7633, ext. 111.

Preble SWCD, 1651 N. Barron St., Eaton, OH 45320; Tel: 937-456-5159; NRCS Office: Tel: 937-456-4211.

Putnam SWCD, 215 S. Oak St., Ottawa, OH 45875; Tel: 419-523-5159.

Richland SWCD, 1495 W. Longview Ave., Ste. 205 B, Mansfield, OH 44906; Tel: 419-747-8686.

Ross SWCD, 475 Western Ave., Ste. H, Chillicothe, OH 45601; Tel: 740-772-4110.

Sandusky SWCD, 2000 Countryside Rd., Fremont, OH 43420; Tel: 419-334-6324; NRCS Office: Tel: 419-334-6330.

Scioto SWCD, 612 6th St., Ste. D, Portsmouth, OH 45662; Tel: 740-355-0505; NRCS Office: Tel: 740-353-8339.

Seneca SWCD, 155 E. Perry St., Tiffin, OH 44883; Tel. 419-447-7073.

Shelby SWCD, 822 Fair Rd., Sidney, OH 45365; Tel: 937-492-4768.

Stark SWCD, 2311 Columbus Rd. NE, Canton, OH 44705; Tel: 330-489-4476, ext. 101.

Summit SWCD, 2795 Front St., Ste. D, Cuyahoga Falls, OH 44221; Tel: 330-929-2871; Fax 330-929-2872; Web Site: <<http://www.members.aol.com/summitswcd/swcd.html>>.

Trumbull SWCD, 140 N. High St., Cortland, OH 44410; Tel: 330-637-2046, ext. 101.

Tuscarawas SWCD, 247 C Stonecreek Rd. NW, New Philadelphia, OH 44663-9998; Tel: 330-339-5584.

Union SWCD, 943 E. Fifth St., Marysville, OH 43040; Tel: 937-642-5871.

Van Wert SWCD, 1354 Ervin Rd., Van Wert, OH 45891; Tel: 419-238-9591.

Vinton SWCD, P.O. Box 494, McArthur, OH 45651-0494; Tel: 740-596-5676.

Warren SWCD, 777 Columbus Ave., Ste. 7, Lebanon, OH 45036; Tel: 513-695-1337; NRCS Office: Tel: 513-695-1336.

Washington SWCD, Rte. 2, Box 1E, Marietta, OH 45750-9614; Tel: 740-373-4857.

Wayne SWCD, County Administration Bldg., 428 W. Liberty St., Wooster, OH 44691; Tel: 330-262-2836; Fax: 330-262-7422; Web Site: <<http://www.bright.net/~swcd>>.

Williams SWCD, 1120 W. High St., Bryan, OH 43506; Tel: 419-636-2349.

Wood SWCD, 1616 E. Wooster St., Unit R 1–B 2, Box N, Bowling Green, OH 43402-3456; Tel: 419-352-5172.

Wyandot SWCD, 97 Houpt Dr. A, Upper Sandusky, OH 43351; Tel: 419-294-2312; NRCS Office: Tel: 419-294-2311.

State

Division of Soil and Water Conservation, Ohio Department of Natural Resources, Fountain Square Ct., Building E-2, Columbus, OH 43224; Tel: 614-265-6610; Fax: 614-262-2064. Web Site: <<http://www.dnr.state.oh.us/odnr/soil+water>>.

National Resources Conservation Service, State Office, 200 N. High St., Columbus, OH 43215-2478; Tel: 614-469-6962; Fax: 614-469-2083.

National

USDA Natural Resources Conservation Service, 14th & Independence Ave., Washington, DC 20250; Web Site: <<http://www.nrcs.usda.gov>>.

(*Source:* 1999 Roster of SWCD Supervisors & Employees, OSWCC, NRCS, ODNR–DSWC, USDA Natural Resources Conservation Service, Lake County SWCD Office, and Web site searches.)

WATERSHED PROTECTION ORGANIZATIONS

A number of organizations have watershed protection as their main interest or mission. These groups can be extremely valuable as advisors, advocates, and expert information sources. Though they vary in levels of staffing, technical expertise, and reference collections (such as model ordinances), their knowledge and assistance can be critical to citizens, local governments, planners, developers, and others in designing comprehensive plans, zoning, and subdivision regulations that reflect the particular needs and characteristics of local watersheds. A selection of local, state, regional, national, and international groups appears below. In addition, Ohio EPA's Division of Surface Water (DSW), maintains a list of watershed protection groups throughout the state. It is available from Laurel Hodory, DSW, OEPA, 122 South Front St., 6th Floor, P.O. Box 1049, Columbus, OH 43216-1049; Tel: 614-644-3448; E-mail: <<laurel.hodory@epa.state.oh.us>>; Web Site: <<http://www.epa. ohio.gov>>.

Local

Chagrin River Land Conservancy. Rich Cochran, Exec. Dir., P.O. Box 148, Chagrin Falls, OH 44022; Tel: 440-247-0880; Fax: 440-247-0881. E-mail: <<crlc148@aol.com>>.

Chagrin River Watershed Partners. Thomas J. Denbow, Exec. Dir., 2705 River Rd., Willoughby Hills, OH 4094-9445; Tel: 440-975-3840; Fax: 440-975-3865; Web Site: <<http://www.crwp.org>>.

Chagrin Watershed Institute. Reini Friebertshauser, University School, 2785 SOM Center Rd., Hunting Valley, OH 44022; Tel: 216-831-2200 or 216-831-1984 ext. 329; Fax: 216-292-7809; Web Site: <<http://cwi.us.edu>>.

Cuyahoga River Remedial Action Program. Kelvin Rogers, Ohio EPA, Division of Surface Water, 2110 E. Aurora Rd., Twinsburg, OH 44087; Tel: 330-963-1117; Fax: 330-487-0769; E-mail:

<<kelvin.rogers@epa.state.oh.us>>;Web Site: <<http://www.
chagrin.epa.Ohio.gov/programs/rap/cuyahoga.html>>..

Friends of the Black River. George Espy, Seventh Generation, 25
Lake St., Elyria, OH 44035; Tel: 440-322-4187; Fax: 440-322-1785;
E-mail: <<SevnGen@aol.com>>.

Friends of the Crooked River. Elaine Marsh, 2390 Kensington,
Akron, OH 44333; Tel: 330-666-4026; Fax: 330-657-2955; E-mail:
<<ohgreenway@aol.com>>.

Grand River Watershed Partners. Chuck Ashcroft, Exec. Dir.,
Lake Erie College, Austin Hall, Room 314-Box M25, 391 West
Washington St., Painesville, OH 44077; Tel/Fax: 440-639-4773;
E-mail: <<grandriver@ncweb.com>>.

Little Miami, Inc. Eric Partee, 6040 Price Rd., Milford, OH 45150;
tel: 513-965-9344; Fax: 513-965-9344.

Little Miami River Partnership. John Kellis, Miami RC&D, 777
Columbus Ave., Ste. 5B, Lebanon, OH 45036; Tel: 937-933-1187;
Fax: 937-933-2943.

Olentangy Watershed Alliance. Richard Tuttle, 311 Central Ave.,
Delaware, OH 43015.

Olentangy River Valley Association. Laurie Konan, P.O. Box
411, Delaware, OH 43015; Tel: 419-223-0040.

Upper Cuyahoga Association. Charles P. English, 4129 Dudley
Rd., Mantua, OH 44155; Tel: 330-274-2746.

Upper Cuyahoga River Watershed Task Force. Kim Coy, 1570
Ravenna, Rd., Kent, OH 44240;

State

Green Environmental Coalition, Inc., P.O. Box 266, Yellow
Springs, OH 45387; E-mail: <<gec@greenlink.org>>; Web Site:
<<http://www.grenlink.org/gec>>.

Rivers Unlimited. 1207 Grandview Ave., Suite 302, Columbus,
OH 43212-3449; Fax: 614-487-7513; E-mail: <<riveruoh@aol.
com>>.; Web Site: <<http://www.greenlink.org/rivers>>.

Regional

Great Lakes Natural Resource Center. National Wildlife Federation, 506 E. Liberty, 2nd Floor, Ann Arbor, MI 48104-2210; Tel: 734-769-3351; Fax: 734-769-1449; E-mail: <<lentz@nwf. org>>; Web Site: <<http://www.nwf.org/greatlakes>>.

National

Conservation Technology Information Center (CTIC). 1220 Potter Dr., Ste. 170, W. Lafayette, IN 47906; Tel: 765-494-9555; Fax: 765-494-5969; download from Web Site: <<http://www.ctic. purdue.edu>>.

National Watershed Network. See contact information, above, for Conservation Technology Information Center.

Surf Your Watershed. Web Site: <<http://www.epa.gov/surf>>.

Terrene Institute. 4 Herbert St., Alexandria, VA 22305; Tel: 703-548-5473; Fax: 703-548-6299; E-mail: <<terrinst@aol.com>>; Web Site: <<http://www.terrene.org>>.

Watershed Information Network. Web Site: <<http://www.epa. gov/win>>.

Watershed Management Council. c/o Public Service Research Program, University of California, Davis, One Shields Ave., Davis, CA 95616-8688; Tel: 510-273-9066; Fax: 510-643-5438; Web Site: <<http://watershed.org>>.

International

Global Rivers Environmental Education Network. Vince Meldrum, Earth Force, 1908 Mount Vernon Ave., Alexandia, VA 22301; Tel: 703-519-6864; Web Site: <<http://www.earthforce. org>>.

International Water Resources Association. IWRA Headquarters, 4535 Faner Hall, Southern Illinois University, Carbondale, IL 62901-4516; Fax: 618-453-2671; Web Site: <<http://www.iwra.siu.edu>>.

World Water Vision. c/o UNESCO, Division of Water Sciences, 1 Rue Miollis, F-75015 Paris, France; Tel: +(33-1)45 68 3928/2904; Fax: +(33-1) 45 68 58 11; Web Site: <<http://www.watervision. org>>.

VI–C: Glossary of Land–Use Terms

(**Authors' Note:** An asterisk marks the name of each land management tool described in Section IV. See page ix for an alphabetical list of tools and their page numbers.)

*Access management: U.S. Department of Transportation standards support community planning efforts to reduce traffic congestion and improve pedestrian and vehicular safety.

Accessory building: A subordinate building detached from, but located on the same lot as, the main building; the use of accessory buildings is incidental to the main building or its use.

Acre: A parcel of land measuring 43,560 square feet (about 208 feet by 208 feet); also equivalent to about 4,840 square yards, 160 square rods, 0.405 hectares, or 4,047 square meters.

*Agricultural conservation easement: Conservation easements that specifically restrict farmland from development and give farmers income, property, and estate tax reductions.

*Agricultural district: A legal designation that allows qualifying farmers to defer utility assessments if farming is continued on the land.

*Agricultural economic development: The creation and stimulation of new marketing strategies to improve the sales and profitability of agricultural products promote the goal of farmland preservation.

Agricultural values: Based upon soil type and the market for the commodity produced from agricultural lands.

*Agricultural zoning: A method for protecting agricultural land use by stipulating minimum lot sizes or limitations on nonfarm uses.

Amenities: Features which add to the pleasant or attractive appearance of a development, such as underground utilities, buffer zones, or landscaping.

Agriculture: The use of land for farming, dairying, pasturage, apiculture (bees), aquaculture (fish, mussels), horticulture, floriculture, viticulture (grapes), and animal and poultry husbandry; includes the necessary accessory uses for packing, treating, or storing the produce from these activities.

Annexation: The process by which an area of land in a township is incorporated as a part of a municipality.

Aquifer: A geologic formation that carries water in sufficient quantity to supply water for drinking and other uses. Aquifers usually are comprised of saturated sands, gravel, and cavernous and vesicular rock.

Aquifer recharge area: The surface area through which precipitation passes to replenish subsurface water–bearing strata of permeable rock, gravel, or sand.

Area variance: A variance that exempts a landowner from specific zoning requirements, allowing the owner to forego such conditions as area specifications for buffers and setbacks.

*Bargain sale: The sale of land to a conservation organization at less than market value.

Best management practices (BMPs): Pollution prevention measures to reduce runoff and other detrimental effects from storm water, soil erosion, animal wastes, and other discharges, prescribed by *Rainwater and Land Development, Ohio's Standards for Storm Water Management, Land Development, and Urban Stream Protection,* Ohio Department of Natural Resources; Contact: Dan Mecklenburg, Tel: 614-265-6610.

*Brownfields: Lands contaminated by spills or leaks of either hazardous materials or petroleum. Ohio's Voluntary Action Program focuses on restoring brownfields, thereby reducing sprawl, retaining jobs for inner cities, and slowing industrial development of farmland and sensitive natural areas.

*Capital improvement programming: The scheduling of budgetary expenditures for infrastructure, thereby guiding and pacing development.

City: An incorporated municipality with a population of 5,000 or more as determined by the most recent federal census.

*Cluster development zoning: A plan which concentrates development on one part of a property in order to protect the remainder of the parcel as open space without changing the overall density of the development.

Clustering: Concentrating the total allowable dwelling units on a tract of land into higher densities on a smaller portion of the tract, leaving the remaining land as open space, e.g., in a five–acre minimum lot zoned area, 10 units could be constructed on 50 acres; but, by clustering, 10 units could be constructed on, say, 20 acres (thereby increasing the density by allowing minimum two–acre lots), while leaving the remaining 30 acres as common open space for all to share. The total number of dwelling units remains unchanged.

Code: The written zoning code, enabled by the state's legislation, that is organized by numbered sections. The code regulates the use of buildings, public facilities, population densities, sets building standards, and establishes many other terms that govern land use.

Commercial district: That zoning area designated for community services, general business, interchange of services, and commercial recreation.

Compensable regulation: A local government option that provides landowners with monetary compensation if land–use regulations unfairly reduce their property values.

Conditional use permit: A permit issued by the zoning administrator upon approval by the Zoning Board of Appeals to allow a use other than a principally permitted use. The permit is generally provided on the condition that the applicant meets certain additional requirements.

Conditional zoning: When an owner's request for a permit conflicts with existing zoning ordinances, a zoning board may grant the permit if the owner meets specific requirements, sometimes resulting in "conditional zoning." It requires the owner to meet previously unstated conditions in return for an exemption from the section of the ordinance in conflict with the intended land use.

*Conservation development zoning: A type of cluster development which emphasizes a planned unit development for preserving open space, wetlands, natural landscaping, floodplains, and other prioritized resources, as well as for preventing storm water runoff.

*Conservation easement: A legal agreement between a landowner and a qualified conservation agency that transfers development rights from the owner to the agency to protect natural or historic features in perpetuity.

*Conservation Reserve Program: A program that pays farmers to convert erodible cropland to vegetative cover.

*Cooperative agreement: An agreement between two or more organizations to share in financing, maintaining, or managing a property.

*Current Agricultural Use Value: A program that calculates farmland value based on soil type and product markets rather than on development values, thereby reducing taxes on agricultural land.

Detachment: The removal of land from a municipality and placement back in the township.

Developer: A person or company who coordinates the ownership, financing, designing, and other activities necessary to bring about subdivision and construction of infrastructure on land for a new purpose, generally residential, commercial, or industrial.

Development: The actions taken to acquire a zoning permit, special–use permit, conditional–use permit, or sign permit. Also refers to land that has been cleared or that has had residential, commercial, or business structures erected on it.

Development values: The economic worth of land based upon the fair market price of land after improvements have been added, such as residential dwellings and commercial or industrial structures.

District: A part, zone, or geographic area within the municipality within which certain zoning or development regulations apply.

Dwelling unit: The space in a dwelling comprises the living, dining, sleeping area, and auxiliary cooking, bathing, and storage space for one family.

Easement: Written authorization by a property owner for the use of a designated part of the property by another or others for a specified purpose, such as recreation or utility lines. In a conservation easement, a property owner relinquishes certain rights to use the land to protect its resources.

Economic Unit: Such units may consist of land parcels separated from one another physically, but if they are farmed by the same people using the same equipment, then the parcels are treated as an economic unit.

Ecosystem: A community of plant and animal populations, the physical and chemical components of that community, and the interrelationships among these living and nonliving parts.

Eminent domain: The right of a government unit to take private property for public use, with appropriate compensation to the owner.

*Environmental impact ordinance: An assessment of the potential harmful effects of a pending development upon the environment so that steps to prevent damage can be taken before the project begins.

Environmentally sensitive: Areas so designated include wetlands, steep slopes, waterways, underground water recharge areas, shores, natural plant and animal habitats, etc., that are easily disturbed by development.

*Estate management strategies: To help preserve family lands, including farmland, a number of estate management strategies may be enacted during a landowner's lifetime or upon death.

*Exactions: Compensation a community requires of a developer as part of the approval of a proposed development project. Exactions may take the form of facilities, land, or an actual dollar payment. They may be incorporated into the community's zoning code or resolution, or negotiated on a project–by–project basis.

Exempted: In reference to school districts, "exempted" districts are those which are free of supervision by the county government, which supervises and provides state–mandated services to the county's school districts.

*Farmland Protection Program: A federal program matching state funds to purchase conservation easements on prime farmlands.

Fee simple acquisition: The purchase of property through cash payment.

Fee simple interest: Absolute ownership of land with unrestricted rights of disposition—i.e., the owner has the right to control, use, and transfer the property at will. Fee simple ownership describes the possession of all rights to property except those reserved to the state. Deed titles can include special provisions on any of these partial rights, such as restriction of building lot size.

Fen: A peat–accumulating wetland with marsh–like plants.

Flood plain: Areas adjacent to watercourses which may be inundated during a 100–year flood, or base flood, as designated by the U.S. Department of Housing and Urban Development's "Flood Boundary and Floodway Map."

*Forest Tax: A program that reduces property taxes if the owner maintains approved forest management practices on the land.

Front lot line: The lot line separating an interior lot from the street upon which it abuts, or the shortest lot line of a corner lot which abuts upon a street.

Geographic Information System (GIS): A computerized method of mapping soils, parcels, roads, waterways, sewer lines, buildings, zoning districts, and locating other resources or subjects from orbiting satellites.

Gift credit: A dollar or in–kind matching equivalent required to secure funds. Gifts or donations of land, for example, may qualify as in–kind equivalents toward the matching requirement.

*Growth management: Pacing the rate of development or controlling the location of development so that laws can be passed on a very selective basis to manage a community's growth.

Habitat: The total requirement of plants and animals to sustain their species, including food, light, heat, cover, water, and opportunities for breeding replacement individuals of the population. The term usually describes a region and its characteristics with respect to a single population, whether plant or animal.

Historic area: A district or zone designated by a local, state, or federal authority within which the buildings or places are important because of their association with history; their unique architecture; their relationship to a related park or square to be preserved; and / or those areas developed according to a fixed plan based on cultural, historical, or architectural purposes.

Home rule: Home Rule Charter for counties, Home Rule Authority for villages and cities, and Limited Home Rule Authority for townships is allowed under Ohio law. This gives local governments more authority and discretion in governing their jurisdictions than the General Law. (See Section VI for details.)

*Impact fees: Fees required of a developer that are based on a formula applied equally to all equivalent development projects.

Impervious surface: A ground cover, such as cement or asphalt, on sidewalks, roads, or parking lots, through which water cannot penetrate to the soil. Even soils themselves may be impervious, such as those composed of hard-packed clay, and may prevent water from being absorbed, leading to runoff.

Improvements: The actions taken to prepare undeveloped land for occupancy or developed land for a different use. These actions can include clearing the land; building infrastructure, such as roads and waterlines; constructing homes or industrial and commercial buildings; and adding recreational facilities and other amenities.

Industrial district: These districts are designated as light manufacturing, heavy manufacturing, research and development, and industrial parks.

Infrastructure: In residential, commercial, and industrial areas, for example, infrastructure refers to such features as streets, curbing, sidewalks, electric utilities, water, sewage, and other public services.

Installment sale: In a bargain sale, for example, the landowner and the recipient organization may negotiate terms in which the property is transferred over an extended period of time rather than all at once.

Land: Used in various ways, land may refer to soil; the ground surface itself; a space on the earth, a bounded area, a subdivision, a tract, parcel, a lot; an open space; the physical elements below ground, such as minerals and water.

*Land and Water Conservation Fund: A 50% / 50% matching fund program to expand and improve public outdoor recreation areas.

*Land banking: The obtaining, holding, and subsequent release of lands by a local government for controlled development or for conservation purposes.

Land exchange: A public agency or nonprofit organization can exchange developable land for land with high conservation value; such a transaction is called a "land exchange."

Land trust: A private, nonprofit organization that protects natural and cultural resources through conservation easements, land acquisition, and education.

Large–Lot Zoning: A requirement that each new house be constructed on a minimum number of acres, generally at least 5 or more.

Limited development: The development of one portion of a property to finance the protection of another portion.

Map: A drawing or other representation that shows the geographic, topographic, or other physical features of an area of land.

Merger: Under Ohio law, an existing municipality (i.e., a city or a village) can join with a remaining unincorporated area of a township. (Compare "annexation" and "detachment.")

Metropolitan planning organizations (MPOs): In 1962 Metropolitan planning organizations were created to oversee federal transportation issues in urbanized and contiguous areas of 50,000 people or more. Less populated areas were overseen by the Ohio Department of Transportation. Some MPOs remain separately housed, while others have joined their planning commissions.

Mitigation: The process of offsetting damages, often to the environment, from destruction or contamination. Mitigation can include repair, replacement, cleanup, reconstruction, or other methods to restore conditions to their previous undisturbed state.

Moratoria: Legal actions that temporarily freeze development so that adequate planning and follow–up ordinances can be put into place.

Municipality: See "City" and "Village."

National Conservation Buffer Initiative: Farmland buffers that reduce runoff and soil erosion and increase wildlife habitat qualify for financial assistance from state and federal programs.

National Pollutant Discharge Elimination System: The 1972 Clean Water Act imposes pollutant discharge limits and monitoring requirements on point–source dischargers.

Natural Resources Conservation Service: Formerly the Soil Conservation Service, the Natural Resources Conservation Service is an agency of the United States Department of Agriculture.

Open spaces: An area substantially open to the sky; it includes the natural environmental features, such as water areas, and may include recreational facilities. (NOTE: although paved areas may be open expanses, most zoning regulations do not include them under the definition of open space.)

Ordinance: Generically, an ordinance is a law. A "code of ordinances" would include the zoning code of a municipality. Called a "resolution" by townships and counties.

*Outright donation: The donation of land to a qualified charitable land conservation management organization.

*Outright purchase: The acquisition of lakeshores, river corridors, or other lands by individuals, land trusts, government organizations, and others for the benefit of the public.

*Overlay zoning: An overlay of additional land–use restrictions on top of existing ones to protect specific resources such as riparian areas (see below), reservoirs, and historic districts.

Parcel: See "Lot"

*Performance zoning: A requirement that any new development be reviewed based on its projected impact on specific features of the community, such as farming, traffic flow, and storm water management.

Plan: Usually refers to drawings and accompanying documents of a proposed design or other work to be undertaken.

*Planned unit development zoning: A mechanism for cluster development zoning and conservation development zoning in the Ohio Revised Code that may allow more creative designs and mixed use plans.

Plat: A map of a lot, parcel, subdivision, or development area on which the lines of each physical unit are shown by accurate distances and bearings.

Point system: Sometimes used in performance zoning, a point system assigns numerical values to impacts caused by development on a community's resources. When all points are added up, projects are approved, or they may be conditionally approved pending revision, or rejected outright.

Preacquisition: A technique whereby one organization, usually a private land trust, buys a property and holds it until another organization, usually a government agency, can allocate the funds to place it under permanent protection.

Preservation: Leaving a resource undisturbed and free from harm or damage, such as preserving wetlands by forbidding development on or near them. While preservation is often used interchangeably with "conservation," the latter differs by implying the prudent use of a resource.

Prime farmland: Farmland classified by the Natural Resources Conservation Service as best for row, forage, and fiber crop production. Factors include level of topography, drainage, moisture supply, soil texture and depth, and susceptibility to erosion and runoff. Essentially, prime farmland also allows least cost to the farmer and least cost to the natural resources. For the USDA's specifications for prime farmland, see its document, *USDA-SCS, 1982 NRI,* available through the USDA Web Site: <<http://www.usda.gov>>.

Principal building: That building which is the primary center for permitted uses, including all parts connected by common walls and a continuous roof.

Purchase / leaseback: An arrangement whereby a community may purchase a natural area from its owner and then either lease it back with special lease restrictions or sell it back with deed restrictions designed to protect the natural features of the property.

*Purchase of development rights (PDR): A public / private government initiative that acquires the development rights of property to limit development.

*Quarter / Quarter Zoning: A specification that limits nonfarm development to one house per 40 acres, that is, ¼ of ¼ of the original 640–acre tract.

Rear lot line: A lot line parallel or within 45 degrees of being parallel, to the front lot line.

Regulations: Those enforceable rules of the municipality and that part of the zoning code which state, for example, the exact footage of setbacks or the height of dwelling units or the width of streets.

Remediation: Often confused with "cleanup," "remediation" means to resolve a problem (its root source is the word "remedy"). For example, a deed restriction on a former brownfield property might ensure that the property is used only for industrial purposes, never for residential. The problem has been remedied, but no cleanup took place. On another property, such as a residential area, cleanup might be the remedy.

Reserved life estate: Under this arrangement, a landowner donates the property to a conservation organization but retains the right of lifetime use.

Resolution: A formal vote of intention, opinion, or declaration by townships and counties (called an "ordinance" by municipalities).

Revolving fund: A conservation fund used to purchase land or easements. Money spent from the fund is replenished through donations or through selling the land to another conservation organization or, most often, a government agency.

Right–of–first–refusal: An agreement between a landowner and a land trust or other prospective buyer that gives the trust a chance to match any third party offer to buy a property in question.

Right–of–way: A strip of land occupied by, or intended to be occupied by, a street, crosswalk, walkway, or other public improvement for travel or access.

Rights: ("The Bundle of Rights Concept of Property") The rights of real property owners are the rights to use, lease, and to dispose of rights as one wishes. The right of use gives the subordinate the rights to improve, harvest, cultivate, cross over, or not to use at all. The right to lease means the right to lease for cash, as well as to hold a cash–share lease or third and fourth leases, a crop share lease, a one–year lease, and/or a perpetual lease. The right of disposition is comprised of the rights to sell all or part of a property, to bequeath it, to mortgage it, and to establish trusts on it.

Riparian areas: The banks of riverbeds, wetlands, ponds and lakes, defined by varying distances from the water. As of 1999, the U.S. Army Corps of Engineers is developing specific scientific criteria relating to soil type, bank cover, slope, and other factors to help planning agencies develop riparian area regulations that will withstand legal challenges.

Scenic: A view or landscape that is visually attractive.

Set back: The minimum distance by which any building or structure can be separated from a lot line.

Side lot line: A lot line that is neither a front nor a rear lot line.

Sign: Any device that is sufficiently visible to persons not located on the lot to attract their attention or communicate information to them.

*Sliding scale zoning: The enactment of a ratio of dwelling units to land acreage that concentrates development on smaller lots by increasing the minimum lot size for houses built on larger parcels.

Smart growth: A long-range, state government coordinated plan which documents development of an incentive-based state investment program that targets growth–related expenditures to locally designated compact growth areas.[1] (Compare "sustainability.")

Soil Conservation Service: Now renamed the Natural Resources Conservation Service, an agency of the United States Department of Agriculture.

*Special designation: The protection of scenic river corridors and other valuable resources through state or federal recognition and technical assistance.

Special districts: A special district is a government entity that functions independently of other governing bodies and is responsible for performing specific tasks and oversight deemed essential to the community's well being. Special districts include watershed districts, park districts, regional library districts, port authorities, joint economic development zones, soil and water conservation districts, and conservancy districts (to control flood, sewage, water supplies).

Stand: Usually referring to trees, a number of plants growing in a continuous area, for example, "a stand of hardwoods" or "a stand of timber."

Steep slopes: Hillsides, cliffs, and other sharply angled terrain.

*Storm water management — NPDES Phase II: Small municipalities and small construction sites previously exempted under NPDES Phase I will now be required to develop and implement storm water management programs.

Subdivision: The division of a tract of land into two or more lots, building sites, or other divisions–any one of which is under five acres–for the purpose of sale or of building a development. Some subdivision regulations refer to "minor subdivisions," simple lot splits in which each lot uses existing frontage, and "major subdivisions," lot splits requiring a new public or private road to afford access to all of the lots.

Sustainability: "Sustainable development is one of those rare ideas that could dramatically change the way we look at 'what is' and 'what could be.' It is about doing things in ways that work for the long run because they are better from every point of view—better economically, environmentally, and socially. Sustainable development challenges us to envision a society superior to today's society, and to make it a reality for our children and grandchildren."[2] (President's Council on Sustainable Development)

Taking: A local government "takes" property without landowner compensation, a violation of the Fifth Amendment of the Constitution.

Takings Laws: Proposed bills to compensate property owners for drops in the value of their property that might be attributed to government regulation. Texas has passed a law requiring payment with a minimum drop in property value of 25%. Under the Fifth Amendment, no one has an absolute right to use their land in a way that may harm the public health or welfare, or that damages the quality of life of neighboring landowners, or of the community as a whole. As of September 1999, the House Judiciary Committee's Constitution Subcommittee is scheduled to hold hearings on H R 2372, introduced in June by Florida Representative Canady. His bill "creates new opportunities for developers and other private landowners to bring 'takings' claims, which seek compensation for not polluting or not building on protected land." (In 1997, nearly identical legislation was introduced.) The current bill "would allow developers to circumvent local zoning procedures to sue towns, cities, and counties for alleged takings directly in federal court."[3]

Total maximum daily loads: Wasteload (point sources) and load (nonpoint sources) allocations refer to amounts of pollutants that can be discharged without violating water quality standards.

Township: All land areas in a county not incorporated into municipalities (cities and villages). Township governing powers granted under the Ohio Constitution include levying taxes, suing and being sued, maintaining roads and cemeteries, provision of police and fire protection, etc. In September 1991, township Home Rule, or "limited self–government," became law in Ohio, granting townships additional governing powers. By special provision under Ohio law, townships of 25,000 residents may incorporate as cities even if they are within three miles of an existing municipality.

Tract: An indefinite stretch or a bounded piece of land. In subdivisions, a tract is often divided into individual "lots."

*Transfer of development rights: A technique for guiding growth away from sensitive resources and toward controlled development centers through the transfer of development rights from one area to another.

*Transportation enhancements (ISTEA & TEA–21): The federal highway transportation program contributes funds to enhance cultural, aesthetic, and environmental aspects of local transportation and transit systems.

Utility facilities: Any above–ground structures or facilities used for production, generation, transmission, delivery, collection, or storage of water, sewage, electricity, gas, oil, or electronic signals.

Variance: A modification of the zoning regulation, permitted where a literal interpretation of the Zoning Code would result in unnecessary hardship as a result of some peculiar or unique condition or circumstance pertaining to the case.

Village: An incorporated area with a population under 5,000 as determined by the most recent federal census. New villages may be formed (incorporated) by the majority of land owners' successful petition to the county commissioners. Such a proposed village must not be within three miles of an existing municipality, and the proposed area must be at least two square miles in size, with a population of 600 people per square mile and an assessed property value of at least $2,000 per person. Villages automatically become cities upon reaching a population of 5,000 or more. Villages may dissolve as incorporated areas through the petition and election process.[4]

Watershed: An area where precipitation falls and then drains to a common body of water, such as a river system, wetland, or lake.

Wellhead protection: A plan to (1) determine the area collecting water for a public well, (2) identify the pollution sources within that area, and (3) detect, prevent, and remediate potential contamination to the collecting area.

Wetlands: Wetlands are of two major types, coastal (estuarine) and freshwater. Some familiar kinds within those categories are marshes, swamps, fens, bogs, tidal marshes, and prairie potholes. Some are permanently flooded or saturated, while others may experience a range of flooding or saturation that may be described from "regularly" to "irregularly" inundated or saturated. Water sources for wetlands may be lakes, ponds, groundwater, tides, rain, and runoff. Wetlands are key to biological diversity because they are the breeding grounds and homes for an immensely diverse number of plants and animals. They also help control floodwaters, provide recreational facilities, and help improve water quality by concentrating harmful chemicals or removing excessive nutrients from polluted waters. (See "wetlands delineation," below.)

Wetlands delineation: The 1972 Federal Water Pollution Control Act (the Clean Water Act) gave the U.S. Army Corps of Engineers and the U.S. Environmental Protection Agency authority to regulate pollution of waters in the U.S., a power subsequently extended by court decisions to include all wetlands of the U.S. In 1993 Congress asked the National Academy of Science to clarify the issues around the wetlands delineation controversy. Through the National Research Council, the Academy presented the following definition to Congress on May 9, 1995, and released it to the public in September 1995 as "Wetlands Characteristics and Boundaries":

> A wetland is an ecosystem that depends on constant or recurrent shallow inundation or saturation at or near the surface of the substrate. The minimum essential characteristics of a wetland are recurrent, sustained inundation or saturation at or near the surface and the presence of physical, chemical, and biological features reflective of recurrent, sustained inundation or saturation. Common diagnostic features of wetlands are hydric soils and hydrophytic vegetation. These features will be present except where specific physicochemical, biotic, or anthropogenic factors have removed them or prevented their development.

This definition of wetlands delineation has not changed as of September 1999.

*Wetlands mitigation and banking: When wetlands, which prevent pollution, flooding, and provide habitat, are irrevocably lost to dredge or fill, constructed or restored replacement wetlands may be purchased to maintain their net value to the country.

*Wetlands Reserve Program: Federal program with state partnering to restore the functions and values of wetlands and to preserve riparian areas through payments to landowners for conservation easements and wetland reconstruction practices.

*Wildlife Habitat Incentives Program: Private landowners may improve habitat for wildlife and fisheries with federal cost–sharing funds awarded after installation.

Zoning inspector: A position usually appointed by the mayor or equivalent head of a political unit (e.g., board of township trustees, board of county commissioners) to administer and enforce zoning regulations and related ordinances (resolutions).

Zoning board of appeals: Usually comprised of a group of five individuals on the board, appointed by the mayor or other governing individual or body. The responsibility of such boards is to review applications for variances and exceptions and then decide whether there is legitimate reason to grant the request for a permit.

Zoning commission: Appointed by township trustees and county commissioners to advise them, respectively, on zoning issues. The zoning commission prepares zoning resolutions, amends zoning codes and maps, and holds public hearings on zoning matters.

Zoning permit: A permit issued by the land–use administrator authorizing the recipient to use property in accord with requirements of the Zoning Code.

NOTES

[1] EcoCity Cleveland, *EcoCity Cleveland Journal* (Fall 1998), 3.

[2] Ibid, 3.

[3] National Resources Defense Council, "Legislative Watch," 1. Downloaded September 21, 1999 from Web Site: <<http://www.nrdc.org/field/state/html>>.

[4] Terry Jacobs, ed., "Article 2—Definitions," *Ohio Model Zoning Code* (Columbus, OH: Ohio Department of Development, 1989), 9.

VI–D: Map of Ohio Counties

Map courtesy of the Division of Geological Survey, Ohio
Department of Natural Resources, 4383 Fountain Square Drive,
Columbus, OH 43224-1362; Tel: 614-265-6576; Fax: 614-447-
1918; Web Site: <<http://www.dnr.state.oh.us/odnr/geo_survey>>.

INDEX

Note: Boldfaced page numbers below refer to the full description of a given land management tool in Section IV.

1996 Farm Bill, 98, 102, 127
30–year easement, 121
30–year WRP conservation easements, 122
A Green Plan Primer, 313
Acadia Cliffs, 285, 288
access management, 59, **61-67**, 357
Access Management: A Solution to Urban Traffic Congestion, 67
accessory building, 357
ACE. See "agricultural conservation easement."
action–based watershed plan, 16
Adams County, 284, 290, 336
Adding Value for Sustainability, 310
agrarian lands, 141
Agricultural Business Enhancement Center, 299
agricultural conservation easement, 33, **35-38**, 70, 113, 141, 218, 357
agricultural district, 59, **68-72**, 94, 155-156, 158, 172, 357
agricultural economic development, 59, **73-79**, 357
agricultural operations, 75, 139
Agricultural Pollution Abatement Cost Sharing Program, 245
Agricultural Preservation Restriction Program, 143
agricultural use, 59, 68, 94, 96-98, 103, 121, 126, 141, 142, 155, 156, 360
agricultural values, 95, 101, 357
agricultural zoning, 25, 70, 71, 153, **155-159**, 166, 200, 357
agriculture, 4, 19, 27, 35, 68, 73, 75, 77-78, 94-95, 98, 141, 157, 167, 170, 179, 203, 251-254, 261, 262, 310, 315, 318, 320, 357
agritourism, 75
A Guide to Developing Local Watershed Action Plans in Ohio, 16, 20, 245
Akron, OH, 139-140, 213-215, 280
Akron water supply, 140
Allen County, OH, 285, 291, 336
allocating state and federal transportation money, 18
Alpine Charter Township, 182
American Electric Power Company, 39
American Farmland, 37-38, 79
American Farmland Trust, 8, 20, 37, 38, 71, 72, 76, 79, 101, 102, 139, 143, 158, 168, 180, 181, 183, 184, 190, 203, 221, 256, 262, 302, 310
American Forests, 310
American Littoral Society, 310
American Planning Association, 6, 7, 143, 173, 178, 181, 183, 190, 191, 198, 203, 207, 210, 220, 234, 235, 310, 317
American Rivers, 310
American Society for Environmental History, 311
American Society of Landscape Architects, 311
annexation, 138, 224, 227, 228, 358, 364
annual exclusion, 46, 47
antidegradation policy, 16
aquatic buffers, 16
aquatic life habitats, 16
aquifers, 5, 141, 172, 358

Ashland County, OH, 285, 291
Ashtabula County, OH, 132, 285, 291, 322, 336
Ashtabula County Metropolitan Park District, 132
Association for Conservation Information, 311
Athens County, OH, 262, 285, 291, 336
Audubon Islands, 287
Audubon Society, 42, 56, 120, 286, 288, 300, 302, 316
Aurora, OH, 56, 208, 210
backage roads, 62
Bainbridge Township, OH, 25, 161-162, 267
bargain sale, 33, **39-40**, 49, 358, 363
Belmont County, OH, 285, 291, 336
best management practices (BMPs), 61-62, 90-91, 110-113, 197, 246, 247, 358
better site design, 113
Big & Little Darby Creek, 290
Big Island wetland mitigation bank, 118
biological diversity, 18, 371
bioregional planning, 12, 18, 19
Blackbrook Audubon Society, 300
Block Island, Rhode Island, 137
BMPs. See "best management practices."
board of zoning appeals, 28, 175, 176, 226-228, 231-233
bonds, 6, 36, 81, 99, 135, 226, 239, 259, 322
brownfields, 6, 59, **80-86**, 149, 202, 358
browsers, Internet, 254, 256-258
Buckeye Hills RC&D, 346
Bucks County, PA, 172
buffers, 15, 16, 88-91, 106-109, 163, 358, 364
bundle of rights concept of property, 41, 141, 218, 367
Bureau of Land Management (BLM), 302, 311
business planning and capital investment, 73
Butler County, OH, 285, 291, 322, 337
California Center for Land Recycling, 311
California Environmental Resources Evaluation System (CERES), 311
capital improvement programming, 185, **187-191**, 358
case histories, 37, 39, 43, 48, 50, 95, 104, 118, 123, 126, 132, 143, 161, 164, 167, 169, 172, 177, 179, 182, 188, 192, 197, 205, 208, 219
CAUV. See "current agricultural use value."
Center for Environmental Information & Statistics, 311
Center for Field Research, 242
Center for Livable Communities, 311
Center for Neighborhood Technology, 311
Center for Watershed Protection, 16, 113, 311
Center of Excellence for Sustainable Development, 312
CERES. See "California Environmental Resources Evaluation System."
Chagrin River, 15, 20, 50, 52, 53, 109, 112-114, 275, 276, 290, 300, 354
Chagrin River Land Conservancy, 50, 275, 354
Chagrin River Watershed, 15, 20, 109, 112-114, 300, 354
Chagrin River Watershed Partners, 15, 20, 109, 112-114, 300, 354
Chagrin Watershed Institute, 300, 354
Champaign County, OH, 263, 285, 291, 337
Chardon Township, OH, 167, 168
Chardon, OH, 205, 206
charitable gift, 39, 46, 57, 132

Charles Stewart Mott Foundation, 242
Chesapeake Bay, 88
Citizens' Bioregional Plan for Northeast Ohio, 8, 17, 18, 21
Citizens' Network for Sustainable Development (CitNet), 312
civil liability, 80, 83
civil penalties, 234
Clark County, OH, 285, 291, 322, 337
Clean Water Act, 16, 365, 371
Clear Creek, 57, 286
clearing and sediment control plan, 197
Clermont County, OH, 285, 289, 292, 322, 337
Clermont County Parks, 285, 289
Cleveland Community Development Network, 300
Cleveland Foundation, 242
Cleveland Neighborhood Development Corporation, 300
Cleveland Restoration Society, 274, 300, 301
Clinton County, OH, 11, 14, 20, 285, 292, 322, 337
cluster development zoning, 28-29, 52, 153, **160-162**, 163-164, 166, 168, 176,
    182, 219, 358-359, 365
coastal zones, 5, 49
Columbiana County, OH, 83, 85, 285, 292, 322, 337
Columbiana County Port Authority, 83, 85
combined sewer overflows, 139
commercial development, 35, 99
commercial district, 359
Commodity Credit Corporation, 87, 98
Common Pleas Court of Clinton County, Ohio, 14
community development block grants, 81
Community of Science, 242
Community Rights Council, 312
Community Service, Inc., 302
community supported agriculture (CSA), 75, 77, 237, 251-253, 315
Community Sustainability Resource Institute, 202, 319
compensable regulation, 359
compensatory mitigation, 115, 116, 118, 119
compensatory mitigation requirements, 115
comprehensive plans and planning, 11-15, 17, 19, 25-27, 29-30, 112, 134,
    149, 167, 170, 172, 176, 187, 188, 199-201, 205, 200, 208, 210-
    219, 229, 230
Concern, Inc., 202, 312
Concord Township, OH, 113
conditional use permit, 359
conditional zoning, 200, 231-233, 359
Consensus Agreement on Model Development Principles to Protect
    OurStreams, Lakes, and Wetlands, 16, 112
conservancies, 49, 116
conservancy districts, 141, 223, 229, 237, 259, 368
conservation buffers, 106, 107
conservation development zoning, 28, 29, 31, 52, **163-165**, 176, 359, 365
Conservation Development Resource Manual, 31, 165
conservation easements, 35-37, **41-45**, 46, 49, 52-53, 55-56, 98-101, 119,
    121-123, 141, 160, 278, 289, 357, 359-361, 364, 372
Conservation Easements: How They Can Work for You, 58
Conservation Ecology, 312, 314
conservation of natural areas (habitat for nature), 16

conservation priority area, 88
Conservation Reserve Enhancement Program (CREP), 90-91, 93, 108
Conservation Reserve Program (CRP), 43, 59, **87-93**, 98, 106-108, 123, 125, 245,360
Conservation Technology Information Center, 168, 312, 356
construction of streets, 30
construction site owners and operators, 110
construction site storm water runoff ordinance, 111
continuous sign–up (Conservation Reserve Program), 89, 91, 107, 108
contour grass strips, 106
contour mapping of terrain, 11
control of road siting, 18
converted cropland, 122
cooperative agreement, 49, 98, 185, **192-195**, 360
Cooperative State Research, Education, and Extension Service, 87
Corps of Engineers. See "U. S. Army Corps of Engineers."
costs of community services, 7, 166
Council of Michigan Foundations, 243
Council on Foundations, 240
counties, 12, 15, 27-28, 30, 74, 76, 94, 96, 141, 143, 156, 165, 174, 200, 223-224, 226-229, 237, 316, 335, 362, 365, 367, 373
Countryside Program, 31, 165, 300
county board of zoning appeals, 226
County Commissioners' Association of Ohio, 302
county park districts (Ohio Revised Code 1545), 322
county zoning, 28, 29, 226, 227, 229, 338
"covenant not to sue," 83-84
Crane Hollow Inc., 289
Crawford County, OH, 285, 292, 337
Crawford Park District, 285, 289, 323
creation of new wetlands, 115
CREP. See "Conservation Reserve Enhanced Program."
criminal fines, 234
critical environmental areas, 196
Crossroads RC&D, 346
cross–wind trap strips, 106
CRP. See "Conservation Reserve Program."
CSA. See "community supported agriculture."
current agricultural use value (CAUV), 59, 68-70, **94-97**, 103, 121, 126, 141, 142, 155-156, 360
Cuyahoga River, 139, 140, 278, 290, 300, 354, 355
Cuyahoga River Remedial Action Program, 300, 354
Cuyahoga Valley Association, 301
Cuyahoga Valley National Recreation Area, 333
Darke County, OH, 285, 292, 323, 337
Dayton, OH, 148, 149
deed restrictions, 80-81, 83, 141-142, 220, 234, 366-367
Deer Creek, 328, 329, 331
Delaware Agricultural Lands Foundation, 70, 71
Delaware County, OH, 285, 292, 338
dependence on the automobile, 18
design and construction costs, 118
designated management agencies, 17
detachment, 224, 227, 228, 360, 364

development, 5, 7, 12-19, 25-30, 35-36, 40-41, 43, 52-56, 61, 64-65, 73-76,
    82, 110-111, 113, 115, 134-135, 138-139, 141-143, 156-165,
    171-172, 176-178, 187-188, 196-197, 199-202, 202-210, 218-221,
    335, 357, 360
development impact fees regulation, 206, 207
development rights, 25, 36, 43, 48, 70, 71, 129, 138, 141-144, 156, 185,
    218-221, 359, 366, 370
development values, 68, 141-142, 360
Devonshire Meadows, 164
direct marketing of agricultural products, 74-76
disturbance of soils, 111
diversification of agricultural products, 75
Division of Air Pollution Control, Ohio EPA 307
Division of Civilian Conservation, Ohio DNR, 303
Division of Drinking & Ground Waters, Ohio EPA, 307
Division of Emergency & Remedial Response, Ohio EPA, 307
Division of Engineering, Ohio DNR, 303
Division of Engineering Policy, Ohio DOT, 305
Division of Environmental & Financial Assistance, Ohio EPA, 307
Division of Environmental Services, Ohio EPA, 307
Division of Forestry, Ohio DNR, 103-105, 247, 283, 303
Division of Geological Survey, Ohio DNR, 303, 373
Division of Hazardous Waste Management, Ohio EPA, 307
Division of Mines & Reclamation, Ohio DNR, 304
Division of Multi-Modal Planning and Programs, Ohio DOT, 305
Division of Natural Areas & Preserves, Ohio DNR, 40, 44, 58, 212, 215-216,
    284, 289-290, 304
Division of Oil & Gas, Ohio DNR, 304
Division of Parks & Recreation, Ohio DNR, 304
Division of Real Estate & Land Management, Ohio DNR, 133, 246, 304
Division of Recycling & Litter Prevention, Ohio DNR, 304
Division of Soil and Water Conservation, Ohio DNR, 124, 246 247, 304, 347
Division of Solid & Infectious Waste Management, Ohio EPA, 307
Division of Surface Water, Ohio EPA, 16, 20, 198, 246, 247, 307, 354
Division of Water, Ohio DNR, 261, 304, 356
Division of Watercraft, Ohio DNR, 304
Division of Wildlife, Ohio DNR, 118, 285, 288, 289, 304
Donors Forum of Chicago, 243
drinking water, 82, 139
driveways, 61-65
dwelling unit, 172, 201, 360
Eagle Creek, 276
Earth Day Coalition, 301
Earth Island Institute, 312
Earth Island Journal, 312
easements, 25, 33, 35-37, 41-44, 46, 48-49, 52-53, 55-56, 58, 70, 98-100,
    119, 121-123, 126, 160, 218, 357, 359-360
EBI. See "environmental benefits index."
EcoAction 2000—Ontario region, 245
Ecocity Cleveland, 6-8, 18, 21, 301, 372
EcoCity Cleveland Journal, 7, 8, 21, 301, 372
economic development, 7, 73-76, 78, 81, 134, 290, 299, 335, 357, 368
ecosystem, 239, 243, 244, 278, 361, 371
Ecotrust, 312
Elimination of Illicit Discharges to the MS4, 111

Ellison Creek, 113
eminent domain, 27, 35, 36, 69, 70, 134, 137, 141, 155, 227, 361
enforcement and penalties for zoning violations, 233
enhancing aesthetics, 121
enhancing existing wetlands, 115
Enterprise Center for Economic Development, 299
environmental benefits index (EBI), 87, 88
Environmental Council of the States, 312
Environmental Defense Fund, 313
environmental impact ordinance, 185, **196-198**, 361
Environmental Law Foundation, 313
Environmental Organizations Web Directory, 313
Environmental Protection Agency (EPA), 16, 110-111, 113, 120, 149, 170,
       198, 206, 244, 246-249, 300, 307, 311, 313, 319, 354-356
Environmental Quality Incentives Program, 106, 245
environmentally sensitive areas, 17, 52-53, 87, 138-139, 169, 176, 187, 218,
       361
EPA. See "Environmental Protection Agency."
EPA–designated wellhead protection areas, 90
Erie Basin RC&D, 346
Erie County, OH, 292, 338
Erie MetroParks, 285, 289, 323
erosion and sediment control, 16, 198
estate management strategies, 33, 44, **46-48,** 51, 55, 58, 361
estate planning, 44, 46-48, 51, 58
exactions, 185, 204, 205, 207, 361
exempted districts, 223, 361
expanding opportunities for environmental education, 121
extension offices. See "Ohio State University Extension."
Fairfield County, OH, 57, 286, 293, 323, 338
Farm Bill of 1996, 125
farm bureaus, 237, 261
Farm Service Agency, 87, 88, 92, 93, 121, 245, 247, 302
Farm*A*Syst, 313
farmed wetlands, 121, 122
Farmers' Market Directory, 1999 Edition, 313
farmers' markets, 74, 76, 79, 237, 262-274
Farming on the Edge, 8
farmland and farms, 3-7, 14, 19, 36-37, 68, 88-102, 106-109, 141-143,
       155-159, 166, 179-184, 199-200, 218-221, 251-253, 262-274, 366
Farmland Information Center, American Farmland Trust, 20, 36-37, 71-73, 79,
       102, 158, 166, 168, 199, 203, 221
farmland loss, 3, 19, 190
farmland preservation planning, 30
Farmland Protection Program, 36, 43, 59, 71, **98-102**, 361
farmland that has become a wetland as a result of flooding, 122
Federal Agriculture Improvement and Reform Act, 87, 98
Federal Information Exchange, 245
Federal Water Pollution Control Act Amendments of 1972, 115
fee simple acquisition, 137, 361
fee simple interest, 361
fen, 285-288, 362
field borders, 106
field windbreaks, 89, 90, 106, 108
filter strips, 88-91, 106, 108, 109

filtering sediment from runoff water, 121
Findlay, OH, 65, 66
flood plains, 163, 169, 362
flood water retention, 121
flood zones, 5
Food Security Act of 1985, 87, 121
forest tax, 59, **103-105**, 362
forestry and forests, 12, 77, 87, 103-105, 138-139, 170, 237, 247, 254, 261,
    276, 283, 303, 310
Forum: Habitat on Developing Countries, 321
four major zoning districts, 28
FPP. See "Farmland Protection Program."
Franklin County, OH, 20, 57, 118, 169, 170, 285-286, 293, 323, 345
Friends of the Black River, 355
Friends of the Crooked River, 301, 355
Friends of Wetlands, 301
front lot line, 362, 366
frontage, 62, 63, 65, 69, 139, 149, 369
Fulton County, OH, 286, 293, 338
*Functional Assessment of Mitigation Wetlands in Ohio: Comparisons with
    Natural Systems*, 117
funding for land protection projects, 17, 37, 71, 95, 98-99, 122-123, 125, 131-
    132, 135, 145-150, 188, 193, 195, 200, 239-249, 280, 308,
Gahanna City Parks, 286, 289
Garden State Preservation Trust Act, 99
Gates Mills Land Conservancy, 52, 53, 276
Geauga County, OH, 50, 104, 105, 113, 126, 167, 205, 293, 338
general law, 224, 225, 229, 363
geographic information system (GIS), 362
geologic areas, 5
George Gund Foundation, 240, 243
German Marshall Fund of the United States, 243
gift credit, 132, 362
Gil Friend & Associates—Strategic Sustainability, 313
GLIN. See "Great Lakes Information Network."
Global Rivers Environmental Education Network, 356
glossary of land–use terms, 49, 237, 357
Grand River, 43, 44, 132, 162, 276, 290, 355
Grand River Watershed Partners, 276, 355
grass waterways, 89, 106, 108-109
Great Lakes, 19, 00, 120, 213, 240 241, 248, 301, 313, 317, 321, 356
Great Lakes / Big Rivers, 241
Great Lakes Commission, 241, 301, 313
Great Lakes Information Network (GLIN), 241-242, 301
Great Lakes Natural Resource Center, 356
Great Lakes Protection Fund, 240, 243
Great Lakes United, 313
Green Environmental Coalition, Inc., 355
Greenbelt, 18, 286
Greene County, OH, 266, 286, 289, 293, 323, 338
Greene County Park District, 286, 289, 323
Greenville Creek River, 290
ground water recharge, 121
groundwater, 5, 11, 17, 26, 49, 82, 163, 166, 168, 171, 371
grower cooperatives, 76

growth management, 103, 173, 178, 185, **199-203**, 210, 219, 221, 321, 362
Growth Management Act, 200
Guidebook of Financial Tools, 313
habitat, 4, 5, 16, 40, 42, 53-54, 57, 87, 90-92, 106, 121, 125-127, 192-194, 321, 364,
Hamilton County, OH, 286, 289, 293, 323, 339
Hamilton County Park District, 286, 289, 323
Hancock County, OH, 66
Hardin County, OH, 286, 294, 323, 339
Harpersfield Covered Bridge Metropolitan Park, 132
harvesting timber, 123
health, safety, and morals, 13
Heart of Ohio RC&D, 346
Heartland Development, Inc., 53
Hebron wetland mitigation bank, 118
Hermitage Builders, Inc., 113
high priority conservation, 89, 108
Highland County, OH, 286, 294, 339
Hiram, OH, 77-78
historic & legislative basis for land–use decisions in Ohio, 227
historic area, 362
historic preservation resources, 237, 274
historic, cultural, and scenic sites, 5
Home Builders Association, 118, 206
Hocking County, OH, 286, 294, 339
Hocking River, 57
home rule, 205, 224-226, 229, 230, 362, 370
home rule authority, 224, 225, 362
home rule charter, 224, 229, 362
home sewage, 17
how your local government works with respect to land use, 223
Hudson, OH, 66, 170, 201-203, 209, 216, 275, 277
human resources, 335
Huron County, OH, 286, 294, 324, 339
hydrology, 11, 12, 15, 122
Illinois Humanities Council, 243
impact fees and exactions, 185, 188, **204-207**, 363
impact zoning, 171
impaired water body segments, 16
Impervious surfaces, 111, 172, 363
improving migratory and other wildlife habitat, 121
increasing open space, 121
Indigo Development—Industrial Ecology Research Center, 314
industrial district, 363
Information Center for Economic Developers, 314
infrastructure and infrastructure costs, 3, 13, 26, 71, 81, 98, 134, 137, 139, 148-149, 162, 166-167, 187, 190, 199-201, 204, 358, 360, 363
installment sale, 39, 363
Institute for Conservation Leadership, 314
institutional dischargers, 111
Intermodal Surface Transportation Efficiency Act (ISTEA), 21, 101, 112, 129, 145-146, 370
International City / County Management Association, 315, 321
International Council for Local Environmental Initiatives, 321
International Joint Commission, 321

International Water Resources Association, 356
Internet, 75, 79, 237, 240, 242, 245, 251, 254-258, 261, 274, 279, 313, 328,
    334, 345
Internet browsers, 257
Internet search engines, 257
Internet service providers, 256-258
inventories of plant and animal life, 11
Island Press, 140, 143, 173, 178, 203, 210, 220, 221, 314
ISTEA. See "Intermodal Surface Efficiency Transportation."
Izaak Walton League of America, 314
Jackson County, OH, 287, 294, 339
Jefferson County, OH, 157, 294, 324, 339
John D. & Catherine T. MacArthur Foundation, 244
Journal of Conservation Ecology, 314
Journal of Industrial Ecology, 314
Joyce Foundation, 243
Kent County, MI, 179, 182
Kent Environmental Council, 301
Kokosing River, 290
Olentangy River Valley Association, 355
Know Your Ohio Government, 234
Knox County, OH, 287, 294, 324, 340
Ladd Natural Bridge Nature Preserve, 215, 288
LaDue Reservoir, 139
Lake County, OH, 43, 44, 95-97, 113, 191-194, 287, 294, 340, 354
Lake County Nursery, 95-96
Lake Erie, 39, 82, 90, 93, 106-109, 240, 244, 276, 329-332, 355
Lake Erie Buffer Program, 106
Lake Erie Protection Fund, 109, 240, 244
Lake Erie watershed, 90, 93, 106, 108
Lake Metroparks, 44, 192-194, 324
Lake Rockwell, 139, 140
land and land issues, 4, 11-12, 363
land acquisition policies and procedures, 140
land and water conservation fund, 129, **131-133**, 363
land banking, 129, **134-136**, 254, 363
land conservation, 14, 16, 31, 44, 58, 365
land exchange, 49, 364
land trust, 33, 35, 39-42, 44, **49-51**, 52, 54, 58, 116, 237, 239, 275-276, 278-
    279, 314, 321-322, 364-367
Land Trust Alliance, 44, 51, 279, 314
land–use analysis, 17
Land Use and Community Alliance Service, 314
Land Use Forum Network, Inc. (LUFNET), 314
land–use planning, 158
Land Use Regulations Supporting Access Management, 62, 63, 67
lands adjacent to protected wetlands, 123
landscaping, 30, 147, 163, 280, 357, 359
LandWorks, 101
large–lot zoning, 153, 160, **166-168**, 364
large–scale wetlands, 117
Lawrence County, OH, 287, 294, 324, 340
League of Conservation Voters, 314
League of Women Voters, 234, 302, 315
lease of development rights, 142

levies, 26, 226
LGC Reports, 315
Licking County, OH, 65, 281, 287, 295, 340
limited development, 29, 33, 49, **52-54**, 163, 179, 364
limited self–government, 370
Lincoln Institute of Land Policy, 135, 136, 162, 220, 315
Little Beaver Creek, 277, 290
Little Miami River, 290
Little Miami River Partnership, 355
Little Miami, Inc., 355
livable communities, 18, 143, 311
Livable Places Update, 315
livestock, 69, 75, 91, 139, 155, 261
living snow fences, 89, 106
loan programs and economic development, 74
Local Government Commission, 310, 311, 315
Local Government Environmental Assistance Network, 315
local ordinances, 204
local referendum, 28
Logan County, OH, 268, 287, 295
Long Island Sound, 88
loss of farmland, 27, 28
lot development (habitat for people), 16
lot splits, 64, 183, 369
low density zoning, 166
Lucas County, OH, 287, 295, 340, 344
Madison County, OH, 123, 287, 295, 324, 340
Madison Township, OH, 70
Mahoning County, OH, 287, 295, 340
maps and land–use, 64, 66-67, 136, 169, 174-175, 183, 209, 231-233, 237,
        241, 262, 313, 362, 364-365, 373
map of Ohio counties, 373
marital deduction, 46, 47
market value of land, 36, 39, 40, 56, 70, 117, 141, 218, 358
marketing strategies, 73, 75, 357
marketing agricultural products to restaurants and food retailers, 74
Martha's Vineyard, MA, 135, 136
Martha's Vineyard Land Bank, 135, 136
Maryland Agricultural Land Preservation Foundation, 101, 220
Maryland Economic Growth, Resource Protection, and Planning Act, 200
Massachusetts, 31, 73, 134-137, 143, 191, 310, 314, 316, 317
Maumee River, 290
Maumee Valley RC&D, 346
Mayo Law Firm, 51, 279, 315
McHenry County, IL, 156, 157
measurable slope, 11
Medina County, OH, 17, 18, 277, 287, 295, 324, 341
Mercer County, OH, 287, 295, 341
merger, 227, 228, 364
Metropolitan Park District of Columbus & Franklin Co., 289
Metropolitan Park District of the Toledo Area, 287, 289
metropolitan planning organizations (MPO), 17, 78, 146, 237, 253,279-281,
        364
Miami County, OH, 177, 287, 289, 296, 325, 341
Miami County Park District, 287, 289, 325

Miami Valley RC&D, 346
Michigan Organic Farm and Food Alliance (MOFFA), 315
Midpeninsula Open Space District, 140
Mid–Ohio Regional Planning Commission, 169, 281, 341
Minnesota's Community–Based Planning Act, 200
minor subdivision & lot splits, 64
mitigation, 36, 59, 115-120, 146, 147, 171, 187, 205, 280, 364, 372
mitigation banks, 115-119
mixed land uses, 18
Model Agricultural Zoning Ordinance, Lancaster County, Pennsylvania, 71
Model Conservation Easement and Historic Preservation Easement, 44
model ordinances, 15-16, 156, 169, 170, 172, 354
Monroe County, OH, 269, 287, 296, 325, 341
Montgomery County, MD, 219
moratoria, 185, **208-210**, 364
municipal corporations, 224
MPO. See "metropolitan planning organization."
municipal zoning, 27, 172, 227-230
municipalities, 12-13, 27-28, 110-112, 223-232, 364
Munisource Web Site, 203, 315
museums, 116, 147, 280
Nantucket, MA, 134, 135, 137
Nantucket Land Bank Act of Massachusetts, 134
Nantucket Land Commission, 135
National Agricultural Library, 315, 320
National Association of Conservation Districts, 316
National Association of Counties, 316
National Association of State Park Directors, 316
National Association of Towns & Townships, 316
National Audubon Society, 120, 302, 316
National Civic League, 316
National Conservation Buffer Initiative (NCBI), 59, 92, **106-109**, 364
National Environmental Education and Training Foundation, 244
National Fish and Wildlife Foundation, 244
National Ground Water Association, 316
National Library for the Environment, 316
National Marine Fisheries Service, 115, 116
National Park Service, 131, 192, 212-214, 216-217, 274-275, 303, 309, 333-334
National Park Trust, 316
National Parks and Conservation Association, 316
National Pollutant Discharge Elimination System (NPDES), 110-112, 114, 365, 369
National Register of Historic Places, 213, 274, 275
National Resources Conservation Service, State Office, 353
National Science Foundation, 245, 248
National Trust for Historic Preservation, 317
National Watershed Network, 356
National Wildlife Federation, 317, 356
natural areas, 16, 18, 29, 40, 44, 58, 112, 156, 212-213, 215-216, 275, 277, 279, 284, 289, 290, 304, 317, 358
Natural Areas Association, 317
natural features, 26, 29, 113, 160, 162, 163, 177, 243, 366
natural landscaping, 163, 359

Natural Resources Conservation Service (NRCS), 4, 16, 35, 44, 87-88, 91, 98, 102, 107, 109, 116, 125, 246, 346-347, 353, 365-366, 368
Natural Resources Defense Council, 168, 317
nature preserves, 212, 237, 284-288
NatureWorks, 122, 124, 246
NCBI. See "National Conservation Buffer Initiative."
NEFCO. See "Northeast Ohio Four County Regional Planning & Development Organization."
New Jersey State Development and Redevelopment Plan, 200
NOACA. See "Northeast Ohio Areawide Coordinating Agency."
"no further action" letter, 80
Nonpoint Source Education Grants, 246
Nonpoint Source Watershed Grants Program, 246
non–nursery farmers, 96
Northcoast Perennials Nursery, 70
Northeast Ohio Four County Regional Planning & Development Organization, 16, 342-345
Northeast Ohio Areawide Coordinating Agency, 16-17, 20, 146, 226, 281, 335, 337-338, 340-342
Northwest Area Foundation, 244
Notice of Intent (NOI), 110, 114
Novak Sanctuary, 56
no–net–loss in wetland function and acreage, 116
NPDES. See "National Pollutant Discharge Elimination System."
NPDES Phase II. See "National Pollutant Discharge Elimination System."
nuisance complaints, 155
Oberlin Sustainable Agriculture Project, 78, 79, 253
Oberlin, OH, 78
ODNR. See "Ohio Department of Natural Resources."
OEPA. See "Ohio Environmental Protection Agency."
Office of Environmental Education, 307
Office of Farmland Preservation, 7, 8, 101, 302
Office of Pollution Prevention, 307
Office of Public Information & Communications, 305
OGRIP. See "Ohio Geographically Referenced Information Program."
Ohio & Erie Canal, 19, 213-215, 217, 303
Ohio & Erie Canal Association, 214, 217
Ohio & Erie Canal Corridor Coalition, 214, 215, 303
Ohio & Erie Canal National Heritage Corridor, 19, 213, 214, 303
Ohio Canal Corridor, 214, 215, 217, 303
Ohio Coastal Resource Management Project, 303
Ohio Department of Agriculture, 6, 79, 303
Ohio Department of Development, 31, 84, 235, 303, 309, 372
Ohio Department of Natural Resources, 16, 40, 44, 58, 91-93, 103-105, 114, 116, 118, 121-122, 124, 131-133, 198, 211-212, 215-216, 245-247, 283, 289, 290, 303, 328, 334, 347, 353, 358, 373
Ohio Department of Tax Equalization, 94
Ohio Department of Transportation (ODOT), 61-62, 65-67, 146, 149, 279, 305, 364
Ohio DNR. See "Ohio Department of Natural Resources."
Ohio Ecological Food and Farm Association, 306
Ohio Environmental Education Fund, 248, 308

Ohio Environmental Protection Agency (OEPA, Ohio EPA), 16, 20, 80-86,
110, 113-114, 116, 120, 240, 246-248, 300, 307-308, 354
Ohio EPA. See "Ohio Environmental Protection Agency."
Ohio Farmers' Markets, 74, 79, 262-274
Ohio Forest Tax Law, 103, 105
Ohio Fund for the Environment, 308
Ohio Geographically Referenced Information Program (OGRIP), 309
Ohio Government Information and Services, 309
Ohio Historic Preservation Office, 170, 216, 275
Ohio Historical Society, 212, 274, 285, 289
Ohio Historical Society / Cedar Bog, 289
Ohio Home Builders Association, 118
Ohio Housing Research Network, 3
Ohio Housing Trust Fund, 6
Ohio Kentucky Regional Council of Governments (OKI), 61, 67
Ohio Natural Areas Program, 212, 213
Ohio Natural Landmark, 215
Ohio Rail Development Commission, 305
Ohio Revised Code (ORC), 12, 14, 28, 31, 41, 62, 68-69, 94, 96, 155, 158,
163, 174, 224, 226-230, 234-235, 335-336
Ohio River Valley Water Sanitation Commission, 309
Ohio Rural Zoning Handbook, Fourth Edition, 31, 235, 309
Ohio Scenic Rivers Program, 211, 289-290
Ohio State University Extension, 7, 16, 19, 20, 31, 51, 72, 78-79, 85, 97, 144,
159, 162, 165, 235, 237, 290-299
Ohio State University, Department of Agricultural Economics, 309
Ohio Township Association, 309
Ohio Valley RC&D, 346
Ohio Water Environment Association, 309
Ohio Water Pollution Control Loan Fund, 246
Ohio Water Service Company, 132
Ohio Wetlands Foundation, 118-120
Ohio's forests, 237, 282-283
Ohio's nature preserves, 237, 284-288
Ohio's scenic rivers, 237, 289
Olentangy River, 290
Olentangy Watershed Alliance, 355
open space, 4, 25-27, 29-30, 50, 52, 160-165, 172, 182, 188, 219, 365
optional or alternative plan laws, 224
ORC. See "Ohio Revised Code."
ordinances, 28, 111, 156-157, 169, 172, 185, 196-198, 201-203, 205-207,
209, 227, 229-231, 234, 361, 365, 367
organizations & publications with land–use interests, 300
Orion Afield, 317
Orion Society, 317
Ottawa County, OH, 287, 296, 325, 342
outmigration, 3, 4, 18, 27
outright donation, 33, 39, 46, 48, 49, 52, **55-58**, 365
outright purchase, 25, 54, 129, **137-140**, 142, 365
overlay district, 66, 67, 164, 175
overlay zoning, 62, 65, 66, 153, 164, **169-170**, 196, 365
package plants, 17
park districts, 15, 19, 140, 141, 223, 237, 322, 326, 328, 368
parking lots, 16, 30, 112, 363

parks, 25, 26, 30, 58, 111, 131, 137, 147, 188, 193, 202-205, 237, 280, 285,
    286, 289, 304, 316, 322, 327-328, 363
pasture, 122
PCBs (polychlorinated biphenyls), 84
PDR. See "Purchase of Development Rights."
performance zoning, 153, **171-173**, 365, 366
performance zoning model ordinance, 172
permanent easement, 121
Perry, OH, 44, 95
petitions, 229, 232
Pew Charitable Trusts, 244
Pickaway County, OH, 287, 297, 343
Pickerel Creek Wildlife Area, 40
Pike County, OH, 287, 297, 343
planned unit development, 25, 28, 29, 153, 160-161, 163-165, **174-178**, 196,
    209, 359, 365
Planners Press, 173, 190, 210, 317
planning, 7, 11-20, 25-30, 365
Planning Commissioners Journal, 317
planning commissions & councils—county & regional, 237, 335
planning for agricultural viability, 73
plats, 63, 64, 157, 209, 228, 365
PL–566 Small Watershed program, 246
police power, 27, 187, 205
pollution prevention and good housekeeping, 111
Portage County, OH, 139, 279, 287, 297, 325, 343
post–construction storm water management ordinance, 111
Prairie Pothole region, 88
preacquisition, 49, 366
Preble County, OH, 157, 158, 288, 297, 343
preconstruction review, 111
preferential utility rates, 81
preservation of land issues, 29-30, 42, 50, 70, 91, 101, 147- 148, 167, 176,
    179, 212, 215, 274-275, 366
preservation of aquatic resources, 117
Preservation Resource Center of Northeastern Ohio, 274, 300, 301
*Preserving Family Lands: Book I—Essential Tax Strategies for the
    Landowner*, 44, 48, 51, 54
Preserving Family Lands: Book II—More Planing Strategies for the Future, 46,
    48, 51
previously restored wetlands, 123
prime farmland, 4, 106, 143, 179, 180, 366
production forestland, 122
professional inventories of community resources, 11
Project for Public Spaces, Inc., 317
Protecting Coastal and Wetland Resources: A Guide for Local Governments,
    170, 198
protection of natural resources, 29
public hearings, 28, 111, 158, 209, 225, 228, 230, 231, 232, 372
Public Interest Center (Media & Public Involvement), 305
public wastewater treatment, 17
PUD. See "planned unit development zoning."
purchase of development rights (PDR), 43, 48, 70-71, 129, **141-144**, 156, 366
purchasing cooperatives, 76

quarter / quarter zoning, 153, **179-181**, 366
Rails–to–Trails Conservancy, 318
Rainwater and Land Development, Ohio's Standards for Storm Water
    Management, Land Development, and Urban Stream Protection,
    114, 198, 358
Ramapo Township, NY, 201
rangeland, 122
rear lot line, 366, 368
recreational uses of land, 76, 131-132, 146-147, 170, 196, 204-205
redevelopment, 80-83, 85, 111, 134, 188, 200
reducing the costs of production, 76
regional greenbelt, 18
regional planning, 12, 16, 20, 28, 30, 146, 169, 226, 231-232, 279, 281-282,
    335-345
regional planning commission, 16, 28, 30, 169, 226, 231, 232, 281, 335-345
regulations and land–use, 30, 61-67, 110, 113, 169, 171-172, 174-177, 199,
    200, 228-230, 359, 367
remediation of land, 82, 83, 367
Reminderville, OH, 138
Renew America, 318
reserved life estate, 57, 367
residential districts, 164, 167, 168
residential streets and parking lots (habitat for cars), 16
resolutions and land–use, 26, 28, 155, 162-163, 174-175, 206, 225, 227-233,
    361, 365, 367, 372
resource conservation & development councils, 237, 346-347
Resource Renewal Institute, 318
restoration cost–share agreement, 122
restoring former wetlands, 115, 123
revolving fund, 49, 367
revolving loans, 81
rezoning, 157, 158, 164, 174, 175, 209, 210
Richfield Township, 164
Richland County, OH, 281, 288, 297, 325, 343
rights, 35, 41, 43, 125, 138, 141-143, 212, 215, 218-221, 227, 367
right–of–first–refusal, 367
right–of–way, 240, 367
riparian areas, 26, 88-91, 106, 111, 122-124, 367-368
riparian buffers, 88-91, 106, 108, 109
river corridors, 5, 137, 141, 365, 368
River Network, 318
Rivers Unlimited, 355
Rivers, Trails, and Conservation Assistance Program, 214, 216, 309
Rocky Mountain Institute, 318
Ross County, OH, 271, 288, 297, 325, 343
runoff, 4, 16, 87, 89- 90, 106, 111-113, 121, 139, 147, 164, 168, 171-172,
    196-197, 280, 358-359, 363-364, 366, 371
rural character, 161, 163, 275
rural zoning regulations, 27
Russell Land Conservancy, 50
Russell Township, 50, 327
S.B. 223, 141
salt–tolerant vegetation, 89
Sandusky River, 290

Sandy Ridge wetland mitigation bank, 118
SARE. See "Sustainable Agriculture Research & Education Program."
scenic areas, 4, 5, 11, 42, 44, 49, 53, 56-57, 134-135, 140, 146-148, 167,
        169, 170, 211-212, 216, 218, 237, 276, 280, 289, 290, 318, 368
Scenic America, 318
scenic rivers, 44, 211, 216, 237, 289, 290
Scenic Rivers Act of 1986, 289
school districts, 223, 226, 361
scientific justification for recommendations in the comprehensive plan, 11
Scioto County, OH, 288, 297, 343
Section 108 loans, 81
Section 314 (Clean Lakes), 246
Section 319 Nonpoint Source, 247
Section 404 Program, 115
sediment control programs, 17
Sell What You Sow! The Grower's Guide to Successful Produce Marketing,
        318
Seneca County, OH, 288, 297, 325
separate storm sewer systems, 110, 111
septic tanks, 139
set back, 180, 368
Seventh Generation, 301, 355
sewage plants, 139
sewers, 3, 18, 30
shallow water areas for wildlife, 89, 91, 106
Sharing the Harvest: A Guide to Community-Supported Agriculture, 318
Shelby County, OH, 288, 297, 325, 344
shelter belts, 89
side lot line, 368
sidewalks, 16, 30, 149, 188, 363
Sierra Club, 301, 309, 318
signs and signage, 73, 89, 360, 368
Silver Creek Farm, 77, 253, 271
single–user mitigation banks, 116
site design, 113
site inspections, 111, 233
site plans, 30, 61, 63-64, 114, 171, 209
six steps of a local comprehensive planning, 25
Slate Run wetland mitigation bank, 118
sliding scale zoning, 153, **182-184**, 368
slopes, 4, 5, 163, 164, 171, 176, 361, 368
small construction sites, 110, 111, 369
small municipalities, 110, 111, 197, 369
smart growth, 5-8, 139, 200, 254, 318, 321, 368
Smart Growth Network, 318
Society for Ecological Restoration, 319
soil and water conservation districts, 44, 76, 88, 101, 125, 223, 226, 237, 347-
        354
Soil and Water Conservation Society, 319
Soil Conservation Service, 179, 347, 365, 368
soil erosion, 87, 91, 106, 197, 247, 358, 364
soil types, 26
Southern Ohio Port Authority, 84, 86
special designation, 19, 185, 192, **211- 217**, 303, 368

special districts, 36, 141, 189, 196, 223, 226, 259, 322, 368
sprawl, 3-5, 7, 18, 19, 25, 27, 61, 82, 143, 179, 182, 201, 210, 358
Stark County, OH, 214, 281, 288, 326, 344
State and Local Government Commission of Ohio, 310
State Bond Issue 1, 246
State Cost Share Program (House Bill 88), 247
state forests, 282-283
State Highway Access Management Manual, 61, 62, 66, 67
State of Ohio Board of Landscape Architect Examiners, 310
Statewide Comprehensive Outdoor Recreation Plan, 131
steep slopes, 4, 5, 164, 171, 176, 361, 368
stewardship of the land, 6, 16, 40, 57, 99, 106, 191, 194, 247, 277
Stewardship Incentives Program, 106, 247
Stillwater River, 290
storm sewer systems, 110, 111
storm water discharge sources, 110
storm water management, 16, 17, 59, 110-112, 114, 197, 198, 358, 365, 369
storm water management—NPDES Phase II, **110-114**, 197, 369
storm water management plan, 110-112, 197
storm water permits, 17, 110, 114
storm water pollution, 110-112
Storm Water Pollution Prevention Plans (SWP3s), 111
Stratford Ecological Center, 285, 289
streambank plantings, 106
subdivision regulations, 12, 23, 25, 30, 61, 63-66, 176, 177, 196, 354, 369
subdivisions, 12, 23, 25, 30, 61-66, 113, 157, 160-162, 172, 176 177, 196,
        200, 209, 223, 232-233, 354, 360, 363, 365, 369
Summit County, OH, 138, 139, 224, 288, 298, 324, 344
Surf Your Watershed, 319, 356
surface water, 16, 20, 91, 110, 168, 198, 246, 247, 307, 354
sustainability, 73, 202, 247, 310, 313, 319, 368, 369
Sustainable Agriculture Network, 320
Sustainable Agriculture Research & Education Program (SARE), 78, 251-252,
        310, 315, 320
Sustainable Communities Resource Collaborative, 319
Sustainable Conservation, 53, 54, 319
sustainable development challenge grants, 247
Sustainable Earth, Inc., 319
SWCD. See "soil and water conservation district."
system development charge, 206
taking of land, 41, 46, 167, 176, 179, 369
takings laws, 369
tax abatements, 81
tax increment financing, 81
taxes and land issues, 6, 14, 25-26, 31, 36, 49, 55, 70, 83, 95-96, 103, 139-
        140, 142, 204, 215, 218, 226, 259, 322, 360, 362, 370
TDR. See "transfer of development rights."
TEA–21. See "Transportation Equity Act."
Terrene Institute, 319, 356
The Back Forty, 311
The Conservation Fund, 53, 312
The Farmer's Guide to the Internet, 254, 313
The Foundation Center, 241
The Many Faces of Community Supported Agriculture (CSA), 253, 315

The Nature Conservancy, 40, 42-44, 54, 57, 58, 278, 284-285, 287-289, 302, 317
The Ohio Zoning and Land Use Survey, 15
The Orion Society, 317
The Trust for Public Land, 50, 51
The Wilderness Society, 321
Three Eagles wetland mitigation bank, 118, 119
Tinker's Creek, 333
Title I Public Works Grants, 81
Title IX Economic Adjustment Assistance, 81
Top of Ohio RC&D, 346
total maximum daily loads, 369
Township Park Districts (Ohio Revised Code 511), 326
township zoning, 28, 162-164, 228-230
townships, 13-15, 19, 27-30, 50, 70, 155-157, 161-164, 172, 174, 176, 223-230, 370
townships and subdivision regulations, 30
traffic and traffic flow, 61-67, 145, 148-149, 171, 204, 206, 207, 240, 357, 365
transfer of development rights (TDR), 25, 185, **218- 221**, 370
transit enhancements, 145-147, 280
Transportation and Community System Preservation Pilot Program, 147, 150-151
transportation enhancements, 17, 129, **145-151**, 279, 370
Transportation Equity Act (TEA–21), 129, 145-148, 150-151, 370
Trout Unlimited, 319
Troy, OH, 177, 178
Trust for Public Land, 50, 51, 54, 278, 301, 319
Twinsburg, OH, 138, 139
U.S. Army Corps of Engineers, 115-117, 119, 367, 371
U.S. Census of Agriculture, 3
U.S. Department of Agriculture (USDA), 79, 87-88, 102, 107, 109, 121-122, 124-127, 179, 195, 245, 248, 251, 262, 274, 313, 315, 319, 320, 347, 353-354, 366
U.S. Department of Agriculture's Forest Service, 284
U.S. Environmental Protection Agency, 115, 116, 311, 371
U.S. Fish and Wildlife Service, 115
U.S. Inland Waterways Commission, 15
underlying geology of land, 11
Union County, OH, 272, 288, 298, 344
upgrading water quality, 121
Upper Cuyahoga Association, 278, 355
Upper Cuyahoga River, 139, 140, 278, 290, 355
Upper Cuyahoga River Watershed Task Force, 355
urban conservation buffer program, 107
Urban Land Institute, 178, 321
urban population movements, 28
Urban Setting Designation, 81-82, 85
urban sprawl, 61, 143, 179, 182
USDA. See "U.S. Department of Agriculture."
USDA Nonprofit Gateway, 248
utility assessments, 68-70, 357
utility facilities, 370
VAP. See "Voluntary Action Program."
variance, 64, 231, 232, 358, 370

vegetation, 5, 29, 89, 90, 111, 371
vegetative barriers, 106
Vermont Housing and Conservation Board, 100
vetoing highway and transit projects, 18
viewscapes, 163
villages, 52, 53, 68, 149-151, 191, 205-207, 223, 225, 228, 231-232, 234, 276, 364, 370
Voluntary Action Program (VAP), 80-86, 358
Warren County, OH, 288, 298, 326, 345
Washington County, OH, 215, 288, 298, 345
Water Environment Federation, 321
water flow (hydrology), 11
water lines, 30
Water Pollution Control Loan Fund, 81, 84, 246
water quality, 11, 15-17, 19, 26, 53, 81-87, 88, 90-91, 109, 113, 117, 121, 124, 195, 211, 226, 246, 369, 371
water supply, 16, 90, 139, 140
Watershed Information Network, 356
Watershed Institute, 53, 300, 354
Watershed Management Council, 356
watershed planning, 12, 15-16
watershed protection, 16, 20, 113, 114, 126, 165, 237, 311, 354
Watershed protection organizations, 20, 237, 354
watersheds and land–use issues, 12, 15-16, 19, 53, 88, 90-91, 106-109, 111-114, 116-117, 126, 139, 197, 223, 370-371
Wayne County, OH, 201, 203, 288, 298, 326, 345
Wayne National Forest, 284
wellhead protection, 82, 90, 106, 108, 246, 371
wells, 82, 90, 132, 161, 163
Western Lake Erie watershed, 90, 93, 108
Western Reserve RC&D, 347
Westlake, OH, 205
wetland conservation, 123
wetland functions and values, 123
wetlands, 5, 16, 115-125, 164-165, 198, 218, 243, 371-372
Wetlands Assistance Guide—General Landowner Options, 58
wetlands delineation, 193, 371
wetlands farmed under natural conditions, 122
wetlands mitigation and banking, 50, **115-120**, 119, 372
wetlands preservation in perpetuity, 119
Wetlands Reserve Program (WRP), 43, 59, 98, 106, 108, **121-124**, 125, 247, 372
WHIP. See "Wildlife Habitat Incentives Program."
White Oaks property, 139
Wilderness Land Trust, 321
Wildlife Habitat Council, 321
Wildlife Habitat Incentives Program (WHIP), 59, **125-127**, 372
William Ellsbury Benua and Emily Platt Benua Nature Preserve, 57
Williams County, OH, 273, 288, 298, 345
Wilson Township, Clinton County, Ohio, 14
Wood County, OH, 108
Woodmere Village, OH, 149, 151
World Water Vision, 356
World Wide Web, 237, 240, 254-256

WRP. See "Wetlands Reserve Program.."
Zoar, OH, 213
zoning and land–use decisions, 12-15, 25-31, 61-62, 65-66, 112, 155-184,
        200-202, 208-210, 224-234, 372
zoning administrator, 359
zoning and subdivision regulations, 12, 23, 25
zoning boards and boards of appeal, 229, 359, 372
zoning commissions, 28, 61, 161, 162, 164, 175, 226-232, 372
zoning inspectors, 28, 168, 202, 227-230, 232, 233, 338, 372
zoning map, 174, 175, 209, 233
zoning permit, 233, 360, 372
zoning regulations, 27-28, 61, 138, 162, 169, 171-172, 174, 179, 229-230,
        365, 372